Jι

*Pluralist Democracy
in the United States*

PLURALIST DEMOCRACY
IN
THE UNITED STATES:

Conflict and Consent

ROBERT A. DAHL

Yale University

RAND MCNALLY & COMPANY   CHICAGO

RAND MᶜNALLY POLITICAL SCIENCE SERIES

Morton Grodzins, Advisory Editor

This book is dedicated to
those who have contributed nothing to the writing of it
but much to what I have written in it:
my teachers,
P.I.D.
and
F.W.C.,
and
my students

ACKNOWLEDGMENTS

I N ADDITION TO the lasting and immeasurable debt to his own teachers and his students which everyone who teaches must surely incur, a debt I have recorded on an earlier page, I should like to acknowledge my obligations to all the others who have helped me to complete this book. Most of these must go nameless here; though some are mentioned in footnotes—all those, I hope, from whom I have drawn directly—it is obvious to me that the number of writers who have shaped what I have written far exceeds the small portion I have cited.

In addition to these general debts, I have incurred some great and specific ones toward friends who have made substantial and direct contributions. William Mitchell, Nelson Polsby, H. Douglas Price, Austin Ranney, and Aaron Wildavsky read and commented on a preliminary draft of the whole manuscript, except for Chapters 15 and 16 which I added in response to suggestions from several of them. C. Vann Woodward, on whose writings I had already drawn heavily in writing Chapter 12, was kind enough to read and comment on that chapter. Likewise, Philip Taft, whose works are the principal sources for Chapter 17, generously went over that chapter in detail.

The reader will never know from what errors, omissions, obscurities and misinterpretations he has been saved by these friendly critics. Whatever lapses may still remain (for which I, of course, assume all responsibility), I am deeply grateful to each of them for his help.

I also appreciate the generosity of the authors and publishers who have allowed me to draw heavily on their works for the cases discussed in Chapter 16: Raymond Wolfinger and David B. Filvaroff for providing me with the materials on the passage of the Civil Rights Act of 1964 from their unpublished research on that series of events; Anthony Lewis and Random House for material from Gideon's Trumpet; Aaron Wildavsky and the Yale University Press for material from Dixon-Yates; and

Raymond A. Bauer, Ithiel de Sola Pool, and Lewis Anthony Dexter, together with Atherton Press, for material from *American Business and Public Policy*.

I am indebted to Daniel Lewis and Miss Barbara Fisher for their assistance on tables, charts, and citations, to Mr. Harry Meyer for helping me to bring up to date the tables in Chapter 6, and to Mrs. Robert C. Holle for typing many of the chapters.

Miss Marianne Clark of Rand McNally has edited the manuscript and guided it through the pitfalls of printing with skill, delicacy, and judgment.

My wife Mary has made her contributions in countless ways from the day in an apartment in Rome when she typed the opening page of a barely legible draft of an early chapter down to reading the last batch of page proof in North Haven some years later. I am reassured to know that my most attentive and most important reader likes our book.

ROBERT A. DAHL

NORTH HAVEN, CONN., 1966

CONTENTS

[viii]

FIGURES AND TABLES

[xiv]

[xv]

Part One

How and why a pluralist democracy emerged on the American continent

I

CONFLICT AND CONSENT

O N SEPTEMBER 17, 1787, some thirty-nine men, having completed
their labors in Philadelphia, signed their names to a short
document that bore a title as spare and simple as the text itself.
The Constitution of the United States had taken almost four months in
the drafting, and more centuries to prepare than anyone then or later
could precisely estimate. In addition to the thirty-nine signers, there were
present at the ceremonies a few men who refused to sign; several other
disgruntled colleagues, having failed to achieve the document they
wanted, had already departed for their homes in discontent. Nonetheless,
the prevailing mood must have been one of satisfaction and optimism.
One of those present, James Madison, recorded in his journal:

> Whilst the last members were signing it Doctor Franklin look-
> ing toward the Presidents Chair, at the back of which a rising
> sun happened to be painted, observed to a few members near
> him, that Painters found it difficult to distinguish in their art a
> rising from a setting sun. 'I have,' said he, 'often and often in
> the course of the Session, and the vicissitudes of my hopes and
> fears as to its issue, looked at that behind the President without
> being able to tell whether it was rising or setting: But now at
> length I have the happiness to know that it is a rising and not a
> setting Sun.'[1]

1. From "Debates in the Federal Convention of 1787 as reported by James
    Madison" in *Documents Illustrative of the Formation of the Union of the
    American States*, Government Printing Office, Washington, 1927, (hereaft-
    er cited as *Documents*), 745.

Almost three quarters of a century after on a late afternoon in April, shore batteries commanded by General G. T. Beauregard split the afternoon quiet of Charleston, South Carolina, as they suddenly commenced firing on a fort in the harbor. Not particularly important in itself, the fort had become a symbol, though evidently a symbol that meant different things to different men in the North and in the South: To many Northerners the fort stood for the supremacy of national power over local rebellion. To many Southerners it represented an alien threat to a desirable way of life. In the four years following that April afternoon, more than one out of every ten men in the United States died in a grim and bloody war.

Now, a century after the fall of Fort Sumter, Americans continue to be fascinated—indeed, seem ever more fascinated—by that Civil War which we so often refer to, rightly, as tragic. While the American Civil War is absorbing for many reasons, to the student of politics it is interesting because it dramatizes so sharply both the failure and the success of the American political system and thereby some of the central problems of any political system. *Failure*, because there can be no more convincing evidence of the breakdown of a political system than reversion to the barbarism of internal war, particularly among a people of the same origins and language, already become a nation after living under the same government for nearly three quarters of a century, or if we count the Colonial period, for two centuries. *Success*, however, because the Civil War has been the only major breakdown in our political institutions during two centuries of continuous development in the arts of operating, on a national scale, a democratic republic in which unity yields to diversity, and diversity to unity: not without strain and conflict, to be sure, but without extensive civil strife or the introduction of those poisonous hatreds and resentments that seep through a system until it collapses in paralysis or in violent paroxysm.

The American Civil War is interesting also because it reminds the students of politics that many of the essential problems of politics are ancient, general, and persistent. A particular political system, such as ours, can be interpreted as a way of coping with these recurring problems. Some of the ways a political system deals with problems may be unique, some commonplace. Because it meets its problems in a particular time and place with a special body of past experience to go on, each political system is unique; so too the American system is unique. But because some problems have recurred ever since civilized men have tried to live together, every political system—and this is true of ours—has had

[4]

to deal with some of the same problems. Its solutions may be unique; the basic questions are not. What are some of these that Americans, like other peoples, have had to meet?

How to Handle Conflict

Much as we often yearn for solitude and enjoy its blessings when we are lucky enough to have them, one characteristic of mankind for the last ten thousand years, and no doubt the last hundred thousand, is a marked preference for living together in some kind of community, however small or rudimentary. The advantages of cooperation and community life are so numerous and so obvious that they must have been evident to man from earliest times. By now, our ancestors have closed off the choice; for most of us the option of total isolation from a community is, realistically speaking, no longer open.

Nonetheless, however strongly human beings are driven to seek the company of one another, and despite millenia of practice, they have never discovered a way in which they can live together without conflict—that is, without creating situations in which one individual wishes to follow a line of action that would make it difficult or impossible for someone else to pursue his own desires. Conflict seems to be an inescapable aspect of community and hence of being human. Why conflict seems inescapable is a question that has troubled many people, philosophers, theologians, historians, social scientists, and, doubtless, a great many ordinary people who have not recorded their musings. James Madison, who perhaps more than any other single individual gave shape to the American constitutional system, held that conflict was built into the very nature of man. Men have diverse abilities, he wrote in *The Federalist*, and these in turn produce diverse interests:

> . . . As long as the reason of man continues fallible, and he is at liberty to exercise it, different opinions will be formed. . . . A zeal for different opinions concerning religion, concerning government, and many other points, as well of speculation as of practice; an attachment to different leaders ambitiously contending for pre-eminence and power; or to persons of other descriptions whose fortunes have been interesting to the human passions, have, in turn, divided mankind into parties, inflamed

[5]

them with mutual animosity, and rendered them much more disposed to vex and oppress each other than to co-operate for their common good. . . . A landed interest, a manufacturing interest, a mercantile interest, a moneyed interest, with many lesser interests, grow up of necessity in civilized nations, and divide them into different classes, actuated by different sentiments and views.[2]

Whatever the explanation for conflict may be, and Madison's is but one among many, its existence is one of the prime facts of all community life. Yet if this were the only fact, then human life would truly fit that famous pattern described by the English political philosopher, Thomas Hobbes, in his great and controversial book, *Leviathan* (1651). Hobbes describes mankind in a state of nature:

In such condition, there is no place for industry; because the fruit thereof is uncertain: and consequently no culture of the earth; no navigation, nor use of the commodities that may be imported by sea; no commodious building; no instruments of moving, and removing, such things as require much force; no knowledge of the face of the earth; no account of time; no arts; no letters, no society; and which is worst of all, continual fear, and danger of violent death and the life of man, solitary, poor, nasty, brutish, and short.[3]

But life is not so dismal. A condition of totally unregulated conflict is, as Hobbes himself argued, obviously incompatible with community life. Along with the deep human need for living in communion with fellow men, and alongside the inevitable conflicts that are generated whenever human beings try to live together, as far back into man's past as one can pry there have also been traces of a search for ways by which conflicts within a community can be settled without extensive violence and bloodshed, according to standards of justice, held, at the very least, among those who enforce the rules. We cannot pause to probe the mystery; but the evidence is so great that we can safely accept it as a fact.

Thus man's existence as a social being—social animal, if you prefer —is conditioned by a set of contradictory tendencies that, taken altogether, make him a member of some political system:

2. *The Federalist,* New York; The Modern Library, n. d., pp. 55–56. Madison's famous passages in *The Federalist,* too long to include here, are worth reading in full; they are reproduced in the appendix to this chapter.
3. *Leviathan,* New York, The Macmillan Company, 1947, p. 82.

(1) *His need* for human fellowship creates communities.
(2) *But he is* unable to live with others without conflict.
(3) *Hence* communities search for ways of adjusting conflicts so that community life will be possible and tolerable.

The third stage in this dialectic is the turning point from man as a social animal to man as a political animal. For if conflicts are to be settled, somewhere in the community there must be individuals or groups with enough authority or power to secure—if need be to compel—a settlement: to make sure that the parties to a conflict abide by the judgment of the ruler, the will of God, existing rules, their own agreement, or law. At any rate, human communities do not seem ever to have existed without some such powers—without, that is, political institutions.

Who Ought to Govern?

It is impossible to say when men first became conscious of their political institutions. We know that for at least two thousand years before the first settlers came to America there had been in the Western world a distinct consciousness of political systems and an awareness of differences among them. During these twenty centuries men asked questions about politics, particularly during eras of great change and crisis when old systems confronted new ones. It is not a great step from becoming keenly aware that communities do have and probably must have governments—institutions for settling conflicts, enforcing rules, and perhaps even making rules—to the question, "Who ought to govern?" Because this question—like many other questions about politics— is likely to come to the fore in times of political disturbance and change, it was one of the most important questions that confronted the Founders gathered in Philadelphia in 1787 to discuss constitutional problems. As we shall see in the next chapter, they were by no means agreed on an answer. For they reflected, among other influences, the history of ancient controversies, controversies that still persist in our own day and will not die, I imagine, as long as men continue to ask questions.

Although the question, Who ought to govern? had been answered in many different ways, two sorts of replies were particularly significant in 1787 and remain so down to the present day. One, which we may call the aristocratic point of view, holds that government should be in the hands of those who are best qualified to govern because of their special virtues and knowledge and that the number of these properly qualified rulers is, in any community, almost certain to be a minority. The other, the democratic point of view, holds that everyone should govern since, ideally, no adult should be governed without his consent; that political virtue and wisdom are not lodged exclusively in any identifiable group of persons; and that if consent is to mean anything, every adult must be quite free to participate in all political decisions without fear or favor.

The debate between those who espouse these conflicting doctrines would not have endured so long if each viewpoint did not have a good deal to be said for it—and each runs into some rather serious problems.

The aristocratic solution (which has nothing intrinsically to do with birth) is frequently used, even in democracies, for governing organizations where superior skills are crucial to the success of the organization and where, it is supposed, these superior skills can be more or less definitely defined and identified. In the early years of the Civil War many units elected their commanding officers; but the results were generally thought to be disastrous, and today even the most ardent exponents of democratic doctrine do not defend this method of governing military units. The perennial appeal of the aristocratic answer, then, is that it focuses directly on the problems of fitness to rule and stresses the importance of having good leadership, of giving authority to *skillful*, *wise*, and *virtuous* men (or women). Leadership is a persistent problem in all political systems—not least in democracies.

Yet it is one thing to govern a family, a ship, an army, a business firm, or a government bureau—and quite another to govern a community or a nation. As a matter of fact even in those institutions where 'aristocratic' solutions are supposed to work best, they have often produced notoriously incompetent leaders. Whatever may be the justification for the aristocratic solution for providing leadership in certain situations, there are four major objections to applying the aristocratic doctrine to the political system of an entire community.

First, the standards of skill, wisdom, and virtue required are unclear. Men of great learning are not always virtuous, and men of virtue are not always learned. After nearly twenty-five centuries, almost the only people who seem to be convinced of the advantages of being ruled by philosopher-kings are . . . a few philosophers. Though indispensable as advisers and occasionally skillful in politics, scholars as a group have not greatly impressed others with their competence as rulers. The skills of the businessman or military leader are highly specialized, and very different from those required in government: Ulysses S. Grant, a great general, and Herbert Hoover, a great businessman, were not great Presidents. In sum, it is easy to propose in the groves of academe that the skillful, wise, and virtuous should rule; but it is difficult to establish practical criteria for identifying persons with superior skill, wisdom, and virtue in politics. There seems to be a very strong and very human tendency to solve the problem by defining skill, wisdom, and virtue in the image of one's own self, group, or class. Was it by chance that Plato, a philosopher, concluded that the best rulers would be philosophers?

In the second place, even if the criteria were much clearer than they are, how are these criteria to be applied? How are the rulers to be selected? In a mad scramble for power, the wise and virtuous are likely to be trampled to death. Popular election would turn the whole process upside down. Hereditary aristocracies have always been subject to the great gamble of genetics and early environment; there is no guarantee that the first born son of a wise and virtuous father may not be a dullard, or a scoundrel, or both. One might propose that the rulers should be chosen by the wise and virtuous. But of course this only pushes the problem one stage farther back: Who is wise and virtuous enough to choose the wise and virtuous men who will choose the rulers?

Third, can a process designed to select only the wise and virtuous also insure that the leaders so chosen have widespread consent for their government? If it is said that surely the wise and virtuous would have general consent for their rule, then why not adopt the democratic solution and allow the people to choose their leaders? If, on the other hand, one objects that the people might not choose wise and virtuous leaders, then, since they are not the choice of and by people must they be imposed on the people? If so, would not the attempt to impose leaders on the people degenerate into a trial by battle in which the strongest, not the wisest and most virtuous, would win?

Finally, even if the skillful, wise, and virtuous could somehow be chosen as rulers, how can we be sure that they will not be corrupted by power? Lord Acton's famous proposition about power is, surely, an overstatement;[4] wags have sometimes proposed that it be amended to read: 'Power corrupts, and the absence of power corrupts absolutely.' Nonetheless, the dangers created by the mysterious alchemy of power are too familiar to be laughed aside.

To suppose, as many people do, that the argument for government by superior beings is as obsolete as the thick walls of a medieval fortress is to overlook the fact that many of the arguments for rule by an elite of unusual virtues and talents have been employed by some powerful twentieth century opponents of democracy, namely, Fascists, Nazis, and Com-

4. See the analysis of Arnold Rogow and Harold D. Lasswell, *Power, Corruption and Rectitude*, Englewood Cliffs, N.J.; Prentice Hall, 1963.

munists. Plato might be horrified to hear a defense of aristocracy from such sources; still, the idea obviously continues to have great appeal.

For anyone convinced by these objections to aristocratic government, the main alternative in the United States ever since Colonial times has always been popular government. In the eyes of the democrat, no one group can be found with such clearly superior talent and virtue to entitle it to rule. In the proper conditions—and it is the job of a democracy to foster and maintain these conditions—practically everyone has sufficient knowledge and virtue to share, directly or indirectly, in the task of governing. In any case, even though I may lack technical knowledge as to the best or most efficient means, is anyone else likely to know better than I what ends are best for me?

However, every species of government has its special problems. These are some questions that an advocate of popular government must face up to honestly:

¶ How is it possible to provide and maintain a real equality of influence and power over government? Underneath all the trappings and rituals of democracy, won't power be concentrated in the hands of a minority—men of great wealth, or political skill, or determination, or simply with better opportunities?

¶ If everyone is to have an equal say, how can the decisions of the government be made with sufficient knowledge and expertness? Aren't the problems of modern governments too complex for ordinary citizens to understand—particularly if they devote only a small part of their time to the effort of understanding the issues?

¶ How can a popular government act vigorously, speedily, and decisively, particularly in crises? Can a popular government have a strong, energetic executive? If not, how can it survive? If so, will he not be a source of great danger?

¶ How can a system of popular government ever cope with the twin problems of faction: On the one hand, how can larger groups with the greatest number of votes be prevented from exploiting and tyrannizing smaller groups with fewer votes? On the other hand, will there not be constant dissension, unrest, and even subversion by discontented minorities who find their aims thwarted by more populous groups?

¶ Can a system really operate with the consent of *all?* Isn't this necessarily only a cloak for the interests of those who rule, whether these are a majority or some oligarchy that manages to dominate by accumulating the resources with which to rule?

These are not abstract questions but live issues. They were very much alive to the Founders in 1787; they had less experience to build on than we, and much of their experience suggested pessimistic answers. In one way or another every popular government must surmount these problems, else it ceases to exist as a popular government. To cast an eye toward the travail of new nations is to see how difficult the problems are. But we need not look so far afield: these problems were not solved, once and for all, when the thirty-nine men at Philadelphia signed The Constitution of the United States.

In the course of this book, I shall come back to these questions on numerous occasions. The last two—the problem of faction and the problem of consent—are particularly thorny and complex. It may prove helpful to explore these briefly now, so that we can gain some perspective on the solutions put forward by the American political system.

The Dangers of Faction

Nothing weighed more heavily on the minds of the Founders than the dangers of faction. In an impressive and justly famous analysis (that foreshadowed the remarks quoted above from The Federalist), James Madison expressed during the second week of the Constitutional Convention a concern that must have been widely shared among the other delegates:

> All civilized Societies would be divided into different Sects, Factions & interests as they happened to consist of rich & poor, debtors & creditors, the landed, the manufacturing, the commercial interests, the inhabitants of this district or that district, the followers of this political leader or that political leader, the disciples of this religious Sect or that religious Sect.[5]

Madison took it for granted, then, that cleavages could occur in many ways; economic relationships, geographical location, religious feelings, even loyalties to particular leaders, all could lead to conflict. And what

5. *Documents*, p. 162.

would restrain one faction in its struggles with another? Honesty? Reputation? Conscience? Religion? In Madison's view, all limits to faction that depend, like these, on the willingness of an individual or a group to exercise self-restraint are bound to be inadequate.

Like most of the other delegates, Madison was more inclined to stress the dangers that could arise from a willful or tempestuous majority than from a minority; for he assumed that in a republic a majority could more easily have its own way. But he was not unmindful of the possibility that minority factions might also threaten a republic.

> . . . According to the Republican theory indeed, Right & power both being vested in the majority, are held to be synonymous. According to fact & experience, a minority may in an appeal to force be an over-match for the majority. 1. If the minority happen to include all such as possess the skill & habits of military life, with such as possess the great pecuniary resources, one third may conquer the remaining two thirds. 2. one third of those who participate in the choice of rulers may be rendered a majority by the accession of those whose poverty disqualifies them from a suffrage, & who for obvious reasons may be more ready to join the standard of sedition than that of the established Government. 3. where slavery exists, the Republican Theory becomes still more fallacious.[6]

Precisely what are the dangers of faction that preoccupied the Founders? Curiously enough, none of the men at the Convention ever seems to have stated exactly what he had in mind. On this question even the clearest minds, like those of Madison and Wilson, gave forth cloudy answers. When the delegates descended from vague generalities to concrete cases, the examples they chose generally involved attempts to change the distribution of property. In fact, a careful reading of the record of debates suggests the cynical answer that when the delegates at the Constitutional Convention spoke of the dangers of faction they were usually thinking of attacks on property—their own. Here, for example, is what Madison said at one point:

> . . . No agrarian attempts have yet been made in this Country, but symptoms, of a leveling spirit, as we have understood, have sufficiently appeared in certain quarters to give notice of the future danger. How is this danger to be guarded agst. on repub-

6. *Ibid.*, p. 230.

lican principles? How is the danger in all cases of interested coalitions to oppress the minority to be guarded ag^{st}?[7]

With the aid of the experience that has accumulated since 1787, perhaps men today can see the problem of faction more clearly than the delegates to the Convention were able to do. We have learned some hard lessons. When someone says he opposes factions and parties, what he usually means, it seems, is that he opposes every faction, every party, every interest—except his own. If one believes that policies proposed by others will deprive him of something he values, or if he so strongly believes his own policies are right that he would impose them on other people no matter what they prefer, he finds it easy to define what the others wish to do as tyranny and what he himself wishes to do as obvious justice.

Many of the concrete concerns of the Founders were, I believe, of this kind. To some extent, they elevated their own privileges into universal matters of abstract and universal right; groups who might interfere with their privileges were, in their eyes, dangerous factions. In this respect they carried partisan attitudes into the Convention, yet were usually unaware that they did so. They were not necessarily cynical, but merely human. (Does one have a right to expect more from men simply because they make a constitution?)

Yet it is too facile to jump to the conclusion that the fear of faction expressed by the Founders represented nothing more than sordid self-interest. Whatever their motives and biases may have been, whatever the extent to which they were influenced by their own socio-economic positions and ideological perspectives, the problem they confronted was genuine, important, timely, persistent and worthy of the concern they gave it. For the problem of faction is simply the mirror image of the problem of gaining consent—of governing with the consent of the governed. And governing with the consent of the governed, as we shall see in a moment, has values both ideal and practical. Goals of personal freedom, human dignity, enlightened self-interest, and political stability all justify a serious concern for gaining consent, and hence for keeping conflict within bounds, so that in the best of circumstances all citizens will feel that what they hold most dear is respected and protected by the government—while even in the worst of circumstances they will feel that the laws are at least tolerable, and do not encourage disloyalty, violence, or civil wars.

As practical men, the Founders were concerned lest conflicts get out

7. *Ibid.*, pp. 280–281.

[13]

of hand. Faction had been the bane of previous republics; faction was a worrisome fact of recent experience; and faction would be a standing danger to the new republic.

> ... In Greece & Rome the rich & poor, the creditors & debtors, as well as the patricians & plebians alternately oppressed each other with equal unmercifulness. What a source of oppression was the relation between the parent cities of Rome, Athens & Carthage, & their respective provinces: the former possessing the power, & the latter being sufficiently distinguished to be separate objects of it? Why was America so justly apprehensive of Parliamentary injustice? Because G. Britain had a separate interest real or supposed, & if her authority had been admitted, could have pursued that interest at our expense. We have seen the mere distinction of colour made in the most enlightened period of time, a ground of the most oppressive dominion ever exercised by man over man. What has been the source of those unjust laws complained of among ourselves? Has it not been the real or supposed interest of the major number? Debtors have defrauded their creditors. The landed interest has borne hard on the mercantile interest. The Holders of one species of property have thrown a disproportion of taxes on the holders of another species.[8]

Yet, being realists, they also knew that conflict is inevitable. Conflict, as Madison said, is sown in the nature of man. An autocratic government might suppress the symptoms of conflict, as modern dictators have succeeded in doing; but even an autocracy cannot eliminate the causes. By establishing a republic in which citizens would enjoy a large measure of personal freedom, the Founders were bound to make it easy for conflict to erupt. How, then, was conflict to be managed? How could it be moderated so that it would not wreck the new Republic? How could government be carried on with something like the general consent of the people? These were the genuine problems of faction that transcended personal or group interests.

With the Consent of All

How can any government operate with "the consent of all"? This

8. Documents, pp. 162–163.

expression is one that Americans fell into the habit of using quite early in their national history.

> *Resolved* (declared the First Continental Congress on October 14, 1774) *that the inhabitants of the English colonies in North America, by the immutable laws of nature . . . are entitled to life, liberty, and property: and they have never ceded to any foreign power whatever, a right to dispose of either without their consent.*

> *We hold these truths to be self evident* (declared the Second Continental Congress on July 14, 1776) *that all men are created equal, that they are endowed by their Creator with certain inalienable Rights, that among these are Life, Liberty, and the pursuit of Happiness.—That to secure these rights, Governments are instituted among men, deriving their just powers from the consent of the governed.*

By now the phrase comes so easily to the lips of an American that few ever pause to ask *why* governments should or *how* they can rest on the consent of all.

There are at least four reasons for insisting that governments ought, ideally, to derive their just powers from the consent of the governed. First, government without consent is inconsistent with personal freedom. To the extent that I am compelled to obey man-made rules that do not have my moral approval, I am not a free man. To be sure, personal freedom is an exacting demand; complete personal freedom is probably impossible to achieve. Nonetheless, one who believes in the value of individual freedom may reasonably hold that so far as possible no adult human being should ever be governed without his consent.

Second, government without one's consent can be an affront to human dignity and respect. We see this most vividly in extreme cases—the hapless victim in a concentration camp, who is subjected to the utmost humiliation, degradation, deprivation, and torture, loses thereby a part of his humanity.

Third, one may demand solely out of self-interest that a government rest on consent. For one might reason as follows: Certainly I do not want the government to act without my approval. But since I am not nor am I likely to be a dictator or even a member of a ruling oligarchy, perhaps the safest way to insure that the government will have my approval is to insist that it must have the approval of everyone. Reasoning from

[15]

self-interest is not generally thought to be quite as noble as reasoning from general principles of freedom and dignity. Nonetheless we should rejoice, I believe, whenever freedom and dignity are supported by widespread self-interest; for nothing is quite so strong a buttress to social institutions as a firm foundation in self-interest.

Finally, one may insist on consent because one thinks that governments "deriving their just powers from the consent of the governed" are more likely to be stable and durable. There are innumerable reasons why one may want stable government, including the fact that revolutions are very uncertain affairs; with a few exceptions, among which, happily, the American Revolution may be counted, those who start the first fires of a revolution are consumed in the holocaust. To control the course of a revolution is almost as difficult as to direct the path of a tornado. Whatever the reasons why one may want stability in government, it is reasonable to suppose that a government is less likely to create hostility, frustration, and resentment—sentiments that breed revolution—if it acts with the approval of its citizens than if it does not. Common sense and modern history both lend substance to this judgment; in the past century the most durable governments in the world have rested on widespread suffrage and other institutions for popular control.

But if it is relatively easy to say *why* governments should derive their just powers from the consent of the governed, it is very much more difficult to say *how* they can do so. The difficulty stems from that inescapable element of conflict in the human condition: People living together simply will not always agree. When people disagree, how can a decision be based on the consent of all? Since political philosophers, like architects, sometimes conceal their failures behind a handsome façade, the unwary student may conclude that the solution would be clear if he only understood the philosophers better. In this case, however, modesty may be misplaced; although political philosophers have long wrestled with the problem, the disagreeable fact remains that they have not been able to prescribe a perfect solution except under certain highly improbable circumstances.

The obvious way out, of course, is to eliminate conflict. This happy solution is characteristic of many literary Utopias, where social life is downright inhuman in its lack of conflict. Utopianism of this genre appears in unsuspected places: Karl Marx was a militant critic of the Utopian socialists of an earlier generation, yet he evidently thought that his famous dialectic—"All history is the history of class conflict"—would for all practical purposes come to an end in a communist society: there would be no need for a state because there would be no significant conflicts.

If one concludes that complete agreement is a hopeless objective and not necessarily a very desirable one, then one must search elsewhere for a solution to the problem of consent. A second way out is to search for specific policies that every citizen approves of, even though he may have disagreed, initially, with his fellow citizens. It is not absurd, surely, to suppose that conflict can sometimes be transmuted into decisions that have the approval of everyone. Perhaps all of us have had experiences of this kind, particularly when we try to arrive at decisions within some group where everyone else shares our fundamental values, even though we may differ on specific questions. There is something of this idea behind Rousseau's much disputed notion of a General Will that bespeaks more truly what we believe than we always do ourselves. Yet the difficulty with all solutions along these lines is that decisions rarely do receive unanimous approval. Do I consent to decisions with which I disagree? Who is a better judge than I of what my 'will', my policy, really is? Should anyone else have the authority to proclaim that a policy really has my consent? Although a distinction can be made between what I really believe is best and what I momentarily think or say is best, a good deal of experience suggests that to allow someone else to make this distinction for me is very dangerous. A tyrant might insist that he has my consent for all he does, though I deny it, because he knows better than I what I really want. When an individual says he disapproves of the policies of the government, even when they have the blessings of an enlightened dictator or an enlightened majority, the safest course in practise, I believe, is to postulate that he knows his own mind. Otherwise, government by consent is likely to degenerate into a mere ritualistic formula.

Even if people cannot always agree on specific policies, however, a third solution is to gain their consent for a *process*. It is perfectly reasonable of me to say that I approve of the process by which certain kinds of decisions are made, even if I do not always like the specific results. Thus the consent of the governed may be interpreted to mean their approval of the processes by which decisions are arrived at and their willingness to abide by these decisions even when these seem wrong.

But what kind of a process shall I require? If I hold that no one can, as a general matter, know my goals and values better than I myself, then no doubt I will insist that the process of making decisions must provide me with a full opportunity to make my views known; and even if I am willing to leave details to experts, I do not want anyone else to have more power over the decision, in the last say, than I do. A solution along these lines might well appeal to me as the best attainable, given the inescapable conditions mentioned earlier: that my need for human fellowship impels me to live in a society, that I cannot live with others without sometimes disagreeing with them, and that I must therefore find some way to adjust our conflicts that will appeal to all of us as fair.

This solution is, in fact, what links consent with democracy. In the real world, of course, democracies never quite satisfy all the conditions implied by this solution; but it serves as one standard against which to measure their success and failure.

The Sovereign Majority

But how is this solution to be applied? What kind of process will insure that I shall have a full opportunity to make my views known, and that no one else will have more power over decisions, in the last say, than I do?

There are a number of different answers to these questions, and it is with two of these that we are concerned. Purely as a matter of abstract theory, the one is admirably clear and explicit; this is decision-making by the sovereign majority. Yet no country seems to have adopted this method in entirety. The other is in greater or lesser degree the pattern that seems to have evolved in the countries we usually call 'democratic.' Yet the pattern is so blurred and chaotic—and there are so many variations from country to country—that it is difficult to describe.

Does the difference between these two kinds of answers reflect a conflict of ideals or only the familiar conflict between ideals and reality? Perhaps a bit of both. What an 'ideal democracy' would be is a subject of interminable dispute. One is tempted to say that there are as many different visions of what democracy ought to be as there are individuals who think about the matter. Because the advocates of each vision shape their definitions to fit their ideals, the world of political thought and political rhetoric is over-populated with definitions of the term 'democracy.'

I want to refrain here from adding to this definitional explosion. I shall speak of the American political system with terms that Americans themselves have used for generations—a democracy, a republic, or a democratic republic. One may if he chooses quarrel with my use of these terms, but he will find me an unwilling contestant, for I do not wish to argue overmuch about terms in this book. Without trying to decide, then, which of the different visions of democracy is more truly democratic, let me nonetheless describe two of these: decision-making by the sovereign majority, and pluralistic democracy.

In the vision of democracy as decision-making by the sovereign majority, the citizens of a given country all approve of the principle of majority rule, according to which all conflicts over the policies of government are settled, sooner or later, by a majority of citizens or voters—either directly in a public assembly or in a referendum, or indirectly through elected representatives. A person who approves of the principle of majority rule need not go so far as to assume, as Rousseau is often interpreted as saying, that a majority mysteriously reveals the 'real' will even of the minority who would prefer a different policy. Nor does one need to assume that every policy preferred by a majority is bound to be morally right. One need not even believe that the principle of majority rule is the best principle for every political system. Although people sometimes lay down these exaggerated requirements, none of them seems to be demanded either by strict logic or by inference from actual experience. To approve of a system that applies the principle of majority rule, evidently one needs only to believe that during this historical period and in this particular society the principle represents the fullest attainable achievement of one's values. An American is not logically inconsistent if he holds that majority rule is not the best principle to apply in the Congo. For it would be entirely consistent to argue that the workability and acceptability of majority rule depends upon the existence of conditions that may or may not be present in a specific society.

In fact, the straightforward application of the principle of the sovereign majority to all questions of public significance is, as a practical matter, not likely to receive everyone's continuing approval—except under unusual circumstances. While a citizen may make certain allowances for majority decisions that displease him, the more frequently he expects to be in a minority, the less likely he is to accept the principle of majority rule. One can, perhaps, accept calmly the prospect of being in a minority so long as the issues are trivial. But the more important the issues, the more difficult it is to accept defeat by a hostile majority. The more I expect that majorities are going to insist on policies that conflict with my most cherished values, the more likely I am to oppose the principle of majority rule. Surely few people would be so loyal to the abstract principle as to approve of it even if they expected it to lead regularly to repugnant policies. At some point even the most convinced adherent of majority rule will give up in despair. In a nation of convinced anti-Semites and religious bigots, a modern Jefferson might be compelled to oppose the principle of the sovereign majority. In short, continuing and universal approval of the principle of majority rule requires a high degree of consensus among all the citizens as to what the policies of government should be.

It seems reasonable to conjecture that the more diverse the beliefs held among a body of people, the less likely it is that they will approve of the idea of making decisions by majority rule. To the extent that this conjecture is valid, it is a severe restriction on the principle of rule by a sovereign majority, particularly in modern heterogeneous societies. For it seems entirely reasonable to hold that diversity of beliefs is likely to be greater the larger the number of citizens, the bigger the territory over which they are spread, and the greater the distinctions of race, ethnic group, regional culture, occupation, social class, income, property, and so on. Some advocates of rule by the sovereign majority have therefore argued, as Rousseau did, that majority decisions would be acceptable only among very small and highly homogeneous bodies of people, groups no larger perhaps than a town or a very small city. According to this view, nations even as small as Norway, and certainly as large as the United States, are unsuitable for democracy.

One possible way to maintain homogeneity would be to eliminate all dissenting minorities who would object to the decisions of a majority. In Athens the Ecclesia—the sovereign town meeting composed theoretically of all adult citizens—had the power of ostracism, by which it could banish an unpopular citizen from Athens for ten years. Rousseau evidently believed that homogeneity would be maintained if dissident citizens had the right to emigrate—presumably to a more sympathetic community. Another possibility, a painful one to Americans, is secession. Yet all of these solutions entail serious practical and moral difficulties, particularly in the modern world. Emigration, for example, can be a staggering price to pay simply for being in a minority; must the price of one's beliefs depend solely on the numbers who happen to share them? Yet if emigration is purely optional, who would emigrate? Many dissenters would remain to deny the legitimacy of majority rule as it applies to them. Shall we then expel these dissenters in order to maintain consensus? To expel an individual from a community is not difficult; American communities have often done so, sometimes with the aid of tar and feathers. But to expel a significant minority that does not chose to depart in peace can mean civil war. It might be said that a discontented minority can be permitted to separate amicably by the simple expedient of redrawing the boundary lines and thus creating a new and independent state. But should every minority that wishes to do so be allowed to secede in full possession of the territory in which they happen to reside, even if this has been so integrated into the economy, transportation system, defenses, and sense of nationhood of the larger country that its loss would be a serious blow? Such forbearance and generosity are unlikely. In any case, what is to be the fate of a minority within a minority, as in the case of Negroes in the South? And of minorities that are not geographically separated but intermixed, like Jehovah's Witnesses?

For Americans these questions are more than rhetorical; here, secession was proposed and rejected as a practical solution by a civil war. Lincoln's first inaugural address pierced the logic of secession:

> Plainly, the central idea of secession is the essence of anarchy. A majority held in restraint by constitutional checks and limitations, and always changing easily with deliberate changes of popular opinions and sentiments, is the only true sovereign of a free people. Whoever rejects it does, of necessity, fly to anarchy or to despotism. Unanimity is impossible; the rule of a minority, as a permanent arrangement, is wholly inadmissible; so that, rejecting the majority principle, anarchy or despotism in some form is all that is left.[9]

But even civil war did not finally settle the debate about the proper scope and limits of rule by majorities in the United States.

There is one further difficulty in the application of majority rule that is of special significance to Americans. That some people may have voted in the distant past to accept the Constitution of the United States —as a rather small proportion of the population did in 1787-8, and as the people or their representatives did in the territories prior to entering the Union—is surely no reason why we, today, should feel bound to accept their verdict: not, at any rate, if we demand continuing 'consent' to the processes of government. Ideally, then, every new generation must be free to refuse its consent to the old rules and to make new ones. The Declaration of Independence contains these ringing phrases:

> That whenever any Form of Government becomes destructive of these ends, (Life, Liberty, and the pursuit of Happiness) it is the Right of the People to alter or to abolish it, and to institute a new Government, laying its foundation on such principles and organizing its powers in such form, as to them shall seem most likely to effect their Safety and Happiness.

Seventy years later, confronted by secession, and on the eve of war, in the inauguration speech from which I quoted a moment ago, Lincoln reaffirmed this principle:

9. Carl Sandburg, Abraham Lincoln, The War Years, vol. I, New York, Harcourt Brace & Co., 1939, p. 132.

[21]

This country, with its institutions, belongs to the people who inhabit it. Whenever they shall grow weary of the existing government, they can exercise their constitutional right of amending it, or their revolutionary right to dismember or over-throw it.[10]

But "the People" is an ambiguous phrase. Do these famous words mean that whenever a majority is discontented with the government it should be free to change it? If they are not permitted to do so, then can we say that they have given their approval, in any realistic sense, to the processes of government? Yet if every majority must be free to alter the rules of government, what is the significance of a "Constitution"? How can a constitution be more binding than ordinary law? Is there no legiti-mate way by which groups smaller than a majority can receive guarantees that the rules they agree to abide by will be more or less permanent and will not change at the whim of the next legislature?

These are difficult questions to answer, and no answers seem to command universal agreement.[11] To gain "the consent of all" consis-tently applying the principle that the majority should be sovereign gives rise to serious problems, both logical and practical. Perhaps under certain unusual conditions, such as a very high degree of homogeneity, among a very small body of citizens, these problems could be solved.

In practise, however, popular governments have moved toward a rather different solution.

A Pluralistic Solution

The practical solutions that democratic countries have evolved are a good deal less clear than a straightforward application of the principle of majority rule. These solutions seem less 'logical,' less coherent, more untidy, and a good deal more attainable. Patterns of democratic govern-ment do not reflect a logically conceived philosophical plan so much as a series of responses to problems of diversity and conflict, by leaders who have sought to build and maintain a nation, to gain the loyalty and

10.   *Ibid.*, p. 133.
11.   *Cf.* Hanna Pîtkin, "Obligations and Consent," *American Political Science Review*, December, 1965, 990–1000; March, 1966, 39–52.

obedience of citizens, to win general and continuing approval of political institutions, and at the same time to conform to aspirations for democracy. However, some common elements can be discovered.

For one thing, in practise, countries with democratic regimes use force, just as other regimes do, to repel threats to the integrity of the national territory. Consequently secession is, as a practical matter, usually either impossible or extremely costly. (Colonies thought to lie outside the territory of the 'nation' may, of course, be granted independence.) To a considerable extent, then, large minorities are virtually 'compelled' to remain within the territorial limits of the nation. To make compulsory citizenship tolerable, great efforts are made to create and sustain a common sense of nationhood, so that minorities of all kinds will identify themselves with the nation. Hence secession or mass emigration are not usually thought of as practical alternatives.

Second, many matters of policy—religious beliefs and practises, for example—are effectively outside the legal authority of any government. Often they are placed beyond the legal authority of government through understandings and agreements widely shared and respected. In many cases these understandings and agreements are expressed in written constitutions that cannot be quickly or easily amended. Such a constitution is regarded as peculiarly binding; and ordinary laws that run counter to the constitution will be invalid, or, at the very least, subject to special scrutiny.

Third, a great many questions of policy are placed in the hands of private, semi-public, and local governmental organizations such as churches, families, business firms, trade unions, towns, cities, provinces, and the like. These questions of policy, like those left to individuals, are also effectively beyond the reach of national majorities, the national legislature, or indeed any national policy-makers acting in their legal and official capacities. In fact, whenever uniform policies are likely to be costly, difficult, or troublesome, in pluralistic democracies the tendency is to find ways by which these policies can be made by smaller groups of like-minded people who enjoy a high degree of legal independence.

Fourth, whenever a group of people believe that they are adversely affected by national policies or are about to be, they generally have extensive opportunities for presenting their case and for negotiations that may produce a more acceptable alternative. In some cases, they may have enough power to delay, to obstruct, and even to veto the attempt to impose policies on them.

Now in addition to all these characteristics, the United States has limited the sovereignty of the majority in still other ways. In fact, the United States has gone so far in this direction that it is sometimes called a pluralistic system, a term I propose to use here.

The fundamental axiom in the theory and practise of American pluralism is, I believe, this: Instead of a single center of sovereign power there must be multiple centers of power, none of which is or can be wholly sovereign. Although the only legitimate sovereign is the people, in the perspective of American pluralism even the people ought never to be an absolute sovereign; consequently no part of the people, such as a majority, ought to be absolutely sovereign.

Why this axiom? The theory and practise of American pluralism tend to assume, as I see it, that the existence of multiple centers of power, none of which is wholly sovereign, will help (may indeed be necessary) to tame power, to secure the consent of all, and to settle conflicts peacefully:

¶ Because one center of power is set against another, power itself will be tamed, civilized, controlled, and limited to decent human purposes, while coercion, the most evil form of power, will be reduced to a minimum.

¶ Because even minorities are provided with opportunities to veto solutions they strongly object to, the consent of all will be won in the long run.

¶ Because constant negotiations among different centers of power are necessary in order to make decisions, citizens and leaders will perfect the precious art of dealing peacefully with their conflicts, and not merely to the benefit of one partisan but to the mutual benefit of all the parties to a conflict.

These are, I think, the basic postulates and even the unconscious ways of thought that are central to the American attempt to cope with the inescapable problems of power, conflict, and consent. How a system reflecting these views came about, how its main institutions operate, what forces sustain it, and how it meets the problems of power, conflict, and consent are the subjects of this book.

Appendix

James Madison on factions:

. . . . . As long as the reason of man continues fallible, and he as at liberty to exercise it, different opinions will be formed. As long as the connection subsists between his reason and his self-love, his opinions and his passions will have a re-ciprocal influence on each other; and the former will be objects to which the latter will attach themselves. The diversity in the faculties of men, from which the rights of property originate, is not less an unsuperable obstacle to a uniformity of interests. The protection of these faculties is the first object of government. From the pro-tection of different and unequal faculties of acquiring property, the possession of different degrees and kinds of property immediately results; and from the influence of these on the sentiments and views of the respective proprietors, ensues a division of the society into different interests and parties.

The latent causes of faction are thus sown in the nature of man; and we see them everywhere brought into different degrees of activity, according to the different circumstances of civil society. A zeal for different opinions concerning religion, con-cerning government, and many other points, as well of speculation as of practice; an attachment to different leaders ambitiously contending for pre-eminence and power; or to persons of other descriptions whose fortunes have been interesting to the human passions, have, in turn, divided mankind into parties, inflamed them with mutual animosity, and rendered them much more disposed to vex and oppress each other than to co-operate for their common good. So strong is this propensity of mankind to fall into mutual animosities, that where no substantial occasion presents itself, the most frivolous and fanciful distinctions have been sufficient to kindle their unfriendly passions and excite their most violent conflicts. But the most common and durable source of factions has been the various and unequal distribution of property. Those who hold and those who are without property have ever formed distinct interests in society. Those who are creditors, and those who are debtors, fall under a like dis-crimination. A landed interest, a manufacturing interest, a mercantile interest, a moneyed interest, with many lesser interests, grow up of necessity in civilized nations, and divide them into different classes, actuated by different sentiments and views. The regulation of these various and interfering interests forms the principal task of modern legislation, and involves the spirit of party and faction in the necessary and ordinary operations of government. *The Federalist*, New York, The Modern Library, n.d. pp. 55–56.

2

"A REPUBLIC—IF YOU CAN KEEP IT"

I N SOME NOTES made by Dr. James McHenry, who attended the Convention as a delegate from Maryland, we find an anecdote as it was evidently written down shortly after the delegates ended their work in September, 1787:

> A lady asked Dr. Franklin Well Doctor what have we got a republic or a monarchy. A republic replied the Doctor if you can keep it.[1]

"A republic—if you can keep it." The results of the Convention could not have been put more succinctly.

For the Constitution proposed by the men at the Convention was both an end and a beginning. It was the culmination of a slow, steady, and gradual growth in America of institutions, practises, and ideas favorable to popular government. It was the beginning of a new period in which these institutions, practises, and ideas were to be tested and vigorously expanded.

The men at the Constitutional Convention did not create a republic. They helped one to emerge. No group of men can create popular government unless the people and their existing institutions are ripe for it. By 1787 Americans were ready for a republic; so much so that sooner or later, one is tempted to conjecture, a republic would surely

1. *Documents, op. cit.,* 952.

[26]

have grown up on this soil. The men who worked in Philadelphia through the summer of 1787 did not—could not—give final shape to the American political system, nor even to the constitutional foundations. The shape of our system was bound to be influenced by other men, by social and economic conditions, by the beliefs and attitudes of Americans, by events beyond the control of the handful of men in Independence Hall meeting week after week in the face of summer's heat and flaring tempers. Yet if it is easy to exaggerate the work of the Convention, or of any constitutional convention, it would be wrong to minimize the consequences of that Convention. For the framework of government proposed by the men in Philadelphia, and in due course accepted by the states and the people, was a unique framework. Once it was put into effect, it was bound to influence the specific ways in which popular government would or could develop in the new United States. If the American political system today is different in some important respects from any other system, this is, at least in part, a result of the *particular* pattern of representative government that grew out of the beliefs, the proposals, the matters of agreement and conflict, the discussions, and the compromises of the Convention. It is a result, too, of the fact that Americans of later generations continued to value, and so to preserve, many of the major aspects of the pattern shaped at the Convention.

Were the Founders Conservatives or Revolutionaries?

The Constitutional Convention, curiously enough, has been described both as a revolutionary body and as a conservative one. There is truth in both views.

Until the year 1787, the entire history of mankind had never witnessed a single case of successful and enduring representative republic over a large area. This was a fact of which every man at the Convention was well aware. If a delegate did not happen to know it when he arrived in Philadelphia, he learned it soon enough, for it was on the minds and lips of all the greater leaders of the Convention. Some of the men who came to Philadelphia—most of them, as it turned out—had in view something that had never been done before. Democracy, though rare, was not new. But to expand representative democracy over a vast domain —that would be a new and revolutionary undertaking.

Although the Founders were uncertain as to how many people there were in the thirteen states, they evidently assumed that the total population was something between 2.5 and 3 million. One compilation used at the Convention counted 2.6 million whites and a half million Negroes. (These were conservative estimates: The federal census of 1790 showed a total population just under 4 million.) Already the number of free white male citizens was fifteen to twenty times as large as in Athens at the time of Pericles. As Charles Pinckney of South Carolina pointed out in the early weeks of the Convention, "The United States include a territory of about 1500 miles in length, and in breadth about 400."[2] The State of New York alone was larger than the whole Greek mainland, larger than the entire Swiss Confederacy, larger than the Dutch Confederacy. And the men in Philadelphia took it for granted that in both population and territory the United States would expand—ultimately, perhaps, into a country of unbelievable vastness.

All the experience furnished by history seemed to foredoom an attempt to establish a national government on republican principles over such a great domain.

More than twenty centuries earlier, the citizens of many Greek city states—especially Athens—participated in political decisions to an extent

2. Most of what we know about the debates is found in Madison's detailed, full, and apparently scrupulous "Notes of Debates," which he wrote down each day but which he did not revise until after he retired from the Presidency in 1817, and which were not finally published until 1840. The official record was little more than a list of votes taken. In addition to Madison, six other delegates kept notes, but none were as detailed as his. All of these notes are collected in *Documents Illustrative of the Formation of the Union of the American States*, selected, arranged, and indexed by Charles C. Tansill (Government Printing Office, Washington, 1927) cited here as *Documents*. The quotation above is at p. 805.

A shorter collection of materials, including an extensive though incomplete selection from Madison's notes, may be found in *The Federal Convention and the Formation of the Union of the American States*, edited, with an introduction by Winton U. Solberg, New York, Liberal Arts Press, 1958. Saul K. Padover has arranged Madison's report on the debates according to topics (and has excluded some material) in *To Secure These Blessings*, New York, Washington Square Press, Ridge Press, 1962. This is the most convenient arrangement of the debates available.

A particularly compact and relevant analysis of the Constitutional Convention is Arthur N. Holcombe, *Our Most Perfect Union, From Eighteenth-Century Principles to Twentieth-Century Practise*, Cambridge, Harvard University Press, 1950, esp. ch. 2.

that probably has never existed since. Athenian politics was virtually a permanent town meeting. Yet the Greeks, for all their political genius, failed to create a federal system that would link one city with another in a representative democracy.[3] Indeed, they seem always to have held fast to their belief that citizenship was meaningless unless it provided for direct participation and control over political decisions. Their inability to develop a wider sense of citizenship and to create a larger Hellenic state in which the perennial wars of Greek against Greek would be eliminated led in time to their subjection, first by the Macedonians and then by the Romans.

More than any other people before, and more than most since, the Romans learned the complex arts of managing a single government over a large area. The Republic of Rome endured for nearly five centuries. The history of that Republic was as familiar to the men at the Convention as our own national history is to us, for their education had typically included a study of the classics; and they were always quick to cite Roman experience. They knew, then, that the Republic had been initially a city government, and that the Romans had been generous in extending the privileges of citizenship throughout the Italian peninsula, and that they had attempted (being a conservative people) to adapt the institutions of the city to the government of the new and greater Rome. Yet the Founders also knew that the Romans never did create an effective system of representation.

The Founders also knew that some of the cities of medieval Italy were, like Florence, republics. But Italy had never developed a national government; in *The Prince*, Machiavelli (1469-1527) had concluded pessimistically that Italy was incapable of a republic and that only a

3. The Greeks knew direct democracy, of course, and they seem to have known representative governments of a sort, but not the combination of the two in a representative democracy. They constructed leagues, alliances, and confederacies, most of which were short-lived; but whether any of these had central legislatures consisting of representatives who were chosen by the people and who could make laws binding on the citizens of each city seems somewhat doubtful, though the matter is by no means certain. Whatever may have been the historical reality, the fact is that the Greeks left no legacy of specific principles of representative democracy comparable in the slightest way to the Athenian view that only direct democracy on a small scale was truly worthwhile. The interested reader should consult J. A. O. Larsen, *Representative Government in Greek and Roman History*, Berkeley and Los Angeles, University of California Press, 1966; Walter R. Agard, *What Democracy Meant to the Greeks*, Madison, University of Wisconsin Press, 1965; H. D. F. Kitto, *The Greeks*, Baltimore, Penguin Books, 1951, chs. 5 and 9.

vigorous and even tyrannical leader could ever bring peace and unity to Italy. Before the eighteenth century, the most extensive development of democracy had occurred among the rural cantons of Switzerland, which of all modern countries can rightly claim to have had a lengthier experience with democratic institutions than the United States. In 1787, however, Switzerland was still a confederacy in which the cantons were sovereign states; their central 'national' assembly, the Diet, had virtually no power. If the men at the Convention had wanted a confederacy, they need not have come to Philadelphia at all. The Articles of Confederation already provided at least as much of a central government as the Swiss then enjoyed. Yet it was precisely because they were in various degrees discontented with the weak confederacy of the Articles that these Americans had assembled. The Swiss example, like Greece, told a good deal about the prospects of democracy on a small scale. But it did not provide a model for a representative republic in a new and extensive nation. Nor, in this respect, was the Netherlands any more useful; for there, too, the oligarchical republics in the provinces were for all practical purposes wholly sovereign.

What the Founders proposed to do, then, had never been done before. More than that, a fair reading of a familiar body of historical experience would suggest that their efforts were more likely to fail than to succeed. You can have republican government in a canton, a city, or perhaps even a small state, historical experience seemed to say, but you cannot have it over a large area. Republics can link themselves into a confederacy with a weak central government; but if you want a strong central government you cannot have a republic. The Founders—with, to be sure, some fears—rejected this dilemma and proposed to establish the first great republic. In this perspective, then, the Founders were indeed revolutionaries.

Yet as revolutionaries they seem oddly out of place. They were, it is true, a youthful group. Nearly 40 per cent were not over forty years old, and three-quarters of them were under fifty. Some of the most vigorous leaders at the Convention were surprisingly young. James Madison was thirty-six, Gouverneur Morris was thirty-five, Alexander Hamilton was thirty-two, and Charles Pinckney was twenty-nine.

Nonetheless, most of them had already had extensive and often even distinguished public careers. Many had acquired experience and reputation during the Revolutionary War. With few exceptions they were substantial and well known figures in their states; some were respected throughout all thirteen states; and the fame of a few, like Franklin and Washington, extended to Europe. Most of them were moderately well-to-do: a few were exceedingly wealthy by the standards of the time. John Rutledge and Pierce Butler of South Carolina were big planters and could be counted on to defend the interests of the planting and slave-holding aristocracy of that state. Gouverneur Morris of Pennsylvania was a wealthy financier and a conservative aristocrat. Although Nathaniel Gorham of Massachusetts had started his business career as apprentice to a merchant, by 1787 he was one of the leading businessmen in his state.

They were, then, a respectable group. Sixty per cent of them were lawyers; an incredibly high proportion for those times—nearly half—were college graduates.

Although they may have seemed revolutionary to Europeans, in their American setting they were not so daring. To be sure, a national government constructed on republican principles was a new experiment for Americans and for the world, but by 1787 representative governments were already well established at the state level. The long period of colonial rule, extending over a century and a half, had given the people in the colonies considerable training in the skills required to operate a representative government. Despite the myths that have since grown up, the colonies had enjoyed an astounding measure of self-government. One house of a colonial legislature was invariably elected by the voters; the second house was sometimes appointed by the first; and in two states, Connecticut and Rhode Island, the governor was elected by the voters. Where the governor was appointed by the King, conflicts between governor and legislature contributed to the development of the arts of managing representative institutions. Since the legislature usually controlled the purse-strings and voted the governor's salary, even a royal governor could sometimes be outmaneuvered.

Just how many people were eligible to vote in colonial elections has been a matter of debate. For many years it was assumed that property requirements restricted the vote to a small and wealthy minority; but recent research indicates that in most of the colonies from half to three-quarters of the white adult males must have been eligible to vote in the years before the Revolution.[4] In Massachusetts, possibly as many as 95 per cent of the adult males could vote.[5]

How did the men at the Convention look upon this strong tide of

4. Chilton Williamson, *American Suffrage from Property to Democracy 1760–1860*, Princeton, N.J., Princeton University Press, 1960, ch. 2.
5. Robert E. Brown, *Middle–Class Democracy and the Revolution in Massachusetts, 1691–1780*, Ithaca, New York, Cornell University Press, 1955, pp. 49–50.

representative democracy? Some scholars have argued—implicitly or explicitly—that the Constitution was the work of a small group of wealthy aristocrats who wished to stem the rapid advance of democracy in the states by constructing a strong national government that would protect the economic interests of large planters, speculators, financiers, merchants and shippers from their natural enemies, the small farmers, who made up the overwhelming majority of the population of the United States, and the mechanics and artisans in the cities, who, though still a small minority, nevertheless were a potential threat to the well-to-do.[6]

In recent years, however, this view of the Convention and its fruits has been subject to extensive criticism. Although a fair assessment of this controversy is impossible in a short space, the criticisms cannot easily be turned aside. If the Founders were engaged in an anti-democratic counter-revolution, how did it happen that the Constitution was approved by eleven states within the following year? The answer had once been that a large part of the adult males were disfranchised by property requirements; hence the conventions held in the various states to approve or disapprove the Constitution were easily rigged by the same aristocratic minority whose representatives had drafted the Constitution. But more recent evidence, as we have just seen, seems to indicate that the suffrage was in fact rather widely held in most of the states. If the small farmers who comprised the overwhelming bulk of the population were opposed to the Constitution they must have been very apathetic or confused, because they evidently did not turn out in large numbers to vote against it.

In the second place, in a surprisingly short time the arrangements provided for in the Constitution seem to have acquired very widespread approval among the general population. In fact, one of the most influential people at the Convention, James Madison, was soon to become the main leader in Congress of the very forces—the small farmers— who, according to the theory, were defeated at the Convention by the

6. The famous pioneering study in this vein was Charles Beard, *An Economic Interpretation of the Constitution*, New York, Macmillan, 1913. Many later historians adopted, expanded, or developed views implicitly contained in Beard's analysis. See, particularly, Merrill Jensen, *The Articles of Confederation*, Madison, University of Wisconsin Press, 1940, and *The New Nation*, New York, Knopf, 1950. Beard was severely attacked by Robert Brown, *Beard and the Constitution*, 1956, and in turn defended by Lee Benson, *Turner & Beard, American Historical Writing Reconsidered*, New York, The Free Press of Glencoe, 1960. A succinct and judicious evaluation of the debate is contained in Edmund S. Morgan, *The Birth of the Republic, 1763–89*, Chicago, University of Chicago Press, 1956.

aristocratic counter-revolution. Yet Madison, like Jefferson, was a staunch supporter of the Constitution; and there is no persuasive evidence that their supporters, the small farmers, were less so. In fact, it was not the small farmers or artisans who displayed the most opposition to the Constitution during the following generation, but a wealthy minority who distrusted democracy and disliked the power given to the people under the new republic.

Finally, on a number of key issues, including the issue of democracy versus aristocracy, the men at the Convention were not of one mind. Although most of them agreed on the need for a stronger central government, they disagreed—as we shall see in a moment—on the extent to which a strengthened central government should be under the influence of the people. If the framework of government they finally proposed showed what the Founders could agree on, it also reflected their disagreements and conflicts.

Indeed, as one reads Madison's reports of the debates at the Convention, one senses two rather different levels of debate. At one level there were practical problems of designing a system of government that would not only have the approval of the delegates and of the States but would work well enough to endure: Should there be one executive or three? How many representatives should there be in the legislative body? What specific powers should be given to Congress?

But underlying and greatly influencing the debates on practical matters, there were differences in political objectives that seemed to reflect differences in political ideas and ideology, for the Founders simply were not of one mind in their beliefs as to what kind of political system was desirable, possible, or likely to endure in America.

The controversy over the private political objectives of the Founders cannot be settled here, and perhaps may never be settled. Yet it is perfectly clear from what the delegates said during the Convention, and from their conduct in later years, that they disagreed in a number of important ways. In fact, there seem to have been four general issues on which they were sharply divided. How each person stood on these general questions appears to have influenced his stand on the more concrete and practical problems of designing a framework of government.

These four general questions were: (1) Was the new republic to be essentially democratic or essentially aristocratic? (2) Was it to have a strong national government, or was it to be a confederacy? (3) What should be the relative power in the new republic of the small states and the large states? (4) How far should one go in compromising his views on these questions in order to arrive at an agreement?

[33]

Disagreement on the answers to these questions did not end when the Founders completed the writing of the Constitution, nor when the Constitution was adopted by the states and put into effect. On the contrary, conflicting answers to these questions continued to reappear in American politics. Nearly all of the great conflicts that have wracked the country since 1787 have raised these questions anew. In fact, the differences in viewpoint expressed during the Convention continue to appear in American politics right down to the present day.

Democracy or Aristocracy?

Thanks to a rule of secrecy that was adopted by the Convention at the third meeting, the delegates were free to ventilate their opinions with unusual candor. Probably they would not have spoken so frankly outside the closed doors of Independence Hall. Fortunately, then, the records of the Convention enable us to learn something about the real beliefs of the delegates. Secrecy was, no doubt, of particular value to those delegates who distrusted popular government and yearned for some kind of aristocratic republic in which the rich and the well born would occupy a special place. These delegates might not have dared to admit in public what they were willing to affirm in private.

The most articulate spokesmen for an aristocratic republic were Gouverneur Morris of Pennsylvania, Rufus King of Massachusetts, and of course Alexander Hamilton of New York (whose influence was greatly reduced, however, by his extreme proposals and his fitful attendance.) One of the delegates from Georgia, William Pierce, contributed little to the Convention but left a good deal to posterity, for he made some vivid sketches of the delegates, from which we learn that

> Mr. Gouverneur Morris is one of those Genius's in whom
> every species of talents combine to render him conspicuous and
> flourishing in public debate:—He winds through all the mazes
> of rhetoric, and throws around him such a glare that he charms,
> captivates, and leads away the senses of all who hear him. With
> an infinite streach of fancy he brings to view things when he is
> engaged in deep argumentation, that render all the labor of
> reasoning easy and pleasing. But with all these powers he is
> fickle and inconsistant,—never pursuing one train of thinking,

—nor ever regular. He has gone through a very extensive course of reading, and is acquainted with all the sciences. No Man has more wit,—nor can any one engage the attention more than Mr. Morris. He was bred to the Law, but I am told he disliked the profession, and turned Merchant. He is engaged in some great mercantile matters with his namesake Mr. Robert Morris. This Gentleman is about 38 years old, he has been unfortunate in losing one of his Legs, and getting all the flesh taken off his right arm by a scald, when a youth.[7]

Morris's view on the Senate are a good example of his attitudes. Although he did not maintain a consistent position as to how the Senators should be chosen, he was unvarying in his views as to the proper role of the Senate:

It is confessed, on all hands, that the second branch ought to be a check on the first—for without its having this effect it is perfectly useless.—The first branch, originating from the people, will ever be subject to precipitancy, changeability, and excess. Experience evinces the truth of this remark without having recourse to reading. This can only be checked by ability and virtue in the second branch. On your present system, can you suppose that one branch will possess it more than the others? The second branch ought to be composed of men of great and established property—an aristocracy. Men, who from pride will support consistency and permanency; and to make them completely independent, they must be chosen for life, or they will be a useless body. Such an aristocratic body will keep down the turbulency of democracy. But if you elect them for a shorter period, they will be only a name, and we had better be without them. Thus constituted, I hope they will show us the weight of aristocracy.[8]

Hamilton was a great admirer of the British Constitution as it existed (or rather as he believed it to exist) in the eighteenth century. "In his private opinion," Madison reports him as saying "he had no scruple in declaring . . . that the British Govt was the best in the world: and that he doubted much whether any thing short of it would

7. *Documents*, pp. 101, 102
8. *Ibid.*, p. 838. The quotation is from the notes of Robert Yates, a delegate from New York.

[35]

do in America."[9] Accordingly, Hamilton proposed to emulate the British system as closely as possible in designing a new constitution for Americans. An Assembly elected by the people would take the place of the House of Commons. Corresponding to the House of Lords—"a most noble institution"—, he proposed a Senate elected for life "or at least during good behavior." The absence of a monarch was annoying. "As to the Executive, it seemed to be admitted that no good one could be established on Republican principles . . . The English model was the only good one on the subject . . . Let the Executive also be for life."[10]

The most consistent spokesmen at the Convention in behalf of popular control were James Wilson of Pennsylvania, George Mason of Virginia, and James Madison.

Of these, Wilson seems to have had the deepest confidence in popular government and the most clear-cut vision of what a democratic republic should and would be. Wilson was a Scot who had attended the University of Saint Andrews, before emigrating to America, where he had taken up the practice of law. He was described by Pierce as follows:

> Mr. Wilson ranks among the foremost in legal and political knowledge. He has joined to a fine genius all that can set him off and show him to advantage. He is well acquainted with Man, and understands all the passions that influence him. Government seems to have been his peculiar Study, all the political institutions of the World he knows in detail, and can trace stages of the Grecian commonwealth down to the present time. No man is more clear, copious, and comprehensive than Mr. Wilson, yet he is no great Orator. He draws attention not by the charm of his eloquence, but by the force of his reasoning. He is about 45 years old.[11]

Early in the Convention, Wilson announced that "he was for raising the federal pyramid to a considerable altitude, and for that reason wished to give it as broad a basis as possible. No government could long subsist without the confidence of the people. In a republican Government this

9. *Ibid.*, p. 220.
10. *Documents*, pp. 221–222. In the plan he submitted on June 18, the Senate and the Executive were to serve "during good behavior," which ordinarily would mean for life (pp. 224–225). The notes kept by Yates of New York confirm Madison's account. See *Documents*, pp. 781–782; for various texts of Hamilton's plan of government, see pp. 979, 988.
11. *Ibid.*, p. 101.

confidence was peculiarly essential."[12] Wilson urged that not only the lower house but also the Senate and the President should be chosen by the people.[13]

Wilson represented at best a small minority. At the other extreme, the ardent aristocrats were also a rather tiny group. Although decisions on specific questions were often influenced by considerations that had little to do with a delegate's preference for democracy or aristocracy, there were several issues on which the differences showed up most clearly. These were whether either the President or members of the Senate should have a limited term or hold office for life or good behavior, and whether the right to vote should be constitutionally restricted to free holders or property owners of some sort. On these issues Wilson, Mason, and Madison took a democratic position, while on all three of them Morris favored the aristocratic view (Table 2.1).

It falsifies history, then, to assume that the delegates at the Convention were in substantial agreement on the alternatives of a democratic republic versus an aristocratic republic. Clearly they were not. Yet it is also easy to exaggerate the extent of their differences. Although some delegates advocated a democratic republic and others an aristocratic republic, most of them were probably ranged somewhere between Wilson at one pole and Morris or Hamilton at the other. Mason, who stood with Wilson on the three issues listed in Table 2.1, frequently took less

Table 2.1 *Three Issues in the Constitutional Convention*

	LIMITED TERM FOR PRESIDENT	LIMITED TERM FOR SENATORS	A CONSTITUTION WITHOUT RESTRICTIONS ON SUFFRAGE
Wilson	Yes	Yes	Yes
Mason	Yes	Yes	Yes
Madison	Yes	Yes	Yes[a]
Hamilton	No	No	?[b]
G. Morris	No[c]	No	No[d]

[a] Madison's views are not entirely clear. On July 26 he opposed restricting the suffrage to freeholders. On August 7 he seemed to lean in that direction. Cf. *Documents*, pp. 489, 935.

[b] Hamilton was absent during these discussions.

[c] At first Gouverneur Morris strongly supported a motion to give the executive tenure "during good behavior." "This is the way to get a good Government." *Documents*, p. 396. A week later, he seemed to have doubts. *Ibid.*, p. 447. But he generally opposed efforts to limit the term of the President. E.g. pp. 453, 458.

[d] Favored restricting the suffrage to freeholders. *Documents*, pp. 489, 935.

12. *Ibid.*, p. 126.
13. *Ibid.*, pp. 209–211.

advanced positions on other issues. Madison, perhaps the most conservative of the three men, was evidently near the midpoint of the Convention. If he was as democratic as Wilson on some issues, on others such as limiting the suffrage to freeholders or advocating definite constitutional protections for wealth and property he was conservative enough to maintain the confidence of pro-aristocratic delegates like Morris.

On two important questions involving democracy, nearly all the delegates were in agreement. First, with only a few exceptions, they believed that the new national government should contain an important element of popular government. Even Morris and Hamilton wanted one branch chosen by the people. To be sure, a few delegates, like the South Carolinians Pierce Butler and Charles Cotesworth Pinckney, went so far as to oppose the election of the lower house by the people; they wanted even this choice to be filtered through the state legislatures. But their views do not seem to have had much influence on the Convention.

Second, evidently every delegate was firmly opposed to a national government in which the representatives elected by the voters would have full constitutional authority to enact any laws whatsoever. A follower of Rousseau might have said, "Let there be no constitutional restrictions on what the people (or, in practise, a majority of their representatives) can do." An unusually doctrinaire follower of Rousseau might have added, "For the people can do no wrong." A more moderate follower might have said, "The people or their representatives from time to time may—nay, probably will—pass bad laws. But it is better that the people should have the chance to learn from their errors than that they should be prevented from acting in ways they think best. After all, men who frame constitutions are also human, and times do change. By putting restrictions into a Constitution the framers may prevent not only a bad law today but also a good law tomorrow."

No delegate to the Convention ever advanced arguments remotely like these. If one had, his arguments would have fallen on deaf ears. One reason was purely practical. The task, as the delegates saw it, was to enlarge the powers of the national government; yet there was much opposition to a more powerful national government. The defenders of the Articles of Confederation would undoubtedly put up a very stiff fight against the new constitution. To give unlimited powers to a majority of elected representatives was exactly equivalent to giving unlimited constitutional authority to the national government. But an unlimited national government in any form would surely be turned down in every state. The most that the Convention could do, therefore, would be to frame a national government with definitely circumscribed authority.

In addition to this practical reason, there were others of a more philosophic cast. Whether democrats or aristocrats, the men at the Convention shared a hard-headed, unsentimental, skeptical view of man's ability to withstand the temptations of power. They took it for granted that men are easily corrupted by power; to any man with great power, they might have said, self-restraint is a fragile dike. The best way to prevent the abuse of power, then, was not to trust in human character but to limit the legal authority allocated to any person and to set one power over against another.

"Men love power," said Hamilton . . . "Give all power to the many, they will oppress the few. Give all power to the few, they will oppress the many. Both therefore ought to have power, that they may defend itself against the other."[14] "The Rich," Gouverneur Morris said, and well he knew, "will strive to establish their dominion and enslave the rest. They always did. They always will. The proper security against them is to form them into a separate interest. The two forces (the rich and the poor) will then controul each other."[15] Mason announced that "he went on a principle often advanced and in which he concurred, that 'a majority when interested will oppress the minority.' "[16] Wilson, that unwavering advocate of a democratic republic, said:

> Despotism comes on Mankind in different shapes, sometimes in an Executive, sometimes in a Military one. Is there no danger of a Legislative despotism? Theory and practise both proclaim it. If the Legislative authority be not restrained, there can be neither liberty nor stability . . . In a single House there is no check, but the inadequate one, of the virtue & good sense of those who compose it.[17]

It was not enough, then, to construct a national government with definite but limited legal authority. The potential abuse of power had somehow to be checked. How was this to be accomplished? The answers that came from the Convention can be summarized in three prescriptions.

1. *The principle of limited authority.* Since the virtues and wisdom of men are not powerful enough to prevent their

14. *Ibid.*, pp. 217–221.
15. *Ibid.*, p. 319.
16. *Ibid.*, p. 587.
17. *Ibid.*, pp. 212, 213.

abusing their power, no person, official, or group—whether a minority or a majority—should ever be allowed to have unlimited legal authority. In other words, legal authority should always be strictly limited.

2. *The principle of balanced authority.* Since purely legal or even constitutional restraints, standing by themselves, are sure to prove inadequate, whenever authority is allocated by law or constitution to one official or body—whether representing a minority or a majority—that authority must be counter-balanced (to some degree) by allocating authority to some other official or body.

3. *The principal of political pluralism.* Since even legal and constitutional arrangements will be subverted if some citizens or groups of citizens gain disproportionate opportunities for power in comparison with other citizens, the potential power of one citizen or group must be balanced by the potential power of other citizens.

From the first two principles it followed that the legal authority of the proposed national government should be carefully defined and limited, and that the authority allocated by the Constitution to one branch or body should be offset by authority allocated to another.

The Constitution reflects these two principles in a great variety of ways:

¶ It preserves the states as fixed elements in a federal system.
¶ It yields to the Congress specific, not unlimited, legal powers (Article I, Section 8).
¶ It specifically denies to the Congress legal authority of some kinds (Article I, Section 9).
¶ It provides for a Congress consisting of two separate and rather independent branches, whose members have somewhat different qualifications and were until 1913 chosen by different means (Article I, Sections 1, 2, 3).
¶ It forbids members of Congress from holding executive offices during the period for which they are elected, thus making it difficult for the President to influence them by appointing them to high offices in the Executive Branch (Article I, Section 6).
¶ It provides for a President elected for a fixed term independently of Congress and bars Congress from shortening his

tenure (except by impeachment) and from increasing or decreasing his salary during his four-year term (Article II, Section 1).

¶ It assigns to the President definite but limited legal authority, including a veto of laws passed by Congress (Article II, Section 2).

¶ It provides for a Judicial Branch substantially independent of both President and Congress (Article III).

¶ It makes amendments to the Constitution difficult by requiring approval of two-thirds the members of each house, and of three-fourths of the States (Article V).

Moreover, when in 1791 the Bill of Rights filled one of the great gaps in the Constitution, it amplified these principles by imposing further specific restraints on the Congress, by guaranteeing a number of individual rights, and by re-emphasizing (in the Tenth Amendment) the limited and federal character of the political system.

The third principle, Political Pluralism, is more vague and more difficult to execute than the others. It draws strength less from the Constitution than from 'politics,' less from laws than from social and economic forces, less from officials than from citizens. Its application, therefore, does not depend as much on what the Convention did as on what the country that existed outside the Convention has done; and less on the delegates than on the generations to come. Nevertheless the formulation of the principle goes back to the Convention, and specifically to Madison who, in a brilliant analysis during the second week of the Convention, sought to meet head-on the charge by the aristocratic faction that a democratic republic would open the door to oppression by the majority:

. . . *The lesson we are to draw* (Madison admitted) . . . *is that where a majority are united by a common sentiment, and have an opportunity, the rights of the minor party become insecure. In a Republican Gov.ᵗ the Majority if united have always an opportunity. The only remedy is to enlarge the sphere, & thereby divide the community into so great a number of interests & parties, that in the I.ˢᵗ place a majority will not be likely at the same moment to have a common interest separate from that of the whole or of the minority; and in the 2ⁿᵈ, place, that in case they sh.ᵈ have such an interest, they may not be apt to be united in the pursuit of it. It was incumbent on us*

[41]

*then to try this remedy, and with that view to frame a republi-
can system on such a scale & in such a form as will controul all
the evils w.*^{ch} *have been experienced.*[18]

Madison must have liked this passage: he inserted it almost unchanged in Federalist paper #10. There it has become famous. Madison
had a right to be pleased with his words, for he had set forth a new
political principle.

A Confederacy or a National Republic?

A month after the delegates got down to business, one of them, Dr.
William Johnson of Connecticut, observed,

> . . . *The controversy must be endless whilst Gentlemen differ
> in the grounds of the arguments; Those on one side considering
> the States as districts of people composing one political Society;
> those on the other considering them as so many political
> societies.*[19]

Johnson (whom Pierce described as "a character much celebrated
for his legal knowledge . . . [who] . . . possesses a very strong and enlightened understanding") had put his finger squarely on one of the
central issues of the Convention. Were Americans in the process of
becoming a single people? Or were they thirteen separate peoples? Were
they one nation—or several nations? Would they be served best by a new
and vigorous national government—or by a confederation of state governments united by a relatively weak central government?

Nearly every delegate, to be sure, professed to be in favor of a federal
system. But the word 'federal' was no more than a label. The trouble was
that they did not agree on what a 'federal' system was or should be.
"Great latitude," Hamilton told the delegates, "therefore must be given
to the signification of the term."[20]

On the one side were a number of the most distinguished delegates
at the Convention—Madison, Wilson, Hamilton, Gouverneur Morris,

18. *Ibid.,* p. 163.
19. *Ibid.,* p. 297.
20. *Ibid.,* p. 216.

Rufus King—who wanted to create a strong national government.

> . . . Bad Govern.*ts* [said Wilson] are of two sorts. I. that which
> does too little. 2. that which does too much: that which fails
> thro' weakness; and that which destroys thro' oppression. Un-
> der which of these evils do the U. States at present groan?
> under the weakness and inefficiency of its Govern.*t* To remedy
> this weakness we have been sent to this Convention.[21]

This group of delegates—one might call them National Federalists
—had three distinct objects in mind. First, they sought a definite and
considerable increase in the powers of the national government. Since
practically everyone at the Convention agreed that the national government should be strengthened, the differences among the delegates on
this score were a matter of degree. But matters of degree are extraordinarily important: after all, the difference between jumping into a hot bath,
an icy lake, or a tub of boiling water is only a matter of degree.

In the second place, the National Federalists wanted a central
government that had legal authority over individual citizens. To National Federalists it was a fatal flaw in the Articles of Confederation that the
Congress had no authority over individuals; that Congress could act only
through the States themselves. Clearly it is one thing to compel an
individual to obey laws passed by the national government; but it is quite
another to compel a state. The disobedience of individuals can generally
be met by police, by courts, by fines and imprisonments; the disobedience of a state creates the terrifying choice of governmental impotence or
civil war.

Finally, the National Federalists wanted a national government that
directly represented individual citizens and not simply the states. The
central government, in their view, should be responsive to the citizens of
the United States, not just to the States.

Some of the delegates—the State Federalists, let us call them—were
very strongly opposed to all these objectives of the National Federalists.
One of the State Federalists, Lansing of New York, announced during
the fourth week:

> . . . I am clearly of opinion that I am not authorized to accede
> to a system which will annihilate the State governments and
> the Virginia plan [i.e., the plan supported by the National
> Federalists] is declarative of such extinction . . . Can we ex-

21. *Ibid.*, p. 308.

pect that thirteen States will surrender their governments up to a national plan?[22]

In fact, Lansing and his fellow New Yorker, Yates, left the Convention not long after, protesting that state sovereignty would be destroyed under a national government.

Luther Martin of Maryland presented the most extensive case for State Federalism. ". . . At great length and with great eagerness," Madison noted, he argued "that the General Gov.ᵗ was meant merely to preserve the State Govern.ᵗˢ: not to govern individuals: that its powers ought to be kept within narrow limits; . . . that the States like individuals were in a State of nature equally sovereign & free."[23] "This," Madison added in one of his rare editorial comments, "was the substance of the residue of his discourse which was delivered with much diffuseness & considerable vehemence."[24] Like Lansing and Yates, Martin quit the convention and fought bitterly in Maryland against the adoption of the Constitution.

Most of the delegates agreed with the State Federalists on two points. First, the states had to be preserved as constituent and important elements in a federal system. In this sense, almost everyone was a 'Federalist.' Hamilton, as usual, was a lonely exception; of all the National Federalists he was the most extreme, for he was quite willing to see the States abolished.[25] But Hamilton's views found little support. As Johnson of Connecticut dryly remarked: "A gentleman from New York, with boldness and decision, proposed a system totally different . . . ; and though he has been praised by every body, he has been supported by none."[26]

Second, there was the age-old conviction that a republic could not function over a large area. Madison had tried to blunt this point by arguing, as we have seen, that size was less a vice than a virtue. Yet the worry about size continued. "The largest states," Ellsworth of Connecticut observed, singling out Virginia and Massachusetts for special atten-

---

22. *Ibid.*, p. 787. This comment is found in the notes of delegate Yates, which were later transcribed by Lansing himself.
23. *Ibid.*, pp. 287, 288.
24. *Ibid.*, p. 290.
25. See his discussion and his plan in *Documents*, pp. 215 ff., and his subsequent remark quoted in Madison's notes: "As States, he thought they ought to be abolished. But he admitted the necessity of leaving in them, subordinate jurisdictions." *Ibid.*, p. 238.
26. *Ibid.*, p. 791.

tion, "are the worst governed."[27] Although the delegates from these states denied the specific charge, the general point was admitted even by the most enthusiastic National Federalists:

Hamilton, on July 16: *The extent of the Country to be governed discouraged him . . . This view of the subject almost led him to despair that a Republican Gov^t. could be established over so great an extent.*[28]

Wilson, on June 25: *When he considered the amazing extent of Country—the immense population which is to fill it, the influence which the Gov^t. we are to form will have, not only on the present generation of our people & their multiplied posterity, but on the whole Globe, he was lost in the magnitude of the object.*[29]

Gouverneur Morris, on July 19: *It has been a maxim in Political Science that Republican Government is not adapted to a large extent of Country because the energy of the Executive Magistracy can not reach the extreme parts of it. Our Country is an extensive one.*[30]

Because they had no relevant experience to go on, the delegates continued throughout the Convention to express worries like these. They saw that they were fleeing from known evils toward dangers both known and unsuspected. But had they given less weight to the existing disadvantages and more to the dangers in a cloudy future, they would never have drafted a new constitution.

The confirmed and intransigeant State Federalists were a small minority among the delegates. Although the Articles of Confederation had many supporters outside the Convention, obviously the ardent State Federalists were not well represented at the Convention. Many of the leading opponents of radical change did not attend. Rhode Island, a stronghold of State Federalism, did not even send a delegation, and she refused to ratify the Constitution until 1790 (when it was already in effect). Delegates like Yates and Lansing left in anger, and subsequently fought the ratification of the Constitution in their own states.

The National Federalists were evidently much closer to the main body of the delegates than were the extreme State Federalists. National

27. *Ibid.*, p. 276.
28. *Ibid.*, pp. 219–220.
29. *Ibid.*, p. 274.
30. *Ibid.*, p. 408.

Federalism cut across the other principle cleavages and united men who disagreed on other questions. Thus the aims of National Federalism were shared by the leaders of both the democratic faction and the aristocratic faction. The principal spokesmen for National Federalism were Wilson, Mason, and Madison, who supported a democratic republic, and Gouverneur Morris, Hamilton, and King, who supported an aristocratic republic. National Federalism was not, as is sometimes supposed, exclusively an aristocratic aim nor an aristocratic doctrine: it was, and continued to be, advocated by those who believed in a democratic republic. Andrew Jackson and Abraham Lincoln did not have to invent National Federalism; they simply took it ready-made from the doctrines that prevailed at the Convention. The State Federalists, by contrast, were not only a minority at the Convention; if they were not already a minority in the nation—a question much disputed by historians—they were soon to become so; and they have remained a dissenting minority ever since.

Nor was the conflict between National Federalists and State Federalists, as is often thought, simply a mirror image of the contest between large states and small. New York, the fourth largest state, was represented not only by Hamilton, perhaps the most extreme National Federalist in the Convention, but also by Lansing and Yates, who were so extreme in their support for State Federalism that they left the Convention and opposed the Constitution. The fifth largest state, Maryland, sent both Luther Martin, an extreme State Federalist, and Daniel Carroll, a National Federalist. The three smallest states were Delaware, Rhode Island, and Georgia. Delaware, the smallest, was represented by (among others) Read, who agreed with Hamilton that the states "must be done away."[31] Rhode Island, the second smallest, sent no delegates. The third smallest, Georgia, sent Pierce, a National Federalist.

In the end, the National Federalists won a clear-cut victory. The Constitution contains all three of their principle objectives.

First, the new national government was endowed with a set of broad legal powers. Two of these, the power to tax and to regulate interstate commerce, were very comprehensive—or at least they could be so interpreted. The Congress, said the Constitution,

> . . . shall have the power
> To lay and collect taxes, duties, imposts and excises; to pay the debts and provide for the common defense and general welfare of the United States.
> . . .

31. *Ibid.*, p. 299.

To regulate commerce with foreign nations, and among the several states, and with the Indian tribes (Article I, Sec. 8).

As legislation of a century later was to show, these two powers were ample enough to permit extensive regulation of the economy. Under the first, for example, the production and sale of agricultural products would one day be so minutely controlled that a tobacco grower in North Carolina could not bring to market more than his allotted quota of tobacco. Under the second, even strikes by elevator operators in New York City would someday fall under the jurisdiction of the national government.

The new central government was given exclusive constitutional authority to coin money and issue currency. It could borrow money on its own credit. It could regulate bankruptcies. For all practical purposes, it had exclusive control over foreign relations, over the military establishment, over the declaration and conduct of war. It could establish a national judiciary with jurisdiction over all cases arising under the Constitution, laws of Congress, or treaties, and over a number of other matters as well. In a sweeping grant (as if to leave no doubts), the Congress was authorized "to make all Laws which shall be necessary and proper for carrying into Execution the foregoing powers, and all other Powers vested by this Constitution in the Government of the United States, or in any Department or Officer thereof" (Article I, Section 8, 10).

In the second place, all of these powers gave the national government legal authority over individual citizens. The President and the Congress would not have to work through the agency of state governments; they could deal directly with the individual citizens of the United States. To avoid all doubt on this crucial point, the Founders took pains to spell it out:

> *This Constitution, and the laws of the United States which shall be made in Pursuance thereof; and all Treaties made, or which shall be made, under the Authority of the United States, shall be the supreme Law of the Land; and the Judges in every State shall be bound thereby, any Thing in the Constitution or Laws of any State to the Contrary notwithstanding* (Article VI).

Finally, the National Federalists insured that American citizens would be directly represented in the national government. They beat off all attempts to have the members of the lower house appointed by the state legislatures, and spelled out their victory in these words:

The House of Representatives shall be composed of Members chosen every second year by the People of the several States, and the Electors in each State shall have the Qualifications requisite for Electors of the most numerous Branch of the State Legislature (Article I, Sec. 2).

The manner in which the President was to be chosen (as we shall see in Chapter 4) was one of the most difficult practical problems that confronted the Convention. Though they changed their minds several times, in the end they decided that even the President would be chosen by the people of the United States, though in a manner that seemed somewhat more indirect to the delegates than it ever proved to be in practise (Article II, Sec. 1).

The states were represented, then, only in the Senate. After lengthy and often bitter controversy, it was finally agreed that the Senators should be chosen by the state legislatures. (Article I, Section 3). As it turned out, however, even this solution proved impractical, for it merely succeeded in converting the elections to the state legislatures into indirect senatorial elections. Nonetheless, the anomaly remained until 1913, when the Seventeenth Amendment provided for the direct election of Senators by the people.

Equal States or Equal Citizens?

If there were to be a strong national government (as the National Federalists proposed), how should the various states share their control over the new government—equally, as under the existing Articles? By wealth or taxes, as had sometimes been proposed? Or according to population? This question provoked the bitterest controversy at the Convention— and perhaps the most pointless.

The story of this famous conflict and the final compromise has been told many times. Right at the beginning, on May 29, John Randolph of Virginia introduced a plan of government that favored National Federalism. This proposal, which quickly gained the name of the Virginia Plan, had the backing of the National Federalists, the advantage of a head start, and at once became the basis of nearly all the later work of the Convention. The second item in the Virginia Plan provided "that the rights of suffrage in the national legislature ought to be proportioned to

[48]

the quotas of contribution (i.e., taxes) or to the number of free inhabitants as the one or the other rule may seem best in different cases." On the basis of taxes, Virginia might have had sixteen representatives to one for Georgia.[32] On the basis of population, the disparity would have been less—about seven to one.[33] Naturally delegates from some of the small states objected. On June 15 they made their counter-move through Paterson of New Jersey, who presented a rival plan that would have left the existing system of equal state representation untouched.[34]

Although Paterson's New Jersey Plan was soon rejected, the conflict over representation remained to plague the Convention. At times, indeed, it looked as if the problem could not possibly be solved. The issue came up repeatedly; summer came on; tempers grew frayed; and delegates talked angrily of ending the Convention, going home, leaving the country with nothing but the old Articles. There were even hints and veiled threats of disrupting the existing Confederation. Some delegates from small states threatened their opponents from the large states by alluding to the possibility of foreign intervention. In a menacing outburst Bedford of Delaware clashed with Rufus King of Massachusetts.

BEDFORD . . . *We have been told with a dictatorial air that this is the last moment for a fair trial in favor of good Government. It will be the last indeed if the propositions reported from the Committee go forth to the people. I am under no apprehensions. The Large States dare not dissolve the Confederation. If they do the small ones will find some foreign ally of more honor and good faith, who will take them by the hand and do them justice . . .*

KING . . . *I can not sit down, without taking some notice of the language of the honorable gentleman from Delaware. It was not I that uttered . . . dictatorial language. This intemperance has marked the honorable gentleman himself. It was not I who with a vehemence unprecedented in this House, declared himself ready to turn his hopes from our common Country, and court the protection of some foreign hand. This too was the language of the Honbl member himself. I am grieved that such a thought has entered into his heart. I am more grieved that*

32. Based on a congressional recommendation for tax quotas in 1785. See *The Federal Convention and the Formation of the Union of the American States*, Winton U. Solberg, ed., New York, 1958, p. 407.
33. The delegates used various population estimates, all differing by some margin from the subsequent census of 1790. Moreover, the question whether slaves were to be counted would effect the representation of the Southern states. For population estimates, see Solberg, *op. cit*,. Appendix II, pp. 407 ff.
34. *Documents*, pp. 204–207.

such an expression has dropped from his lips. The gentleman can only excuse it to himself on the score of passion. For myself whatever might be my distress, I would never court relief from a foreign power.[35]

Delegates from the large states in turn drew dismal pictures of the sad fate of small states if the United States were to dissolve. Both sides were intransigeant. A delegate from Delaware had reminded the Convention at the end of its first week of work that should there be any change from the existing system of representation—that is, any departure from an equal weight for each state—"it might become their duty to retire from the Convention."[36] If the states were not given equal weight in the new government, Paterson of New Jersey warned, "N. Jersey will never confederate . . . She would be swallowed up. He [Paterson] had rather submit to a monarch, to a despot, than to such a fate. He would not only oppose the plan here but on his return home do everything in his power to defeat it there."[37] The other side seems equally committed. It was his "firm belief," said Rufus King, "that Mas.^{ts} would never be prevailed on to yield to an equality of votes" in the Senate.[38] Madison "entreated the gentlemen representing the small states to renounce a principle wch was confessedly unjust [and] which c.^{d} never be admitted . . ."[39]

On June 29, the advocates of equal representations suffered their first defeat. On that day, by a vote of six states to four, the delegates rejected the principle of equal state representation in the lower house (Table 2.2). From this time forward, the question centered on the Senate. On July 2, over a proposal by Ellsworth of Connecticut that each state should have one vote in the Senate, the Convention split in two. Five states supported Ellsworth's motion, five opposed it, and one was divided (Table 2.2). The Convention, split asunder, agreed to appoint a committee. The committee, consisting of one member from each state, reported back three days later with the recommendation "that in the 2^d branch each State shall have an equal vote".[40] On July 7 the decisive vote was taken on the committee report. Among the delegations that had fought against this principle, only Virginia, Pennsylvania, and South Carolina held firm to the last. North Carolina now swung to the

35. *Ibid.*, pp. 316–317. In the original, Madison puts these speeches in the third person.
36. *Ibid.*, p. 123.
37. *Ibid.*, p. 183.
38. *Ibid.*, p. 378.
39. *Ibid.*, p. 300.
40. *Ibid.*, p. 324.

other side. The vote of Massachusetts was lost because the delegates from Massachusetts were split. Georgia was also divided. Six states favored the compromise (Table 2.2). Thus, the issue was put to rest by a compromise that had little to be said for it except for one extremely important virtue: its acceptability.

Though equal state representation has sometimes been hailed as a great constitutional principle, Hamilton's judgment of the controversy was not far off the mark: "The truth is," he said, with the cruel candor of youth that made him both feared and admired, "it is a contest for power, not for liberty."[41] Because the conflict was dramatic and dangerous, and because it had the happy ending Americans firmly believe in, it has been

Table 2.2   Votes in the Constitutional Convention on the Issue
of Equal Representation for the States.

STATES	IN THE HOUSE	IN THE SENATE	
	June 29	July 2	July 7
Solid "Yes"			
Connecticut	Yes	Yes	Yes
New York	Yes	Yes	Yes
New Jersey	Yes	Yes	Yes
Delaware	Yes	Yes	Yes
Solid "No"			
Virginia	No	No	No
Pennsylvania	No	No	No
South Carolina	No	No	No
Waverers			
Maryland	Divided	Yes	Yes
North Carolina	No	No	Yes
Massachusetts	No	No	Divided
Georgia	No	Divided	Divided
Yes	4	5	6
No	6	5	3
Divided	1	1	2
	11*	11*	11*

*Rhode Island sent no delegates. Those from New Hampshire arrived later.
SOURCES: Documents, 303, 324, 340

41. Ibid., p. 301.

given an importance by later generations out of all proportion to its intrinsic significance. For the advocates of equal representation were defending a principle that events were to make obsolete.

Men like Madison and Wilson foresaw this with considerable clarity. "Can we forget for whom we are forming a Government?" Wilson asked. "Is it for men or for the imaginary beings called *States?*"[42] "Was a combination to be apprehended from the mere circumstance of equality of size?"[43] Madison asked.

> . . . *Experience suggested no such danger. The journals of Cong.ˢ did not present any peculiar association of these States in the votes recorded . . . Experience rather taught a contrary lesson . . . the States were divided into different interests not by their difference of size, but by other circumstances. . .*[44]

Madison proved to be right. There has, in fact, never been a significant conflict between the citizens of small states and the citizens of large states. Or, to put it in another way, there has been no important controversy in the United States that has not cut squarely across the people in both small states and large.

Nonetheless, equal representation of states in the Senate was firmly written into the Constitution (Article I, Section 3). And those delegates like Madison and Wilson who had so vigorously opposed a bad principle preferred compromise to a dissolution of the union, swallowed their bitterness, and accepted defeat—though they always refused to concede that the outcome was anything more exalted than an unprincipled bargain that had to be accepted, not because it was just, but merely because the alternatives were still more unpleasant.

The Politics of Compromise versus the Politics of Political Purity

Were men like Madison and Wilson right to have accepted a compro-

42. *Ibid.*, p. 307.
43. *Ibid.*, p. 292.
44. *Ibid.*, pp. 292, 310.

mise that violated their principles? Should they have left the Convention in indignation, like Lansing, Yates, and Luther Martin? Should they have refused to sign the document because they did not subscribe to everything in it, as Randolph and Gerry did? Should they have refused to support it, as Mason did, because of scruples about the way the proposed Constitution "had been formed without the knowledge or idea of the people"?[45]

Questions like these are easy to answer if one has very weak principles of conduct—or very strong ones. To the man of weak principle, compromise is an easy path so long as one gains even a little in the bargain. To the man of rigid morality, the answer is equally obvious: it is better not to agree at all than to agree to an imperfect bargain.

But the problem is not just a personal affair, a matter of private morality. Since the way a political leader answers these questions may greatly affect the rest of us, the problem is also a public affair.

Lying between the simple extremes of unprincipled politics and rigid morality is a domain of action that has been called the ethics of responsibility: meaning by this term an attempt to weigh the consequences of each alternative as intelligently as possible, and then to choose the best available. Acting according to the ethics of responsibility, a political leader cannot enjoy the luxury of rejecting an imperfect compromise, even a highly imperfect compromise, so long as that compromise represents the best possible alternative presented by the world as it happens to be. Irresponsibility, in this view, consists not in making concessions, but in making unnecessary concessions; not in making imperfect bargains, but in failing to make the best possible bargains; not in adhering strictly to principles, but in holding rigidly to one principle at excessive costs to other principles. One may be irresponsible, then, not merely from a want of principles but also from a want of intelligence and knowledge of the real world: in the ethics of responsibility it is important not only to know what one wants but also to know exactly what one must do to get it, and what it will cost, not merely in money but in other values.

What is sometimes called the Anglo-American political tradition has, at its best, accented the ethics of responsibility. If that tradition has rejected wholly unprincipled and unscrupulous politics as an aim unworthy of the political calling, it has also rejected fanaticism and rigidity as too simple for the complex world of political decisions. If sheer opportunism is ignoble, rigid morality in politics is dangerous and inapplicable.

Now the men at the Convention were English (Wilson was a Scot)

45. See below, pp. 145, 146.

before they were American. Whatever else they were they were not fanatics. Nor were they mere opportunists. They were above all realists, who knew or believed they knew the rough boundaries of the politically possible: yet, I have suggested, they were principled realists who sought to achieve their aims with the imperfect materials at hand. When the committee appointed to examine the thorny question of equal representation in the Senate reported back to the Convention, Mason probably expressed the sentiments of most of the delegates when he said:

> . . . There must be some accommodation on this point. However liable the Report might be to objections, he thought it preferable to an appeal to the world by different sides, as had been talked of by some Gentlemen . . . He would bury his bones in this City rather than expose his Country to the Consequences of a dissolution of the Convention without any thing being done.[46]

Thus the men at the Convention bequeathed more than a Constitution. In what they did there, and in what they did in public life in later years, they also helped to shape a way of entering into political decisions and evaluating political institutions that is as much a part of the American political system as the Constitution.

The Uncompleted Agenda

As the years passed, and the Constitution took an exalted place in the American creed alongside a faith in the virtues of democracy, the Founders came to be treated less as men than as gods. And since what followed from their labors turned out to be a democracy, it was often supposed, and still is, that they had 'created' a democracy in the United States—or, at any rate, a democratic republic. More than a century later, when critics like Charles Beard punctured the myth by showing that they were not only men but men with investments, it came to be intellectually fashionable to hold that the Founders really carried through a kind of aristocratic counter-revolution that somehow was converted, nonetheless, into a democratic republic as time wore on.

A more exact interpretation than either of these would, surely, be

46. *Documents*, pp. 329, 330.

this: The Founders did not create either a democratic republic or an aristocratic republic. Whatever their intentions were—as we have seen they did not agree on these—what they did was to create a framework of government which, once it had been accepted, might become either an aristocratic republic or a democratic republic. Which it was to be depended not on what any group of men could do in three or four months at a Convention in Philadelphia, but on what was to happen later, over years and decades and perhaps centuries, among men outside the Convention and generations still unborn. And what these men, these Americans then living and yet to be born would do, in turn depended on many factors— factors that no one at the Convention could control or even predict, some of which are even today little understood.

One thing is perfectly clear now, even if it was not so clear at the time. Given the right conditions, the framework of government they had created could become the government of a democratic republic. And it did.

3

THE SILENT REVOLUTION: PROOF OF THE IMPOSSIBLE

In 1835 an English visitor to the United States, Harriet Martineau, paid a visit to James Madison, who was then 84 and within a year of his death. "Mr. Madison remarked to me," she wrote later, "that the United States had been 'useful in proving things before held impossible.' "[1]

This view of the American experience was not uncommon in the nineteenth century. It attracted foreigners like Alexis de Tocqueville and Miss Martineau to the United States in order to unravel the mystery.

> . . . The experiment of the particular constitution of the United States may fail [Miss Martineau went on to say]; but the great principle which, whether successfully or not, it strives to embody,—the capacity of mankind for self-government,—is established for ever. It has, as Mr. Madison said, proved a thing previously held impossible.[2]

That a large democratic republic existed on American soil was a palpable, uncontestable, and implacable fact of the nineteenth century. This undeniable presence was visible proof that a democratic republic was no merely Utopian idea. Yet the proof generated a mystery: What was required for such an experiment to succeed? And why had the Americans been able to prove the impossible?

1. Harriet Martineau, *Society in America*, S. M. Lipset, ed., Garden City, N.Y., Anchor Books, 1962, p. 57.
2. *Ibid.*, p. 58.

Democracy or Aristocracy?

The Constitutional Convention, we have just seen, created an instrument of government that could have been adapted to either an aristocratic republic or a democratic republic. The direction in which the new system was to develop was not wholly within the control of any constitutional convention. As Alexis de Tocqueville wrote in 1835,

> . . . Mexico, which is not less fortunately situated than the Anglo-American Union, has adopted these same laws [i.e., the Federal Constitution] but is unable to accustom itself to the government of democracy. Some other cause is therefore at work, independently of physical circumstances and peculiar laws, which enables the democracy to rule in the United States.[3]

In recent times, too, we have relearned the ancient lesson that a constitution is a frail barrier along the path of an aspiring dictator who has a large and disciplined following.

Proper constitutional agreements are, obviously, necessary conditions for a democratic republic. One cannot have democracy if there are no elections, no legislatures, no legal rights to speak freely about politics, no courts to enforce these rights. But it is equally obvious that constitutional arrangements are not sufficient to insure democracy. For there must also be suitable social and economic conditions, and appropriate beliefs, among the citizens. Thanks to greater experience with democratic government, the task of drafting a democratic constitution is, nowadays, very much easier than it was in 1789. But it is as difficult as ever to insure the proper socio-economic conditions and beliefs.

Consider two problems. First, the problem of power. In order for a satisfactory approximation of democracy to exist, power over government must not be distributed too unequally among the citizens. One of the most important contributions to the wide diffusion of power over government is broad suffrage. But standing alone even universal suffrage is insufficient, for legal equality in the voting booth can be nullified by inequalities outside. Imagine an agricultural society, for example, where a tiny group of people owns all the land; where these people control the police, the military, the newspapers; the radio; and where the great bulk of the population consists of uneducated agricultural laborers dependent for their livelihood on the few landowners. Is it likely that the introduc-

3. *Democracy in America*, New York, Vintage Books, 1955, Vol. I, p. 333.

tion of universal suffrage and a democratic constitution would, by themselves, produce a durable democratic republic?

Second, there is the problem of unity and diversity, of consensus and conflict. Even if power were equally distributed, a democracy might nonetheless be destroyed from internal dissension. A minority, outvoted, might grow to prefer dictatorship to the prospect of obeying laws passed and enforced by the representatives of a hostile majority.

Now it happened, for causes with which the Founders had very little to do, that conditions in the United States were unusually favorable for a solution to both these problems. Had they been less favorable, the American experience might only have added new evidence that a thing previously held impossible was indeed impossible.

In fact, then, what produced democracy in America was not so much the American Revolution and the Constitutional Convention as the underlying forces that facilitated a second, silent revolution.

Equalities

With few exceptions, Europeans who came to the United States during the first half of the nineteenth century were struck by the degree of political, social, and economic equality among Americans. Tocqueville made this observation the very kernel of his famous analysis of American democracy. Some foreign visitors were charmed, some were offended, but all agreed that the prevalence of equality was truly astounding.

Even when considered in the most cautious light, Tocqueville's conclusion appears to be correct: the world had never before witnessed so much equality of condition as existed in America. In everything that one says on this topic, of course one is bound to except the Negroes, particularly the great bulk who were slaves in the southern states. This is no slight exception, and I shall return to it more than once in the course of this book. Therefore, it is well to keep in mind that I speak at the moment only of the free white population. Among these there was not only a fair approximation to universal male suffrage, but evidently an amazing degree of social and economic equality as well. At the Convention, Charles Pinckney had portrayed Americans in words that were to be echoed two generations later by Tocqueville.

> . . . Among [Americans] there are fewer distinctions of fortune

and less of rank, than among the inhabitants of any other nation . . . Equality is . . . the leading feature of the United
States.[4]

And Pinckney, like Tocqueville, pointed to the principle reason, the
availability of land:

> . . . This equality is likely to continue, because in a new Coun-
> try, possessing immense tracts of uncultivated lands, where
> every temptation is offered to emigration and where industry
> must be rewarded with competency, there will be few poor,
> and few dependent.[5]

If Pinckney's statement stood alone, we could count it as the kind of
exaggerated rhetoric about equality that Americans seem to enjoy hearing themselves say to one another. But Pinckney's observation in 1787
was also Tocqueville's in 1832. Democracy in America begins with this
sentence:

> Among the novel objects that attracted my attention
> during my stay in the United States nothing struck me more
> forcibly than the general equality of condition among the
> people. I readily discovered the prodigious influence that this
> primary fact exercises on the whole course of society; it gives a
> peculiar direction to public opinion and a peculiar tenor to the
> laws; it imparts new maxims to the governing authorities and
> peculiar habits to the governed. I soon perceived that the
> influence of this fact extends far beyond the political character
> and the laws of the country, and that it has no less effect on
> civil society than on government; it creates opinions, gives birth
> to new sentiments, founds novel customs, and modifies whatev-
> er it does not produce. The more I advanced in the study of
> American society, the more I perceived that this equality of
> condition is the fundamental fact from which all others seem to
> be derived and the central point at which all my observations
> constantly terminated [emphasis added].[6]

4. Documents, pp. 267, 270.
5. Ibid., p. 267.
6. Vol. I, p. 3. On this general point and its bearing on American development, see Louis Hartz, The Liberal Tradition in America, New York, Harcourt, Brace, 1955.

Unfortunately the kinds of statistical information one would need in order to make these observations more precise is lacking.[7] Yet one fact is beyond argument: during the first half century of experience under the new Constitution, the United States was a country of farmers. Until 1840, seven out of ten workers were engaged in farming; in the two decades before the Civil War the proportion fell, but even in 1860, six out of every ten were in agriculture. Americans were, therefore, a rural people. In 1790, only 5 per cent of the population lived in places with 2,500 inhabitants or more. In the 1830s, when Tocqueville and Harriet Martineau visited the United States, the proportion was about 10 per cent. As late as 1860, it was only 20 per cent.[8]

Unfortunately we can only guess at the distribution of property ownership. But observers agreed that among this vast farming population, property was, thanks to the availability of land, widely diffused. Tocqueville and Martineau found few rich and few poor, even though frontier families sometimes lived under the most miserable conditions, particularly during their first years. Because land was plentiful in relation to the population, labor was relatively scarce; society put a premium on a man's labor. In the towns and cities, wages were relatively high. In the countryside, sons of farmers found it possible to acquire their own farms. The European practise of keeping landed estates intact by passing them on to the eldest son was uncommon; even among the land-rich Patroons of New York, Miss Martineau reported, the practise was disappearing.[9]

Equality extended in other directions, too. In a nation of farmers, there was no peasantry, and not even any tradition of peasantry in the European sense. Large landed estates existed, to be sure, particularly in the South; but it was extremely difficult to keep free white farm labor from leaving. "The people of the United States," Miss Martineau observed, "choose to be proprietors of land, not tenants."[10] The large governmental establishments of the centralized European monarchies scarcely existed in the United States of 1831; in a population of over thirteen million only 11,491 persons were employed by the federal government

7. See, however, Ralph L. Andreano, "Trends and Variations in Economic Welfare in the United States before the Civil War," in *New Views on American Economic Development*, ed. by Andreano, Cambridge, Schenkman Publishing Co., 1965, 131–167.

8. *Historical Statistics of the United States*, Prepared by the Bureau of the Census, with the Cooperation of the Social Science Research Council, Washington, D.C., U.S. Government Printing Office, 1961, p. 9, Series A 34–50; p. 72, Series D 36–45.

9. Harriet Martineau, *op. cit.*, p. 264.

10. *Ibid.*, p. 179.

—and of these, nearly nine thousand were in the Post Office[11] and therefore dispersed throughout the country. The vast private corporations created by industrial capitalism had not yet arrived; the giant factories, the great financiers, the urban proletariat, the army of clerks and white collar workers—these were still unknown. Nearly everyone, according to Tocqueville, had at least a modest education: though he encountered few great scholars in his travels, he also found few wholly uneducated people. In fact, though illiteracy was high among Negro slaves, among the whites, it was exceedingly low for the time; between 1840-1860, the U.S. Census reported that among white people twenty years of age or over, only about one in ten could not read and write.[12]

Given the substantial degree of equality that prevailed in property, incomes, wealth, control over economic enterprise, and education, it is not surprising that there was also a remarkable degree of equality in social relations among Americans. Europeans were frequently struck by the comparative weakness of social barriers among Americans, particularly outside the Eastern cities, and most notably in the agricultural West. Even servants did not give the deference to which an Englishman or European was accustomed. Yet Miss Martineau, perhaps too generously, insisted that "the manners of the Americans [in America] are the best I ever saw."[13] Indeed, among Americans then, as now, even family relationships were conducted with an astonishing amount of equality. The lack of strong parental domination, the tendency of parents to rely more on persuasion than severe punishment, and the free and easy ways of American children were as evident to Tocqueville and Harriet Martineau in the 1830s as they are to foreign visitors today. "For my own part," said Miss Martineau, "I delight in the American children"; but (it is only fair to add) what she found charming, many others saw as insolence and lack of proper deference toward adults. Both Tocqueville and Miss Martineau concluded that the family was a kind of miniature training ground in "democratic" attitudes.

Just as striking to the foreigner as all other aspects of equality was the extent to which Americans seemed to believe that equality was a virtue. Americans seemed not only to accept a high degree of political, social, and economic equality as a plain fact of life; to them it was also a value. No doubt there was a good deal of rhetoric, muddle-headedness, and hypocrisy in the widespread emphasis by Americans on the virtues of equality. But thoughtful foreigners like Tocqueville and Harriet Mart-

11. *Historical Statistics*, p. 710, Series Y 241–250.
12. *Ibid.*, p. 206.
13. Harriet Martineau, *op. cit.*, p. 272.

ineau held that the American belief in equality went far deeper than mere cant; to a greater extent than in any other society up until that time, it seemed to them, Americans, taken in the large, believed that in essential value as a human being, one person was very much like another. Sixty years after Tocqueville and Martineau, another famous observer from abroad, Bryce, emphasized the same point in a happy metaphor:

> . . . In America men hold others to be at bottom exactly the same as themselves. If a man is enormously rich . . . or if he is a great orator . . . or a great soldier . . . or a great writer . . . or a President, so much the better for him. He is an object of interest, perhaps of admiration, possibly even of reverence. But he is deemed to be still of the same flesh and blood as other men. The admiration felt for him may be a reason for going to see him and longing to shake hands with him. But it is not a reason for bowing down to him, or addressing him in deferential terms, or treating him as if he was porcelain and yourself only earthenware.[14]

Inequalities

Since so much of all that has just been said about equality in agrarian America has long since passed into American mythology to provide us with gilt aplenty for our Golden Age, it might have been superfluous to emphasize the matter so strongly, except for one thing: Unlike many other American myths, this particular one seems to have been substantially true. And unless we realize how extensive was the equality of condition among Americans—to use the phrase of both Pinckney and Tocqueville—in the first half century or so after the men at the Convention completed their labors, we shall not be able to understand why democratic political institutions took root so readily on this soil and survived through some severe hard times.

However, if equality prevailed among Americans to a degree that had not been matched anywhere up to that time (and perhaps has not been matched since even in the United States), there were nonetheless

14. James Bryce, *The American Commonwealth*, London and New York, Macmillan and Co., 1889, 2 vol., vol. II, p. 606.

important exceptions, and these the myth makers usually forget to mention. Some of these exceptions were to threaten the system at its foundations; not even in our time have we seen the last of them.

In the first place, if social classes in the harsh European fashion were absent in America, rudimentary forms of social stratification existed among the white population, most markedly in the old cities along the eastern seaboard and in the South. Harriet Martineau had some strong words to say about the snobbery she encountered among "those who consider themselves the aristocracy of the United States: the wealthy and showy citizens of the Atlantic ports . . . I was told a great deal about 'the first people in Boston': which is perhaps as aristocratic, vain, and vulgar a city, as described by its own 'first people', as any in the world."[15] Were these rudimentary social classes merely a legacy of the past—or, worse, a foreshadowing of the future? Was equality only a fleeting aspect of American life? Would 'equality of condition' become more and more a myth, a dream about a vanished Golden Age? And would the new American aristocrats look with disdain on the political institutions of a democratic republic? Harriet Martineau was, as usual, optimistic:

> . . . Such an aristocracy must remain otherwise too insignificant to be dangerous. It cannot choose its own members, restrict its own numbers, or keep its gentility from contamination; for it must be perpetuated, not by hereditary transmission, but by accessions from below. Grocers grow rich, and mechanics become governors of States; and happily there is no law, nor reason, nor desire that it should be otherwise. This little cloud will always overhang the republic, like the perpetual vapour which hovers over Niagara, thrown up by the force and regularity of the movement below.[16]

To the extent that social equality reflected a general equality in property, wealth, and control over economic enterprise, the pervasive equality that seemed to be so characteristic of American agrarian society rested upon a transitory phenomenon—the fact that Americans were predominantly a nation of farmers in a country where there was a vast supply of cheap land. But if Americans became a nation of businessmen and employees, what then? In 1800 about 10 per cent of the people in the labor force were employees. In 1860 the number had grown to 60 per

15. Harriet Martineau, op. cit., p. 260.
16. Ibid., p. 263.

cent. By 1960, 90 per cent would be working for others.[17] What would happen when agrarian capitalism gave way to business capitalism? One answer was at least suggested by those parts of the United States where this had already occurred.

For urban business enterprise—commerce, banking, manufacturing —provided the second important source of inequalities.[18] To be sure, business enterprise was still small; it was confined to a few cities. But it was exactly in the cities that the consequences were evident: disparities of wealth, the sharper delineation of social 'classes,' greater possibilities of political corruption. This was why men like Jefferson and Madison often argued that the United States should if possible remain a nation of farmers and that business enterprise should not be encouraged; for they held that the equality of condition necessary to a democratic republic could not be maintained in a society that was based on business rather than on small farmers.

Was there any ground for the Jeffersonian dream of an agrarian democracy or for the fear that business enterprise and manufacturing would endanger democracy? Farmers are not necessarily more knowledgeable, upright, or more civic-minded than city dwellers[19]; and a nation of landlords and peasants would surely be no Eden for democrats. Yet a country made up exclusively of small farmers is likely to be a country where equality prevails. The kernel of truth in the myth, then was this:

17. Stanley Lebergott, "Labor Force Mobility and Employment" in Andreano, op. cit., 362–276, at p. 369.

18. Criticism of snobbery and anti-democratic sentiments among the new wealthy strata was strongly emphasized in a volume by another person of foreign origin, Francis J. Grund, a Viennese who became an American citizen—and an enthusiastic one. He exposed the anti-democratic snobbery of some Americans in his *Aristocracy in America*, first published in London in 1839, New York, Harper Torchbooks, 1959. "The *moveable*, moneyed aristocracy of our times," he wrote, "I consider as the greatest enemy of mankind" (p. 163). Yet he concluded on an optimistic note: "What is termed 'the aristocracy of America'—that is, a considerable portion of all people worth from fifty to an hundred thousand dollars,—are, owing to the growing power of the West, a most harmless, though I cannot say 'inoffensive,' part of the population . . . In politics they are the most implacable enemies of democracy; which, with them, is synonymous with mob-governments and anarchy. They are for a *strong* administration, made out of their own party; and would hardly object to royalty, if the King would support himself out of his private chest . . . In all other respects their political opinions do not seriously differ from those of the mass of the people . . . " (p. 301).

19. In fact, whenever measurable differences in the performance of civic duties

A nation of small farmers would almost automatically preserve a high degree of economic, social, and political equality. By contrast, the development of commerce, industry, manufacturers, and banking on a large scale was bound to generate inequalities—in wealth, income, control over economic enterprise, social status, knowledge, skill, and, because of these, in power too. Although Jefferson and Madison did not accurately foresee the shape of the future, they were right in their conjecture that the expansion of commerce and industry would create a serious problem for American democracy; in the cities of the eastern seaboard, in fact, it had already done so in their own day.

The third exception to the prevalence of social, economic, and political equality was, as I have already said, the Negro. Whether he was free or slave, he discovered that the prevailing practises of the white man placed him in a position of social, economic, and political subordination. Yet Negroes were no trifling minority; from 1800-1860 they were 15 to 20 per cent of the population of the United States; in the South, one out of every three persons was a slave (Tables 3.1, 3.2).

In a society that preached equality and to a surprising extent practised what it preached, slavery was an anomaly; and everyone knew it. It had been a sore issue at the Constitutional Convention. Yet no one wanted to face the issue squarely, then or later, for everyone knew it was explosive. When Harriet Martineau entered the United States in 1834,

can be found, American farmers tend to come off rather badly in comparison with city dwellers. Whether this was true in the early nineteenth century, we cannot say. In recent times, farmers seem to have been less interested in politics, felt less involved, and been less likely to vote than urban residents; among city people, only the unskilled workers show so little interest, involvement, and participation. Compared with city people today, farmers do not write or wire their Congressmen or Senators as often; they are less likely to be asked by others to express their political views; they express a weaker sense of citizen duty; they feel less confident and effective in politics; they are less likely than white collar workers to have opinions on international and domestic issues, and have no opinions about as frequently as blue collar workers. Nor can the differences be explained by educational inequalities, for even when we compare citizens with the same general level of education—grade school, or high school, or college— the differences tend to remain. In general, on all the measures, farmers trail behind professional people, businessmen, and white collar workers and usually a bit behind skilled workers; the only urban group they often exceed, and not by much, are the unskilled laborers. For evidence, see Robert A. Lane, *Political Life*, Glencoe, Ill., The Free Press, 1959, pp. 68, 91; V. O. Key, Jr., *Public Opinion and American Democracy*, New York, Knopf, 1961, pp. 326, 329, 333; and Angus Campbell, Phillip E. Converse, Warren E. Miller, Donald E. Stokes, *The American Voter*, New York, 1960, p. 411.

Table 3.1   Negro Population in the United States, 1800 to 1860

	TOTAL POPULATION	NEGRO	
		Total	Slave
	(000)	(000)	(000)
1800	5297	1002	894
1810	7224	1378	1191
1820	9618	1772	1538
1830	12901	2328	2009
1840	17120	2874	2487
1850	23261	3639	3205
1860	31513	4442	3954

SOURCE: *Historical Statistics of the United States, Colonial Times to 1957*, U.S. Department of Commerce, Bureau of the Census, Washington, D.C., Government Printing Office, 1961, Series A34-50; A59-70. For 1800 and 1810, figures used for Negroes are for nonwhites.

Table 3.2   Negro Population in the South, 1800 to 1860

	TOTAL POPULATION	NEGRO	
		TOTAL	SLAVE
	(000)	(000)	(000)
1800	2,622	918	857
1810	3,461	1,268	1,160
1820	4,419	1,643	1,508
1830	5,707	2,162	1,980
1840	6,950	2,642	2,428
1850	8,983	3,352	3,117
1860	11,133	4,097	3,838

SOURCE: *Historical Statistics*, p. 12, Series A 95-122

. . . there was an absolute and almost ominous silence in Congress about slavery. Almost every leading man told me in conversation that it was the grand question of all; that every member's mind was full of it; that nearly all other questions were much affected, or wholly determined by it; yet no one even alluded to it in public.[20]

In 1836, the House of Representatives even went so far as to adopt a Gag Rule, as it came to be called, preventing the House from considering "all

20.   Harriet Martineau, *op. cit.*, pp. 78–79.

petitions, memorials, resolutions, propositions, or papers relating in any way or to any extent whatever to the subject of slavery or the abolition of slavery."[21]

The subjection of the Negro, a monument to inequality, cast a dark shadow over American democracy. For one thing, an ideology that justified slavery was difficult to reconcile with an ideology that made virtues of equality, liberty, and democracy. Yet the bare-faced contradiction was too much to live with. There began, as a result, that strange effort to construct an ideology that justified both democracy and slavery, a task (carried on most enthusiastically, but not exclusively in the South) that proved to be one long travail of tortured logic and denial of humanity to the Negro—whatever the cost to fact, reason, and sentiments of humanity.

But slavery weighed heavily on American democracy in another way: as a source of conflict that went beyond the capacities of democratic institutions to handle peacefully. Long before the Civil War, many observers like Tocqueville foresaw with clear foreboding that if anything should split the nation asunder, it would be slavery.

Among the various sources of inequalities, another kind of difference that contributed heavily to political inequality among Americans was a difference in political interest, activity, and skill. Men may have equal legal rights and, roughly, equal political resources; but if some use their resources to the full, and others not at all, then the first group is likely to exert more influence than the second. Yet in every political system, even in democratic ones, some citizens are much less interested and active in politics than others. The apathetic citizens disfranchise themselves; the active citizens gain power. Among Americans, as among other peoples, these differences are pronounced.

Or is this only a recent development? Were the early years of the Republic, as our myth makers tell us, a political Golden Age when citizens were far more interested and active in politics than they are today? Although we do not have nearly enough data or the right kinds to permit us to speak with confidence, the myth does not seem to survive a critical examination. Unfortunately, Tocqueville, a shrewd observer of many things, contributed to the myth by describing the American as extraordinarily concerned with politics. "To take a hand in the regulation of society and to discuss it is his biggest concern and, so to speak, the only pleasure an American knows."[22] Tocqueville's observations, however,

21. Richard B. Morris, Encyclopedia of American History, New York, Harper and Bros., 1953, p. 179.
22. Alexis de Tocqueville, Democracy in America, New York, Knopf, 1945, Phillips Bradley, ed., vol. I, p. 250.

ran counter to those of Harriet Martineau, who was in the United States at almost the same time and for a longer period. In fact she wrote a special section on "Apathy in Citizenship."[23] Half a century later, another Englishman, James Bryce, came to the same conclusion:

> The citizen has little time to think about political problems. Engrossing all the working hours, his avocation leaves him only stray moments for this fundamental duty . . . He has not leisure to do it for himself, and must practically lean upon and follow his party. It astonished me in 1870 and 1881 to find how small a part politics played in conversation among the best educated classes and generally in the cities.[24]

These are impressions. An examination of the number of people who have voted in presidential elections indicates several conclusions. First, the percentage of the *total population* voting in presidential elections rose rapidly until 1840 and then remained rather stable until

23.   Harriet Martineau, *op. cit.*, pp. 106–108.
24.   James Bryce, *The American Commonwealth*, London, New York, Macmillan, 1910, 2 vols., vol. II, p. 291.

FIGURE 3.1—PERCENT OF TOTAL POPULATION VOTING IN PRESIDENTIAL ELECTION, 1824-1952

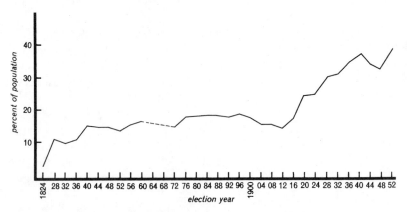

SOURCE: Robert Lane, *Political Life*, Glenco. The Free Press, 1962, p. 20.

[68]

the Civil War. After the Civil War the proportion increased slightly, no doubt because of the newly enfranchised Negroes. From 1896 to 1912, the proportion declined, probably because of the great influx of immigrants, many of whom did not vote; with the general enfranchisement of women in 1920, the proportion rose to new heights (Figure 3.1). Thus the percentage of the total population voting in presidential elections has actually increased over the whole period.

However, over against rising percentage of voters in the population there was also a countertrend: for the number of persons *eligible* to vote seems to have increased more rapidly than the number of persons who *actually* voted (Table 3.3 and Figure 3.2). Thus the proportion of the electorate that does not bother to go to the polls has been higher in the twentieth century than in the nineteenth. Does this mean that there has been a general increase in citizen apathy? Not exactly. For what seems to have happened, at least in part, is that the franchise was broadened to include groups that were hitherto excluded—particularly Negroes and women—and among these new groups there is markedly less voting (for a variety of reasons) than among others. Thus, the rate of voting is lower among women than among men, and, even in the North, lower among Negroes than among whites. In addition, the influx of immigrants in the

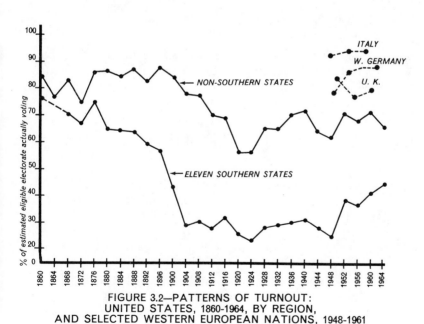

FIGURE 3.2—PATTERNS OF TURNOUT:
UNITED STATES, 1860-1964, BY REGION,
AND SELECTED WESTERN EUROPEAN NATIONS, 1948-1961

Table 3.3. *Decline and Partial Resurgence: Mean Levels of National Turnout and Drop-Off by Periods, 1848–1962**

PERIOD (PRESIDENTIAL YEARS)	MEAN ESTIMATED TURNOUT	PERIOD (OFF-YEARS)	MEAN ESTIMATED TURNOUT	MEAN DROP-OFF
	(%)		(%)	(%)
1848–1872	75.1	1850–1874	65.2	7.0
1876–1896	78.5	1878–1898	62.8	15.2
1900–1916	64.8	1902–1918	47.9	22.4
1920–1928	51.7	1922–1930	35.2	28.7
1932–1944	59.1	1934–1946	41.0	27.8
1948–1960	60.3	1950–1962	44.1	24.9

*Off-year turnout data based on total vote for congressional candidates in off years.
SOURCE: Walter Dean Burnham, "The Changing Shape of the American Political Universe," *The American Political Science Review*, Vol. LIX (March, 1965), No. 1, p. 10.

late nineteenth century probably increased somewhat the number who became eligible to vote but did not always make use of this right. In general then, the franchise was extended to groups of people who were probably even more inclined to political passivity in the nineteenth century than they are now. However, the data are shaky, for it is difficult to arrive at reliable historical estimates of the numbers actually eligible to vote in all the states.

One cannot be entirely sure, then, that the myth is false; but it is not sustained by the evidence now at hand. In any case, it is quite clear that then, as now, only a small percentage of citizens gave much time to politics; only a few were willing to make a career out of politics; and it was these professional politicians who, then as now, organized and controlled those vital instruments of democratic politics, the political parties.

To sum up, foreigners and Americans were correct, beyond any doubt, in portraying the United States as a land where social, economic, and political equality prevailed to an unusual degree; in fact, Tocqueville was surely right in believing that the degree of equality in condition among Americans was not only unusual but unique among all civilized peoples.

It was the conditions of American life, then, that settled the debate at the Convention. The Constitution may not have been radically democratic; American agrarian society was. In a different environment, the Constitution might have permitted an aristocracy, an oligarchy, a plutocracy to rule the republic; after the Civil War, Americans were to see how far a plutocracy could go in acquiring power in spite of—or even with the help of—the constitutional framework. But in the critical early years, democracy was able to flourish because political equality was sustained by an extraordinary degree of social and economic equality.

There were, as we have seen, sources of inequality—slavery, rudimentary social classes in the cities, the economic and social institutions of commercial and industrial capitalism, and political apathy. These were storing up problems for the future.

Unity

For a democratic republic to survive, political equality is not enough. Political equals may quarrel: quarreling may bring civil strife. The policies of a majority may seem oppressive to a minority: the minority may revolt. Consent, you may remember, has a practical side: if the laws passed by the representatives of a majority fail to gain the tacit 'consent' of a large minority, a democracy is likely to be ripped apart.

In this case, too, destiny seemed to favor American democracy, for during the first half century under the new Constitution, there were powerful forces uniting Americans, forces strong enough to overcome centrifugal tendencies toward disintegration. To begin with, the social, ethnic, and economic homogeneity of the people, the very equality of condition we spoke of a moment ago, helped to minimize conflict. Most people pursued essentially the same way of life, the life of the small farmer, and they substantially agreed on the values of that way of life.

> . . . *The possession of land is the aim of all action, generally speaking, and the cure of all social evils, among men in the United States* [Harriet Martineau wrote]. *If a man is disappointed in politics or love, he goes and buys land. If he disgraces himself, he betakes himself to a lot in the west. If the demand for any article of manufacture slackens, the operatives drop into the unsettled lands. If a citizen's neighbors rise above him in the towns, he betakes himself where he can be monarch of all he surveys. An artisan works, that he may die on land of his own. He is frugal, that he may enable his son to be a landowner. Farmers' daughters go into factories that they may*

clear off the mortgage from their fathers' farms; that they may
be independent landowners again.[25]

A second factor that probably helped to soften conflict was the
general prosperity that marked American life then as it has since. Prosperity was not, to be sure, universal. Farming in New England had already begun its long, inexorable, and painful decline. "I met with no
class in the United States so anxious about the means of living as the
farmers of New England," wrote Miss Martineau.[26] Yet the prevailing
prosperity and material well-being of Americans struck Europeans
sharply. Labor was in short supply; extended unemployment was perhaps
rarer than it is today; wages were high; real incomes were relatively high
and increasing; property ownership was widespread.[27] Whether this material prosperity had anything to do with the cheerfulness and good
humor that were often ascribed to Americans is hard to say, but no
doubt material well-being helped to prevent the accumulation of the
bitter resentments and hatreds that arise when one sector of a society is
subjected to the degradations of permanent poverty and the frustrations
of lifelong want.

In the third place, Americans seem quickly to have developed a
remarkable similarity in their attitudes and beliefs. Unfortunately, we
have no more than impressionistic evidence to go on; despite many
learned attempts to do so, no one can say with much confidence what
the content of these beliefs actually was. Judging from contemporary
descriptions, and particularly from Tocqueville, most Americans seemed
to affirm the virtues of equality and democracy. Not all, to be sure, were
equally fervent; nor was public utterance always the same as private
belief; and practise did not necessarily correspond perfectly with belief.
Both Tocqueville and Martineau found skepticism and cynicism about
democracy among the wealthy strata of the population. Nonetheless no
sharp ideological cleavage between supporters and opponents of democracy was visible, simply because the opponents were too few and too
fearful of the opinions of the rest.

Americans also came to agree very quickly on the virtues of their
constitutional system. The reverence of Americans for the Constitution,
an attitude that has at different times puzzled, astonished, amused, and
irritated foreign observers, evidently developed rapidly. Within an unbe-
lievably short time, hardly more than a decade, Americans no longer debated seriously whether their constitutional system was good or bad; it

25. Harriet Martineau, op. cit., p. 168.
26. Ibid., p. 169.
27. See the essays by Andreano and Lebergott, cited above, fns. 7 and 17.

appeared to be a postulate almost universally subscribed to that the American Constitution was a good one, if not in fact the best in the world. Americans ceased to be divided over questions of constitutional structure. There was, however, one aspect of the Constitution on which Americans did not wholly agree, and that was the full nature of the powers granted to the federal government. Yet even in this case the debate was not so much over the virtues of the Constitution, per se, as whether this or that interpretation of the Constitution was the correct one. Very early, therefore, a familiar semantic device appeared in American politics that continues down to the present time. To question the Constitution itself was taboo; one argued instead over what the Constitution 'really' meant. In this way it was possible to isolate the Constitution from political debate.

Not only Tocqueville but also the political practises of that time suggest that Americans also tended to agree on the virtues of political compromise. Tocqueville remarked on the self-restraint of Americans, on their reluctance not to push a good point too far.

With exceptional speed, Americans also developed a sense of nationhood. If it is difficult to be sure what the content of American beliefs is or has been, it is even harder to determine the exact nature of American Nationalism. That such a nationalism exists is, however, beyond doubt, and evidently it came about surprisingly soon. Foreigners and Americans alike began to observe from the time of the Revolution onward that Americans seemed to feel themselves more and more to be a distinct people, a unique people, not Englishmen now, nor Canadians, nor Frenchmen, nor Mexicans, nor any other people but Americans.[28] Americans soon gained a reputation among Europeans for being touchy about the virtues of the United States and even for a sort of national vanity. Traveling abroad, blow-hard Americans often alienated foreigners, as they have done ever since; while on this side of the Atlantic, the visitor who implied that the United States had any blemishes was likely to stir up a resentful counterattack.

There is perhaps no more vivid description of this unity of beliefs than Tocqueville's summary:

> The observer who examines what is passing in the United States . . . will readily discover that their inhabitants, though divided into twenty-four distinct sovereignties, still constitute a

28. An unusual attempt to trace the development of a sense of national identity among Americans from 1735–1775 will be found in Richard L. Merritt, *Symbols of American Community, 1735–1775*, New Haven, Yale University Press, 1966.

single people; and he may perhaps be led to think that the Anglo-American Union is more truly a united society than some nations of Europe which live under the same legislation and the same prince.

Although the Anglo-Americans have several religious sects, they all regard religion in the same manner. They are not always agreed upon the measures that are most conducive to good government, and they vary upon some of the forms of government which it is expedient to adopt; but they are unanimous upon the general principles that ought to rule human society. From Maine to the Floridas, and from the Missouri to the Atlantic Ocean, the people are held to be the source of all legitimate power. The same notions are entertained respecting liberty and equality, the liberty of the press, the right of association, the jury, and the responsibility of the agents of government.

If we turn from their political and religious opinions to the moral and philosophical principles that regulate the daily actions of life and govern their conduct, we still find the same uniformity. The Anglo-Americans acknowledge the moral authority of the reason of the community as they acknowledge the political authority of the mass of citizens; and they hold that public opinion is the surest arbiter of what is lawful or forbidden, true or false. The majority of them believe that a man by following his own interest, rightly understood, will be led to do what is just and good. They hold that every man is born in possession of the right of self-government, and that no one has the right of constraining his fellow creatures to be happy. They have all a lively faith in the perfectibility of man, they judge that the diffusion of knowledge must necessarily be advantageous, and the consequences of ignorance fatal; they all consider society as a body in a state of improvement, humanity as a changing scene, in which nothing is, or ought to be, permanent; and they admit that what appears to them today to be good, may be superseded by something better tomorrow. I do not give all these opinions as true, but as American opinions.

Not only are the Anglo-Americans united by these common opinions, but they are separated from all other nations by a feeling of pride. For the last fifty years no pains have been spared to convince the inhabitants of the United States that *they are the only religious, enlightened, and free people. They perceive that, for the present, their own democratic institutions prosper, while those of other countries fail; hence they conceive a high opinion of their superiority and are not very remote from believing themselves to be a distinct species of mankind.*[29]

How can one account for the rapid development of a similarity of beliefs and attitudes that has impressed so many visitors to the United States? The social and economic equality of Americans, together with their ethnic homogeneity and a common language undoubtedly helped a great deal: General ideas that appealed to one small farmer were very likely to have an appeal to another. Given a homogeneous population, similarities in beliefs were probably fostered also by physical isolation from Europe, by relatively firm boundaries to the East, North, and South, and by the existence of a unique political system that united Americans in a bold new experiment in self-government. Related to all these factors, there may be another, less flattering reason. A number of European observers, including Tocqueville and Martineau, were struck by the fear Americans displayed of seeming different from one another. To use the modern jargon, Americans often appeared to Europeans as strongly 'conformist' and 'other-directed.' They worried about the opin- ions of their neighbors and were reluctant to express or perhaps even to hold unpopular views. Everyone seemed bent on converging around a common mean.

> . . . *The time will come* (Harriet Martineau wrote of Ameri- cans) *when they will be astonished to discover how they mar their own privileges by allowing themselves less liberty of speech and action than is enjoyed by the inhabitants of coun- tries whose political servitude the Americans justly compassion- ate and despise . . . They may travel over the whole world, and find no society but their own which will submit to the restraint of perpetual caution, and reference to the opinions of others.*[30]

Was the ancient problem of faction solved among Americans, then, by a kind of spontaneous agreement? To suppose so would be to engender another myth. For if the forces making for unity were, luckily for Americans, strong enough to maintain a united country, there were

29. Tocqueville, Vol. 1, 409–410.
30. Harriet Martineau, *op. cit.*, pp. 249–251.

also matters that divided them. If the Americans were in many respects alike, they were not by any means a perfectly homogeneous people, and some of their differences created conflicts. On one issue, time was running out. Barely a generation separated the visits of Alexis de Tocqueville and Harriet Martineau from the outbreak of the American Civil War.

Nonetheless, despite some inequalities, differences and conflicts, American ideas shaped the American environment and the American environment shaped American ideas in a silent revolution that produced an equality of condition, a degree of national unity, and a set of values, which, taken one with the other, could hardly have been more congenial to the emergence of a democratic political order. In these circumstances, almost any constitutional arrangements might have become (somehow) democratic. The question, not wholly resolved at the Constitutional Convention, of whether the United States should be an aristocratic republic or a democratic republic, was thus resolved as Wilson, Madison, and Mason had hoped and planned it would be.

The conditions that helped toward this outcome by no means provided a permanent guarantee that conflicts could be managed peacefully, that widespread consent and loyalty would continue to be forthcoming, and that new social and economic institutions would be as congenial to democracy as the old. But they did provide strong foundations for a democratic order during one of the most critical periods any nation ever faces—its early years.

Part Two

How American political institutions evolved and how they contribute to pluralist democracy

4

THE PRESIDENCY

Introduction

FOR MANY A FERVENT PROPONENT of democracy, it is awkward to admit that a 'democratic' system needs leaders. For the admission seems to imply that the people are not wholly capable of governing themselves. Yet every political system with more than a handful of citizens has to provide for governmental functions that the whole people are unable or unwilling to perform individually or collectively. Among the most important of these functions are to work out specific proposals of policies that the government should adopt; to insure that these policies are properly executed; to undertake emergency actions, especially on matters of war and foreign affairs; and to perform certain kinds of symbolic functions—as symbolic head of the state for internal and for international purposes and as spokesman for and representative of unity. These functions are carried on in democratic systems (as in other systems) by political leaders.

If the need for leadership in a democracy is much more widely accepted today than it was earlier, this is partly because experience with democratic institutions has made the need for leadership obvious to almost everyone. There is also a second, and in some ways more interesting, reason: The leaders developed in and by democracies have come to be among their proudest symbols. When an American is asked to say who this country's greatest men have been, the chances are that he will at once think of our Presidents;[1] a British citizen is likely to name prime

1. Although today's children and adolescents, it seems, are much less likely to choose Washington as the person they would most like to resemble than children two or three generations ago. Cf. Fred I. Greenstein, "New Light on Changing American Values: A Forgotten Body of Survey Data." *Social Forces*, vol. 42 (1964), 441–450.

ministers as once he would have named kings. When Americans are asked in Gallup polls what living man they admire the most, the name of their current President invariably tops the list, followed by the names of living past Presidents, presidential candidates, and other political leaders.[2] Presidents' wives are named among the most admired women.[3] The mourning that followed the assassination of President Kennedy and the death of Winston Churchill suggest the deep emotional ties that leaders in democracies sometimes have with their people, or an allied people.[4]

In American life, far and away the most important political leader is, of course, the President. As a contribution to the art of politics, the American Presidency is unique. The institution was not at the outset a copy of anything else; nor, despite a number of attempts, has it been successfully copied elsewhere.[5] What makes the American Presidency unique is its particular and peculiar combination of characteristics. Unlike a prime minister, the President is not elected by the legislature but by the people (despite the electoral college, an irrelevancy from the very beginning). In some ways and at some times, the President is extraordinarily powerful; yet in many ways and at many times, his power is—as every President sooner or later discovers—severely limited. Great hierarchical authority has been vested in the President by the Constitution, by the Supreme Court, and by historical evolution; yet every President must spend much of his time bargaining with other political leaders to obtain only a small part of what he wants. Except perhaps for the Supreme Court, no institution plays so important a symbolic role in American political life; particularly in times of crisis the President symbolizes the nation. Yet a President is inescapably a partisan; he is the head of a political party and up to his ears in partisan politics.

2. E.g., The ten men most admired by Americans in 1965 were Lyndon B. Johnson, Dwight D. Eisenhower, Robert F. Kennedy, Rev. Billy Graham, Pope Paul VI, Martin Luther King, Richard M. Nixon, Hubert H. Humphrey, Barry M. Goldwater, Harry S. Truman. Source: American Institute of Public Opinion. Gallup poll, for release Jan. 2, 1966.
3. Ibid., for release Jan. 31, 1965.
4. Among the ten men most admired by Americans "between 1953 and 1960, Churchill was second only to the U.S. President, Dwight Eisenhower. In 1961, he was third, behind President John Kennedy and former President Eisenhower, as he was in the following year, 1962. In 1963, he placed third behind President Lyndon Johnson and Eisenhower." Source: American Institute of Public Opinion. Gallup poll for release Jan. 29, 1965.
5. President Charles de Gaulle in the Fifth Republic of France is in some ways similar to a strong American President. But there are also many differences. And it is not yet clear whether de Gaulle's presidency will prove to be unique in French history.

This unique institution was one of the more successful products of the Constitutional Convention. Yet, detached observers might quite reasonably have voted it the institution least likely to succeed. For it was the institution about which the men at the Convention were most confused; they least understood it, they foresaw its development unclearly, and they left its design uncompleted in the Constitution they created.

The modern Presidency, then, is the end-product of the imprecise but not totally pliable pattern created by the Constitution, and of the play of historical forces upon that loose and yielding office.

At the Convention: the Paucity of Models

To understand the Presidency it is instructive to put ourselves briefly in the shoes of the men at the Convention. That some functions of leadership had to be performed in the political system for which they were designing a constitution, these men were both too practical and too versed in political experience to doubt. They knew they had to design the office of "national executive," "executive magistracy," "magistrate," or "executive," as they referred to it at various times.

Yet how were they to create an "executive magistrate" who would perform whatever functions the other institutions could not properly execute and who at the same time would not be a political monstrosity? In 1787, the problem was far more baffling than it would be today, because the democratic executive was all but unknown. A popularly elected President was a novelty; the chief alternative solution, a prime minister chosen by the parliament, had not yet emerged in its modern democratic form even in Britain.

Every problem was unsolved, every proposal debatable, every solution risky. How many executives should there be: one or several? How should the executive be chosen? For how long? What should the qualifications be for executive office? What constitutional powers and limits were required? Whatever was written into the Constitution, what would be the real role of the executive in the new political system? The answers necessarily had to be highly speculative.

HOW MANY. It is true that earlier republics furnished some experience, but republican executives had generally been collegial, consisting of several men, each of whom served as a check on the others. This was the famous solution of the Roman Republic. Although the plural executive is designed to solve one problem, it creates another. The plural executive may help to prevent any single man from gaining too much power; yet where one executive checks another, decisions may be paralyzed. That system must, therefore, avoid great emergencies, particularly those requiring decisive action in international affairs and war; or else, as in the Roman Republic, it must have some provision for a temporary 'dictator' armed with emergency powers.

Because of these disadvantages, the plural executive is rarely used in modern democracies. Switzerland has employed it most successfully— but Switzerland is small, maintains a vigorous neutrality, remains free of alliances and international organizations, and avoids war. In 1951, one of the few constitutional democracies of Latin America, Uruguay, shifted from a presidential executive to a nine-member council; Uruguay, like Switzerland, is small and peaceful; even so, in 1966, Uruguay decided to restore the single executive. No other nation has chosen the collegial form, though the cabinet system bears a superficial resemblance to it.

The idea of a plural executive had little support at the Convention. Randolph of Virginia

> . . . strenuously opposed a unity in the Executive magistracy. He regarded it as the foetus of monarchy . . . He could not see why the great requisites for the Executive department, vigor, despatch and responsibility could not be found in three men, as well as in one man.[6]

But Randolph won few converts. After all, the Articles of Confederation had followed the pattern of the ancient republics; the only executive provided for in the Articles was a committee, appointed by Congress, "to sit in the recess of congress, to be denominated 'A committee of the States,' and to consist of one delegate from each state." Not even Randolph wanted to duplicate that feeble system in the new Constitution. In their own constitutions, the states (except for Pennsylvania) had settled, nominally, for a single executive—though often he was so hedged around by a legislative council that the executive was in fact collegial. One famous republic, it is true, had in outward form a single executive: the Doge of Venice. That Republic, the longest-lived republic in history, was after some seven or eight centuries approaching its final coup de grace at the hands of Napoleon. But the Doge was virtually all

6. *Documents*, p. 132.

figurehead and no power; executive authority was in fact lodged in numerous councils, commissions, and officials.

Whatever the reasons, the proposal for a single executive was agreed to in the early days of the convention. It was almost the only question having to do with the Presidency on which the Convention, having once made a decision, did not later change its mind.[7]

HOW LONG?   In the absence of an appropriate model for a republican executive, the most visible alternative was the form that all members of the Convention knew best: an hereditary monarchy. Yet it was precisely because this solution was barred to them by their own beliefs and the attitudes of the country—". . . There was not a one-thousandth part of our fellow citizens who were not against every approach toward monarchy," said Gerry—that there existed the vacuum they had to fill. To Alexander Hamilton—if we can rely on Madison's notes—a republic was inherently a second-best form of government because, unlike a monarchy, it could provide no good solution to the problem of the executive:

> As to the executive, (Madison reports Hamilton as saying on June 18) it seemed to be admitted that no good one could be established on republican principles. Was not this giving up the merits of the question; for can there be a good government without a good executive? The English model was the only good one on this subject. The hereditary interest of the king was so interwoven with that of the nation, and his personal emoluments so great, that he was placed above the danger of being corrupted from abroad—and at the same time was both sufficiently independent and sufficiently controuled, to answer the purpose of the institution at home . . . What is the inference from all these observations? That we ought to go as far in order to attain stability and permanency, as republican principles will admit. Let one branch of the legislature hold their places for life, or at least during good behavior. Let the executive also be for life.[8]

One weak spot of Hamilton's argument was, as everyone knew, the

---

7.   No one except Randolph spoke against the single executive. Three states—New York, Delaware, and Maryland—voted against it on the decisive vote of June 4. Virginia voted for it, although the delegation was split down the middle: Madison, Washington, and two others favored the single executive; Randolph, Mason, and Blair opposed it. Documents, p. 132.

8.   Documents, pp. 221–222.

simple matter of genes and the accidents of human personality. A great king may have a son less suited to kingship than his own fool. A king famed for his justice may beget a tyrant. To a king of intelligence, vision, courage, and resolution, the mysteries of genes and child-rearing may produce an heir, short-sighted, feckless, weak, and irresolute. Writing some years later, Jefferson reflected on the monarchs of Europe:

> While in Europe, I often amused myself with contemplating the characters of the then reigning sovereigns . . . Louis XVI was a fool, of my own knowledge . . . The King of Spain was a fool, and of Naples the same. They passed their lives in hunting, and despatched two couriers a week, one thousand miles, to let each other know what game they had killed the preceding days. The King of Sardinia was a fool. All these were Bourbons. The queen of Portugal, a Braganza, was an idiot by nature. And so was the King of Denmark. Their sons, as regents, exercised the powers of government. The King of Prussia, successor to the great Frederick, was a mere hog in body as well as in mind. Gustavus of Sweden, and Joseph of Austria, were really crazy, and George of England, you know, was in a straight waistcoat. There remained, then, none but old Catherine, who had been too lately picked up to have lost her common sense . . . These animals had become without mind and powerless; and so will every hereditary monarch be after a few generations . . . And so endeth the book of Kings, from all of whom the Lord deliver us.[9]

The Americans had thrown off one hereditary monarch; it was obvious to all—including Hamilton—that they would not tolerate another.

An executive for life might solve some of these problems; but such a system would create others. To give a man a lifetime in which to accumulate power is dangerous. A lifetime tenure might even be enough to establish a dynasty. Sickness, senility, degeneration, insanity have turned good leaders into evil ones; yet an executive appointed for life might not yield power gladly and might have too much power to be dispossessed without violence. The Roman emperors were the obvious model: They had held office for life. Yet while some of them, like Hadrian, were undoubtedly great leaders and ruled during times of great prosperity and peace, many were brutal tyrants: Caligula, Nero, Commodus, Caracalla.

9. *Thomas Jefferson On Democracy*, selected and arranged by Saul K. Padover, New York, Penguin Books, 1946, p. 26.

An executive chosen for life had no support at the Convention. Even Hamilton, when he got down to his specific proposals, called for an appointment not explicitly for life, but "during good behavior." When James McClurg (a delegate from Virginia whose role at the Convention was brief and unimportant) moved that the executive hold office "during good behavior," the idea won little acclaim. That distinguished advocate of an aristocratic republic, Gouverneur Morris, briefly endorsed it but changed his mind a few days later.[10] Madison tactfully suggested that "respect for the mover entitled his proposition to a fair hearing and discussion."[11]

> . . . He considered an Executive during good behavior as a softer name only for an Executive for life. And that the next would be an easy step to Hereditary Monarchy. If the motion should finally succeed, he might himself live to see such a Revolution. If he did not it was probable his children or grand children would. He trusted there were few men in that house who wished for it. No state he was sure had so far revolted from Republican principles as to have the least bias in its favor.[12]

The proposal was turned down by a close vote—four states in favor, six against—which, according to Madison, grossly exaggerated the actual support the proposal had enjoyed at the Convention. "This vote," he wrote in a comment on his own notes, "is not to be considered as any certain index of opinion, as a number in the affirmative probably had it chiefly in view to alarm those attached to a dependence of the Executive on the Legislature, and thereby facilitate some final arrangement of a contrary tendency. The avowed friends of an Executive, 'during good behaviour' were not more than three or four, nor is it certain they would finally have adhered to such a tenure."[13]

Yet, while this proposal was disposed of fairly easily, the Convention twisted and turned like a man tormented in his sleep by a bad dream as it tried to decide just what term would be proper. On July 24, the Convention had a particularly trying day: Luther Martin proposed a term of eleven years; Gerry suggested fifteen; King, twenty years—"the medium life of princes"; Davie, eight years. After that day's work, the Convention adjourned without having decided anything at all.

10. Cf. *Documents*, pp. 396, 447.
11. *Ibid.*, p. 398.
12. *Ibid.*
13. *Ibid.*, p. 399, fn.

The log of votes in the Convention on the length of term of the President reveals the uncertainty of the delegates:

June 1. Seven-year term, *passed,* 5 states to 4.
June 2. Ineligible for re-election after seven years, *passed,* 7-2.
July 19. Seven-year term, *defeated,* 5-3.
    Six-year term, *passed,* 9-1.
    Ineligibility for a second term, *defeated,* 8-2.
July 26. Seven-year term, with ineligibility for re-election, *passed,* 7-3.
Sept. 6. Seven-year term, *defeated,* 8-3.
    Six-year term, *defeated,* 9-2.
    Four-year term, *passed,* 10-1.

HOW CHOSEN?   But having settled on a four-year term, how was the executive to be chosen? On this question the Convention could never quite make up its mind. Almost to the end, it would move toward a solution and then, on second thought, reverse itself in favor of some different alternative. On no question was experience so uncertain a guide. If ultimately the Convention invented the popularly elected Presidency, it would be excessively charitable to say that the men in Philadelphia foresaw what they were doing.

The most obvious solution in 1787 was the election of the executive by the legislature. This was the essence of the cabinet system that was evolving in Britain. Yet, in 1787, that evolution was far from complete; neither in Britain nor in this country did anyone quite realize how much the Prime Minister was ceasing to be the agent of the King and becoming instead the representative of a parliamentary majority. When one spoke of the British executive in 1787 one still meant the King, not the Prime Minister.

In the American states, too, under new or revised state constitutions the governor was generally chosen by the legislature. Yet the experience of the various states suggested some of the disadvantages of that solution: If the executive were elected by the legislature, what was to prevent him from becoming a mere creature of that body? To some of the men at the Convention, this was exactly what was needed. Thus Sherman of Connecticut "was for the appointment by the legislature and for making him absolutely dependent on that body, as it was the will of that which was to be executed. An independence of the executive on the supreme legislature was in his opinion the very essence of tyranny, if there was any such thing."[14] Was Sherman thinking of his own state—one of the few in which the governor was popularly elected?

The main reason those who opposed election by the Congress gave for their opposition was a fear that the executive would be too weak. The chief spokesman for an aristocratic republic, Gouverneur Morris, joined with the spokesmen for the democratic republic, Madison and Wilson, in opposing election by the Congress. But to find an alternative was infinitely more difficult. If the executive were elected by the people, as Wilson proposed, would he not then be too dependent on the whims of popular majorities? And could the people possibly know enough to make a wise choice? Even to Mason, who usually favored the more democratic solutions, it seemed "as unnatural to refer the choice of a proper character for chief magistrate to the people as it would be to refer a trial of colors to a blind man. The extent of the country renders it impossible that the people can have the requisite capacity to judge of the respective pretensions of the candidates."[15]

Thus the argument went on. Every possible solution seemed fatally flawed. Should the President be chosen by the Congress? by the Senate only? by the people? by the state governors? by the state legislatures? by electors chosen by the people? As Madison wearily concluded in late July, "There are objections against every mode that has been, or perhaps can be proposed."[16]

The United States came within a hair's breath of adopting a kind of parliamentary system. The Virginia plan had proposed that the executive be chosen by the national legislature. Only July 17 this mode was unanimously agreed to. It won another trial vote, 6-3, on July 26. As late as August 24 the Convention voted against an attempt to substitute election by the people or by electors for choice by the legislature. Yet when a committee reported out on September 4—two weeks before the end of the Convention—it suggested the "electoral college" solution which was embodied in Article II of the Constitution. No one altogether knows what happened in the interval; perhaps many delegates who had earlier voted for election by the legislature were so unsure of their grounds, so weary of the dispute, and so fearful of further haggling and possible deadlock that they eagerly accepted the compromise suggested by the committee. Whatever the reasons, all who struggle today with the task of inventing new political institutions may be comforted by this record of the Convention's torment:

14. *Ibid.,* p. 134.
15. *Ibid.,* pp. 394–395.
16. *Ibid.,* p. 449.

June 2. Virginia plan (Randolph) proposes a national executive "to be chosen by the national legislature." Discussed.

June 2. Wilson's proposal for presidential electors chosen by the people, *defeated* 8-2.

June 9. Gerry's proposal that the executive be chosen "by the executives of the states," *defeated* 9-0.

July 17. Wilson's proposal for election by the people, *defeated* 9-1. Luther Martin's proposal for choice by electors appointed by state legislatures, *defeated* 8-2.

Randolph's original proposal, "to be chosen by the national Legislature," *passed unanimously.*

July 19. Ellsworth's proposal that national executive be chosen by electors appointed by state legislatures, *passed* 6-3 (Massachusetts divided).

July 24. Houston's proposal that "the Executive be appointed by the National Legislature," *passed* 7-4.

July 25. Ellsworth's proposal that "the Executive be appointed by the Legislature" except for re-election "in which case the choice shall be by Electors appointed by the Legislators in the States," *defeated* 7-4.

July 26. A comprehensive resolution on the National Executive proposing among other things that he be "chosen by the National Legislature" *passed* 6-3. (Virginia divided, with Washington and Madison against). This article, as approved, referred to Committee of Detail.

August 6. Constitution as reported by Committee of Detail reads "he shall be elected by ballot by the legislature."

August 24. Carroll's proposal to strike out "by the legislature" and insert "by the people," *defeated*, 9-2.

G. Morris' proposal that the President "shall be chosen by electors," *failed*, 4-4 (Connecticut and Maryland, divided, Massachusetts absent).

September 4. Committee of Eleven, to which this and other sections had been referred, propose essentials of present Constitution: *"Each State shall appoint in such manner as its legislatures may direct,*[17] *a number of electors equal to the whole number of Senators and members of the House of Representatives to which the States may be entitled in the legislature."*

September 6. This proposal *adopted* 9-2.

September 17. Constitution signed; Convention adjourns.

17. For further discussion of this matter, see below, p. 92.

The Unfinished Business

Most modern democracies have rejected the Founders' solution. They have preferred the parliamentary system in which the executive is chosen by and is dependent on the confidence of the national legislature. The difficulty foreseen by the critics of an executive chosen by the Congress —his weakness—has come to pass in some countries and not in others. In Britain, the prime minister gradually emerged as a powerful leader who could count on the disciplined majority that chose him in parliament; in the twentieth century few British cabinets have ever fallen through a vote of no confidence; the prime minister is nearly as secure in his five-year tenure as the President is in his four-year term. A number of other democracies have followed a similar path. However, in France under the Third Republic (1870-1940) and the Fourth (1946-1958), the worst fears of men like Wilson and Madison were vindicated: The cabinet, dependent on parliament, was its creature; governments fell with appalling frequency—about every seven months on the average during the Fourth Republic. The Fifth Republic (1958-) granted great executive authority to General de Gaulle, and in 1962 a constitutional amendment providing for the direct popular election of the president was approved by nearly two-thirds of the voters in a national referendum. A number of other countries that have chosen the parliamentary-cabinet system have had an experience similar to that of France. Some, paradoxically, have had both experiences. In Sweden during the nineteen-year period from 1917-1936, there were eleven governments; yet, since 1936, Swedish cabinets have been remarkably stable and have carried through comprehensive reforms.

If the Convention had adhered to the Virginia plan and thereby left the choice of the executive to the Congress, would the United States have developed a stable and powerful executive like the British prime minister—or, instead, a weak and unstable executive like that of France under the Third and Fourth Republics? It is difficult to say.

But, instead of speculating on that subject, let us take stock of what the Convention did and did not do.

The Convention

¶ Provided unity in the office of chief executive.
¶ Insured that the President would (short of impeachment or death) remain in office for a fixed four-year term. Thus

there would ordinarily be continuity and stability in the executive office at least for four years.

¶ Provided the President with an electoral base, a constituency, independent of the Congress.

¶ Armed the President (Article II) with constitutional powers not dependent on the Congress, the President's electors, the people, or the states. Hence, both in his election and in his powers, the President could be to some degree independent of congressional majorities and of popular opinion.

¶ And placed no limit on the number of times he could be re-elected. (The Twenty-second Amendment, providing that "no person shall be elected to the office of the President more than twice" was not enacted until 1951.)

On the other hand, the Convention

¶ Could not foresee how the election of the President by the method they chose at the ultimate hour would actually work. Would presidential electors tend to speak for aristocracy, and thus choose a man who would be a brake on the Congress and the people? Or would they themselves be agents of popular majorities and choose Presidents who appealed to the populace rather than to elite groups?

¶ Did not provide for a method by which conflicts between the President and the other branches might be resolved, other than by the cumbersome and unlikely process of impeachment or, somehow, through elections. Conflict between executive and legislature was, in the eyes of most of the men at the Convention, not wholly undesirable; conflict was the essence of the rationale for separation of powers. But would conflict between President and Congress lead to unproductive stalemate?

¶ Could not know how weak or powerful the President's office they had created would become in actual practice. Would his independence and unity be sufficient to keep him from being a mere weak creature of the Congress? Conversely, might he become so powerful that he would overweigh the 'balances' in the system? Was he, despite all the efforts they had made to prevent it, a potential tyrant? Would he be too powerful—or not powerful enough?

These questions were left to be answered by the Presidents themselves, and the political forces of which they were a part.

The Growth of the Presidential Office

The evolution of the Presidency is the story of a frequent and cumulative
increase in the role—or, better, the roles—that the President can play,
and is expected to play, in the American political system, and, more
recently, in the world. Every 'great' President has left the office somewhat altered and enlarged. The Presidency is like a family dwelling that
each new generation alters and enlarges. Confronted by some new need,
a President adds on a new room, a new wing; what began as a modest
dwelling has become a mansion; every President may not use every room,
but the rooms are available in case of need.

Washington's greatest legacy to future Presidents was, perhaps, in
creating and acting out superbly the symbolic roles that Presidents have
generally played ever since: as head of state for official, semi-official, and
popular functions; as a key spokesman for national unity; as a symbol of
the obligation imposed on all officials, on all Americans, to obey the
Constitution and to behave according to the spirit of constitutionalism.
In playing the role of constitutional monarch to a republic, Washington
was assisted both by his beliefs and by his practices. For he appears to
have believed that the President could and should be free of partisan
attachments. Yet he himself was a staunch Federalist who was prone to
see 'the spirit of party' in others but not in his own administration. "He
is to be blamed," a modern critic has written, "not for allying himself with
a party, but for not knowing that he had done so, and for denouncing
those opposed to his party as opposed to the government. He was most
in the grip of party feeling at the time when he was being represented as
being above it."[18]

It was Washington's practises that helped rescue his image of himself as above partisanship. For in Alexander Hamilton, his Secretary of
the Treasury, Washington had a lieutenant who came as close as any
American cabinet member ever has to being a prime minister to the
President. It was Hamilton who discharged many of the political duties
that later Presidents discharged themselves, and it was therefore Hamil-

18. Joseph Charles, *The Origins of the American Party System*, New York,
Harper Torchbooks, 1956, 1961, p. 44.

[90]

ton, not Washington, who became the prime target of the emerging opposition. It was Hamilton who developed the Administration's major policies, Hamilton who struggled to build a durable presidential coalition, Hamilton who mobilized the Congress on behalf of presidential policies.

Under Jefferson, these roles—constitutional monarch and prime minister, chief magistrate and party leader, President of the country, and head of a faction within the country—were fused.

If every President since Jefferson has played the role of party leader, none has ever performed it with more consummate skill. Before he became President, and as an important instrument in gaining the Presidency, Jefferson and his staunch ally Madison had forged the Republican party (which in due time was to be called the Democratic-Republican, and finally the Democratic Party) as a nation-wide organization with many of the features of modern parties.[19] As President, Jefferson perfected the instrument he had helped to construct. Following the pattern of John Adams, who in the late moments of his Presidency had sought to pack the courts with Federalists, Jefferson now initiated a policy of appointing only trustworthy Republicans to office; justified a policy of removing Federalists from office and replacing them with Republicans; worked closely with the congressional Republican leaders in gaining the support of Congress; and sought to strengthen the national and state party machinery.[20] He was perhaps as professional a party leader as has ever occupied the White House.

Yet if Jefferson saw himself as a spokesman both for the nation as a whole and for the majority (and the party) that elected him, he accepted the fact that he must work in and through the Congress, the only legitimate representative of the popular will. In this respect, Jefferson reflected the traditional republican doctrine expressed by men as unlike as Locke, Rousseau, and the delegates to the Constitutional Convention. This view—it has been called the Whig view—holds that the true representative of the people is the legislature; the task of the executive is to 'execute' the commands of the legislative body. In persisting as long as it did in its original decision to have the chief executive elected by Congress, the Convention was to some extent reflecting this deeply ingrained respect for the representativeness of the legislative body. When Sherman announced that "an independence of the executive on the supreme

19. *Ibid.*, and Noble E. Cunningham, Jr., *The Jeffersonian Republicans in Power, Party Operations 1810–1899*, Chapel Hill, University of North Carolina Press, 1963.
20. *Ibid.*

legislature was in his opinion the very essence of tyranny," he spoke for a powerful tradition. Not even Jefferson claimed that the President might be as representative of the popular will or of a national majority as the Congress.

It was Jackson who proclaimed this role for the President and thereby justified his use of the veto against congressional majorities. Jackson and his followers formulated a revolutionary new concept of the democratic executive: Because in the American system, the national leader elected by and responsible to the people was the only official elected by votes cast over the whole nation, he was therefore the most legitimate representative and spokesman, as no other official could be for the majority of the nation.

As a result of gradual change in the method of electing the President, Jackson had, in fact, rather better grounds for claiming to be the elected spokesman of the nation than Jefferson had. You will recall that the Constitution directs that "each state shall appoint, *in such manner as the legislature thereof may direct,* a number of electors" who, in turn, choose the President (Article II, italics added). At first, in most states the legislatures themselves chose the presidential electors; when Jefferson was named President in 1800, the electors were chosen by the state legislatures rather than the people in ten of the sixteen states. By 1828, however, only two states out of twenty-four (Delaware and South Carolina) still followed the old practise, and when Jackson was re-elected in 1832 the only state in which electors were chosen by the legislature was South Carolina—which, incidentally, stubbornly persisted in its anachronism until 1860.[21] Thus by Jackson's time the electoral college was already becoming an anomalous, quaint, but for the most part reliable way of designating the choice for President. Consequently, in Jackson's view, if there were a clash between President and Congress, the President had as much—if not more—right to speak for the people of the country, or a majority of them, as the Congress.

In accusing him of breaking tradition, Jackson's enemies were correct, even if their language was characteristically intemperate:

> *I look upon Jackson as a detestable, ignorant, reckless, vain and malignant tyrant* . . . . [Chancellor Kent, the distinguished Federalist jurist of New York, wrote in 1834 to his equally distinguished Massachusetts friend, Joseph Story.] *This American elective monarchy frightens me. The experiment, with its*

21. For methods of electing presidential electors, 1788–1836, see *Historical Statistics,* p. 681.

foundations laid on universal suffrage and our unfettered press, is of too violent a nature for our excitable people.

We are in the midst of a revolution [said Clay] hitherto bloodless, but tending rapidly towards a total change of the pure republican character of the government, and to the concentration of all power in the hands of one man.[22]

If the passages seem familiar, even hackneyed, it may be because every strong President since Jackson has provoked similar rhetoric. Jackson's opponents chose to call themselves Whigs in order to emphasize their adherence to the traditional view that the legislature was the supreme representative agency in a republic. They professed to seek a restoration of Jeffersonian republicanism. In 1840, a Whig newspaper thundered:

If ever there was a genuine Republican party in the country it is that party which General Harrison now worthily leads and leads to victory. What are its objects and ends? To restore the Constitution, the charter of public liberty, to authority, to reduce the more the monarch's power of the President of the United States.[23]

Yet, though the Whig view of the Presidency lingered on, and echoes of it are heard occasionally even now, it was Jackson's enlarged conception that has generally prevailed in practice. Jackson's own accomplishments as President were mainly negative; his success depended almost entirely on his use of the executive power and the veto to negate congressional policies rather than on leadership in creating new legislation; yet during his two terms in office he added a spacious new wing to the Presidency. His conception of the role of President as a national leader with his own independent basis of legitimacy in a popular majority has won the support of all our most famous Presidents; it has come to be widely accepted among political leaders and the public; and it has even shaped the development of our other elected chief executives in the state and municipal governments, the governors and mayors.

22. Both quotations in a modern classic on the Presidency, Edward S. Corwin, *The President, Offices, and Powers*, New York, New York University Press, 1948, p. 24.
23. Quoted in Wilfred E. Binkley, *President and Congress*, New York, Alfred A. Knopf, 1947, p. 88.

Jackson's Presidency foreshadowed Lincoln's. When, in 1832, a special convention called by the state legislature of South Carolina adopted an ordinance nullifying the tariff acts of 1828 and 1832, and the state legislature passed laws to enforce this Ordinance of Nullification, Jackson issued a Proclamation to the People of South Carolina that described nullification as an "impractical absurdity," asserted the supremacy of the sovereign and indivisible Federal Government over the states, and denied the right of any state either to disobey Federal laws or to leave the Union. Jackson asked for and received from Congress the authority to enforce revenue laws by military force. But force proved to be unnecessary, the crisis was resolved by a compromise on the tariff, and the questions at issue were postponed, to be confronted by Lincoln when he assumed office in 1861.

It was Lincoln who carried to the outermost boundaries the President's role as leader in times of national emergency. The Roman Republic, you will recall, provided for a short-term dictator to cope with great emergencies. At the Constitutional Convention, which was much concerned, as we have seen, with the danger of creating a tyrant, no one seems to have proposed a grant of 'emergency powers' to the executive —a constitutional lacuna that constitution-makers in other countries were later to fill by various devices, not all of them successful. American Presidents have filled the gap, not by changing the letter of the Constitution but by adding invisible text between the lines.

Lincoln, to be sure, was not the first President to be confronted by a crisis. Jackson, as we just saw, had to meet South Carolina's threat of disobedience. Washington called out troops to put down an insurrection by farmers in western Pennsylvania (who objected to paying an excise tax on the manufacture of whiskey, a tax that fell heavily on backwoods farmers who disposed of their surplus grain by turning it into liquor). Jefferson faced a prolonged international crisis generated by the Napoleonic wars. Madison was President during the new nation's first war, the war of 1812-1814 with Britain. A war with Mexico took place during Polk's Administration.

All of these were modest crises compared with the break-up of the United States. History decreed that it would be Lincoln, a Whig before he was a Republican, who should stretch the Constitution to its very limits—or, to be candid, beyond them. As a Whig, Lincoln had espoused the narrow Whig doctrine on the President; yet Lincoln's inaugural address was no Whig statement: It could have been delivered by Jackson:

... *I hold that, in contemplation of universal law and of the*

Constitution, the United of these States is perpetual . . . It follows from these views that no State upon its own mere motion can lawfully get out of the Union; that resolves and ordinances to that effect are legally void; and that acts of violence . . . against the authority of the United States are insurrectionary or revolutionary.

I therefore consider that, in view of the Constitution and the laws, the Union is unbroken and to the extent of my ability I shall take care, as the Constitution itself expressly enjoins upon me, that the laws of the Union be faithfully executed in all the states. Doing this I deem to be only a simple duty on my part; and I shall perform it, so far as practicable, unless my rightful masters, the American people, shall . . . direct to the contrary.

The chief magistrate derives all his authority from the people . . . His duty is to administer the present government, as it came to his hands, and to transmit it, unimpaired by him, to his successor.[24]

Lincoln's view that the President "derives all his authority from the people" created, for him, a source of authority even more exalted than the Constitution or the Congress; and his view that "the Union" was "perpetual" no doubt justified, to him, violations of the Constitution and disregard for Congressional sentiment. "Was it possible to lose the nation," he asked in 1864, " and yet to preserve the Constitution?"

Perhaps few Presidents have had less of the tyrant in their nature than Lincoln, as much charity, and as little will to dominate for the mere sake of domination. It is these qualities of the man himself, the mixture of great strength with great self-restraint, the compound of resolution and forebearance, that have helped to make him an all but mythical prototype of the great popular leader. And it is because of this, and the cruel choices he faced, that it is less than charitable to be harsh about his methods.

. . . Unquestionably the high-water mark of the exercise of executive power in the United States is found in the administration of Abraham Lincoln (an historian of the Presidency has written). No President before or since has pushed the boundaries of executive power so far over into the legislative sphere.

24. The address is quoted in full in Carl Sandburg, *Abraham Lincoln, The War Years,* New York, Harcourt Brace, 1939, vol. I, pp. 125–135, italics added.

No one can ever know just what Lincoln conceived to be the limits of his powers. Even a partial review of them presents an imposing list of daring adventures. Under the war power he proclaimed the slaves of those in rebellion emancipated. He devised and put into execution his peculiar plan of reconstruction. In disregard of law he increased the army and navy beyond the limits set by statute. The privilege of the writ of habeus corpus was suspended wholesale and martial law declared. Public money in the sum of millions was deliberately spent without congressional appropriation. Nor was any of this done innocently. Lincoln understood his Constitution. He knew, in many cases, just how he was transgressing and his infractions were consequently deliberate. It is all the more astonishing that this audacity was the work of a minority President who performed in the presence of a bitter congressional opposition even in his own party.[25]

If, after Lincoln's death, the Congress and the Whig view of the Presidency reasserted themselves, the role of emergency 'dictator' that Lincoln had created could not be wholly forgotten. Lincoln had acted mainly under two clauses of the Constitution: "The President shall be Commander in Chief of the Army and Navy of the United States . . ." and "he shall take care that the laws be faithfully executed." During the two World Wars, the Cold War that followed the Second World War, the Korean War (1950-1952), American involvement in Vietnam from 1956 onward, and throughout the Cuban crisis of 1962 when the confrontation between the United States and the Soviet Union brought the world to the very gates of the inferno—Presidents Wilson, Franklin Roosevelt, Truman, Eisenhower, Kennedy, and Johnson all drew heavily on these constitutional sources. To constitutional authority, Congress added other powers by delegating through normal statutory law wide discretionary authority to the President, usually but not always for a fixed period. For example, under the Lend-Lease Act of 1940,

> . . . the President was empowered (even before the country was legally at war) to procure any "defense articles" and dispose of them on such terms as he saw fit to "any country whose defense the President deems vital to the defense of the United States." Allocation of material was authorized, price controls set up, plant seizure provided for—all within the discretionary
> 25. Binkley, op. cit., p. 127.

control of the President. Where these and like dispensations were questioned in court, they were always sustained.[26]

Thus the President's war power is a mighty arsenal. Yet it is not unlimited. When Lincoln suspended the writ of habeus corpus (which Article I pretty clearly intended that only Congress could do) he asked rhetorically: "Are all the laws but one to go unexecuted, and the Government itself to go to pieces lest that one be violated?" Nonetheless, the Supreme Court has not always responded to a President's demand that military crisis allows him to stretch the terms of the Constitution. When President Truman, acting without statutory authority, seized the steel mills to forestall a strike during the Korean war, the Supreme Court denied that the constitutional powers of the Chief Executive went so far. Yet the Court was obviously troubled. Four of the nine Justices dissented, and the five Justices in the majority disagreed among themselves as to the grounds for their decision.[27]

To the enormous role of the President as emergency head of the country in war, the exigencies of survival in the modern world have added yet another role of great compass: the nation's leader in foreign affairs. Starting from a rather modest base in the Constitution,[28] the President has become the dominant figure in foreign policy. Woodrow Wilson, who first developed the role in its modern form (and crowned his performance with failure), foresaw (four years before he became President, when the matter was still cloudy) that control over foreign policy would give the President great power as the United States moved from the wings to the center of the world stage.

. . . One of the greatest of the President's powers [he wrote in 1908], [is] . . . his control, which is very absolute, of the foreign relations of the nation. The initiative in foreign affairs, which

26. Charles Black, *Perspectives in Constitutional Law*, Englewood Cliffs, N.J., Prentice-Hall, 1963, p. 73.
27. *Youngstown Sheet and Tube v Sawyer*, 343 U.S. 579 (1952).
28. Article II. Section 1. "The executive Power shall be vested in a President of the United States of America . . . "
Section 2. The President "shall have Power, by and with the Advice and Consent of the Senate, to make Treaties, provided two thirds of the senators present concur; and he shall nominate, and by and with the Advice and Consent of the Senate, shall appoint Ambassadors, other public Ministers and Consuls . . ."
Section 3. . . . "he shall receive Ambassadors and other public Ministers . . ."

[97]

the President possesses without any restrictions whatever, is virtually the power to control them absolutely . . . The President can never again be the mere domestic figure he has been throughout so large a part of our history. The nation has risen to the first rank in power and resources . . . Our President must always, henceforth, be one of the greatest powers of the world, whether he act greatly and wisely or not . . .[29]

After the outbreak of the First World War, Wilson virtually took control of foreign policy into his own hands—so much so that what was to have been his greatest triumph, the Peace Treaty and the League of Nations Covenant, became his greatest defeat at the hands of a hostile Senate. From 1938 onward, as the Second World War drew near, Franklin Roosevelt more and more dominated the foreign relations of the United States. Every President since Roosevelt has had to give a major part of his attention to foreign affairs; Congress, the courts, and the country have long since shown by word and deed that they expect initiative on foreign policy to lie with the Chief Executive.

In this century the President has come to play still another role: The President, not the Congress, now initiates legislation, and a President now normally brings his skills, resources, and prestige to bear on the Congress in order to secure congressional support for his policies. He is often unsuccessful. Yet it is doubtful whether either the Congress or the electorate would now be content with a Chief Executive who adhered faithfully to the Whig view frequently heard in the nineteenth century; the view summed up by Lincoln, for example, when he was a Whig Congressman: "Were I President, I should desire the legislation of the country to rest with Congress, uninfluenced in its origin or progress, and undisturbed by the veto unless in very special and clear cases."[30] Although Lincoln did not practise what he had preached, in the last half of the nineteenth century his successors generally followed the Whig ideal rather than Lincoln's. Even Cleveland, the first member of Jackson's party elected President since before the Civil War and a man whose historical reputation as a vigorous President is strangely unsupported by historical fact, held that it was enough to recommend legislation to the Congress and then to permit that body to go its way without pressure of any kind from the White House.[31]

29. Woodrow Wilson, Constitutional Government in the United States, New York, Columbia University Press, 1908, pp. 77–78.
30. Cited in Corwin, op. cit., p. 381, fn. 60.
31. Binkley, op. cit., p. 178.

Ever since McKinley and Theodore Roosevelt, however, Presidents have taken a much bolder role in legislation. In 1908, Woodrow Wilson formulated a view of the President's role in policy-making that, if daring at one time, has become conventional in this century:
"The Constitution bids him speak, and times of stress and change must more and more thrust upon him the attitude of originator of policies."[32]

Later, as governor of New Jersey, Wilson said:
" . . . a new role, which to many persons seems a little less than unconstitutional, is thrust upon our executives. The people are impatient of a President or a governor who will not formulate a policy and insist upon its adoption."[33] As President, Wilson lived up to his conception; no President since Jefferson worked so closely with his party in Congress nor was more effective in gaining congressional support for his policies: tariff reform, the Federal Reserve Act, the Federal Trade Commission Act, the Clayton Anti-Trust Act.[34]

Wilson's successors, particularly Franklin Roosevelt, Truman, Kennedy, and Johnson, took for granted that they, not Congress, must originate legislation and must use every means at their disposal to secure its adoption by Congress. Thus in securing passage of most of the New Deal legislation, the preponderant influence was that of Franklin Roosevelt.[35] Although even as late as the New Deal, Congressmen occasionally spoke as if the President's role in legislation was a usurpation of their own legitimate authority, objections of this kind have grown less and less audible. The death-knell of the Whig view may have been sounded when Republican congressional leaders complained of President Eisenhower's failure to present them promptly with a full legislative program.

The most recent role in the now vast presidential repertoire is his responsibility as head—if sometimes only nominal head—of the extensive administrative structure that has developed for handling national affairs in this century. In 1901, the federal government had some 231 thousand civilian employees. By 1930 the number had reached 590

32. Wilson, op. cit., p. 73.
33. Quoted in Arthur W. Macmahon, "Woodrow Wilson: Political Leader and Administrator" in Earl Latham, ed., The Philosophy and Policies of Woodrow Wilson, Chicago, University of Chicago Press, 1958, p. 100.
34. Lester V. Chandler, "Wilson's Monetary Reform," and John Perry Miller, "Woodrow Wilson's Contribution to Antitrust Policy," and Richard P. Longaker, "Woodrow Wilson and the Presidency," ibid.
35. See the tabulation in Lawrence H. Chamberlain, The President, Congress and Legislation, New York, Columbia University Press, 1946, p. 450. See also the author's comments, pp. 18–19.

thousand. Under the impact of the New Deal and then the Second World War, civilian federal employment swelled to a total of 3.7 million in 1944, from which it receded to something over two million in the years that followed. Controlling this enormous establishment and meeting his constitutional obligation "to take care that the laws be faithfully executed" is a complex and time-consuming presidential task. Cabinet officers, bureau chiefs, commission heads are powerful men; and it is difficult indeed for the man in the White House to keep track even in a general way of what they are doing, or to secure their compliance with his own policies. Each President brings to this all but impossible task his own techniques and style. None discharges it without failures.

A Success?

Thus the elastic framework the Founders created for the Presidency has been filled out and expanded by the Presidents. Today the Presidency is a result of the forces that have played upon that office: the initial impetus received from the Convention, the men who have held the office, the situations and times in which they have acted, the responses of other leaders and of ordinary citizens.

Undeniably, what has emerged is one of the greatest offices in the world; considering the place of the United States in the world, it is no mere hyperbole to suggest that the American President today is, taken all around, the most important popularly elected official in human history.

But how successful is the Presidency as an office in a democratic republic? To answer this question would require us to place the Presidency in the perspective of other important elements in the American political system that bear heavily upon his power and his actions, particularly the Congress, the courts, elections, political parties, federalism, local governments. Description of these awaits later chapters. It is convenient and perhaps even necessary for clarity that we examine each of these major institutions separately; but like examining the organs of the human body one by one we might end with little sense of how they operate as a system. Hence we need to see the President in the context of political action and policy-making. And that effort I shall postpone until the end of this book.[36] Nonetheless, it is not too soon to deal briefly with two

36. Some readers may therefore find it useful to skip ahead to Chapter 15, where an effort is made to interpret and describe processes of policy-making and the President's varying part in these processes.

questions that bear upon the success of the Presidency as the chief magistrate of a democratic republic. First, given all the roles that the Constitution, the Presidents themselves, and historical developments have thrust upon the President, is the office now too great for one man? If so, what if anything can be done about it? Second, does the office give the incumbent too much power measured by democratic standards—or not enough measured by the demands heaped upon him?

Too Much to Do?

All the roles that have accumulated in the repertory of the President impose a burden that is appallingly difficult to discharge, and perhaps impossible to discharge well. A friendly critic can easily find serious deficiencies in the performance of all our twentieth century Presidents. What human being could fulfill the awesome obligations of that great office?

Proposals are often made for reducing the burdens of the Presidency. Yet workable or acceptable changes promise little relief; and changes that would reduce the scope of the office enough to matter seem unworkable or unacceptable. Thus it has been suggested that the President might give up his symbolic roles: his duties as head of state. But where are these duties to be lodged? Parliamentary democracies solve the problem, at least in part, with a hereditary monarchy or an elected head of state who serves as a figurehead. Thus Britain, Sweden, Norway, Denmark, Holland, and Belgium have all retained their royal families for ceremonial purposes. Australia, Canada, and New Zealand each have a governor general. Switzerland, Germany, Austria, Italy, and India have a ceremonial president. These solutions have worked well. Yet a constitutional monarch is as unacceptable to Americans as it was in 1787. As for the other alternatives, if special ceremonial office were to be created after nearly two centuries under the presidential system, it would probably not work in practise simply because the President's symbolic role is too important to him politically to make him willing to yield its advantages to a figurehead. Would he not, in fact, fight such a constitutional amendment tooth and nail? Moreover, what head of state, ambassador, member of Congress, or plain citizen would sit with a figurehead if he could meet with the real center of authority?

If the ceremonial burdens of the office cannot be lightened, what of the administrative load? It is sometimes suggested that the Vice Presidency be turned into a kind of administrative chief of staff. But the President's burdens arise less from administrative details than from all the decisions he cannot delegate without abdicating his responsibilities. A Vice President who took over the burden of presidential decisions would in effect be another President; surely few Presidents would tolerate such a rival. As for delegating work to subordinates, the President already has a White House staff of more than a thousand employees. He can, if he wishes, create a de facto chief-of-staff, as Eisenhower did with Sherman Adams. But the danger with a chief-of-staff is that the President may become too much his captive; most Presidents are unwilling—rightly, I think—to allow one subordinate such a monopoly over access to him.

It has been suggested that the President make greater use of his Cabinet. Yet it is not clear how this would help. Cabinet officers are appointed for many reasons; they do not necessarily have great administrative skills; they may not always agree with the President on policy; indeed one task of the President, and no easy one, is to make sure that department heads follow his policies. The Cabinet is, in any case, a large and unwieldy collection.

Naive critics sometimes yearn for a President who would be 'above politics.' He could thus give up his role as party leader by yielding this presumably unworthy task to unworthy politicians. This seems to have been, at times, Eisenhower's view of the Presidency: " . . . in the general derogatory sense you can say that, of course, I do not like politics."[37] Yet the result of not liking "politics" was that Eisenhower did not work at the job of party leader; and this in turn resulted, as it would for any President, in a considerable diminution of his authority with Congress.[38] A President who wants to persuade Congress to adopt his program will, above all, execute the role of party leader, as Jefferson, McKinley, Wilson, the two Roosevelts, Truman, Kennedy, and Johnson all did.

The Presidency, then, is unquestionably too great for any man. Yet, for all that, it may be our greatest contribution to the arts of governing a vast republic. No President can ever measure up to its obligations. Yet every one elected to the post adds at least a cubit to his stature in the time that follows the oath of office.

37. Richard E. Neustadt, *Presidential Power, the Politics of Leadership*, New York, John Wiley and Sons, 1960, p. 166.
38. For a concrete example, see the description of the congressional battle over renewing the Reciprocal Trade Act in 1955 in Raymond A. Bauer, Ithiel de Sola Pool, and Lewis A. Dexter, *American Business and Public Policy*, New York, Atherton Press, 1963, ch. 5. See also Chapter 15 below.

No one, then, is really qualified to be President of the United States, least of all now in the last part of the twentieth century. Yet in this period of history, could anyone assume this position who did not believe that it is the world's most important public office or sense, with at least a touch of awe, the rich traditions of an office inextricably intermingled with the history of the nation?

Too Much Power?

The Presidency has evolved into "the vital place of action in the system," as Woodrow Wilson described it.[39] The President is the energizer, the innovator; when energy, skill, and determination are missing in the White House, the system must coast along on past policies. New policies, new legislation depend almost entirely on the President.

What of the President's power?[40] Is he too powerful? Or not powerful enough?

This innocent question, a favorite subject of discussion among those who contemplate the American Presidency, is much more difficult to answer than it seems. It is difficult to answer in part because 'power' is not a simple concept, as it is often assumed to be, but an exceedingly complex and many-sided notion; there are, in practise, no ways of measuring power with satisfactory precision. Moreover, even for a crude answer, it is obviously important to specify the time in which the President's actions occur, the situation with which the country is confronted, and the subjects he deals with: what would be considered too much presidential power in peacetime might be too little in war-time. Finally, what criteria are we to use for determining 'too much' or 'too little'?

Throughout the history of the Presidency, there have been many fluctuations in the extent to which the President initiates policies and secures their adoption and enforcement by the national government. Lincoln, as we have seen, all but single-handedly determined policies bearing on the war and the South. On Lincoln's death a reaction against executive power set in, and from Grant's inauguration until McKinley entered the White House in 1897, the Presidency was eclipsed by Congress. McKinley's Presidency may be regarded as the beginning of a long-run increase in presidential control over policy-making. This secular

39. Wilson, op. cit., p. 73.
40. This question is taken up again in Chapter 15.

increase in presidential power has been marked, however, by significant fluctuations caused both by the man and the circumstances. In emergencies such as the Great Depression and particularly in wartime, Presidents have inevitably expanded their untrammeled control over policy. The man himself—his skills, energy, style, and goals—also makes a difference. A student of the Presidency has compared Franklin Roosevelt and Dwight Eisenhower:

> . . . Roosevelt's methods were the product of his insights, his incentives, and his confidence. No President in this century has had a sharper sense of personal power, a sense of what it is and where it comes from; none has had more hunger for it, few have had more use for it, and only one or two could match his faith in his own competence to use it. Perception and desire and self-confidence, combined, produced their own reward. No modern President has been more nearly master in the White House.

> . . . With Eisenhower, seemingly, the case is quite opposite . . . Through Eisenhower's first six years his power sense was blunt in almost the degree that F.D.R.'s was sharp. As late as 1958 he had not quite got over "shocked surprise" that orders did not carry themselves out. Apparently he could not quite absorb the notion that effective power had to be extracted out of other men's self-interest; neither did he quite absorb the notion that nobody else's interest could be wholly like his own. And he seems to have been unaware of all his natural advantages in turning different interests toward his own.[41]

A President who is reluctant to develop the potential power of the office, or does not know how to, is obviously likely to be less influential than one who both wants and knows how to increase and retain presidential authority.

The President's power also depends on the subject he deals with. In foreign and military affairs, his discretion is often great and sometimes unbounded—or bounded only by his expectations of how other nations, friends or enemies, will react. For better or for worse, then, the President of the United States will for many years to come be in a position to determine the fate of the world by his choice of foreign and military policies. Yet, even with respect to foreign and military affairs, his control

41. Neustadt, op. cit., pp. 161, 163–164.

is by no means unlimited, for he must appeal to the Congress for funds. On appropriations, Congress is still a match for any President: thus most presidential requests for foreign aid have been cut by the Congress, often severely, despite the best efforts of the White House to retain the full amounts requested.

On most questions of domestic policy and sometimes on foreign policy, the President is hedged in by the Congress, the Supreme Court, his own officials, his party leaders, public opinion, the national communications media, and the prospect of coming elections, both presidential and congressional. Observers who look at the Presidency from a distance can easily underestimate how much these factors limit the President's range of action. For years, the Congress rejected presidential proposals on civil rights and medical care. Within three months after President Truman ordered the government to seize the steel industry during the Korean War, the Supreme Court held his action unconstitutional; the steel mills had to be returned at once to private hands. To pick another example from the experience of a strong executive with a penchant for decisive action, Truman dallied month after month before relieving General MacArthur of his command in Korea for failure to execute orders. For not only was MacArthur a distinguished general with a following in Congress and the country, but also, as Truman said later, MacArthur "was a commander in the field. You pick your man, you've got to back him up."[42] A President may have to discard or modify a policy because of negative responses from farmers, doctors, an ethnic group, a region, union leaders, an industry . . . For the publics that comprise 'public opinion' have sanctions: congressional and presidential elections.

What then can we conclude about the President's power? Does the magnitude of his power serve American democracy well or badly?

To begin with, the American President is not more independent of popular, constitutional, or legislative controls than the chief executives of many other modern democracies. Today, Theodore Roosevelt might have to modify his observation that "there inheres in the Presidency more power than in any other office in any great republic or constitutional monarchy of our times."[43] The President is more at the mercy of the Congress than, for example, the British prime minister is at the mercy of parliament. If the President is, or at least can be, more powerful than the premier of the Third and Fourth Republics of France, his discretion is more limited than that of President de Gaulle in the Fifth Republic.

42. *Ibid.*, where the incident is described and analyzed in considerable detail.
43. Quoted in John Blum, *The Republican Roosevelt*, New York, Atheneum, 1963, p. 107.

A more relevant criterion, however, is whether the Presidency has accumulated such massive resources of power that a skillful President can, on important issues, act counter to the preferences of a congressional majority or majority opinion in the country; or, worse, can systematically manipulate congressional and public opinion in order to achieve his purposes. That the President sometimes chooses policies that do not have the support of congressional majorities is undeniable. But for the most part he must do so negatively, as Jackson did, by means of the veto. It is exceedingly difficult, perhaps impossible, for him to persist in positive policies that a majority in both houses of Congress oppose, for the Congress has too many ways of getting revenge on the President: investigating committees, denial of funds, rejection of appointments, and the ultimate threat, impeachment. Moreover, a President who defies Congress cannot succeed in his defiance unless he and his policy have more support in the influential publics of the nation than the Congressmen he opposes. A President who persists in opposing *both* the Congress *and* a large fraction of articulate opinion is headed for certain defeat, one way or another.

Because American politics is more a matter of articulate and influential minorities than of cohesive majorities, it is by no means easy to tell at any given moment whether the President or the Congress has the greater public support in a conflict. In pressing a controversial policy, a President always assumes the risk of miscalculating congressional or public opinion. Can he warp public or congressional opinion to his own desires? That the President has enormous resources for influencing opinion is obvious: his prestige, the constant attention focussed on him by all the media of communications, his unequalled access to information. By holding a press conference, as Franklin Roosevelt demonstrated, the President can, in effect, write an editorial on behalf of his policies in every newspaper in the country, even those hostile to him. Yet his prestige is a fragile thing, as Gallup polls have shown over the last several decades. Perhaps no better record of how limited is his ability to manipulate public opinion at will can be found than the testimony of these polls (Figure 4.1). His slightest mistakes are ruthlessly exploited—usually exaggerated—by the opposition; the least breath of scandal is turned against him; and if he claims the benefits of good times when they occur during his Administration, he is also a handy target for resentment when the economy declines or things go badly in international politics (which, sooner or later, they do). As for Congress, the limits of the President's capacity for bending that stubborn body to his desires are demonstrated by the frequency with which Congress rejects his legislative proposals.

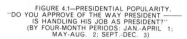

FIGURE 4.1—PRESIDENTIAL POPULARITY.
"DO YOU APPROVE OF THE WAY PRESIDENT ———
IS HANDLING HIS JOB AS PRESIDENT?"
(BY FOUR-MONTH PERIODS: JAN.-APRIL 1;
MAY-AUG. 2; SEPT.-DEC. 3)

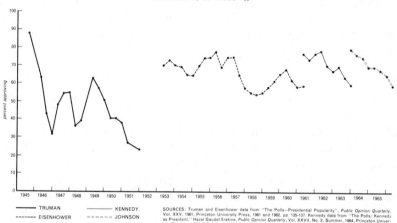

——— TRUMAN   ——— KENNEDY
------- EISENHOWER   ====== JOHNSON

SOURCES: Truman and Eisenhower data from "The Polls—Presidential Popularity", *Public Opinion Quarterly*, Vol. XXV, 1961, Princeton University Press, 1961 and 1962, pp. 135-137. Kennedy data from "The Polls: Kennedy as President," Hazel Gaudet Erskine, *Public Opinion Quarterly*, Vol. XXVII, No. 2, Summer, 1964, Princeton University Press, pp. 334-335. Johnson data from Gallup Political Index, Report No. 6, November, 1965, p. 3.

Yet even if the President's power is limited, have Americans by demanding too much of the President made the office too powerful? In a democratic republic should any single citizen, no matter what his office, be as powerful as the President of the United States? A modern description of the British monarchy in the early eighteenth century seems uncomfortably close to fitting the American Presidency in the twentieth:

Despite the numerous limitations placed upon the royal power since 1660, the king remained the dominant figure in political life. The Constitution endowed the monarch, as chief executive, with control of Government patronage and national policy, a share in one or both of which is ever the goal of the aspiring politician. He who would secure place, honour, pension, or other favor must go to Court. He who would influence the great decisions of state must first convince His Majesty. It should be said, however, that in neither of these areas was royal power absolute . . . Though the Constitution made no distinction between royal policy and national policy, the king could not carry out decisions strenuously disapproved by a parlia-

[107]

mentary majority and devoid of the necessary financial support. On the other hand, to obtain a favour or to implement a design opposed by the monarch was extremely difficult. Nothing but heavy pressure from external circumstances could ordinarily force the king to act against his will. If not absolute, therefore, royal control of policy and patronage was at once so extensive in its scope, so pervasive in its influence, and so concentrated in the king's person that politics inevitably revolved about the throne.[44]

The twentieth century has seen the emergence of powerful leaders in democracies and dictatorships alike: Roosevelt, Churchill, Nehru, Adenauer, de Gaulle; Stalin, Khrushchev, Hitler, Mussolini, Mao Tse-Tung. This phenomenon has been interpreted as the re-emergence of the Prince, the rebirth in a new guise of monarchy, the age of Caesars.

In an age of Caesars, should the Presidency be scaled down to more nearly human proportions? Can it be? How, and at what price?

Like most students of the Presidency, most Americans seem to agree that the office has served the Republic well. From its first beginnings, it has been in perpetual evolution; there is little room for doubt that this great political office will continue to evolve. In what ways? Though we can now see the office of the President far more clearly than the men could who tried to design it in 1787, like them we cannot foresee clearly the shape that office will take in the future. But we can be sure that the future character of pluralistic democracy in the United States will depend heavily on the way the Presidency evolves.

44. Archibald S. Foord, *His Majesty's Opposition 1714–1830*, Oxford, Oxford University Press, 1964, pp. 16–17.

5

THE CONGRESS

I F THE PRESIDENT has become the main source of drive, energy, and leadership in the American political system, what functions does the Congress perform?

The Congress and the Convention

The design of the Congress presented the Convention not only with some of its easiest problems but also with a few of its thorniest ones. That there must be a legislative body was a matter beyond debate. That it must consist of two houses; that one of these must represent 'the people'; that the national legislature must have power to make national law; that this body would be the chief if not, in fact, the exclusive source of national law, other than the Constitution itself; that it would serve as a check on the President—these propositions were not seriously contested.

So far, then, as the intentions of the Convention are clear, the minimum functions of the Congress were three: to make national laws, to represent 'the people,' and to check and control the power of the Chief Executive. These functions were obviously inter-related. Given the political ideas prevalent in the United States at that time, and in the Convention, the only legitimate source of new laws, other than amendments to the Constitution, would be the legislature. Most of the delegates doubtless took it for granted that policy-making would consist almost entirely of law-making, that proposals for new laws would originate in the legislature, which would examine these proposals, act on them and, if it so decided, give them the necessary stamp of legality. To make policy was to make law; to make law was to legislate; and only a legislature could legislate. Q.E.D.

Essentially what gave legitimacy to a legislature in the law-making process was its representative character. The legislature was to represent, to stand for, to serve on behalf of the citizens of the United States.

That the Congress should (and would) also serve as a check on the Chief Executive followed from the general principle of pitting one part of government against another: "by so contriving the interior structure of the government as that its several constituent parts may, by their mutual relations, be the means of keeping each other in their proper places," as the authors of *The Federalist* were to put it.[1]

While the delegates no doubt took this checking role of the Congress for granted, they said surprisingly little about it at the Convention. In the light of later developments, this is a curious omission—probably accounted for in two ways. In the first place, the delegates saw the legislature as the most dynamic and most dangerous branch; hence they were preoccupied—one might almost say obsessed—with the problem of building adequate restraints on that body. When they spoke of the relations between Chief Executive and Congress, their concern was invariably with the role of Executive as a check on the Congress, not the other way around.

In the second place, as we saw in the last chapter, throughout most of the Convention it appeared that the President was going to be elected by the Congress. This in itself, it was assumed, would provide a powerful check by legislature on executive; hence the delegates may have taken it for granted that further discussion of the adequacy of Congress' power to check the President was unnecessary. Indeed, the problem, in their eyes, was quite the opposite; if Congress elected the President, would this not give the legislature too much control over the executive, and, conversely, the Executive too little independence of the legislature? In the end, as we know, they solved this problem by creating an Executive elected independently of the Congress.

Yet if the delegates to the Constitutional Convention were evidently in substantial agreement that the national legislature they proposed to create would, at a minimum, make national laws, represent the people of

1. *Federalist* No. 51, *The Federalist*, New York, The Modern Library, n.d., p. 336.

the United States, and help control the Chief Executive, they did not agree on other matters; certain questions that were controversial in 1787 and uneasily decided at the Convention remain controversial today. Nor could the delegates to the Convention accurately foresee the shape of future problems as the United States developed into a great nation and then a world power.

Of the questions left unsettled by the Convention, two are particularly important, and it is these that I propose to explore in the rest of this chapter:

¶ First, even if it be taken for granted that Congress is to 'represent the people,' in some sense, should it represent each citizen equally, or should some minorities or 'interests' be given extra protection by means of extra weight in the national legislature?

¶ Second, if the Congress is to make laws and to check the Executive, how far should its control over policy and appointments extend?

Representation: Majorities and Minorities

Like everyone else who has ever seriously examined the problems of 'representing the people' in a republic, the men at the Convention were confronted by some exceedingly difficult questions. If their compromises helped to shape the American political tradition, their conflicting viewpoints persist within that tradition down to the present day.

The House of Representatives, as Sherman of Connecticut suggested it be named, presented only modest difficulties. Although there was scattered opposition to the idea that one house of Congress was to be elected by the people, that proposal passed early and easily and was never subsequently contested. Yet it seems to have been widely assumed at the Convention that the House of Representatives would be the driving force in the system; that the people's representatives would be turbulent and insistent; that they would represent majorities and would be indifferent to the rights of minorities; that the people would be the winds driving the ship of state and their representatives would be the sails, swelling with every gust. Gouverneur Morris evidently reflected the dominant view when he remarked that "The first branch, originating in the people, will ever be subject to *precipitancy, changeability,* and excess."[2]

It followed that the "popular branch" (like every other branch) must be hedged in by constraints: by the Constitution itself, the President, the courts, the states, and, not least, the other house of Congress.

It was in the composition of the other house that the Convention faced one of its most difficult problems, to which it gave a compromise solution that a majority of the delegates probably opposed in principle but had to accept out of expediency. The problem had two sides, one intellectual and the other political. Although the second has been much emphasized, the first has been almost ignored. Yet it goes to the heart of a problem still debated in the United States.

The intellectual problem turns on this question: Is it possible to protect minorities by giving them a larger share of representatives in a legislature than they would be entitled to simply by their numbers, without at the same time creating a potential injustice to other minorities or to majorities? The Convention wrestled with this problem, as Americans have ever since; but it cannot be said that the Founders came up with an intellectually defensible solution.

Gouverneur Morris, as might be expected, saw the question as a straightforward one of protecting the rich minority from the 'people' and vice versa. What qualities, he asked, are necessary in the second branch of the Congress if it is to check the excesses of the people's representatives:

> . . . *Abilities and virtue, are equally necessary in both branches. Something more then is now wanted. 1. The checking branch must have a personal interest in checking the other branch, one interest must be opposed to another interest. Vices as they exist, must be turned against each other.*
> *2. It must have great personal property, it must have the aristocratic spirit; it must love to lord it thro' pride . . .*
> *3. It should be independent. To make it independent, it should be for life . . . By thus combining and setting apart, the aristocratic interest, the popular interest will be combined against it. There will be a mutual check and mutual security.*
> *4. An independence for life, involves the necessary permanency . . .*[3]

2. Documents, *op. cit.,* p. 838. The quotation is from the notes of Yates; Madison recorded substantially the same words, p. 319.
3. *Ibid.,* pp. 319–320.

In this blunt view of the ineradicable conflict of social classes, "the rich" versus "the rest," "the aristocratic interest" versus "the popular interest," Morris may have overstated his case, but he undoubtedly reflected a common view.

In a masterly analysis marked by his customary moderation, Madison espoused a not dissimilar point of view; but he arrived at a different solution. One of Madison's most impressive utterances, it is worth reproducing in full:

> . . . In order to judge of the form to be given to this institution, it will be proper to take a view of the ends to be served by it. These were first to protect the people agst. their rulers: secondly to protect the people agst. the transient impressions into which they themselves might be led. A people deliberating in a temperate moment, and with the experience of other nations before them, on the plan of Govt. most likely to secure their happiness, would first be aware, that those chargd. with the public happiness, might betray their trust. An obvious precaution agst. this danger wd. be to divide the trust between different bodies of men, who might watch & check each other. In this they wd. be governed by the same prudence which has prevailed in organizing the subordinate departments of Govt., where all business liable to abuses is made to pass thro' separate hands, the one being a check on the other. It wd. next occur to such a people, that they themselves were liable to temporary errors, thro' want of information as to their true interest, and that men chosen for a short term, & employed but a small portion of that in public affairs, might err from the same cause. This reflection wd. naturally suggest that the Gvt. be so constituted, as that one of its branches might have an oppy [opportunity] of acquiring a competent knowledge of the public interests. Another reflection equally becoming a people on such an occasion, wd. be that they themselves, as well as a numerous body of Representatives, were liable to err also, from fickleness and passion. A necessary fence agst. this danger would be to select a portion of enlightened citizens, whose limited number, and firmness might seasonably interpose agst. impetuous councils. It ought finally to occur to a people deliberating on a Govt. for themselves, that as different interests necessarily result from the liberty meant to be secured, the major interest might under sudden impulses be tempted to commit injustice on the minority. In all civilized Countries the people fall into different

classes havg. a real or supposed difference of interests. There will be creditors & debtors, farmers, merchts, & manufacturers. There will be particularly the distinction of rich & poor. It was true as had been observd. [by Mr. Pinkney] we had not among us those hereditary distinctions, of rank which were a great source of the contests in the ancient Govt. as well as the modern States of Europe, nor those extremes of wealth or poverty which characterize the latter. We cannot however be regarded even at this time, as one homogeneous mass, in which every thing that affects a part will affect in the same manner the whole. In framing a system which we wish to last for ages, we shd. not lose sight of the changes which ages will produce. An increase of population will of necessity increase the proportion of those who will labour under all the hardships of life, & secretly sigh for a more equal distribution of its blessings. These may in time outnumber those who are placed above the feelings of indigence. According to the equal laws of suffrage, the power will slide into the hands of the former. No agrarian attempts have yet been made in this Country, but symtoms, of a leveling spirit, as we have understood, have sufficiently appeared in a certain quarters to give notice of the future danger. How is this danger to be guarded agst. on republican principles? How is the danger in all cases of interested coalitions to oppress the minority to be guarded agst.?[4]

Madison posed the problem clearly. The popular branch might act out of impulse, ignorance, or interest "to commit injustice on the minority." The second branch must therefore be so constituted as to "aid on such emergencies the preponderance of justice by throwing its weight into that scale."[5]

But how was the second branch to be made up? Here was the nub of the difficulty. If the second branch were elected by the people (as Wilson, the most persistent advocate of a democratic republic, proposed) then it would represent the same interests as the other house and would hardly serve as a check on it. Gerry of Massachusetts, worried by the fact that farmers vastly outnumbered businessmen, observed: "To draw both branches from the people will leave no security to the latter [commercial] interest; the people being chiefly composed of the landed interest, and erroneously supposing, that the other interests are adverse to it."

4. *Ibid.*, pp. 279–281.
5. *Ibid.*, p. 169.

What interests were the Senators supposed to represent? Why should *these* particular interests be given special weight? And how were Senators to be chosen to represent these interests? Although the first two questions were logically prior, debate turned almost entirely on the last question. Yet it is the first two that were—and are—most troublesome.

A Compromise Solution

Should a legislature represent interests or individuals? It cannot do both. For if interests are to be given equal representation, then individuals must be denied equal representation. There is no way out of this dilemma. And why should some interests be given more power than others? It might be argued that unless a certain interest were given extra numbers in the legislature, it would be unjustly treated by a legislative majority. This was the essence of Morris' and Madison's argument. Yet, in this solution to the problem of majority 'tyranny,' there are two exceedingly serious difficulties that neither Morris nor Madison dealt with.

First, since almost any minority might be unjustly treated by a majority, it would seem to follow that every minority should be over-represented—doctors, lawyers, college professors, businessmen, trade unionists, cotton farmers, wheat farmers, tobacco farmers, Catholics, Jews, Negroes, 'Wasps' (White Anglo-Saxon Protestants) . . . We quickly arrive at an absurdity. Morris and Madison were rescued from absurdity because of the simplicity of prevailing conceptions of the interests of the country in 1787. Charles Cotesworth Pinckney suggested that "the people of the United States may be divided into three classes—professional men . . . ; commercial men . . . ; the landed interest . . ."[6] This simple scheme was reasonable in 1787; it would be unacceptable today.

Second, if an interest is given special weight, what is to prevent it from using its added power unjustly toward the majority? If a minority has enough representation to prevent a majority from acting unjustly toward it, it will also have enough representation to prevent a majority from acting justly. Are we to suppose that minorities invariably act justly, and majorities never? Neither Morris nor Madison made such an untenable assumption: If, as Morris said, the rich always have and always will "strive to establish their dominion and enslave the rest," what would happen if the rich were given enough power to veto the actions of a

6. *Ibid.,* pp. 271 ff.

[115]

majority that wanted to enact, say, a progressive income tax? Would the rich not use their power in naked self-interest to prevent themselves from being taxed more heavily than others? Or suppose that the rich are mistreating their employees: Is a legislative majority to be prevented from passing laws regulating employer-employee relations, simply because the rich are opposed?

In conceiving of the representation of interests in different houses, men like Morris were reverting to a medieval conception of a parliament that represented the estates of the realm. In Britain there was the House of Lords for Church and aristocracy, the House of Commons for the commoners—though in actual practise in 1787 only a tiny percentage of adult males could vote in elections to that House. Within two years, the King of France was to summon an anachronism that had not met since 1614, the Estates-General, which consisted of the First Estate, or lower clergy, the Second Estate or nobility, and the Third Estate or the 'people.' But the Third Estate lost no time in facilitating a revolution that forever ended the Estates-General in France. In Sweden, four estates— nobility, clergy, burghers, and peasants—had been represented in the Riksdag, or parliament, since the Middle Ages; under the impact of democratic ideas the four estates were finally to be abolished in 1866 and replaced by a bicameral legislature. In 1849, the ruler of Prussia would sway gently with the winds of revolution by providing universal suffrage —combined with a three-class system of voting under which a tiny minority consisting of the richest taxpayers elected one-third of the deputies in indirect elections, a second class of moderately well-to-do citizens elected another third, and the rest of the population, more than 80 per cent of the taxpayers, chose the remaining third. ("It would be difficult to devise an electoral measure," it has been said, "more calculated to alienate the lower classes from the national political system."[7])

It is doubtful whether any members of the Convention, including Morris, entertained ideas of this kind. The Americans, after all, consisted almost entirely of small farmers plus a handful of merchants and artisans. There was no titled aristocracy, as in Britain, no clerical estate, as in France and Sweden. When one got right down to the nub of the matter, by European standards Americans were all commoners. Consequently, although the familiar distinction between the House of Lords and the House of Commons unquestionably influenced the thinking of the Convention about a second chamber, an American version of the House of Lords had to be . . . another House of Commons.

7. Stein Rokkan, "The Comparative Study of Political Participation" in Austin Ranney, ed., *Essays on the Behavioral Study of Politics*, Urbana, University of Illinois Press, 1962, p. 76.

The concrete proposals presented to the Convention were, therefore, tame. Some delegates may have thought that property qualifications could be made higher for Senators; but the point was not pressed, and in the end no property qualifications were set by the Convention for any public office. Some delegates may have envisioned special property qualifications for those who elected the Senators; yet no such requirement was laid down. In the speech of Madison's quoted above, the only specific proposals he makes for insuring the kind of Senate he had in mind is, you will notice, that Senators be elected for a long term—nine years—at a relatively advanced age. As it turned out, their term is for six years and the 'advanced' age is 30—six years younger than Madison himself when he made the speech.

What happened, then, to the idea of representing interests? Probably two things. First, however attractive the idea might have seemed abstractly, concrete proposals to over-represent the rich—this was the only interest that anyone seemed to have in mind—were bound to end in palpable absurdities, fatal unpopularity, or both. In the America of 1787, the rich were not a traditional and legitimate aristocracy; they were never to become so. Even in England by 1787 it is doubtful whether the peerage could have gained by force or persuasion the special place in the British constitutional system it had inherited; instead it had only to hold onto the constitutional position in which it found itself. More than a century would elapse before the ancient power of the peerage over legislation would, for all practical purposes, finally be eliminated.

In the second place, the whole question of the composition of the Senate was abruptly changed from the problem of representing a special economic or class interest, as Morris and Madison had posed it, to the problem of representing a very different sort of interest: that of the smaller states. Madison and Morris, who fiercely opposed equal representation in the Senate for the smaller states and fought for representation according to population until it became clear that their solution might well wreck the whole scheme for a new Constitution, were, in a sense, hoist by their own petard. Having argued that the Senate should protect the minority interest against the majority interest, how were they to meet the arguments of delegates who contended that the smaller states, as an outnumbered minority, needed special protection from the more populous states? "Besides the aristocratic and other interests, which ought to have the means of defending themselves" Johnson of Connecticut reasoned, "the states have their interests as such and are equally entitled to like means."[8]

Wilson, the unswerving democrat (and happily for him a delegate

8. *Documents, op. cit.,* p. 297.

from a large state), encountered no difficulty in disposing of Johnson's argument on abstract democratic principles:

> The gentleman from Connecticut in supposing that the preponderance secured to the majority in the first branch had removed the objections to an equality of votes in the second branch for the security of the minority, narrowed the case extremely. Such an equality will enable the minority to control in all cases whatsoever, the sentiments and interests of the majority. Seven States will control six . . . It would be in the power then of less than ⅓ to overrule ⅔ whenever a question should happen to divide the States in that manner. Can we forget for whom we are forming a government? Is it for men, or for the imaginary beings called States?[9]

Madison found it all the more difficult to counter the small-state argument with a straightforward appeal to the principle of political equality among all citizens, as Wilson had done, because only a few days earlier, as we have just seen, he had asserted the desirability of using the Senate to give minorities special protection from majorities. Madison therefore combined an appeal to the majority principle with a pragmatic argument that there was in fact no small-state interest different from the interests of the large states.

> . . . It was urged continually (Madison said) that an equality of votes in the second branch was not only necessary to secure the small [states] but would be perfectly safe to the large ones whose majority in the first branch was an effectual bulwark. But notwithstanding this apparent defence, the majority of States might still injure the majority of people. 1. They could obstruct the wishes and interests of the majority. 2. They could extort measures repugnant to the wishes and interest of the Majority. 3. They could impose measures adverse thereto; as the second branch will probably exercise some great powers, in which the first will not participate. He admitted that every peculiar interest whether in any class of citizens, or any description of States, ought to be secured as far as possible. Whenever there is danger of attack there ought to be given a constitutional power of defense. But he [Madison] contended that the States were divided into different interests not by their differences of size,

9. Ibid., p. 307.

but by other circumstances; the most material of which resulted partly from climate, but principally from the effects of their having or not having slaves. These two causes concurred in forming the great division of interests in the United States. It did not lie between the large and small states: It lay between Northern and Southern, and if any defensive powere were necessary, it ought to be mutually given to these two inter-ests.[10]

Madison's argument, he must have realized, could equally well be turned against the very position he himself had taken four days earlier. Perhaps it is for this reason that from this day forward it was Madison the democratic-republican and not the Madison fearful of majorities who invariably spoke on the troublesome question of representation in the Senate. From now on, Madison's position on representation in the Senate was usually indistinguishable from Wilson's.

In the end, as we know, the small states won. They did not win because they ever persuaded men like Madison and Morris and least of all Wilson—the great architects of the Constitution—that their position was just. For these men never were converted. As so often happens in political affairs, the small states won simply because of their bargaining power. To Madison, Morris, and Wilson, better a constitution that granted equal representation to states in the Senate than no constitution at all. The bargain was struck. It has held ever since.

The Senate: Bastion of
Which Minorities?

If the House was intended to represent the people and the Senate the states, to what extent has Congress fulfilled these expectations? Indeed, what, or whom, does Congress represent?

To answer these questions is no simple matter. It will help to distin-guish between two aspects of representation. First, different citizens may be unequally represented because the boundaries of legislative constit-uencies—states in the case of Senators and congressional districts in the case of Congressmen—operate so as to over-represent some parts of the

10. *Ibid.*, pp. 310–311.

electorate and to under-represent others. Second, different citizens may be unequally influential with respect to their representatives because they have different political resources or skills: money, information, friendship, access, social standing, and the like.

Consider the first of these problems. In the Senate the people of the smaller states are of course over-represented and the people of the larger states are under-represented; that, after all, was precisely the point of the compromise. Yet the degree of over- and under-representation has increased since 1787. According to the various estimates used at the Convention, the largest state, Virginia, had a population some ten to fifteen times larger than the smallest state, Delaware. According to the Census of 1790, the free population of Virginia was eight times larger than that of Delaware, the total population twelve times.[11] In 1960, the population of New York was almost seventy-five times that of Alaska; the population of California fifty-five times that of Nevada. As Table 5.1 shows, in 1964 twenty-six states with 15 per cent of the electorate furnished a majority of the Senators, while the nine largest states with more than half the electorate had only eighteen Senators out of one hundred.

Table 5.1   Advantage and Disadvantage in the Senate—1964

		STATE ELECTORATE (000)	PERCENTAGES OF TOTAL ELECTORATE	CUMULATIVE PERCENTAGE	INDEX OF ADVANTAGE
1.	Alaska	67	.10	.10	19.7
2.	Nevada	131	.19	.29	10.0
3.	Arkansas	130	.19	.48	10.1
4.	Wyoming	139	.21	.69	9.4
5.	Vermont	163	.24	.93	8.0
6.	Delaware	199	.30	1.23	6.6
7.	Hawaii	230	.34	1.57	5.7
8.	North Dakota	249	.37	1.94	5.3
9.	Montana	277	.41	2.35	4.7
10.	New Hampshire	279	.42	2.77	4.7
11.	Idaho	285	.43	3.20	4.6
12.	South Dakota	288	.43	3.63	4.5
13.	New Mexico	349	.52	4.15	3.7
14.	Mississippi	361	.54	4.69	3.6
15.	Maine	370	.56	5.25	3.5
16.	Rhode Island	373	.56	5.81	3.5
17.	Utah	396	.59	6.40	3.3
18.	South Carolina	436	.66	7.06	3.0
19.	Arizona	461	.69	7.75	2.8

(continued)

11. For estimates at the Convention and 1790 Census, see appendix 2 in Winton U. Solberg, ed., *The Federal Convention and the Formation of the Union of the American States*, New York, Liberal Arts Press, 1958, p. 407.

Table 5.1.   Advantage and Disadvantage in the Senate—1964
(Continued)

	STATE ELECTORATE (000)	PERCENTAGES OF TOTAL ELECTORATE	CUMULATIVE PERCENTAGE	INDEX OF ADVANTAGE
20. Nebraska	561	.84	8.59	2.3
21. Louisiana	601	.91	9.50	2.1
22. Alabama	617	.93	10.43	2.1
23. Colorado	758	1.14	11.57	1.7
24. West Virginia	770	1.16	12.73	1.7
25. Oregon	767	1.16	13.89	1.7
26. Kansas	814	1.23	15.12	1.6
27. Georgia	835	1.26	16.38	1.5
28. Oklahoma	840	1.27	17.65	1.5
29. Virginia	929	1.40	19.05	1.4
30. Kentucky	955	1.44	20.49	1.3
31. Maryland	1,012	1.53	22.02	1.3
32. Tennessee	1,035	1.56	23.58	1.2
33. Iowa	1,142	1.72	25.30	1.1
34. Washington	1,198	1.81	27.11	1.1
35. Connecticut	1,209	1.83	28.94	1.0
36. North Carolina	1,304	1.97	30.91	1.01
37. Florida	1,413	2.13	33.04	.93
38. Minnesota	1,521	2.36	35.40	.86
39. Wisconsin	1,649	2.49	37.89	.80
40. Missouri	1,772	2.68	40.57	.74
41. Indiana	2,073	3.13	43.70	.63
42. Massachusetts	2,108	3.19	46.89	.62
43. Texas	2,617	3.96	50.85	.50
44. New Jersey	2,721	4.12	54.97	.48
45. Michigan	3,060	4.63	59.60	.43
46. Ohio	3,732	5.65	65.25	.35
47. Illinois	4,575	6.92	72.17	.28
48. Pennsylvania	4,676	7.08	79.25	.28
49. New York	6,763	10.24	89.49	.19
50. California	6,823	10.33	99.82	.19

Notes: Mean state electorate, 1964=1,320,000

Index of advantage $= \dfrac{\text{actual representation}}{\text{proportionate representation}}$

$= \dfrac{1/50 \text{ state electorate}}{\text{total electorate}}$

$= \dfrac{\text{mean state electorate}}{\text{state electorate}}$

$= \dfrac{1,320,000}{\text{state electorate}}$

If actual representation=proportionate representation, then the index of advantage=1.

SOURCE: U.S. Bureau of Census, *Statistical Abstract 1965.*

Yet Madison's judgment has been confirmed. The great conflicts have not been between large states and small states. Although there have been many lines of political cleavage in the United States, differences between large states and small states have surely been the least important of these. The tariff, slavery, civil rights, monetary and fiscal problems, taxation, regulation of business, welfare programs, foreign and military policies—none has produced conflicts between large states and small states. It would be difficult to demonstrate, therefore, that the small states have *needed* their extra influence in the Senate in order to protect themselves against the large states.

In the first and second sessions of the Eighty-eighth Congress in 1963-64, the Senate dealt with a wide range of key issues: civil rights, mass transportation, a nuclear test-ban treaty, poverty, foreign aid, medical care for the aged. As Table 5.2 shows, the Senators from the small and the large states voted very much the same way except on three issues. These three issues are revealing. On a motion to invoke cloture (#1), all except two Senators from the large states were in favor of the motion, but those from the small states split 10-10. Senators from small states, it would appear, were more favorable to the added advantage given by the filibuster to their equality of votes in the Senate. On the Mass Transportation Act (#2), the difference was not a function of size but of the degree of urbanization; Senators from states with populations living mostly in towns and rural areas, like Wyoming, Vermont, and New Hampshire, voted solidly against a proposal that would result in few immediate benefits to their own constituents. The difference in the vote on foreign aid (#11) cannot be explained by differences in the size of states. Instead, it seems to have been primarily a clash between liberal, internationalist, and pro-Administration Senators on the one side, and conservative Republicans and Democrats on the other. Republican Senators voted overwhelmingly for the Amendment (24-6), and so did Southern Democrats (13-5); northern Democrats voted against it (27-13).

If the Senate has not had to protect the small states, has it, however, served to protect other minorities? If so, are these particular minorities entitled to special protection? Although the problem is a thorny one, the answer to the first question is probably yes; the answer to the second is, I believe, very much more debatable. Three preliminary observations are in order.[12]

In the first place, the argument for equal representation of states in

12. The following discussion is adapted from my *A Preface to Democratic Theory,* Chicago, University of Chicago Press, 1956, pp. 113–118.

Table 5.2.   How Senators from the ten largest and ten smallest
states voted on 12 key issues, 88th Congress, 1963–1964.

	Issue #											
	1	2	3	4	5	6	7	8	9	10	11	12
Ten Smallest												
For	10	9	12	15	12	18	17	17	18	14	13	12
Against	9	11	8	5	8	2	3	3	2	6	7	8
Ten Largest												
For	18	15	16	15	11	18	18	19	19	16	8	15
Against	2	5	4	5	9	2	2	1	1	4	11	5
Senate												
For	42	52	50	65	47	80	77	71	73	61	50	49
	54	41	34	30	44	19	21	29	27	34	38	44

Notes:
Population range (1960)
   10 smallest states   226-674 thousand
   10 largest states   4.7 to 16.8 million
The issues were those listed in *Congress and the Nation, op. cit.*, as key votes. First
Session:
   1. A motion to invoke cloture (limit debate) on a pending motion to amend the
       Senate rules in order to reduce from ⅔ to ⅗ the number of Senators required
       to bring debate to a close.
   2. Mass Transportation Act of 1963, providing matching grants and other aid to
       local and state governments for the development of urban mass transit systems.
   3. Youth Employment Act, establishing a Youth Conservation Corps and a "Home
       Town Youth Corps" to provide useful work experience for and increase the
       employability of unemployed youths.
   4. Area Redevelopment Act Amendments of 1963, increasing area redevelopment.
   5. National Services Corps Act, authorizing a program of volunteer public service
       and authorizing $15 million for two years.
   6. Limited Nuclear Test-Ban Treaty. Approval of the resolution of ratification.
   7. Passage of the Revenue Act of 1964, reducing personal and corporate income
       taxes.
   8. Civil Rights Act of 1964. Mansfield (D. Montana)—Dirksen (R. Illinois)
       motion that the Senate invoke cloture on the Souther filibuster.
   9. Civil Rights Act of 1964.
  10. Economic Opportunity Act of 1964. Passage of the bill authorizing $947.2
       million in fiscal 1965 for a wide variety of programs to combat poverty.
  11. Foreign Assistance Act of 1964. Mundt (R. South Dakota) amendments to pro-
       vide that loans for commercial enterprises be repaid at a rate three fourths of
       1 percent higher than the rate for Treasury borrowing (thus, about 3⅝ percent)
       and that other foreign aid loans be repaid within 25 years.
  12. Social Security Amendments of 1964. Gore (D. Tenn.) amendment authorizing
       a new program of medical care for persons 65 and over financed through an
       increase in the Social Security tax and wage base and from general revenues.
In counting the votes among the 10 smallest and largest states, Senators listed as
paired for or against or announced for or against are also counted. In the Senate totals,
only actual votes are counted.
   SOURCE: *Congress and the Nation 1945-1964. A Review of Government and Politics
in the Postwar Years*, Washington, D.C., Congressional Quarterly Service, 1965, pp.
92a-93a.

the Senate frequently seems to rest upon a false psychological equation, in which small states are equated with small interests and small interests with small or defenseless persons. Our humanitarian desires to protect relatively defenseless persons from aggression by more powerful individuals are thereby invoked on behalf of small states. But states consist of people; and it is the interests of people we are concerned with. What we need to know, therefore, is what sorts of people are benefited or handicapped by equal representation in the Senate.

I assume that we do not wish to endorse the principle that all small interest-groups must have a veto on policy. For then we could never specify any situations short of unanimity in which a law-making majority should be permitted to act. And thus we would make impossible not merely the operation of the republican principle but government itself. The first to exercise their vetoes might be the gangsters, the murderers, the thieves—in short, the criminal population. The rest of us would not be far behind: capitalists, laborers, farmers, even college professors, the exploiters and the exploited, the social and the anti-social, the sweatshop operator, the labor racketeer, the draft dodger, the income tax evader, and a thousand other groups, would exercise their veto on public policy.

In the second place, we must also avoid the fallacy of assuming that if the Senate represents or over-represents some minorities situated in certain geographical areas in the United States, it necessarily represents all minorities situated in those areas. This is clearly false. There are minorities within minorites. The dominant regional group may be represented in the Senate while the subordinate regional minority is excluded. Hence a Senate veto may merely preserve or extend the control of the dominant regional group over the subordinate minority. The Negroes in the South, and the itinerant farm laborers of the West, are clearly not the minorities who benefit from equal representation in the Senate. It is worth remembering that even in a situation of full political equality, a regional minority protected by equal representation of geographical units in a legislative body would be a majority in its own area; and the defeated minority in that region would be unprotected by equal representation. Indeed, if the minority in the region consisted of individuals with preferences like those of the majority in the whole electorate, equal representation of geographical areas would, paradoxically, divest this regional minority of protection in all cases where positive government action was required to prevent the regional majority from tyrannizing over it.

In the third place, equal representation of geographical units over-represents some minorities concentrated in sparse areas but under-represents those concentrated in heavily populated areas. Moreover, to the extent that a minority is not geographically concentrated, it receives no protection per se from equal state representation. In a society in which all minorities were distributed in equal proportions among the voters of every state, no minority would receive any protection per se from equal state representation. Why, then, this special tenderness toward minorities concentrated geographically in sparse areas?

In sum:

¶ The only minorities protected by equal state representation as such are geographical minorities concentrated in sparse areas.

¶ But some of the minorities in these areas are left unprotected; indeed, representatives of the dominant group may actually use their over-representation in the Senate to bar action intended to guard the unprotected.

¶ Minorities in heavily populated areas are under-represented in a system of equal state representation.

¶ The conclusion seems inevitable that the benefits and disadvantages flowing from equal state representation in the Senate are allocated in an entirely arbitrary fashion and cannot be shown to follow from any general principle.

Representatives of the People

What then of the House? How has it represented the people? The Constitution, you may recall, does not require that House members be elected by districts; it leaves "the times, places, and manner of holding elections for . . . Representatives" to the state legislatures (Article 1, Section 4). In practise the states have been divided by the state legislatures into districts equal, normally, to the number of representatives. Moreover, the same system exists for state legislatures themselves: The state legislators are also elected in districts. Now the obvious consequence of this arrangement is that with changes in population in the states, the heavy hand of history may produce growing disparity between the numbers of citizens in one district and another. This is what happened to

Table 5.3.   Population percentages of largest and smallest districts
of the House of Representatives (following 1961–1962 redistricting).

	LARGEST 20	SMALLEST 20
Urban	43.3%	2.8%
Suburban	36.8	0.5
Rural	19.9	96.7
Total	100%	100%

Note: A city is urban if population exceeds 50,000.
SOURCE: Congressional Quarterly, Special Report, "Congressional Redistricting"
(September 28, 1962), p. 1604

the House of Representatives. (Table 5.3).

Originally, as we have seen, most of the population of the United States lived in rural areas. As the urban dwellers increased and finally outnumbered the rural population, the number of representatives they were granted in the state legislature failed to increase at the same rate. The explanation is simple: Since reapportionment was up to the state legislatures, since any reapportionment could only reduce the proportion of legislators elected by the rural population, and since the existing state legislatures were already controlled or strongly influenced by representatives drawn from rural districts, quite naturally the rural representatives who dominated the state legislatures were unwilling to pass bills providing for the reduction of their own power through reapportionment. Doubtless, too, legislators who favored reapportionment were often dissuaded from attempting to seek a change because their chances for success were negligible, because they feared to incur the hostility of the dominant legislative majority, and even because they did not like to see friends or allies lose their seats in the legislature. Consequently the state legislatures became more and more severely unrepresentative. The cities were, of course, the first to suffer. Beginning in the 1930s, however, as the cities began losing population to the suburbs, it was the suburban areas that were more and more under-represented.[13] By 1962, in only about a quarter of the states were both houses of the legislature apportioned in districts approximately equal to population. In the rest,

13.   On this point, see the data in Edward C. Banfield and James Q. Wilson, City Politics, Cambridge, Harvard University Press, M.I.T. Press, 1963. Table 5, p. 72; and Paul R. David and Ralph Eisenberg, Devaluation of the Urban and Suburban Vote, Charlottesville: University of Virginia Press, 1961.

the districts in one or both houses were markedly unequal in population.[14]

Strongly influenced by rural and small town constituents, the malapportioned state legislatures were reluctant to pass legislation to create congressional districts approximately equal in numbers: for this would decrease the power of the towns and rural areas in electing Congressmen. Hence the House of Representatives came to over-represent the rural and small-town areas at the expense first of the cities and later of the suburbs. In 1960, each state was entitled to one representative for every 410 thousand persons. Yet some representatives came from districts with twice this population, while others were elected in districts with less than half this number. In 1962, there were twenty House districts with a population over 620 thousand, and twenty with a population less than 252 thousand. The largest district in the country (951 thousand) was Dallas, Texas, a rapidly growing city that elected the state's lone Republican Congressman; the Democratic controlled legislature refused to create an additional seat for Dallas. In Detroit, Michigan, a Democratic Congressman represented a district of over 800,000; a Republican Congressman represented the smallest district in the country, a rural area in Michigan with a population of 177 thousand; naturally the Republican legislature failed to reapportion these districts.

As might be expected, the twenty largest districts (the population of which was under-represented) were predominantly urban and suburban, while the twenty smallest districts (whose population was over-represented) were overwhelmingly rural. What this over-representation of the rural and small-town areas meant in practise was that the House somewhat over-represented what might loosely be called 'conservative' attitudes. If the voting records of Congressmen are located on a scale of 'liberalism-conservatism' (there are a number of these, and they generally produce similar results), it is clear that Congressmen from rural and small-town districts in both parties are more 'conservative' than their counterparts from cities and metropolitan areas. (Table 5.4)

Paradoxically, while population changes were making the House less responsive to cities and suburban areas, the same changes were making the Senate more so. For few States lacked one or more big cities and extensive suburban areas; in every state, the rural and small-town population shrank. By 1950, 80 per cent of the people in the Northeast lived

14. See Glendon Schubert and Charles Press, "Measuring Malapportionment," *American Political Science Review*, vol. 58, No. 2 (June, 1964), 302–327; Paul T. David and Ralph Eisenberg, *op. cit.*

Table 5.4. Percentage of 'Liberal'* Representatives by Types of Districts, 1956.

		PERCENT OF 'LIBERALS'
		DEMOCRATS
TYPE OF DISTRICT	REPUBLICANS	(EXCLUDING SOUTH)
I. Primarily rural, containing no city over 25,000	22%	59%
II. Small town, containing no city over 50,000	24	59
III. Mid-urban, containing city of 50,000–200,000	43	81
IV. Metropolitan: containing cities of 200,000 or over (or within such cities)	57	90

*'Liberal': score of 4 or more on New Republic index, based on the votes of the Representative on roll-call votes in the House, 1956.
SOURCE: adapted from V. O. Key, Public Opinion and American Democracy, A. A. Knopf, New York, 1961, pp. 485-486.

in urban areas; in the West, 70 per cent; in the North-Central region, 64 per cent; and in the least urbanized region, the South,[15] just under half. Consequently, while a great many Senators had to be sensitive to the concerns of their urban voters, a substantial number of members of the House could safely ignore the cities and the suburbs.[16]

On the whole, then, far from being a turbulent forum for the people, 'ever subject to precipitancy, changeability, and excess,' the House had become a slightly more conservative institution than the Senate or the Presidency. Its members were more inclined to share the views of farmers and small-town folk than those of the working classes in the cities or the white-collar workers and executives in the suburbs; more likely to think nostalgically of a United States that had disappeared some generations ago than to press vigorously for solutions to problems of the urban America that now existed.

On a number of occasions, citizens in various states appealed to the Supreme Court to remedy the inequalities in representation in state legislatures and in the House of Representatives. But, until 1962, the Court steadily refused to intervene, on the ground that inequitable representation was not a judicial matter but was a "political question"

15. M. Gendell and H. L. Zetterberg, eds. A Sociological Almanac for the United States, New York, the Bedminster Press, 1961, Table 86, p. 83.
16. See Lewis A. Froman, Jr., Congressmen and their Constituencies, Chicago, Rand McNally & Co., 1963, ch. 6, "Why the Senate Is More Liberal than the House."

that could only be remedied by the appropriate political bodies.[17] Because the legislative majorities that controlled these bodies would only decrease their own power by reapportionment, naturally they refused to approve of laws or constitutional amendments that would have remedied the situation. Consequently the position of the Court meant, in effect, that nothing could be done. Beginning in 1962, however, the Court reversed its traditional position in a series of historic decisions that laid down the requirement of "one man, one vote" not only for both houses of all state legislatures but for the U. S. House of Representatives itself.[18]

To the extent that these decisions are adhered to in the coming decades, the House will more nearly fulfill its original and intended role as "representative of the people."

Representation: Formal and Effective

Constitutional rules, laws, and judicial decisions may preserve formal equality in representation by guaranteeing the principle of one man, one vote. But formal equality is not necessarily effective equality. Even if people were to be equally represented in the sense that the House districts and even the states all had equal numbers of citizens, one could not conclude that all citizens would be perfectly equal in their influence on the behavior of their representatives. The influences to which Congress responds, depend on at least three gross factors: the characteristics of the general process of influence, the structure of the influence within the Congress, and the problem of communication.

As a general matter, political influence is a function of one's *resources* (money, information, status, organization, time, energy, friendships, loyalties, etc.), the extent to which one *uses* these resources to gain political influence, and the *skill* with which one uses his resources.[19] Thus, other things being equal, a well-to-do or educated citizen is likely to have more influence than a poor or ignorant citizen. A politically *active* person is likely to be more influential than one who, from lack of interest, lack of concern, or other reasons, makes no attempt to influence Congress. And an individual who is politically sophisticated, who has

17. See, for example, *Colegrove v Green*, 328 U.S. 549 (1946).
18. The leading decisions were *Baker v Carr*, 369 U.S. 186 (1962), *Wesberry v Sanders*, 376 U.S. 1 (1946), and *Reynolds v Sims* 377 U.S. 533 (1964).
19. See Chapter 15, pp. 372 ff.

political know-how, is likely to be more influential than one who does not know how to operate in political affairs.

One of the most palpable facts of life in American society (as, indeed, in all large societies) is that most resources are unequally distributed. Yet it does not follow that Congressmen are invariably responsive to small groups with large resources. In the first place, there is at least one resource that is distributed equally in most states in the North: the legal right to vote. To a Congressman who wants to be re-elected—and few Senators and Representatives do not—one vote counts just as much as another. One indispensable requirement for becoming or remaining a member of Congress is to win more votes than any opponent in an election. Other things being equal, therefore, the Congressman will be more responsive to two potential votes than one, more eager to win the votes of a group of one thousand voters (whose other political resources may be very slender) than a group of one hundred voters (whose political resources may be very large).

In the second place, different resources are generally distributed in different patterns to different groups. Some citizens with a good deal of money and social status do not have much in the way of organization, friendships, and loyalties. A Congressman from a predominantly working-class Polish district would, no doubt, be a good deal more responsive to a Polish ward leader in a working-class neighborhood than to a wealthy suburbanite.

In the third place, dedication, skill, or numbers can compensate for a good deal. A Congressman is likely to be sensitive to a group so intensly committed on a particular issue that they are likely to vote against any candidate who takes the 'wrong' position, as in the case of Negroes on civil rights and integration; or who are highly organized, like the Farm Bureau Federation; or who appear to represent a large body of citizens, like the AFL-CIO.

Although different Congressmen and Senators do not necessarily respond to these various factors in the same way, they do tend to have one strategy in common: Because no one can long remain a Congressman or a Senator if he cannot win an election, all often pay some attention, most of them pay a great deal of attention, and some give paramount attention, to calculating the effects their actions are likely to have on the way their constituents will vote in the next election. The member of Congress lives, like the rest of us, in a world marked by considerable uncertainty and lack of information. He is forced to conjecture, on the basis of his experience and such current information as he may have, as to what these effects will be. Most members of Congress know a good deal about the various ethnic groups, industries, socio-economic groups, and other interests in their state or district; in order to regulate his own conduct in Congress as best he can, a Congressman usually attempts to guess how this or that group will respond.

This strong tendency of members of Congress to pay close attention to their own constituents is fortified by the structure of control in both houses. As compared with party leaders in most other parliaments today, in the Congress the party leaders are relatively weak in *their* resources for influencing congressional members of their parties to vote for the alternatives backed by themselves and by the majority of the party members. (Party leaders are rarely so foolhardy as to back a proposal for which they cannot gain even a majority of the members of their party.) They must rely mainly on persuasion, party loyalty, expectations of reciprocal treatment, and, occasionally, special inducements such as patronage or public works. But none of these is likely to be adequate if a member is persuaded that a vote to support his party will cost him votes among his constituents. For he is concerned about his own re-election. Fortunately for him, the mores of Congress, accepted by the leaders themselves, are perfectly clear on this point: His own re-election comes first.

It might be thought—and indeed it is often supposed—that the member of Congress is therefore nothing but an automatic agent of his constituents. It is conceivable that he might be—in a world of perfect information. But in the real world, communication between constituents and members of Congress is a highly uncertain matter. It is bound to be, in a large country, as one can easily see by performing a simple mental experiment: If every adult in an average Congressional district tried to gain the attention of his representative for half an hour, and if the Congressman were to devote ten hours a day the year round to nothing but communicating with his constituents, it would take a quarter of a century for him to hear all of them!

The fact is, of course, that most people do not communicate with their Congressmen at all. In a typical year, probably something under 15 per cent of the population ever write or talk to a Congressman or any other public official in order to give their opinions on a public issue.[20]

20. Julian L. Woodward and Elmo Roper reported in 1950 that in a national sample of eight thousand adults, 13 per cent said they had "written or talked to a Congressman or other public official to give own opinion on a public issue, one or more times in the past year." "Political Activity of American Citizens," *American Political Science Review*, vol. 44 (December 1950), pp. 872–85. In 1961, the Gallup poll asked its national sample: "During the last 12 months—that is, since September of last year —have you written to a U.S. Congressman or Senator—" Only 9 per cent said yes. Source: American Institute of Public Opinion Release, October 20, 1961.

Many citizens have virtually no knowledge about their Congressmen. In one study it was found that

Of constituents living in Congressional districts where there was a contest between a Republican and a Democrat in 1958 less than one in five said they had read or heard something about both candidates, and well over half conceded they had read or heard nothing about either. . .[21]

The minority of citizens who do try to influence Congress by no means always represent majority opinion. It has been found again and again that certain factors are associated with higher levels of political activity of any kind, and these would apply to efforts to influence Congressmen. Thus the results of a survey in 1950 (Table 5.5) have been confirmed by many studies:[22]

There is still another factor of great importance. People who happen to be aroused about an issue, because their goals, values, prestige, esteem, income, ethnic loyalties or other interests are involved, are, it is obvious, much more likely to influence a Congressman than people who are not aroused. Moreover, because of uncertainties in communication, their activity may make their numbers and resources seem greater than they are. Bauer, Pool, and Dexter found, for example, that businessmen who favored tariff protection were more likely to write their Congressmen in 1954-55 than those who favored tariff reductions; thus, although public sentiment favored a liberal trade policy by about three to one, to Congressmen who surveyed their mail it might have looked as if the public actually favored protectionist policies by two to one.[23]

Given all these difficulties in knowing what a majority of his constit-

21. Warren E. Miller and Donald E. Stokes, "Constituency Influences in Congress," *American Political Science Review* (March, 1963), pp. 45–46, p. 53.
22. See Robert Lane, *Political Life*, Glencoe, The Free Press, 1959, ch. 5; "Who Tries to Influence Public Officials and How Do They Do It?" Robert A. Dahl, *Who Governs?*, New Haven, Yale University Press, 1961; ch. 26. Fred I. Greenstein, *The American Party System and the American People*, Englewood Cliffs, N.J., Prentice-Hall, 1963, ch. 3; Lester Milbrath, *Political Participation*, Chicago, Rand McNally & Co., 1965.
23. R. A. Bauer, I. de Sola Pool, and L. A. Dexter, *American Business and Public Policy, The Politics of Foreign Trade*, New York, Atherton Press, 1963, p. 211. See also Lewis A. Dexter, "What Do Congressmen Hear? and "The Representative and His District," both reprinted in N. W. Polsby, R. A. Dentler, and P. A. Smith, *Politics and Social Life*, Boston, Houghton Mifflin, 1963, pp. 485–513.

Table 5.5. Amount of Political Activity Exhibited by Various Sub-Groups in the Population*

| | % WITHIN EACH SUB-GROUP WHO ARE POLITICALLY | | | |
SUB-GROUPS	VERY ACTIVE	FAIRLY ACTIVE	FAIRLY INACTIVE	VERY INACTIVE
"A" economic level	36%	33%	23%	8%
Executives	34	29	28	9
Professional people	31	32	25	12
Stockholders	28	30	30	12
College educated	24	28	30	18
"B" economic level	24	26	34	16
Republicans	15	21	39	25
Men	13	19	36	32
People 50 years of age and over	12	17	34	37
Peope 35–49 years	11	19	39	31
"C" economic level	11	19	38	32
White people	11	17	36	36
Farmers	11	14	35	40
Independents in politics	10	21	37	32
Total adult population	10	17	35	38
People with only high school education	9	17	40	34
Democrats	9	15	37	39
Non-stockholders	8	15	37	40
Women	8	14	33	45
People 21–34 years of age	8	14	32	46
Laboring people	6	14	37	43
Housewives	6	14	34	46
People with grade school education only	5	11	33	51
Negroes	5	10	25	60
"D" economic level	3	9	31	57

*Eulau, Eldersveld, and Janowitz, eds., *Political Behavior*, Glencoe, Ill., The Free Press, 1956, p. 136.
SOURCE: Woodward and Roper, *op. cit.*, fn. 19.

————•◆•————

uents wants, how closely does a Congressman respond to the views of his constituents? One of the most perceptive observers of Congress, Lewis A. Dexter, suggests the following answer:

> A Congressman's conception of his district confirms itself, to a considerable extent, and may constitute a sort of self-fufilling prophecy.
> A Congressman hears most often from those who agree with him.

Some men automatically interpret what they hear to support their own viewpoints.

In more general terms, what Congressmen hear and how they interpret what they hear depends on who they are.

For any particular Congressman, his interpretation results from his being the particular kind of person he is and is reputed to be.

A Congressman's reputation among those who might want to influence him determines in large measure what actually is said to him.

Some communications tend to be unclear in their meaning. A good deal of so-called 'lobbying' by constituents tends to be nothing more than a social visit and a general discussion.

What the Congressman listens to is partly accidental.

'Pressure' is how you see it. What you call pressure, or what you feel to be pressure, depends on how thick your skin is.

Opportunism, also, is where you see it. Few Congressmen attribute their friends' decisions or their own to opportunism.[24]

Thus it should not be surprising that even a body of men who are relatively eager to respond to constituents, if for no other reason than to be re-elected, are by no means a mirror of the country or even of their own states or districts. Just how closely the members of Congress correspond, in their voting, to the preferences of a majority of their own constituents is not easy to say. The most careful study of this question so far, which compared the views and voting records of one hundred sixteen Congressmen in 1958 with the views of their constituents, revealed a surprisingly low relationship between the majority attitude in each district on social welfare and foreign policy and what the Congressman from that district *thought* was the majority view among his constituents. On the other hand, the Congressmen were much more likely to be correct about the views held by a majority of their constituents on civil rights.[25] The way the Congressmen actually voted corresponded fairly

24. These statements are for the most part verbatim quotations from his article "The Representative and his District" in Polsby, Dentler, and Smith, pp. 495 ff. See also his "What Do Congressmen Hear?" *ibid.*, pp. 485 ff.

25. The correlations between the views of a majority of constituents in a district, and what Congressmen thought a majority believed, were:

On social welfare: 0.17
On foreign policy: 0.19
On civil rights: 0.63

Warren E. Miller and Donald Stokes, "Constituency Influences in Congress," *American Political Science Review* (March 1963), pp. 45–57. Table 1, p. 52.

[134]

closely with the views of a majority of their constituents on matters of civil rights, much less so on matters of social welfare, and not at all on foreign policy.[26]

Perhaps a fair conclusion from rather uncertain evidence is that the average Congressman has a good deal of leeway on many of the questions he must vote on; even on critical issues that seem sharp and salient in Washington, he often has more elbow room than he may suppose. Yet surely Congressmen are right in thinking that they would place themselves in serious jeopardy at the polls if they were to vote counter to the views of a majority of their constituents on any matter that is salient and important to a sizeable share of the voters at home.

Congress as Policy-Maker

The input and output of laws requiring congressional action has become staggering. In the First Congress, one hundred forty-four measures were introduced. Throughout the first twenty-five years of the nineteenth century, the number of measures introduced climbed steadily from one Congress to the next. Nor did the upward trend stop after the initial phase. The number of measures introduced reached its highest point with the Sixty-first Congress (1909-1911) when over 44 thousand measures were introduced. Many of these were 'private bills': claims for property damage or personal injury by government agents, matters of immigration, citizenship, or deportation of specific individuals, corrections of individual military and naval records, private land bills, and the like. Changes in congressional rules (involving, among other things, delegation of many such decisions to executive officials) have reduced the number of private bills. In the second quarter of the twentieth century the number of measures introduced in each Congress varied from a low point of something over eight thousand in the middle of the Second World War to a high point of nearly 25 thousand during the Seventy-first Congress (1929-1931).

The output of public measures has not kept pace with this enor-

26. The correlations between the scale positions of the Congressmen on roll-call votes and the attitudes of their constituents were:
   Social welfare "approximately" 0.3
   Foreign policy 0.09
   Civil rights .57
   Ibid., pp. 49, and 52, fig. 2.

mous input. The First Congress passed a total of one hundred eight public bills. The output of the Congress gradually increased until about 1930, when it seems to have stabilized at a number varying between six hundred and one thousand public measures passed in each Congress.[27]

Congress remains, both formally and actually, a key organ in making laws. In many other democracies the parliament has become a rubber-stamp for the cabinet, or at least a body with a dutiful majority that can be relied on to pass without resistance the measures submitted to it by the cabinet. By comparison, the American Congress is far too independent of the President and the American parties far too heterogeneous, to make this possible here except in rare circumstances. It is true that when Franklin Roosevelt took office in the bleakest days of Great Depression, he found a Congress eager to do his bidding. "The first months of the New Deal," the leading historian of that period has written, "were to an astonishing degree an adventure in unanimity."[28] Yet the honeymoon, the famous Hundred Days, did not last even through the crisis of the Depression. After 1933, Congress gradually recovered self-confidence; and in 1937 Northern Republicans and Southern Democrats forged an alliance that all but brought the period of New Deal reform to an end. Again, from 1963-1965, President Johnson matched Roosevelt's 1933-1937 record for new legislation. Thanks in part to Johnson's exceptional skills with Congress and in part to the crushing Democratic majorities resulting from the 1964 elections (the largest since 1938 in the House and since 1942 in the Senate), one major bill after another passed Congress. But by 1966 Congress was again displaying a less co-operative spirit.

If the Congress continues, then, to be a formidable participant in making laws, certain developments have nonetheless greatly qualified its role. First, as we saw in the preceding chapter, the initiative in legislation has increasingly shifted in this century to the Executive. The Congress no longer expects to originate measures but to pass, veto, or modify laws proposed by the Chief Executive. It is the President, not the Congress, who determines the content and substance of the legislation with which Congress deals. The President is now the motor in the system; the Congress applies the brakes. The President gives what forward movement there is to the system; his is the force of thrust and innovation. The Congress is the force of inertia—a force, it should be said, that means not only restraint but also stability in policies.

27. These figures will be found in *Historical Statistics of the United States,* Washington, D.C., Bureau of the Census, 1960, pp. 689–690.
28. Arthur M. Schlesinger, Jr., *The Coming of the New Deal,* Cambridge, Houghton Mifflin, 1959, p. 423.

Second, as we have also seen, the relative importance of President and Congress in policy-making is not and probably cannot be static. It varies with the circumstances and with the kinds of policies at stake. Although the Congress, despite its reputation to the contrary, sometimes acts with exceptional dispatch, legislatures have never proved as suitable as executives for handling emergency actions. Like all legislatures, Congress is most handicapped in times of crisis and in dealing with military and foreign affairs. On questions where time and secrecy are not of the essence, Congress is much stronger—on legislation having to do with domestic affairs or with aspects of foreign affairs not removed from purview of Congress by the need for speed or circumspection: policies with respect to agriculture, labor, business, taxation, immigration, appropriations, and the like. Finally, on all questions having to do with the distribution of benefits or deprivations, Congress tends to play an important part; even during the Second World War, when it was a matter of deciding how the burdens of war were to be distributed among different groups of Americans, Congress played a pre-eminent role.[29]

In the third place, it must always be kept in mind that laws, these days, are only one part of policy. Many of the most important decisions, particularly in foreign and military affairs, do not require legislation, at least not directly. Sometimes, too, even where legislation is required, the Chief Executive has for all practical purposes already committed the Congress and the country; in these cases Congress may modify but it cannot easily reverse the basic commitment that has been entered into. Thus Congress could play only a passive role in our entry into the Korean war, the increasing U.S. presence in Vietnam from 1956 onward, suspension of nuclear testing by the executive, etc.

Fourth, Congress participates in policy-making in many ways other than by making laws. Its informal participation, usually by consultation between President and congressional leaders, is regular and important. Many actions technically within presidential discretion, frequently including actions on foreign and military affairs, are taken by the President only after he consults with congressional leaders to find out whether he will have adequate support for the decision he proposes to take. If he does not, he may back down. Thus, in 1954, when the fall of the French fortress of Dienbienphu in Indo-China was imminent, a defeat which the French foresaw would mean their collapse in Southeast Asia, President Eisenhower, Secretary of State Dulles, and Admiral Radford, then chairman of the Joint Chiefs of Staff, advocated aiding the French with an air strike by Navy and Air Force planes. In a secret meeting, under question-

29. See Roland Young, *Congressional Politics in the Second World War*, Columbia University Press, New York, 1956.

ing from congressional leaders, including Majority Leader of the Senate Lyndon Johnson, it became apparent that congressional leaders were reluctant to support the action unless the Administration could find allies abroad, particularly Britain. But Britain, too, was reluctant; and in the end the plan was abandoned. Even in this case, in the view of one observer, the President could probably have won congressional support "provided he had asked for it forcefully and explained the facts and their relation to the national interest of the United States." But he did not, and his soundings of congressional opinion evidently did prevent immediate intervention in support of the French.[30] Sometimes the Congress tries to tie the President's hands publicly by passing a resolution, as in the series of resolutions from 1951-1961 in which one or both houses declared, in most cases unanimously, their opposition to admitting Communist China to the U.N. Sometimes, on the other hand, when it suits his purposes, the President openly asks for an expression of congressional approval, as when President Lyndon Johnson obtained a joint resolution indicating congressional support for actions during a crisis in the Gulf of Tonkin in August, 1964. To the discomfiture of some Congressmen, the President later used this resolution as evidence of congressional authorization for his policy of bombing North Vietnam, increasing the number of American troops, and escalating American participation in other ways.

Congressional committees also share with the President a substantial measure of influence over the administrative agencies. Indeed, probably no national legislature in any other democracy has greater influence over bureaucracy, and most have far less. Committees acquire and maintain this influence because they control appropriations and legislation wanted by the agencies. Committee influence over administration is exercised chiefly by means of hearings, both public and off-the-record, and by investigations. Like the President, a congressional committee can often influence policies informally without actually spelling out their demands in a law. This is accomplished by day to day contacts between committee staff and people in the executive agencies, on-site visits, by inspection tours, informal briefings, and the like. It is important to keep in mind, too, that while Presidents, cabinet members, heads of departments, and even bureau chiefs come and go, many ranking members on congressional committees remain in Congress serving on their commit-

30. See Chalmers M. Roberts, "The Day We Didn't Go to War," *The Reporter*, September 14, 1954, pp. 31–35, reprinted in T. J. Lowie, ed., *Legislative Politics USA*, Boston, Little Brown and Co., 1962, pp. 240–248. The quotation is at p. 248.

tees a very long time, during which they acquire a great deal of knowledge and often a proprietary interest in the agencies that fall within the jurisdiction of their committee.

Finally, Congress participates in policy-making in an important indirect way, by serving as a source of information to the public—and sometimes to the executive branch. Congressional debates and discussions, particularly on the floor of the Senate, and the hearings conducted by congressional committees produce a steady flow of reports and news about existing and proposed policies. A committee hearing in which witnesses are heard over weeks, months, and even years is often a vital instrument in calling public attention to an issue and winning support for or against some proposal. Although it is impossible to assess the exact weight such hearings have had, it would be a mistake to under-estimate their importance by looking only for effects on *general* public opinion; for often what committee hearings do is to change, solidify or mobilize the opinions of *specific* publics whose influence is critical to a particular piece of legislation—cotton farmers, the leaders of the AFL-CIO, an ethnic group, bankers, the elderly.

Has Congress Declined as Policy-Maker?

In general, then, it seems fair to conclude that the Congress has about as much weight in policy-making as the national legislature of any other large democracy in the world today—and a good deal more than most.

Nonetheless, one reads and hears a good deal about 'the decline of legislatures' and 'the rise of the executive' in the twentieth century. The growth in authority and power of chief executives has been a worldwide phenomenon. Lament over the "decline" of legislatures can be heard in almost every democracy in the world. In the last several decades there has been a steady ferment of ideas, proposals, and demands for the 'reform' of Congress in order to equip it better to carry out its functions.

As I indicated earlier, it is impossible to measure shifts in quantities of power with much precision. Consequently to decide whether the power of Congress has declined is not as simple as most observers assume. However, it is possible to discern two kinds of historical changes in the character of congressional control.

As a formal institution within which national government policies were initiated and decided, Congress reached its apex in the three decades after the Civil War; indeed, during these years, Congress exercised very nearly a complete monopoly over the initiation and determination of national policy. For some time Congress also enjoyed a virtually complete control even over presidential appointments. The control of the President over policy and appointments had begun to recede immediately after Lincoln's death. The Whig view of the ascendancy of Congress over President was pushed to its outermost limits by the radical Republicans who dominated the House of Representatives under the leadership of Thaddeus Stevens.[31] In order to tie the hands of the President, in 1867 the Congress passed (over Johnson's veto) a Tenure of Office Act that was designed to prevent the President from removing officials (including Cabinet officers) without the consent of the Senate. Johnson, who rightly believed that the act was unconstitutional, chose to defy Congress and dismiss his Secretary of War, Stanton, who was openly disloyal to him. The House then voted 126 to 47 to impeach the President. As everyone knows, Johnson escaped conviction in the Senate by only one vote. Had he been convicted, it is conceivable that the United States would have changed, de facto, to a parliamentary system under which the President would be dependent on the continuing 'confidence' of the Congress, lacking which he would be impeached.

Although Johnson escaped conviction, the Congress nonetheless became the center of energy in the system. Under President Grant, control over both policies and appointments fell exclusively into the hands of Congress; the President became little more than a tarnished figurehead.

". . . The predominant and controlling force, the centre and source of all motive and of all regulative power," observed a young historian and political scientist named Woodrow Wilson in 1885, "is Congress."[32]

Congress' monopoly of control was exercised chiefly through its innumerable committees; de facto control was lodged with the committee chairmen, each lord of his own domain, and with leaders elected in the party caucus, most notably the Speaker of the House, who toward the end of the century became a personage as important as the President —and a good deal more powerful with respect to legislation.

President after President yielded control over policy without a murmur. The Whig view was gospel to the Presidents themselves. This was the age of industrial growth, new fortunes, the worship of business suc-

31. See Fawn M. Brodie, *Thaddeus Stevens, Scourge of the South*, New York, W. W. Norton and Company, 1959, pp. 324 ff.
32. *Congressional Government*, republished in 1956, New York, Meridian Books, p. 31.

cess, and a widespread faith in the virtues, of an uncontrolled economy, particularly in the Republican Party, which controlled the White House throughout most of this period. The ascendant political forces of the day had no broad program of legislation or reform to enact; vigorous government was a danger; a weak President controlled by a Congress concerned more with patronage than with broad legislative programs provided a political system perfectly adapted to the purposes of business, so long as corruption did not interfere with profits or alienate the growing middle classes.[33]

The resurgence of the Presidency from the nadir reached under Grant was gradual. It may seem unbelievable today, but the greatest battles between President and Congress during this period resulted from the attempts of Presidents Hayes, Garfield, and Cleveland to regain from the Senate control over their own Cabinet appointments, an effort in which each succeeded only after considerable travail. But none of these men had the slightest intention of asserting control over policy, which they took for granted was entirely in the domain of the Congress.[34] It was only around the turn of the century, with McKinley and Theodore Roosevelt, that greater control over policy came to be lodged in the White House.

In this sense, then, it is correct to say that the 'power' of Congress over policy and appointments has declined since its apex in the period after the Civil War. In the twentieth century not only has the President broken the monopoly of Congress over policy—and, of course, over appointments—but, as we have seen, he has also largely taken command over the initiation of new policies.

Similarly, the Congress is now a far more active institution, far better equipped to deal with complex matters of public policy, far more deeply involved in an incredible range of important issues than ever it was or could be in the nineteenth century. What has happened is this: In the post-Civil-War period, during a time when the doctrine of complete laissez faire marched triumphant and the foreign policy of the United States limited the country to a role of neutrality and isolation, there was, in plain fact, very little policy for either President or Congress to initiate and to enact. But, in the twentieth century, govern-

33. See E. E. Schattschneider, "United States: The Functional Approach to Party Government," in S. Neumann, ed., *Modern Political Parties*, Chicago, University of Chicago Press, 1956, pp. 194-218, esp. at p. 197.
34. The principal battles over appointments are described in Wilfred E. Binkley, *President and Congress*, New York, Alfred A. Knopf, 1947, ch. VII, pp. 145–167.

ment regulation and control, welfare programs, foreign affairs, military policy, and the taxation and spending measures required for all these purposes have produced a veritable "policy-explosion." If Congress were to do no more than to consider the principal measures submitted to it by the Chief Executive, it would have plenty to do; yet the Congress does considerably more than this.

In this sense, then, the 'power' of Congress has grown: the decisions Congress makes by modifying, passing, or rejecting measures affect all of us, and the whole world, to an incomparably greater extent today than in the nineteenth century. If the Congress had not met after 1868, and had left behind a dutiful caretaker President to enforce existing laws, neither the United States nor the world would have been much different several decades later from what, in fact, they were. But the United States of the 1960s could not possibly have existed legally on the statutes of the 1920s.

In sum, in the post-Civil-War period, Congress enjoyed a monopoly control over policies mostly of trivial importance; today Congress shares with the President control over policies of profound consequence. Congress has, then, both lost and acquired power.

6

THE SUPREME COURT

AN ARISTOCRATIC REPUBLIC might very well have given a Supreme Court the power to nullify laws passed by the representatives of the people. A Supreme Court so armed could shield aristocratic power from popular attack. But because Americans took the path of democracy rather than aristocracy, the extraordinary position of the Supreme Court in the American political system has ever been a source of controversy.

Is the Supreme Court's power of judicial review, as it is called, consistent with a democratic republic? Or is the Supreme Court essentially some sort of aristocratic institution suitable only in an aristocratic republic?

These queries might be dismissed as merely a war of words were it not for the fact that they bring into question the legitimacy of a highly important political institution, the federal judiciary, and hence the claim of that institution to the rational consent, loyalty, and obedience of Americans. If we cannot justify judicial review on grounds consistent with democratic theory and practise, should we allow such a power to exist? Or should we not instead take steps to end it?

There are three general grounds on which one might base a claim to the legitimacy of judicial review: that judicial review is implied by the Constitution, which is itself accepted as legitimate; that it rests on a long-standing tradition that for all practical purposes incorporates judicial review into the constitutional system; and that it is implied by the principles of democratic government.

Because the tradition itself gains acceptibility from a line of reasoning intended to prove that judicial review is implied by the Constitution, the first two grounds tend to be fused into one; let me call this fusion of the two claims the traditional constitutionality of judicial review. The third ground for judicial review, deriving from democratic theory, is, as we shall see, unquestionably the weakest.

The Traditional Constitutionality of Judicial Review

The traditional constitutionality of judicial review must start with the intentions of the men who framed the Constitution, for, if they had never intended judicial review, it would be unreasonable (in the absence of an amendment) to argue that it is implied by the terms of the Constitution! Unfortunately, what the Founding Fathers intended the Supreme Court to be is a highly debated question; even more unfortunately for the clarity of this debate, judging from the records of the Convention, the delegates scarcely discussed the functions of the proposed Court. The discussion most relevant to the question of judicial review was stimulated by a highly controversial provision (ultimately rejected) in the Virginia plan. That provision and the brief but sharp skirmishes it produced are interesting for what they reveal about the intentions, or lack of them, of the Foundling Fathers.

The proposal in question—it was the eighth in the series of resolutions that historians have called the Virginia plan, introduced on May 29 by Randolph of Virginia—provided for a Council of Revision to consist of the President "and a convenient number of the National Judiciary." This Council was to have a veto on laws passed by Congress or by a state legislature. Although the proposal did not say so explicitly, discussion among the delegates reveals their clear understanding that the Council's veto was to be used much as the President has come to use his veto: to block 'bad' laws, even though these might not be unconstitutional. Under Randolph's proposal, the Congress could overcome the Council's veto simply by passing the measure a second time. As to state laws, the plan evidently intended to provide that a state legislature could overcome the veto by passing a measure a second time with a larger than ordinary majority in each house of the state legislature; the exact number or proportion was left blank in Randolph's proposal.

Like the Constitution itself, the Virginia plan said not one word about the power of judicial review as we know it: i.e., the power to decide on the constitutionality of laws. Many delegates distinguished sharply between the power of the courts to declare acts of Congress or the state legislatures *unconstitutional*, and the proposed Council of Revision which was for the purpose of inhibiting 'bad' but not necessarily unconstitutional legislation. A delegate might, then, have taken one of four positions.

1. At least two delegates were against granting the federal judiciary the power to declare laws unconstitutional (i.e., judicial review), and against giving it any voice on policy questions (i.e., the Council of Revision). One was John Mercer of Maryland. As a State Federalist, Mercer probably anticipated the dangers to state power from a federal court when he remarked that he "disapproved of the doctrine that the judges as expositors of the Constitution should have authority to declare a law void. He thought laws ought to be well and cautiously made, and then to be uncontroulable."[1] Mercer—who arrived at the Convention late, left within two weeks in protest against the trend toward National Federalism, refused to sign the finished document, and fought against its ratification—can hardly be regarded as a representative figure of the Convention. Yet he was supported by one of the important men at the Convention, John Dickinson, who confessed that he

> . . . was *strongly impressed with the remark of Mr. Mercer as to the power of the Judges to set aside the law. He thought no such power ought to exist. He was at the same time at a loss what expedient to substitute.*[2]

Some of the other delegates who opposed the Council of Revision may also have been against judicial review; but their remarks are too ambiguous to allow a firm conclusion.[3]

2. At the other extreme, some of the most influential members of the Convention were in favor of giving the judiciary not only the power to declare laws unconstitutional but also a veto over policy questions by means of the Council of Revision. Representatives of this view included two of the strongest advocates of a democratic republic, Wilson and Mason, and one of the most outspoken supporters of an aristocratic

1. *Documents, op. cit.,* p. 548.
2. *Ibid.,* p. 549.
3. Eg., Goram, Strong, Rutledge; see *Documents,* pp. 423–429.

republic, Gouverneur Morris. Madison, too, spoke with great force in behalf of the Council; and while he did not say so explicitly, his arguments do imply that the judiciary would have the power to decide on the constitutionality of laws. These men argued that decisions on constitutionality would not go far enough: for "bad" laws might nonetheless be perfectly constitutional. For example, Wilson, who stubbornly upheld the virtues of the proposed Council of Revision after it was twice voted down, contended:

> . . . It has been said that the Judges, as expositors of the Laws would have an opportunity of defending their constitutional rights. There was weight in this observation; but this power of the judges did not go far enough. Laws may be unjust, may be unwise, may be dangerous, may be destructive; and yet may not be so unconstitutional as to justify the Judges in refusing to give them effect. Let them have a share in the Revisionary power, and they will have an opportunity of taking notice of these characters of a law, and of counteracting, by the weight of their opinions, the improper views of the Legislature.[4]

Mason, Madison, and Gouverneur Morris argued along similar lines.[5] Morris was explicit as to some of the "bad laws" he wanted checked: "Emissions of paper money, largesses to the people—a remission of debts and similar measures . . ."[6]

3. Some delegates could have been *against* judicial review and *for* the Council. Although this alternative seems rather illogical, a case could undoubtedly be made for it, and it is conceivable that a few delegates silently supported it. Yet since no one advocated this position, openly or by indirection, it is reasonable to conclude that none of the delegates adhered to it.

4. Finally, some delegates who believed that the judiciary would have the power to declare laws *unconstitutional* opposed giving the courts the power to veto laws simply on the ground that they were bad laws. These delegates argued that while it was appropriate for judges to decide on the *constitutionality* of laws, they were unsuitable for deciding on the *wisdom* of laws. Although a number of delegates expressed distrust of the courts as policy-makers—more seemed to agree on this than any other point—only two of these explicitly favored judicial review of

4. *Documents*, p. 423.
5. *Ibid.*, pp. 426, 427.
6. *Ibid.*, p. 425.

constitutionality. One of these was the State Federalist, Luther Martin. The other was the National Federalist, Gerry of Massachusetts, who doubted

> ... whether the Judiciary ought to form a part of it [the Council], as they will have a sufficient check against encroachments on their own department by their own exposition of the laws, which involved a power of deciding on their Constitutionality. In some States the Judges had actually set aside laws as being against the Constitution. This was done too with general approbation. It was quite foreign from the nature of ye office to make them judges of the policy of public measures.[7]

Despite the eloquent support given to the idea of a Council of Revision by Wilson, Madison, and Morris, the proposal was decisively rejected. When it was first taken up on June 4, Gerry's substitute motion to give the veto power to the President without the participation of the judges was passed by a vote of eight states to two.[8] Undaunted, two days later, Wilson (Madison seconding his motion) tried again. They gained the support of only three states—Connecticut, New York, and Virginia—and were opposed by eight. Most delegates must have thought the matter firmly settled, but Wilson and Madison evidently felt too strongly to let the idea drop. On July 21, they once more introduced a motion for the Council of Revision. Although they were voted down again, they may have felt that the opposition was softening, for despite the fact the motion received favorable votes only from the same three states as before, two states, Pennsylvania and Georgia, were divided, leaving only four states in opposition. (New Jersey was recorded as "not present.")[9] Heartened, perhaps, by signs that the opposition was weakening, Madison and Wilson tried once more on August 15; but this time the delegates gave them short shrift and voted their motion down 8-3, virtually without debate.[10]

What conclusions as to the intentions of the Founding Fathers can we draw from these debates?

First, the record of the debates leaves their intentions unclear.

7. *Ibid.*, p. 147.
8. *Ibid.*, p. 152.
9. *Ibid.*, p. 429.
10. Of the states originally favoring the proposal, only Virginia remained, Connecticut and New York having deserted to the opposition; however, Virginia was joined this time by Delaware and Maryland. *Documents*, p. 548.

Probably a great many delegates did not have very precise intentions with respect to the powers of the judiciary.

Second, it is a reasonable inference that a majority of the delegates accepted the notion that the federal courts would rule on the constitutionality of state and federal laws involved in cases before them. Some additional though by no means conclusive evidence is provided by the bold and unambiguous stand announced in *Federalist* No. 78—written, ironically, by Hamilton, who had taken no part in the debates on the judiciary:

> . . . By a limited Constitution, I understand one which contains certain specified exceptions to the legislative authority; such, for instance, as that it shall pass no bills of attainder, no ex-post-facto laws, and the like. Limitations of this kind can be preserved in practice no other way than through the medium of courts of justice, whose duty it must be to declare all acts contrary to the manifest tenor of the Constitution void. Without this, all the reservations of particular rights or privileges would amount to nothing.[11]

Third, it is also a reasonable inference that a majority of delegates rejected the notion that judges should participate in policy-making. It was for exactly this reason, it appears, that the Council of Revision was turned down three times. Ever since the Convention defenders of judicial review have generally assumed that judicial review is legitimate only on questions of constitutionality and illegitimate on questions of policy. This is the explicit position of the Supreme Court itself.

In the light of these observations, it is difficult to sustain the view that when Chief Justice John Marshall enunciated the doctrine of judicial review in the famous case of *Marbury v. Madison*[12] on February 24, 1803, he usurped powers that the Founding Fathers had intended to deny to the federal judiciary. Marshall's argument, in fact, adhered closely to the reasoning of Hamilton in *Federalist* No. 78, which was in line, as we have seen, with what one can reasonably infer to have been the dominant view at the Convention.

11. *The Federalist*, New York, The Modern Library, n.d., p. 505.
12. 1 Cranch 1937 (1803). Reams have been filled about this famous case and concerning judicial review. A detailed history of the case itself has been written by a Supreme Court Justice, Mr. Justice Harold Burton, "The Cornerstone of Constitutional Law: the Extraordinary Case of Marbury v. Madison," *American Bar Association Journal* XXXVI (Oct. 1950), pp. 805–883.

Marshall's argument was succint and persuasive:

1. The Constitution is the supreme law of the land, binding on all branches of the government—legislature, executive, the judiciary.

2. The Constitution deliberately establishes a government with limited powers.

3. Consequently "an act of the legislature, repugnant to the constitution, is void." If this were not true, then the government would be unlimited; and the Constitution would be an absurdity.

4. "It is emphatically the province and duty of the judicial department to say what the law is."

5. "So if a law be in opposition to the constitution . . . the court must determine which of these conflicting rules governs the case. This is of the very essence of judicial duty."

6. "If, then, the courts are to regard the constitution, and the constitution is superior to any ordinary act of the legislature, the constitution and not such ordinary act, must govern the case to which they both apply."

7. Hence if a law is repugnant to the Constitution, when that law comes before a court, the judges are duty bound to declare that law void in order to uphold the supremacy of the Constitution.

Marshall's opinion has the majestic finality of Euclid. It has been quoted and paraphrased thousands of times in defense of judicial review, by judges, lawyers, historians, political scientists, and others. From 1803 to 1966, the Supreme Court used the power of judicial review on more than eighty occasions to strike down federal legislation. It has used the power many more times—no one has ever calculated how many—to hold state laws unconstitutional. The Court's actions have invariably been met with protest. Yet more often than not, critics protest a particular decision but not the general principle of judicial review. And the bitterest critics of the Court in one decade are often the Court's boldest defenders in the next.

Thus the principle of judicial review is firmly anchored simultaneously in tradition and a highly compelling rational-legal appeal to the supremacy of the Constitution.

There remains, nonetheless, the nagging question of democracy.

[149]

Democracy and Judicial Review:
A Dialogue

Does the power of judicial review entail a nondemocratic, an aristocratic, even an oligarchic principle of government? The defenders and critics of judicial review have wrestled with this question ever since *Marbury v. Madison*. Jefferson may have had *Marbury v. Madison* in mind when in his old age he wrote to a friend that "the judiciary in the United States is the subtle corps of sappers and miners constantly working underground to undermine the foundations of our confederated republic . . . A judiciary independent of a king or executive alone is a good thing; but independence of the will of the nation is a solecism, at least in a republican government".[13]

The controversy can perhaps be summarized best in a dialogue between a critic and an advocate of judicial review:

CRITIC: I am quite willing to concede that a tradition of constitutionality may convey a measure of legitimacy to judicial review. I contend, nonetheless, that judicial review is undemocratic. After all, most of the people in eighteenth-century Britain no doubt regarded their constitutional system —kings, lords, and all—as legitimate. Yet you would not argue, I'm sure, that eighteenth-century Britain was a democracy. Aristocracies, monarchies, even dictatorships, I suppose, might acquire legitimacy in the eyes of the people they rule; yet they would not be democratic. In different times and places, all sorts of political institutions have acquired a certain degree of legitimacy; yet I would not want many of these institutions in this country, nor, I imagine, would you. I wonder if judicial review hasn't generated a conflict between two different principles of legitimacy accepted by Americans —a conflict between our tradition of constitutionality and our commitment to democracy.

13. Letter to Thomas Ritchie, December 25, 1820, in Paul Leicester Ford, ed., *The Writings of Thomas Jefferson*, New York, G. P. Putnam's Sons, 1899, pp. 170–171, quoted in John R. Schmidhauser, ed., *Constitutional Law in the Political Process*, Chicago, Rand McNally & Co., 1963, pp. 145-146.

ADVOCATE: I do not think so. As Hamilton and Marshall said, ours is a *limited* government; I prefer to call it a libertarian democracy. I don't contend, as Marshall did, that judicial review is inherent in a written constitution; I know as well as you do that a number of other democracies that were not in existence when Marshall wrote his famous opinion now have written constitutions, and yet do not give their courts the power of judicial review. I would contend, however, that the *limited* character of our government is an absolutely essential characteristic. Stripped of its constitutional limitations, ours would be a totally different system. Moreover, we Americans continue to believe strongly in limited government. And judicial review helps to preserve limited government by protecting the Constitution from violations by state governments, by the federal government, or by particular parts of the federal government, such as the Congress. This is why Americans overwhelmingly believe in judicial review. Do you contend that democracy requires *unlimited* government?

CRITIC: You misunderstand me. I know full well that we possess a written Constitution. I realize that someone has to interpret the meaning of what is written in that Constitution. I can see that in the course of events cases come to the courts which depend on what the Constitution means. So, in deciding the cases before them, the courts must interpret the Constitution. Let me remind you, however, that the United States is not the only country in the world with a written constitution. In fact, I believe that every modern democracy in the world except Britain now has a written constitution: Switzerland, Sweden, Norway, The Netherlands, France, Canada, New Zealand, Ireland, Australia, to name a few well-known democratic countries. And all the more recent democracies: West Germany, Austria, Italy, India, Japan, Israel . . . Yet many of them do not have judicial review—and I think it fair to say that not one has a supreme court as powerful as ours.

ADVOCATE: I do not quite see how we could function without judicial review!

CRITIC: What are you afraid of—the American people? But if

the American people wanted unlimited government, do you really think that a few men on our Supreme Court could prevent it? Why, the voters would elect a President and a Congress who would impeach and convict the Justices one day and appoint new ones the next! Limited government exists in this country not because the Supreme Court wants it but because, as you said yourself, we Americans want it. And limited government will cease the day Americans cease to want it, no matter what nine men on a court may say or do. So long as the bulk of the American people want limited government, they will elect representatives to Congress and the Presidency who adhere to this commitment. If Americans should stop wanting limited government, they will elect revolutionaries, and our Constitution will be as dead as the Articles of Confederation. So here is my answer: The best protection for limited government in a democracy, in fact the only protection, consists of the people and their elected representatives. What I am saying is this: Democracy depends on the self-restraint of the people. If they don't exercise self-restraint, you won't have a democracy and no Court can keep it for them. If they do exercise self-restraint, then you don't need to have judicial review.

ADVOCATE: What you say is all very well in the abstract. But remember, ours is also a federal system. Suppose a state government violates the Constitution—for example, by depriving some of its citizens of their right to assemble or to speak freely? A majority of the voters in the United States might oppose the state action, but even if they knew about it —which they probably would not—what could they do?

CRITIC: I admit that federalism complicates matters. Most federal republics, I notice, do have some form of judicial review; in this respect Canada, Australia, and more recently India have all rejected the British pattern. Another federal republic, West Germany, also has judicial review. I am quite willing to endorse the principle, on purely democratic grounds, that national majorities should prevail over state majorities. Even so, I do not see why you couldn't adopt the Swiss pattern; the federal judiciary could review the constitutionality of state laws but not of federal laws.

ADVOCATE: If you need judicial review in order to keep the states from invading the powers of the federal government, doesn't the logic of your argument cut the other way, too? What if the federal government invades the powers of the states?

CRITIC: That might once have been a forceful argument. But is it not true that today the federal government can constitutionally regulate almost anything through its powers over taxation and interstate commerce? If the federal government does not regulate everything, that is only because the President and Congress do not want to do so. Again, you see, restraints depend on the people and their elected representatives, not on the Courts.

ADVOCATE: You ignore the possibility that a demagogic President or a large congressional majority, or both together, might pass laws that would deprive some particular minority of important constitutional rights.

CRITIC: Don't we have periodic elections? If we Americans really believed in these rights, we would vote out such a Congress at the next election. If we did not, I do not see how the Supreme Court could maintain our rights, at least in the long run.

ADVOCATE: In the long run, no. But do we have to forget about the short run? A majority of voters, or a majority of their representatives, might act under the transitory pressures of impulse, passion, hysteria, crisis. Politicians might not be steadily anti-libertarian; yet they might be temporarily so. In such cases the Court could void laws passed during short-run aberrations.

CRITIC: Isn't this the heart of the matter? You assume that a majority of Americans and their elected representatives cannot always be trusted to act within the spirit of limited government or, as you say, libertarian democracy. You believe that when they are misguided, the Supreme Court can maintain the essential conditions of a libertarian democracy by nullifying federal laws contrary to a Constitution designed

[153]

for limited government. I admit that your argument is persuasive. But it raises two problems. First, will the Supreme Court really stand up against a majority in order to protect some embattled minority that is threatened by a federal law, or will it not be moved by much the same passions and prejudices as the majority of people and their representatives? Second, even assuming now that the Court does stand against majorities, will it uphold general and abstract principles of right or justice, or will it instead strike down laws it disapproves on grounds of *policy?* Judges are human. As Jefferson said in 1820: "Our judges are as honest as other men, and not more so. They have, with others, the same passions for party, for power, and the privilege of their corps."[14] Even when judges are not swayed by the same passions and prejudices as a majority, they may be moved by the passions and prejudices of a particular minority. If they use judicial review and the claim of 'constitutionality' simply to impose their own views about good and bad laws, have they not contrived to evolve into exactly the kind of body that your Constitutional Convention thought it was preventing?

ADVOCATE: Well, we both seem to agree on one thing anyway: Americans seem to want judicial review. But if, as you say, they can sweep it aside when they do not want it, how in the world can you argue that there is anything undemocratic about judicial review?

The Supreme Court and Majority Control[15]

What does the record of the Supreme Court reveal? In the course of its one hundred and sixty-seven years, in eighty-five cases, the Court has struck down ninety-four different provisions of federal law as unconstitu-

14.   Letter in Jarvis, 1820, quoted in Padover, ed., *Thomas Jefferson on Democracy*, New York, Penguin Books, Inc., 1946, p. 64.
15.   The following sections are adapted from my article, "Decision-Making in a Democracy: The Role of the Supreme Court as a National Policy-maker," *Journal of Public Law*, vol. 6, (No. 2), Fall, 1957. The data in the tables, however, has been re-computed to bring them up to date and in some cases to correct errors in the original tables.

tional, and by interpretation it has significantly modified a good many more. It might be argued, then, that in all or in a very large number of these cases the Court was, in fact, defending the legitimate constitutional rights of some minority against a 'tyrannical' majority. There are, however, some exceedingly serious difficulties with this interpretation of the Court's activities.

To begin with, it is difficult to determine when any particular Court decision has been at odds with the preferences of a national majority. Adequate evidence is not available, for scientific opinion polls are of relatively recent origin; and, strictly speaking, national elections cannot be interpreted as more than an indication of the first choice of about 40 to 60 per cent of the adult population for certain candidates for public office. The connection between preferences among candidates and preferences among alternative public policies is highly tenuous. On the basis of an election, it is almost never possible to adduce whether a majority does or does not support one of two or more *policy* alternatives about which candidates are divided. For the greater part of the Court's history, then, there is simply no way of establishing with any high degree of confidence whether a given alternative was or was not supported by a majority or a minority of adults or even of voters.

In the absence of relatively direct information, we are thrown back on indirect tests. The ninety-four provisions of federal law that have been declared unconstitutional were, of course, initially passed by majorities of those voting in the Senate and in the House. They also had the President's formal approval. One could, therefore, speak of a majority of those voting in the House and Senate, together with the President, as a 'law-making majority.' It is not easy to determine whether a law-making majority actually coincides with the preferences of a majority of American adults, or even with the preferences of a majority of that half of the adult population which, on the average, votes in congressional elections. Such evidence as we have from opinion polls suggests that Congress is not markedly out of line with public opinion, or at any rate with such public opinion as there is after one discards the answers of people who fall into the category, often large, labelled "no response" or "don't know." If we may, on these somewhat uncertain grounds, take a law-making majority as equivalent to a 'national majority,' then it is possible to test the hypothesis that the Supreme Court is shield and buckler for minorities against tyrannical national majorities.

Under any reasonable assumptions about the nature of the political process, it would appear to be somewhat naive to assume that the Supreme Court either would or could play the role of Galahad. Over the whole history of the Court, one new Justice has been appointed on the average of every twenty-three months. Thus a President can expect to appoint two new Justices during one term of office; and if this were not enough to tip the balance on a normally divided Court, he would be almost certain to succeed in two terms. For example, Hoover made three appointments; Roosevelt, nine; Truman, four; Eisenhower, five; Kennedy in his brief tenure, two. Presidents are not famous for appointing Justices hostile to their own views on public policy; nor could they expect to secure confirmation of a man whose stance on key questions was flagrantly at odds with that of the dominant majority in the Senate. Typically, Justices are men who, prior to appointment, have engaged in public life and have committed themselves publicly on the great questions of the day. As the late Mr. Justice Frankfurter pointed out, a surprisingly large proportion of the Justices, particularly of the great Justices who have left their stamp upon the decisions of the Court, have had little or no prior judicial experience. Nor have the Justices—certainly not the great Justices—been timid men with a passion for anonymity. Indeed, it is not too much to say that if Justices were appointed primarily for their 'judicial' qualities without regard to their basic attitudes on fundamental questions of public policy, the Court could not play the influential role in the American political system that it does in reality play.

It is reasonable to conclude, then, that the policy views dominant on the Court will never be out of line for very long with the policy views dominant among the law-making majorities of the United States. And it would be most unrealistic to suppose that the Court would, for more than a few years at most, stand against any major alternatives sought by a law-making majority. The judicial agonies of the New Deal will, of course, come quickly to mind; but President Franklin D. Roosevelt's difficulties with the Court were truly exceptional. Generalizing over the whole history of the Court, one can say that the chances are about two out of five that a President will make one appointment to the Court in less than a year, two out of three that he will make one within two years, and three out of four that he will make one within three years (Table 6.1). President Roosevelt had unusually bad luck: he had to wait four years for his first appointment; the odds against this long interval are about five to one. With average luck, his battle with the Court would never have occurred; even as it was, although his 'court-packing' proposal did formally fail, by the end of his second term in 1940 Roosevelt had appointed five new Justices and he gained three more the following year:

Table 6.1.   The Interval Between Appointments to the
Supreme Court, 1789–1965

INTERVAL IN YEARS	NUMBER OF APPOINTMENTS	PERCENTAGE OF TOTAL	CUMULATIVE PERCENTAGE
Less than 1 year	38	41	41
1	22	24	65
2	10	11	76
3	9	10	86
4	6	6.5	92.5
5	6	6.5	99
12	1	1	100
Total	92	100	100

Note: The table excludes six Justices appointed in 1789. It includes only Justices who were appointed and confirmed and served on the Court. All data through 1964 are from *Congress and the Nation*, 1452-1453.

Thus by the end of 1941, Mr. Justice Roberts was the only remaining holdover from the pre-Roosevelt era.

It is to be expected, then, that the Court would be least successful in blocking a determined and persistent lawmaking majority on a major policy. Conversely, the Court is most likely to succeed against 'weak' lawmaking majorities: transient majorities in Congress, fragile coalitions, coalitions weakly united upon a policy of subordinate importance or congressional coalitions no longer in existence, as might be the case when a law struck down by the Court had been passed several years earlier.

The Record

An examination of the cases in which the Court has held federal legislation unconstitutional confirms these expectations. Over the whole history of the Court, about half the decisions have been rendered more than four years after the legislation was passed (Table 6.2). Thus the congressional majorities that passed these laws went through at least two elections before the decision was handed down and may well have weakened or disappeared in the interval. In these cases, then, the Court was probably not directly challenging current law-making majorities.

Of the twenty-four laws held unconstitutional within two years,

Table 6.2.   Supreme Court Cases Holding Federal Legislation
Unconstitutional: by time between legislation and decision.

	SUPREME COURT CASES INVOLVING:					
	NEW DEAL				ALL FEDERAL	
NUMBER OF YEARS	LEGISLATION		OTHER		LEGISLATION	
	N.	%	N.	%	N.	%
2 or less	11	92	13	17.5	24	28
3–4	1	8	13	17.5	14	16
5–8	0	0	20	27	20	24
9–12	0	0	10	14	10	12
13–16	0	0	7	10	7	8
17–20	0	0	2	3	2	2
21 or more	0	0	8	11	8	10
Total	12	100%	73	100%	85	100%

eleven were measures enacted in the early years of the New Deal. Indeed, New Deal measures comprise nearly a third of all the legislation that has ever been declared unconstitutional within four years of enactment.

It is illuminating to examine the cases where the Court has acted on legislation within four years of enactment—where the presumption is, that is to say, that the lawmaking majority is not a dead one. Of the twelve New Deal cases, two were, from a policy point of view, trivial; and two although perhaps not trivial, were of minor importance to the New Deal program.[16] A fifth involved the NRA, which was to expire within three weeks of the decision.[17] Insofar as the unconstitutional provisions allowed "codes of fair competition" to be established by industrial groups, it is fair to say that President Roosevelt and his advisers were relieved by the Court's decision of a policy that they had come to find increasingly embarrassing. In view of the tenacity with which FDR held to his major program, there can hardly be any doubt that, had he wanted to pursue the policy objective involved in the NRA codes, as he did for example with the labor provisions, he would not have been stopped by

16.   Booth v United States, 291 U.S. 339 (1934), involved a reduction in the pay of retired judges. Lynch v United States, 292 U.S. 571 (1934), repealed laws granting to veterans rights to yearly renewable term insurance; there were only twenty-nine policies outstanding in 1932. Hopkins Federal Savings & Loan Assn' v Cleary, 296 U.S. 315 (1935), granted permission to state building and loan associations to convert to federal ones on a vote of 51 per cent or more of votes cast at a legal meeting. Ashton v Cameron County Water Improvement District, 298 U.S. 513 (1936), permitted municipalities to petition federal courts for bankruptcy proceedings.

17.   Schechter Poultry Corp. v United States, 295 U.S. 495 (1935).

the Court's special theory of the Constitution. As to the seven other cases,[18] it is entirely correct to say, I think, that whatever some of the eminent Justices might have thought during their fleeting moments of glory, they did not succeed in interposing a barrier to the achievement of the objectives of the legislation; and in a few years most of the constitutional dogma on which they rested their opposition to the New Deal had been unceremoniously swept under the rug.

The remainder of the thirty-eight cases where the Court has declared legislation unconstitutional within four years of enactment tend to fall into two rather distinct groups: those involving legislation that could reasonably be regarded as important *from the point of view of the law-making majority* and those involving minor legislation. Although the one category merges into the other, so that some legislation must be classified rather arbitrarily, probably there will be little disagreement with classifying the specific legislative provisions involved in eleven cases as essentially minor from the point of view of the law-making majority (however important they may have been as constitutional interpretations).[19] The specific legislative provisions involved in the remaining fifteen cases are by no means of uniform importance, but with one or two possible exceptions it seems reasonable to classify them as major policy issues from the point of view of the law-making majority[20]. We would expect that cases

18. *United States v Butler*, 297 U.S. 1 (1936) *Perry v United States*, 294 U.S. 330 (1935); *Panama Refining Co. v Ryan*, 293 U.S. 388 (1935); *Railroad Retirement Board v Alton R. Co.*, 295 U.S. 330 (1935); *Louisville Joint Stock Land Bank v Radford*, 295 U.S. 555 (1935); *Rickert Rice Mills v Fontenot*, 297 U.S. 110 (1936); *Carter v Carter Coal Co.*, 298 U.S. 238 (1936).

19. *United States v Dewitt*, 9 Wall. (U.S.) 41 (1870); *Gordon v United States*, 2 Wall. (U.S.) 561 (1865); *Monongahela Navigation Co. v United States*, 148 U.S. 312 (1893); *Wong Wing v United States*, 163 U.S. 228 (1896); *Fairbank v United States*, 181 U.S. 283 (1901); *Rassmussen v United States*, 197 U.S. 516 (1905); *Muskrat v United States*, 219.

20. *Ex parte Garland*, 4 Wall. (U.S.) 333 (1867); *United States v Klein*, 13 Wall. (U.S.) 128 (1872); *Pollack v Farmers' Loan & Trust Co.*, 157 U.S. 429 (1895), rehearing granted 158 U.S.. 601 (1895); *Employers' Liability Cases*, 207 U.S. 463 (1908); *Keller v United States*, 213 U.S. 138 (1909); *Hammer v Dagenhart*, 247 U.S. 251 (1918); *Eisner v Macomber*, 252 U.S. 189 (1920); *Knickerbocker Ice Co. v Stewart*, 253 U.S. 149 (1920); *United States v Cohen Grocery Co.*, 255 U.S. 81 (1921); *Weeds, Inc. v United States*, 255 U.S. 109 (1921); *Bailey v Drexel Furniture Co.*, 259 U.S. 20 (1922); *Hill v Wallace*, 259 U.S. 44 (1922); *Washington v Dawson & Co.*, 264 U.S. 219 (1924); *Trusler v Crooks*, 269 U.S. 475 (1926).

Table 6.3. Number of Cases Involving Legislative Policy Other than Those Arising Under New Deal Legislation Holding Legislation Unconstitutional Within Four Years After Enactment.

INTERVAL IN YEARS	MAJOR POLICY	MINOR POLICY	TOTAL
2 or less	11	2	13
3 to 4	4	9	13
Total	15	11	26

involving major legislative policy would be propelled to the Court much more rapidly than cases involving minor policy, and, as the table above shows, this is in fact what happens (Table 6.3).

Thus a law-making majority with major policy objectives in mind usually has an opportunity to seek ways of overcoming the Court's veto. It is an interesting and highly significant fact that Congress and the President do generally succeed in overcoming a hostile Court on major policy issues (Table 6.4). It is particularly instructive to examine the cases involving major policy. In two cases involving legislation enacted by radical Republican Congresses to punish supporters of the Confederacy during the Civil War, the Court faced a rapidly crumbling majority whose death knell as an effective national force was sounded after the

21.   a. *Pollock v Farmers' Loan & Trust Co.*, 157 U.S. 429 (1895); *Employers' Liability Cases*, 207 U.S. 463 (1908); *Keller v United States*, 213 U.S. 138 (1909) *Hammer v Dagenhart*, 247 U.S. 251 (1918); *Bailey v Drexel Furniture Co.*, 259 U.S. 20 (1922); *Trusler v Crooks*, 269 U.S. 475 (1926); *Hill v Wallace*, 259 U.S. 44 (1922); *Knickerbocker Ice Co. v Stewart*, 253 U.S. 149 (1920); *Washington v Dawson & Co.*, 264 U.S. 219 (1924).
b. *Ex parte Garland*, 4 Wall. (U.S.) 333 (1867); *United States v Klein*, 13 Wall. (U.S.) 128 (1872).
c. *United States v Cohen Grocery Co.*, 255 U.S. 81 (1921); *Weeds, Inc. v United States*, 255 U.S. 109 (1921); *Eisner v Macomber*, 252 U.S. 189 (1920).
d. *Gordon v United States*, 2 Wall. (U.S.) 561 (1865); *Evans v Gore*, 253 U.S. 245 (1920).
e. *United States v Dewitt*, 9 Wall, (U.S.) 41 (1870); *Monongahela Navigation Co. v United States*, 148 U.S. 312 (1893); *Wong Wing v United States*, 163 U.S. 228 (1896); *Fairbank v United States*, 181 U.S. 283 (1901); *Rassmussen v United States*, 197 U.S. 516 (1905); *Muskrat v United States*, 219 U.S. 346 (1911); *Choate v Trapp*, 224 U.S. 665 (1912); *United States v Lovett*, 328 U.S. 303 (1946).
f. *Untermyer v Anderson*, 276 U.S. 440 (1928).

Table 6.4. *Type of Congressional Action Following Supreme Court Decisions Holding Legislation Unconstitutional Within Four Years After Enactment (Other than New Deal Legislation).*

CONGRESSIONAL ACTION	MAJOR POLICY	MINOR POLICY	TOTAL
Reverses Court's Policy	10a	2d	12
Changes Own Policy	2b	0	2
None	0	8e	8
Unclear	3c	1f	4
Total	15	11	26

Note: For the cases in each category, see footnote 21.

election of 1876.[22] Three cases are difficult to classify and I have labelled them "unclear." Of these, two were decisions made in 1921 involving a 1919 amendment to the Lever Act to control prices.[23] The legislation was important, and the provision in question was clearly struck down, but the Lever Act terminated three days after the decision and Congress did not return to the subject of price control until the Second World War, when it experienced no constitutional difficulties arising from these cases (which were primarily concerned with the lack of an ascertainable standard of guilt). The third case in this category successfully eliminated stock dividends from the scope of the Sixteenth Amendment, although a year later Congress enacted legislation taxing the actual income from such stocks.[24]

The remaining ten cases were ultimately followed by a reversal of the actual policy results of the Court's action, although not necessarily of the specific constitutional interpretation. In four cases,[25] the policy consequences of the Court's decision were overcome in less than a year. The other six required a long struggle. Workmen's compensation for longshoremen and harbor workers was invalidated by the Court in 1920;[26] in 1922 Congress passed a new law which was, in its turn,

22. Ex parte *Garland*, 4 Wall. (U.S.) 333 (1867); *United States v Klein*, 13 Wall. (U.S.) 128 (1872).

23. *United States v Cohen Grocery Co.*, 255 U.S. 81 (1921); *Weeds, Inc. v United States*, 255 U.S. 109 (1921).

24. *Eisner v Macomber*, 252 U.S. 189 (1920).

25. Employers' Liability Cases, 207 U.S. 463 (1908); *Keller v United States*, 213 U.S. 138 (1909); *Trusler v Crooks*, 269 U.S. 475 (1926); *Hill v Wallace*, 259 U.S. 44 (1922).

26. *Knickerbocker Ice Co. v Stewart*, 253 U.S. 149 (1920).

knocked down by the Court in 1924;[27] in 1927 Congress passed a third law, which was finally upheld in 1932.[28] The notorious income tax cases of 1895[29] were first somewhat narrowed by the Court itself;[30] the Sixteenth Amendment was recommended by President Taft in 1909 and was ratified in 1913, some eighteen years after the Court's decisions. The two child labor cases represent the most effective battle ever waged by the Court against legislative policy-makers. The original legislation outlawing child labor, based on the commerce clause, was passed in 1916 as part of Wilson's New Freedom. Like Franklin Roosevelt later, Wilson was somewhat unlucky in his Supreme Court appointments; he made only three appointments during his eight years, and one of these was wasted, from a policy point of view, on Mr. Justice McReynolds. Had McReynolds voted 'right,' the subsequent struggle over the problem of child labor need not have occurred, for the decision in 1918 was by a Court divided five to four, McReynolds voting with the majority.[31] Congress moved at once to circumvent the decision by means of the tax power, but in 1922 the Court blocked that approach.[32] In 1924, Congress returned to the engagement with a constitutional amendment that was rapidly endorsed by a number of state legislatures before it began to meet so much resistance in the states remaining that the enterprise miscarried. In 1938, under a second reformist President, new legislation was passed twenty-two years after the first; this a Court with a New Deal majority finally accepted in 1941,[33] and thereby brought to an end a battle that had lasted a full quarter-century.

The entire record of the duel between the Court and the law-making majority, in cases where the Court has held legislation unconstitutional within four years after enactment, is summarized in Table 6.5.

A consideration of the role of the Court as defender of minorities, then, suggests the following conclusions:

First, judicial review is surely inconsistent with democracy to the extent that the Court simply protects the policies of minorities from reversal or regulation by national majorities acting through regular law-making procedures.

27. *Washington* v *Dawson & Co.*, 264 U.S. 219 (1924).
28. *Crowell* v *Benson*, 285 U.S. 22 (1932).
29. *Pollock* v *Farmers' Loan & Trust Co.*, 157 U.S. 429 (1895).
30. *Nicol* v *Ames*, 173 U.S. 509 (1899); *Knowlton* v *Moore*, 178 U.S. 41 (1900); *Patton* v *Brady*, 184 U.S. 608 (1902); *Flint* v *Stone Tracy Co.*, 220 U.S. 107 (1911).
31. *Hammer* v *Dagenhart*, 247 U.S. 251 (1918).
32. *Bailey* v *Drexel Furniture Co.*, 259 U.S. 20 (1922).
33. *United States* v *Darby*, 312 U.S. 100 (1941).

Table 6.5. Type of Congressional Action After Supreme Court Decisions Holding Legislation Unconstitutional Within Four Years After Enactment (Including New Deal Legislation).

CONGRESSIONAL ACTION	MAJOR POLICY	MINOR POLICY	TOTAL
Reverses Court's Policy	17	2	19
None	0	12	12
Other	6*	1	7
Total	23	15	38

*In addition to the actions in Table 6.4 under "Changes Own Policy" and "Unclear," this figure includes the NRA legislation affected by the *Schechter Poultry* case.

Second, however, the frequency and nature of appointments to the Court inhibits it from playing this role, or otherwise protecting minorities against national law-making majorities. National law-making majorities—i.e., coalitions of the President and a majority of each house of Congress—generally have their way.

Third, although the court evidently cannot hold out indefinitely against a persistent law-making majority, in a very small number of important cases it has succeeded in delaying the application of a policy for as long as twenty-five years.

Judges as Policy-Makers

How can we appraise decisions of the third kind just mentioned? It might be argued that the one function of the Court is to protect rights that are in some sense basic or fundamental. Thus (the argument might run), in a country where basic rights are, on the whole, respected, one would expect only a small number of cases where the Court has had to plant itself firmly against a law-making majority. But majorities may, on rare occasions, become 'tyrannical'; when they do, the Court intervenes; and although the constitutional issue may, strictly speaking, be technically open, the Constitution assumes an underlying fundamental body of rights and liberties which the Court guarantees by its decisions.

Even without examining the actual cases, however, it is somewhat unrealistic to suppose that a Court whose members are recruited in the fashion of Supreme Court Justices would long adhere to norms of ab-

[163]

stract Right or Justice substantially at odds with those of a majority of elected leaders. Moreover, in an earlier day it was perhaps easier to believe that certain rights are so natural and self-evident that their fundamental validity is as much a matter of definite knowledge, at least to all reasonable creatures, as the color of a ripe cherry.

But today we know that the line between abstract Right and policy is extremely hard to draw. A policy decision might be defined as an effective choice among alternatives about which there is, at least initially, some uncertainty. This uncertainty may arise because of inadequate information as to (a) the alternatives that are thought to be 'open'; (b) the consequences that will probably ensue from choosing a given alternative; (c) the level of probability that these consequences will actually ensue; and (d) the relative value of the different alternatives.

No one, I imagine, will quarrel with the proposition that the Supreme Court, or indeed any Court, must make and does make policy decisions in this sense. But such a proposition is not really useful to the question before us. What is critical is the extent to which a court can and does make policy decisions by going outside established 'legal' criteria found in precedent, statute, and Constitution. Now in this respect the Supreme Court occupies a most peculiar position, for it is an essential characteristic of the institution that from time to time its members decide cases where legal criteria are not in any realistic sense adequate to the task. The distinguished legal scholar and member of the Court, the late Mr. Justice Frankfurter, once described the business of the Supreme Court in these words:

> It is essentially accurate to say that the Court's preoccupation today is with the application of rather fundamental aspirations and what Judge Learned Hand calls "moods," embodied in provisions like the due process clauses, which were designed not to be precise and positive directions for rules of action. The judicial process in applying them involves a judgment . . . that is, on the views of the direct representatives of the people in meeting the needs of society, on the views of Presidents and Governors, and by their construction of the will of legislatures the Court breathes life, feeble or strong, into the inert pages of the Constitution and the statute books.[34]

Very often, then, the cases before the Court involve alternatives about which there is severe disagreement in the society, as in the case of

34. Frankfurter, "The Supreme Court in the Mirror of Justices," 105 U. of Pa. Law Review 781, 793 (1957).

segregation or economic regulation; the very setting of the case is, then, "political." Moreover, these are usually cases where competent students of constitutional law, including the learned Justices of the Supreme Court themselves, disagree; where the words of the Constitution are general, vague, ambiguous, or not clearly applicable; where precedent may be found on both sides; and where experts differ in predicting the consequences of the various alternatives or the degree of probability that the possible consequences will actually ensue. Typically, in other words, although there may be considerable agreement as to the alternatives thought to be open, there is very serious disagreement—both as to questions of fact bearing on consequences and probabilities and as to questions of value.

If the Court were assumed to be a 'political' institution, no particular problems would arise, for it would be taken for granted that the members of the Court would resolve questions of fact and value by introducing assumptions derived from their own predispositions or those of influential clienteles and constituents. However, since much of the legitimacy of the Court's decisions rests upon the belief that it is not a political institution but exclusively a legal one, to accept the Court as a political institution would solve one set of problems at the price of creating another. Nonetheless, if it is true that the nature of the cases arriving before the Court is sometimes of the kind I have described, then the Court cannot act strictly as a legal institution. It must, that is to say, choose among controversial alternatives of public policy by appealing to at least some criteria of acceptability on questions of fact and value that cannot be found in or deduced from precedent, statute and Constitution.

In making these choices does the Court rise to a level of abstract Right or Justice above the level of mere policy? The best rebuttal to this view of the Court will be found in the record of the Court's decisions. Surely the six cases referred to a moment ago, where the policy consequences of the Court's decisions were overcome only after long battles, will scarcely appeal to many contemporary minds as evidence for the proposition under examination. A natural right to employ child labor in mills and mines? To be free of income taxes by the federal government? To employ longshoremen and harbor workers without the protection of workmen's compensation? The Court itself did not rely upon such arguments in these cases, and it would do no credit to their opinions to reconstruct them along such lines.

So far, however, our evidence has been drawn from cases in which the Court has held legislation unconstitutional within four years after enactment. What of the other forty cases? Do we have evidence in these that the Court has protected fundamental or natural rights and liberties against the dead hand of some past tyranny by the lawmakers? The evidence is not impressive. In the history of the Court there has never been a single case arising under the First Amendment in which the Court has held federal legislation unconstitutional.[35] If we turn from these fundamental liberties of religion, speech, press, and assembly, we do find a handful of cases—something less than ten—arising under Amendments Four to Seven in which the Court has declared acts unconstitutional that might properly be regarded as involving rather basic liberties.[36] An inspection of these cases leaves the impression that, in all of them, the lawmakers and the Court were not very far apart; moreover, it is doubtful that the fundamental conditions of liberty in this country have been altered by more than a hair's breadth as a result of these decisions.

Over against these decisions we must put the fifteen or so cases in which the Court used the protections of the Fifth, Thirteenth, Fourteenth, and Fifteenth Amendments to preserve the rights and liberties of a relatively privileged group at the expense of the rights and liberties of a submerged group: chiefly slaveholders at the expense of slaves,[37] white people at the expense of colored people,[38] and property holders at the

35. It is at least debatable whether *Aptheker v Secretary of State* 378 U.S. 500 (1964) might be considered an exception. A divided court held that the passport provisions of the Subversive Activities Control Act of 1950 were invalid because they were too broad. If Congress wanted to forbid or regulate travel it would have to be more specific.
36. The candidates for this category would appear to be *Boyd v United States*, 116 U.S. 616 (1886); *Rassmussen v United States*, 197 U.S. 516 (1905); *Wong Wing v United States*, 163 U.S. 228 (1896); *United States v Moreland*, 258 U.S. 433 (1922); *Kirby v United States*, 174 U.S. 47 (1899); *United States v Cohen Grocery Co.*, 255 U.S. 81 (1921); *Weeds, Inc. v United States*, 255 U.S. 109 (1921); *Justices of the Supreme Court v United States ex rel. Murray*, 9 Wall. (U.S.) 274 (1870); *United States ex rel. Toth v Quarles*, 350 U.S. 11 (1955). It would be only fair to add one case not involving the first ten amendments: *U.S. v Brown*, 381 U.S. 437 (1965). Section 504 of the Labor-Management Reporting and Disclosure Act of 1959 made it a crime for a Communist Party member to serve as an officer or an employee (other than in a clerical or custodial position) of a labor organization. By a vote of 5-4 the Court held this section unconstitutional on the rather narrow ground that it constituted a bill of attainder, a holding that rested on the Court's conclusion that the intent of the statute was punitive. The prohibition against bills of attainder is not contained in the Bill of Rights but in Article I, Section 9.
37. *Dred Scott v Sandford*, 19 How. (U.S.) 393 (1857).
38. *United States v Reese*, 92 U.S. 214 (1876); *United States v Harris*, 106 U.S. 629 (1883); *United States v Stanley (Civil Rights Cases)*, 109 U.S.

expense of wage earners and other groups.[39] These cases, unlike the relatively innocuous ones of the preceding set, all involved liberties of genuinely fundamental importance, where an opposite policy would have meant thoroughly basic shifts in the distribution of rights, liberties, and opportunities in the United States—where, moreover, the policies sustained by the Court's action have since been repudiated in every civilized nation of the Western world, including our own. Yet, if our earlier argument is correct, it is futile—precisely because the basic distribution of privilege was at issue—to suppose that the Court could have acted much differently in these areas of policy from the way in which it did in fact act.

Some Conclusions

Thus the role of the Court is not simple; and it is an error to suppose that its functions can be either described or appraised by means of simple concepts drawn from democratic or moral theory. It is possible, nonetheless, to derive a few general conclusions about the Court's role as a policy-making institution.

National politics in the United States, as in other stable democracies, is dominated by relatively cohesive alliances that endure for long periods of time. One recalls the Jeffersonian alliance, the Jacksonian, the extraordinarily long-lived Republican dominance of the post-Civil-War years, and the New Deal alliance shaped by Franklin Roosevelt. Each is marked by a break with past policies, a period of intense struggle, followed by consolidation, and finally decay and disintegration of the alliance.[40]

Except for short-lived transitional periods when the old alliance is disintegrating and the new one is struggling to take control of political institutions, the Supreme Court is inevitably a part of the dominant national alliance. As an element in the political leadership of the dominant alliance, the Court of course supports the major policies of the

3 (1883); *Baldwin v Franks*, 120 U.S. 678 (1887); *James v Bowman*, 190 U.S. 127 (1903); *Hodges v United States*, 203 U.S. 1 (1906); *Butts v Merchants & Miners Transportation Co.*, 230 U.S. 126 (1913).

39. *Monongahela Navigation Co. v United States*, 148 U.S. 312 (1893); *Adair v United States* 208 U.S. 261 (1908); *Adkins v Children's Hospital*, 261 U.S. 525 (1923); *Nichols v Coolidge*, 274 U.S. 531 (1927); *Untermyer v Anderson*, 276 U.S. 440 (1928); *Heiner v Donnan*, 285 U.S. 312 (1932); *Louisville Joint Stock Land Bank v Radford*, 295 U.S. 555 (1935).

40. We return to this point in Chapter 8.

alliance. Acting solely by itself with no support from the President and Congress, the Court is almost powerless to affect the course of national policy.

The Supreme Court is not, however, simply an *agent* of the alliance. It is an essential part of the political leadership and possesses some bases of power of its own, the most important of which is the unique legitimacy attributed to its interpretations of the Constitution. This legitimacy the Court jeopardizes if it flagrantly opposes the major policies of the dominant alliance; such a course of action, as we have seen, is one in which the Court will not normally be tempted to engage.

It follows that within the somewhat narrow limits set by the basic policy goals of the dominant alliance, the Court can make national policy. Its discretion, then, is not unlike that of a powerful committee chairman in Congress who cannot, generally speaking, nullify the basic policies substantially agreed on by the rest of the dominant leadership, but who can, within these limits, often determine important questions of timing, effectiveness, and subordinate policy. Thus the Court is least effective against a current law-making majority—and evidently least inclined to act. It is most effective when it sets the bounds of policy for officials, agencies, state governments, or even regions, a task that has come to occupy a very large part of the Court's business.[41]

Few of the Court's policy decisions can be interpreted sensibly in terms of a 'majority' versus a 'minority.' In this respect the Court is no different from the rest of the political leadership. Generally speaking, policy at the national level is the outcome of conflict, bargaining, and agreement among minorities; the process is neither minority rule nor majority rule but what might better be called *minorities* rule, where one aggregation of minorities achieves policies opposed by another aggregation.

The main objective of presidential leadership is to build a stable and dominant aggregation of minorities with a high probability of winning the Presidency and one or both houses of Congress. Ordinarily the main contribution of the Court is to confer legitimacy on the fundamental policies of the successful coalition.

But if this were the only function of the Supreme Court, would it have acquired the standing it has among Americans? In fact, at its best—

41. "Constitutional law and cases with constitutional undertones are of course still very important, with almost one-fourth of the cases in which written opinions were filed (in recent years) involving such questions. Review of administrative action . . . constitutes the largest category of the Court's work, comprising one-third of the total cases decided on the merits. The remaining . . . categories of litigation . . . all involve largely public law questions." Frankfurter, *op. cit.*

and the Court is not always at its best—the Court does more than merely confer legitimacy on the dominant national coalition. For one thing, by the way it interprets and modifies national laws, perhaps but not necessarily by holding them unconstitutional, the Supreme Court sometimes serves as a guide and even a pioneer in arriving at different standards of fair play and individual right than have resulted, or are likely to result, from the interplay of the other political forces. Thus in recent years the Court has modified by interpretation or declared unconstitutional provisions of federal law restricting the rights of unpopular and even widely detested minorities—military deserters, Communists, and alleged bootleggers, for example.[42] The judges, after all, inherit an ancient tradition and an acknowledged role in setting higher standards of justice and right than the majority of citizens or their representatives might otherwise demand. If the standards of justice propounded by the Court are to prevail, for reasons we have already examined they cannot be too remote from general standards of fairness and individual right among Americans; but, though some citizens may protest, most Americans are too attached to the Court to want it stripped of its power.

There are times, too, when the other political forces are too divided to arrive at decisions on certain key questions. At very great risk, the Court can intervene in such cases; and sometimes it may even succeed in establishing policy where President and Congress are unable to do so. Probably in such cases it can succeed only if its action conforms to a widespread set of explicit or implicit norms held by the political leadership: norms which are not strong enough or are not distributed in such a way as to insure the existence of an effective law-making majority but are nonetheless sufficiently powerful to prevent any successful attack on the legitimacy and power of the Court. This is probably the explanation for the relatively successful work of the Court in enlarging the freedom of Negroes to vote during the past three decades and in its famous school integration decisions,[43] and the reapportionment cases mentioned in Chapter 5.[44]

42. *Trop v Dulles*, 356 U.S. 86 (1958); *Kennedy v Mendoza-Martinez*, 372 U.S. 147 (1963); *Schneider v Rusk*, 377 U.S. 163 (1964); *Aptheker v Secretary of State*, 378 U.S. 500 (1964); *U.S. v Brown* 381 U.S. 437; *Alberston v Subversive Activities Control Bd.*, Sup. Ct. 194 (1965); *U.S. v Romano*, 86 Sup. Ct. 279 (1965).

43. *Rice v Elmore*, 165 F.2d 387 (C.A. 4th, 1947), cert. denied 333 U.S. 875 (1948); *United States v Classic*, 313 U.S. 299 (1941); *Smith v All-wright*, 321 U.S. 649 (1944); *Grovey v Townsend*, 295 U.S. 45 (1935); *Brown v Board of Education*, 347 U.S. 483 (1954); *Bolling v Sharpe*, 347 U.S. 497 (1954).

44. See p. 129, fn. 18.

Yet the Court does even more than this. Considered as a political system, democracy is a set of basic procedures for arriving at decisions. The operation of these procedures presupposes the existence of certain rights, obligations, liberties, and restraints; in short, certain patterns of behavior. The existence of these patterns of behavior in turn presupposes widespread agreement (particularly among the politically active and influential segments of the population) on the validity and propriety of the behavior. Although its record is by no means lacking in serious blemishes, at its best the Court operates to confer legitimacy, not simply on the particular and parochial policies of the dominant political alliance, but upon the basic patterns of behavior required for the operation of a democracy.

Yet in order to confer legitimacy, the Court must itself possess legitimacy. For in a political society thoroughly permeated by the democratic ethos, where the legitimacy of every political institution depends finally on its consistency with democracy, the legitimacy of judicial review and the Court's exercise of that power must stem from the presumption that the Court is ultimately subject to popular control. The more the Court exercises self-restraint and the less it challenges the policies of law-making majorities, the less the need or the impulse to subject it to popular controls. The more active the Court is in contesting the policies of law-making majorities, the more visible becomes the slender basis of its legitimacy in a democratic system, and the greater the efforts will be to bring the Court's policies into conformity with those enacted by lawmaking majorities.

To the extent that the Supreme Court accepts the policies of lawmaking majorities, then, it retains its own legitimacy and its power to confer legitimacy on policies; yet to that extent it fails to protect minorities from control or regulation by national majorities. To the extent that it opposes the policies of national law-making majorities in order to protect minorities, it threatens its own legitimacy. This is the inescapable paradox of judicial review in a democratic political order.

7

THE OTHER
NINETY THOUSAND
GOVERNMENTS

ALTHOUGH THE NATIONAL GOVERNMENT is only one of many governments that Americans support, it is the largest, most inclusive, and
most powerful of all the governments within the United States.
The national government receives from most Americans a greater share of their loyalty, obedience, affection, and taxes than any other
government. It is without much question the dominant government in
the American democratic republic.

The national government is one out of more than ninety thousand
governments of all kinds existing within the boundaries of the United
States (Table 7.1). Of these, more than a third are school districts,
although the number of these has declined precipitously since the 1930s.
Even if we ignore school and special districts and consider only general
territorial governments, the states, counties, municipalities, townships,
and towns have numbered altogether close to 38 thousand for the last
thirty or forty years.

These territorial governments below the national level are of bewildering variety and complexity. The governments of the fifty states constitute a vast field in themselves.[1] The thousands of towns and cities create

1. As one can readily see by consulting the following: Herbert Jacob and
Kenneth N. Vines, eds., *Politics in the American States, A Comparative
Analysis*, Boston, Little Brown, 1965; V. O. Key, Jr., *American State
Politics An Introduction*, New York, Alfred A. Knopf, 1949; Duane Lock-
ard, *New England State Politics*, Princeton, Princeton University Press,
1959; John R. Fenton, *Politics in the Border States*, New Orleans, The
Hauser Press, 1957.

Table 7.1. Number and Type of Governmental Units in the United States, Selected Years, 1942–62

| | NUMBER | | | CHANGE | |
UNIT OF GOVERNMENT	1942	1957	1962	1942-57	1942-62
U.S. Government	1	1	1	0	0
States	48	48	50	0 +	2
Counties	3,050	3,047	3,043	− 3	− 7
Municipalities	16,220	17,183	17,997	+ 963	+ 1,777
Towns and townships	18,919	17,198	17,144	− 1,721	− 1,775
School districts[a]	108,579	50,446	34,678	−58,133	−73,901
Special districts	8,299	14,405	18,323	+ 6,106	+10,024
Total	155,116	102,328	91,236	−52,788	−63,880

SOURCES: U.S. Census Bureau, *1957 Census of Governments*, Vol. 1, No. 1, "Government in the United States," p. 1; *1962 Census of Governments*, Vol 1, "Governmental Organization," p. 1.

[a]This counts only the so-called "independent" school districts. Another 2,341 'dependent' school systems were in operation in 1962, administered by county, city, or town governments. In four states (Virginia, Hawaii, North Carolina, Maryland) there are no independent school districts; in twenty-three states independent districts are responsible for all public schools; in the remaining twenty-three states, the situation is 'mixed.' *Ibid.*, p. 4.

a political tapestry even more complex. It has been estimated, to take one example, that the metropolitan area around New York City alone includes 1,467 "distinct political entities."[2] A recent monumental study entitled *Governing New York City*[3] runs (as befits the largest city in the country) to over eight hundred pages.[4]

What contributions do territorial governments below the national level make to the American democracy? If one tries to imagine how the American political system might operate without them, four possible contributions suggest themselves:

1. By reducing the workload of the national government, they make democratic government at the national level more manageable.

2. Robert C. Wood, *1400 Governments*, Garden City, Doubleday Anchor, 1964.

3. By Wallace Sayre and Herbert Kaufman, New York, Russell Sage Foundation, 1960.

4. Recent attempts to bring order to the complexities of local governments include Edward C. Banfield and James Q. Wilson, *City Politics*, Cambridge, Harvard University Press, 1963; Charles K. Adrian, *Governing Urban America*, 2nd ed., New York, McGraw-Hill, 1961. For a succinct overview of both state and local governments, cf. Herbert Kaufman, *Politics and Policies in State and Local Governments*, Englewood Cliffs, Prentice Hall, 1963.

2. By permitting diversity, they reduce conflicts at the national level and thus make democratic government at the national level more viable.
3. By providing numerous more or less independent or autonomous centers of power throughout the system, they reinforce the principles of Balanced Authority and Political Pluralism discussed in Chapter 2.[5]
4. By facilitating self-government at local levels, they greatly expand the opportunities for learning and practising the ways of democratic government in the United States.

Efficiency, Decentralization,
and Democracy

The imagination boggles at the attempt to conceive of the United States as a democratic country operating at the national level by means of elected leaders and competitive political parties and locally through a centralized bureaucracy, federally appointed and controlled, that would administer tasks now carried on by 38 thousand territorial governments. After all, many important self-governing nations are no larger than our larger states.[6] In fact, in 1961 only 28 out of over 125 independent countries were as large as New York or California.[7]

How would a completely centralized system actually function in the United States? On the one hand, the system might be centralized not only in law but *in fact* as well. In this case, would not the weight of the Chief Executive and the insensitivity of the national bureaucracy to local variation crush out local diversity? What is more, the burdens on national policy-makers—the President, the Congress, the courts, the administrative agencies—would be frightful; to superimpose these new tasks on their present duties (which, we have seen, are already enormous) would surely create a workload well beyond their capacities to handle.

National policy-makers might meet such an impossible work load by either neglecting their duties or delegating decisions to other officials. To

5. P. 56 et seq.
6. James A. Maxwell, *Financing State and Local Governments*, Washington, The Brookings Institution, 1965, p. 29, fn. 22.
7. Bruce M. Russett, et al., *World Handbook of Political and Social Indicators*, New Haven, Yale University Press, 1964, p. 18.

the extent that national officials delegated decisions to other officials who were closer to the local scene, the system might become centralized in law but decentralized in fact. National uniformity would doubtless be too rigid and oppressive to remain tolerable for long. National officials would develop strong but informal local ties. Local pressures would be felt. The wise administrator would learn to adapt his policies to local circumstances. Sooner or later, American citizens might conclude that law should conform more closely to fact. In short: If local governments did not exist, they would quickly be invented.

It might be objected, however, that there is a third alternative, and that this alternative has actually come to pass in the United States: a system decentralized in constitutional and legal form but centralized in fact. It is often said that the rapidly increasing role of the national government has deprived local territorial governments of their older functions; 'the demise of local government' is as common a theme in the United States as 'the rise of the Executive' and 'the decline of Congress.'

Because the degree of centralization or decentralization of an organization has so far proved all but impossible to measure, one cannot meet the argument directly by producing satisfactory evidence on the amount of change in centralization in the political system of the United States over the past half century. But a fairly large number of different indicators do reveal that the role of local governments in American life has actually *expanded* in this century. Evidently what has happened is that all our territorial governments—national, state, and local—have increased their functions; whether it be national, state, or local, every government carries out more tasks today than it did a few generations ago.

For example, the expenditures, revenues, and functions of the state and local governments have steadily grown in recent decades. True, since the high period of the New Deal in 1936, federal expenditures have risen faster than those of the state and local governments. But the lion's share of federal outlays has been consumed by national defense, international relations, space programs, veterans' services, and interest on the public debt. If we eliminate these items, we discover that the difference virtually disappears: In the quarter century from 1938-1963 the expenditures of the federal government increased a little more than eight-fold, the expenditures of state and local governments a little less than eight-fold (Figure 7.1). In 1962, 'obsolete' state and local governments spent far more than the federal government for education, highways, health and hospitals, public welfare, and housing and community development (Figure 7.2). Revenues from strictly state and local sources—that is,

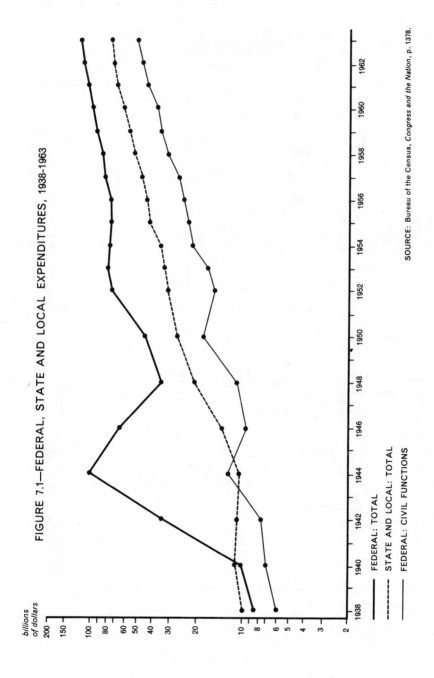

FIGURE 7.1—FEDERAL, STATE AND LOCAL EXPENDITURES, 1938-1963

SOURCE: Bureau of the Census, *Congress and the Nation*, p. 1378.

FEDERAL: TOTAL

STATE AND LOCAL: TOTAL

FEDERAL: CIVIL FUNCTIONS

FIGURE 7.2—GENERAL EXPENDITURE OF THE FEDERAL GOVERNMENT
AND OF STATE AND LOCAL GOVERNMENTS, OTHER THAN
FOR NATIONAL DEFENSE AND INTERNATIONAL DEFENSE
AND INTERNATIONAL RELATIONS, BY FUNCTION: 1962

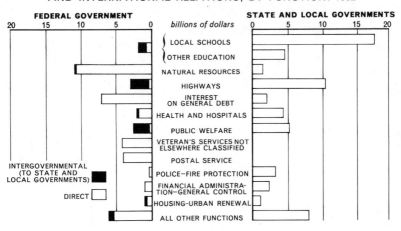

SOURCE: Department of Commerce; *Congress and the Nation*, p. 1380.

FIGURE 7.3—FEDERAL, STATE
AND LOCAL REVENUES, 1938-1963

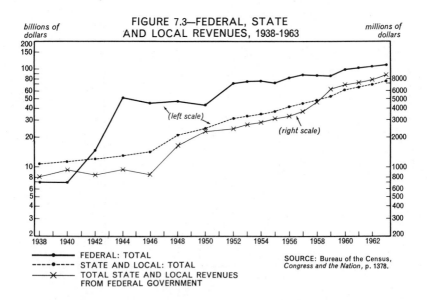

SOURCE: Bureau of the Census,
Congress and the Nation, p. 1378.

excluding all federal grants, which amount to 7.2 per cent of the total in 1938 and 11.6 per cent in 1963—were six and one-half times greater in 1963 than in 1938 (Figure 7.3). Of about 9.7 million civilians employed by government in 1963, about one in four were federal employees; more than one in six were state employees; and something more than one out of two were employed by local governments (Table 7.2).

Far from having lost functions, then, the local governments have been gaining new ones. There is no record that state and local governments spent any funds at all for housing development until 1938, when they spent three million dollars. In 1963 they spent 446 million dollars. The state and local governments are a major factor in the national economy. In 1963 their expenditures for civil functions were equivalent to 11 per cent of the Gross National Product, compared with 4 per cent for the federal government (Table 7.3).

There are then no valid grounds for doubting that both in fact and

Table 7.2. Government Employment (in thousands)

YEAR	FEDERAL	STATE	LOCAL	TOTAL MONTHLY PAYROLL
1940	1,128	N.A.	N.A.	$ 566
1941	1,598	N.A.	N.A.	649
1942	2,664	N.A.	N.A.	880
1943	3,166	N.A.	N.A.	1,084
1944	3,365	N.A.	N.A.	1,103
1945	3,375	N.A.	N.A.	1,110
1946	2,434	804	2,762	1,156
1947	2,002	909	2,880	1,184
1948	2,076	963	3,002	1,329
1949	2,047	1,037	3,119	1,406
1950	2,117	1,057	3,228	1,528
1951	2,515	1,070	3,218	1,865
1952	2,583	1,103	3,418	1,980
1953	2,385	1,129	3,533	3,104
1954	2,373	1,198	3,661	2,103
1955	2,378	1,250	3,804	2,265
1956	2,410	1,322	3,953	2,509
1957	2,439	1,358	4,249	2,533
1958	2,405	1,469	4,423	2,977
1959	2,399	1,518	4,570	3,114
1960	2,421	1,592	4,795	3,333
1961	2,484	1,627	4,990	3,634
1962	2,539	1,680	5,169	3,966
1963	2,548	1,775	5,413	4,264

N.A.—Not available.
SOURCE: Department of Commerce; Congress and the Nation, p. 1393.

Table 7.3.   General Expenditure for Civil Functions by All Levels
of Government as Percentage of Gross National Product, Selected
Years, 1902–63

(Money amounts in billions of dollars)

YEAR	GNP	Expenditures as Percentage of GNP		
		FEDERAL	STATE-LOCAL	TOTAL
1902	$ 21.6	1.1	4.7	5.8
1927	96.3	1.5	7.5	9.0
1938	85.2	5.9	10.3	16.2
1948	259.4	3.4	6.8	10.2
1963	583.9	4.0	11.1	15.1

SOURCE: Maxwell, op. cit. Appendix Table A-1, A-3. Intergovernmental payments are
charged to the level of government making final disbursement.

in law the local territorial governments of the United States assume a
huge burden, which in their absence would have to be discharged, somehow, by federal officials. It seems reasonable to conclude that in a country as vast and as complex as the United States, local governments are
necessary simply (if for no other reason) in order to achieve a level of
efficiency in government high enough to make democracy at the national
level tolerable. Without the local governments, democratic institutions
at the national level would probably go under from the sheer weight of
their burdens.

One might nonetheless wonder whether local governments in the
United States operate above some minimum level of tolerability. They
may provide enough efficiency to keep the system stumbling along. But
are they anything like as efficient as they should be?

Unfortunately, dear though it be to advocates of governmental reform, the criterion of efficiency does not take one very far. For if efficiency is measured by the ratio of valued 'inputs' to valued 'outputs,' then
to one who believes strongly in the values of democracy, the efficiency
of state and local governments must be measured in large part by comparing their costs, using the term in a very broad sense indeed, against
their contributions to democracy. We remain then pretty much in the
place from which we started. If efficiency is measured by the ratio between actual output and a theoretically maximum output, how are we
to decide what is a theoretical maximum?

It seems perfectly reasonable to ask how well state and local governments perform the various tasks assigned to them by law. Are they

efficient administrative units in the narrow sense that they economize, cut costs, act with expertness and dispatch? The question seems reasonable, but it is nonetheless almost impossible to answer. One must first ask a counter-question: With what are we to compare them? If we compared state and local governments with some theoretical ideal, it would be easy to show that like every other human institution they fall very far short of ideal achievement. But we know this much in advance. We can scarcely compare state and local governments with private firms, because neither the inputs nor the outputs of state and local governments are sufficiently like those of private enterprise to make comparisons valid. How can we compare the relative efficiency of the New York police in controlling crime and traffic with the efficiency of General Motors in producing and marketing automobiles? There seems to be little possibility of a useful or even a meaningful comparison; even those intrepid spirits who would contend that General Motors is the more efficient of the two organizations would not propose, I imagine, to turn the police force of New York over to General Motors.

Can we compare the administrative efficiency of state and local governments with that of federal agencies? Here again we run into formidable problems because of the differences in outputs—the services performed. In any case, an adverse comparison would be highly misleading if it led one to conclude that the federal government would perform local functions more 'efficiently', in the restricted sense, than the local governments themselves.[8] For we need to know what would happen to the present level of efficiency of federal agencies if the federal government were to take on all the additional tasks now performed at local levels; if, in short, the federal civil service bureaucracy were to triple in numbers, from less than one out of twenty-five persons in the civilian labor force to one out of eight.

Perhaps the only way out of this dilemma is to compare similar local units with one another. Yet, given the enormous variety of local governments, even this is a much more formidable enterprise than it might seem.

Thus, despite its glossy appeal, the criterion of efficiency does not take one very far. For appraising governments, 'efficiency' is a concept either too slippery to be meaningful or too precise to be applicable. However, three observations may nevertheless be permissible. First,

8. From this point forward the term 'local governments' means state and local, except where the context clearly implies the more restricted meaning of a city, town, county, etc. There is no generally accepted word to cover both state and local; local, therefore, will have to do the work of two.

American state and local governments have generally lagged behind the federal government in introducing reforms thought to contribute to administrative efficiency: in the development of a neutral and expert civil service, an executive budget, a single chief executive with substantial hierarchical control over administrative agencies, an adequate specialized staff for the chief executive, and so on. Corruption seems to occur more frequently, and on a bigger scale, in local units than in the federal government. Pay scales are lower, both at the start and at the end of one's career.

Second, there are enormous variations among the different units of local government. By almost any objective test, the best local government would be as efficient as any found in the federal government; the worst are appalling. Between the best and the worst, there is a whole universe of types. No one can ever judge the quality of local government in the United States by his experience with one or two units.

Third, whatever weight one may give to local governments as instruments of democracy (we shall proceed to that matter at once), it is obvious that American democracy would be a very different system without local governments that enjoy a great measure of autonomy.

Conflict: Diversity and De-nationalization

If one cannot speak with much confidence about the efficiency of local governments as administrative units, one can say more about their efficiency as instruments of democracy. To begin with, how does the existence of 38 thousand local territorial governments affect the course and severity of political conflicts?

The contributions of local government are I think, two. Local governments make it possible for different groups of citizens to arrive at different solutions to problems. And they reduce the strain on the national political system by keeping many questions out of the national arena.

It is a great and inescapable defect in any system of rule by majorities that on all questions in which the policy of a minority conflicts with the policy preferred by a majority, neither can prevail without frustrating the desires of the other. In this respect the hypothetical universe of democracy is rather different from the hypothetical universe of a free market; the hypothetical citizen is not equivalent to the hypothetical consumer. In a model 'free' market it does not matter that in my role as consumer I prefer buying books to phonograph records, while you prefer records to books. Within broad legal limits, we may both spend our incomes as we please, and the market will respond. In the market, differences among individuals in tastes and values need not lead to conflict among them.

Why not, then, substitute the market for the government? The most important reason is that there are a great many matters which the mechanisms of the marketplace are ill equipped to handle—including the sovereign question as to what should and what should not be left to the market. If I as a citizen wish to raise taxes and spend more money in order to construct new schools, and if you prefer lower taxes and no new schools, we cannot both get what we want. We cannot, that is, if we are in exactly the same political system. But if you and the people who think like you are in one political system, while I and other like-minded people are in another, we can perhaps both have what we want. In this way we could both be free to go our own different ways; both our governments might enjoy the full consent of all its citizens. Here is the kernel of truth in Rousseau's belief that small autonomous democracies consisting of like-minded citizens offer the greatest promise of freedom and self-government.

Their local governments permit Americans to take or to keep many questions out of the great arena of national politics, and therefore out of a strictly either-or kind of conflict; they make it possible for Americans to deal with many problems in different ways, ways presumably more in harmony with local tastes and values than any national solution could possibly be. To this extent, the presence of a vast network of local governments with a good deal of autonomy has probably reduced by a considerable margin the severity of conflict that a wholly national system would run into. By *de-nationalizing* many conflicts, local governments can reduce the strain on national political institutions. The importance of de-nationalizing conflicts can hardly be over-estimated, particularly in a large country like the United States where there is great diversity in resources and local problems.

Yet the experience of the United States with the question of the role of the Negro in American life also suggests some limits on the process of denationalizing conflicts.[9] For some sixty years after the Constitutional Convention, national conflict over slavery was reduced by

9. *Cf.* Chapter 12, below.

de-nationalizing the conflict. All the famous compromises of the pre-Civil War period were agreements to de-nationalize the question of slavery. Within little more than a decade after the end of the Civil War, the issue of the place of the freed Negro was de-nationalized: for another sixty years or more national conflict on this issue was avoided. When the question of the place of Negroes in American life became nationalized, as it did in the 1850s and again a century later in the 1940s, that question turned into one of the most explosive issues in American politics. In the first case, nationalizing the conflict led directly to civil war; in the second, to violence and federal troops, to Little Rock, Freedom Riders, murders in Mississippi, demonstrations, Selma, and passage of Civil Rights Acts in 1957, 1960, 1964 and 1965.

This experience reveals some of the limits to the process of de-nationalizing conflicts. It is quite one thing to de-nationalize a dispute by allowing various groups of like-minded people to follow their own desires; but it is quite another to take a dispute out of the national arena in order to hand it over to local despots, as we Americans did in the case of the Negro for all except a few decades in our national history.

The case of the Negro is, admittedly, an extreme one, and it is worth keeping that fact in mind. It is an extreme case partly because as both slave and freeman, the Negro lacked allies, at least in substantial numbers, outside the South. Members of a minority who feel oppressed in their localities would ordinarily search for allies in the national political arena, and they would count on their allies to keep the dispute alive in the Congress and in presidential elections—in short, to prevent the conflict from becoming fully de-nationalized. Today, Southern Negroes have no lack of allies outside the South—nor, for that matter, in the South itself; consequently it would be impossible to de-nationalize that conflict today.

In some disputes, then, the parties simply will not allow the issue to be cast out of national politics. This is a second limit to the process of de-nationalizing conflicts. The more interwoven the fabric of society, the less likely it is that different localities will be permitted to go their different ways—at least if these ways are very different from one another. The Kansas-Nebraska Act of 1854 was intended by Senator Douglas to put an end to the rising conflict over whether slavery was to be legal in new states carved out of the Western territories; he hoped to de-nationalize the dispute by letting the settlers in each new state decide the matter for themselves. Yet his bill was no sooner law than the political forces of the North and West began to realign themselves. For, while it had once been possible to de-nationalize the issue of slavery in the Old South, it proved impossible to de-nationalize the question of slavery in the territories. (Cf. Chapter 12)

With these reservations in mind, it is nonetheless true that the existence of local government with a considerable measure of autonomy does permit extensive variations among communities in the way they carry on their activities. There are differences in the variety and range of functions. But perhaps more common are differences in levels of expenditure,[10] in emphasis, in administrative and political styles, in the sorts of people who hold office, and in their attitudes. Educational facilities, public health, unemployment compensation, hospital care, city planning, community redevelopment and dozens of other activities vary enormously in quality and quantity from state to state and even from locality to locality. The differences are mainly a function of the resources available; but not entirely. For example, in 1961, state expenditures for public schools were in rough proportion to state income per capita in twenty-seven states, but markedly high in relation to income in eleven states, and markedly low in ten states.[11] Or, to take another example from the field of education, in New England private schools, colleges, and universities have played a much more significant part than they do in the Middle West, where resources have been poured almost exclusively into public education.

American local governments have, then, permitted an important measure of local variety and heterogeneity. In so doing, doubtless they have reduced the strain on national institutions. People are able to work out many of their problems in their states and localities, finding solutions which would lead to interminable debate and conflict if they were imposed uniformly throughout the United States. Even though the most pressing questions of the day cannot be de-nationalized, the existence of local autonomy helps to free the national arena for precisely these 'national' issues.

10. E.g. in 1961, average payments per recipients under six state welfare programs varied as follows:

U.S. Average	$116.68	$67.85	$73.36	$68.19	$65.13	$33.84
High State	178.57	96.51	126.45	132.90	110.76	42.32
Low State	36.38	35.40	38.43	34.85	12.89	21.24

SOURCE: *Politics in the American States, A Comparative Analysis*, Herbert Jacob and Kenneth N. Vines, eds., Boston, Little, Brown and Company, 1965, Table 4, p. 389.

11. Jacob and Vines, *op. cit.*, p. 354, Table 1.

The Distribution of Power
Among Leaders

Alexis de Tocqueville was deeply concerned with discovering the answer to the question: How, if at all, can liberty and democracy be maintained in a society of equals? Tocqueville was both fascinated and repelled by the Janus-face of equality. An increasing equality was, he thought, not only inevitable in America and Europe; it was also a necessary condition for democracy. At the same time, Tocqueville, like Aristotle, believed that extensive political, economic, and social equalities created a natural political environment for the tyrant. Thus he formulated a dilemma for democrats: A necessary condition for democracy is also a condition that facilitates despotism. The whole of the two-volume *Democracy in America* can be read as an exploration of the circumstances in which tyranny might be avoided and liberal democracy preserved in a society of equals.

The problem, as Tocqueville saw it, was this: In a society of equals, there are no intermediate institutions or classes with enough power to prevent the rise of a despot. Having eliminated aristocracy, a society of equals needs institutions to perform the political function that Tocqueville attributed, perhaps, over-generously, to a well established aristocracy —some force to stand in the way of the aspiring despot. In a nation of equals, no individual is strong enough to stop the despot; and citizens are incapable of acting as a body except through leaders. Even should citizens want to oppose the despot (Tocqueville thought that they probably would not), in the absence of an intermediate stratum of leaders they would be impotent. It was a haunting and evocative picture that Tocqueville painted of that peculiar tyranny in which democracy might one day culminate, the tyranny of an equal people united under a popular leader, the special tyranny that was appropriate to democracy because it would thrive on the very equality so indispensable to democracy.

> I think, then, that the species of oppression by which democratic nations are menaced is unlike anything that ever before existed in the world; our contemporaries will find no prototype of it in their memories. I seek in vain for an expression that will accurately convey the whole of the idea I have formed of it; the old words despotism and tyranny are inappropriate: the thing itself is new, and since I cannot name, I must attempt to define it.

I seek to trace the novel features under which despotism may appear in the world. The first thing that strikes the observation is an innumerable multitude of men, all equal and alike, incessantly endeavoring to procure the petty and paltry pleasures with which they glut their lives. Each of them, living apart, is as a stranger to the fate of all the rest; his children and his private friends constitute to him the whole of mankind. As for the rest of his fellow citizens, he is close to them, but does not see them; he touches them, but does not feel them; he exists only in himself and for himself alone; and if his kindred still remain to him, he may be said at any rate to have lost his country.

Above this race of men stands an immense and tutelary power, which takes upon itself alone to secure their gratifications and to watch over their fate. That power is absolute, minute, regular, provident, and mild. It would be like the authority of a parent if, like that authority, its object was to prepare men for manhood; but it seeks, on the contrary, to keep them in perpetual childhood: it is well content that the people should rejoice, provided they think of nothing but rejoicing. For their happiness such a government willingly labors, but it chooses to be the sole agent and the only arbiter of that happiness; it provides for their security, foresees and supplies their necessities, facilitates their pleasures, manages their principal concerns, directs their industry, regulates the descent of property, and subdivides their inheritances: what remains, but to spare them all the care of thinking and all the trouble of living?

Thus it every day renders the exercise of the free agency of man less useful and less frequent; it circumscribes the will within a narrower range and gradually robs a man of all these uses of himself. The principle of equality has prepared men for these things; it has predisposed men to endure them and often to look on them as benefits.

After having thus successively taken each member of the community in its powerful grasp and fashioned him at will, the supreme power then extends its arm over the whole community. It covers the surface of society with a network of small complicated rules, minute and uniform, through which the most original minds and the most energetic characters cannot penetrate, to rise above the crowd. The will of man is not shattered, but softened, bent, and guided; men are seldom forced by it to act, but they are constantly restrained from acting. Such a power does not destroy, but it prevents existence; it does not tyrannize, but it compresses, enervates, extinguishes, and *stupefies a people, till each nation is reduced to nothing better than a flock of timid and industrious animals, of which the government is the shepherd.*[12]

In spite of his melancholic vision of the possible fate of democratic societies, Tocqueville was hopeful about the United States—precisely because Americans had not destroyed the intermediate institutions, the democratic alternatives to aristocracy. Indeed, Americans had not only conserved and strengthened certain old institutions; they had even created some new ones. In the power, autonomy, and self-consciousness of the legal profession, in the freedom of the press, in a variety of private associations, political and non-political, Americans had, he thought, developed their substitutes for the political functions of an aristocracy as an offset to tyranny. Constitutional arrangements themselves had added even more barriers to halt the eager tyrant. Among these constitutionally created barriers were, naturally, the federal system and the tradition of local self-government.

Looking back from our present perspective, what can we say to Tocqueville's judgment? Do state and local governments help to tame our political leaders?

The first and most obvious contribution of local representative institutions is to provide a training ground in which political leaders learn the political arts required in a democratic republic. In Almond's terminology, local institutions carry on the functions of political socialization and recruitment.[13] The enormous number and variety of governments in the United States, many of them with elective offices and many involved in some way with party or factional politics, provide a vast school of politics that turns out a sizeable stratum of sub-leaders with at least modest political skills. Many of the leaders who go into national politics are drawn from this pool of leaders trained in local and state politics; it is this pool, too, that often furnishes the local leaders in moments of emergency—when, for example a possible unjust local regulation threatens to become a reality and citizens feel the need to act.[14]

12. Alexis de Tocqueville, *Democracy in America*, Vol. 2, New York, Vintage Books, 1955, pp. 336–337.
13. Gabriel A. Almond, "A Functional Approach to Competitive Politics," in Almond and Coleman, *The Politics of the Developing Areas*, Princeton University Press, Princeton, New Jersey, 1960.
14. For example, see William K. Muir, Jr., *Defending "The Hill" Against Metal Houses*, ICP case series, No. 26, University of Alabama Press, University of Alabama, 1955, and Dahl, *Who Governs? op. cit.*, pp. 192 *et seq.*

Table 7.4.   U.S. Presidents, 1900–1964: Previous Elective Offices

	STATE LEGISLATURE	GOVERNOR	U.S. CONGRESS HOUSE	SENATE	VICE PRESIDENT
McKinley		*	*		
T. Roosevelt	*	*			
Taft					*
Wilson		*			
Harding	*			*	
Coolidge	*	*			*
Hoover					
F. D. Roosevelt	*	*			
Truman				*	*
Eisenhower					
Kennedy			*	*	
Johnson			*	*	*

Table 7.5.   Experience of Congressional Leaders in State and Local Government

OFFICES HELD	CONGRESSIONAL LEADERS 1903	1963	ADMINISTRATION LEADERS 1903	1963
Any state or local office	75%	64%	49%	17%
Elective local office	55	46	22	5
State legislature	47	30	17	3
Appointive state office	12	10	20	7
Governor	16	9	5	4

SOURCE: Samuel P. Huntington, "Congressional Responses to the Twentieth Century," p. 14, in David B. Truman, ed., The Congress and America's Future, Englewood Cliffs, Prentice Hall, 1965.

Table 7.6.   Roads to the Senate—Last Previous Office Held by Senators with Prior Experience in Office, 1947 through 1957 (Excludes Party Office and Unsuccessful Campaigns)

LAST PREVIOUS OFFICE HELD	PERCENTAGE OF SENATORS
State Governor	22%
U.S. Representative	28
State Legislator	10
Statewide Elective Office	2
Local Elective Office	6
Law-Enforcement Office	15
Administrative Office	17
Congressional Staff	1

Adapted from Donald R. Matthews, U. S. Senators and Their World, Chapel Hill, University of North Carolina Press, 1960, p. 50.
SOURCE: H. Douglas Price, "The Electoral Arena," p. 41 in Truman, op. cit.

Thus, of the twelve men elected President in this century, all except three—Taft, Hoover, and Eisenhower—had previously held elective political office. Of the nine with experience in an elective office, six had held office as governor or member of the state legislature (Table 7.4). A large proportion of congressional leaders have also held a state office of some kind, usually an elective office (Table 7.5).

Just as being Senator or Governor is the best public position from which to win the Presidency, so, too, the Senate itself recruits a large share of its membership from the House and from state or local offices (Table 7.6).

Most state governors first learn their craft in state and local politics. Out of almost one thousand governors elected in the United States from 1870–1950, slightly over half had previously been in the state legislature, a fifth had held local elective office, and nearly a fifth had held some statewide elective office.[15]

The state and local governments also help to provide a secure base to which opposition may retire when it has suffered defeat elsewhere, in order to sally forth and challenge their opponents at the next election. If the two major parties are highly competitive at the national level, perhaps the weaker competition and even the numerous local party monopolies are the price to be paid. In the thirty-six-year period from Mc-Kinley's election in 1896 to Franklin Roosevelt's election in 1932, the Democratic party enjoyed only eight years in the White House; it had a majority in the Senate during only six years. Yet, thanks to their secure fortress in the South and their bastions in northern cities like New York, Boston, and Chicago, they remained a formidable party at every election and were able to organize the national campaign in 1932 that brought Roosevelt into office for the first of his four terms. The Republicans recovered from the devastation of Roosevelt's famous landslide in 1936 because their state and local party strongholds were never completely over-run. By 1938 they were, in coalition with Southern Democrats, powerful enough to bring further New Deal reforms to a halt. Within individual states the situation is often much the same: The party or faction that controls the state house encounters its toughest opposition in the big cities.

Finally, the state and local governments have helped to maintain the American pattern of pluralistic power. Political power is pluralistic in the sense that there exist many different sets of leaders; each set has

15. Joseph A. Schlesinger, *How They Became Governor*, East Lansing, Governmental Research Bureau, 1957, p. 11. See also his *Ambition and Politics: Political Careers in the United States*, Chicago, Rand McNally, 1966.

somewhat different objectives from the others, each has access to its own political resources, each is relatively independent of the others. There does not exist a single set of all-powerful leaders who are wholly agreed on their major goals and who have enough power to achieve their major goals. Ordinarily, the making of government policies requires a coalition of different sets of leaders who have diverging goals. In this situation, it is probably easier for leaders to be effective in a negative way, by blocking other leaders, than in a positive way, by achieving their own goals. Positive leadership generally requires action by the chief executive, the President, governor, or mayor; it is the chief executive who can give impetus and drive to the system, who is the coalition builder and the central coordinator.

The state and local governments have undoubtedly contributed to this pattern, though it is not easy to distinguish the special effects of federalism and local representative institutions. State and local governments have provided a number of centers of power whose autonomy is strongly protected by constitutional and political traditions. A governor of a state or the mayor of a large city may not be the political equal of a President (at least not often); but he is most assuredly not a subordinate. In dealing with a governor or a mayor, a President rarely if ever commands; he negotiates; he may even plead. Here, then, is a part of the intermediate stratum of leadership that Tocqueville looked to as a barrier to tyranny.

The state and local governments have contributed something further to the pluralistic pattern of power. They have increased the options available to citizens. Citizens who find one group of leaders unsympathetic to their wishes can often turn to another group that influences a different level or sector of government. Thus a group that finds its needs ignored at the local level may turn to the state or to the federal government; the system also works the other way round. In its earlier years, for example, the American labor movement, often blocked in its efforts to win national legislation, turned to state governments to lead the way in the regulations of the working day, workmen's compensation, employment of women and children, and unemployment compensation. In recent decades, it has more often concentrated its efforts for positive gains on the national government, where it is assured of more sympathetic attention than in many of the states.[16] At the state level, the labor movement has grown more concerned with occasional negative actions— such as blocking laws limiting the right to strike.

It is permissible, certainly, to argue over the merits of this pluralistic

16.   *Cf.* Chapter 16, below.

distribution of power. It makes for a politics that depends more upon bargaining than upon hierarchy; that resolves conflicts more by negotiation and compromise than by unilateral decision; that brings about reform more through mutual adjustment and a gradual accumulation of incremental changes than through sweeping programs of comprehensive and coordinated reconstruction. As in other political systems, leaders seek to accumulate power. But the system rarely yields unchecked power to leaders, and rarely leaves any group of citizens powerless. To this extent, the accent of the system is not so much on power as on consent.

Self-Government: The Darker Side

How much do the state and local governments contribute to democracy by enlarging the area of self-government? In particular, to what extent do local elections help citizens to participate in local decisions and to elect leaders responsive to their wishes?

As with the criterion of efficiency, the problem posed by these questions is to find a suitable yardstick with which we can compare local governments.

There can be no question that local governments fall very far short of ideal democracy. But perhaps a more useful comparison is with the national government, since both sets of governments exist within the same general political culture and society. In two respects, local politics in the United States seem to operate at lower levels of performance than national politics. In the first place, party competition is weaker at local levels than at the national level. The frequency of two-party competition, in fact, is roughly correlated with the size of the political unit: it declines from the national arena to statewide contests for U.S. Senator, governor and other statewide elective offices, and declines again from statewide elections to contests in smaller units—congressional districts, cities, and towns. Though we do not have the data one would need to confirm the hunch, there is every reason to suppose that two-party competition is rarest of all in the smallest units: wards, councilmanic districts, state legislative districts, and the like. To overstate the point: Effective contests for office and votes in a larger area do not result from effective electoral contests between the parties in the smaller areas; they are produced by parties that are highly unequal in strength in the smaller units. The smaller the area, evidently, the more difficult it is for oppositions to challenge incumbents by presenting a rival slate at elections.

The principle that the smaller the area the less the chances of two-party competition is quite evident from the data. Nationally, the Democratic and Republican parties are highly competitive. The Presidency is contested vigorously in great nationwide campaigns; the outcome is always to some extent in doubt; over the years the Presidency shifts back and forth from one party to the other. The Congress, too, is the site of considerable party competition. Neither party can take for granted that it will control either the Presidency or the Congress after the next election.

In many states, though by no means all, party competition is a good deal weaker than it is in the national arena. For example, between 1914 and 1954, in six states of the Old South the Republicans did not win a single election for governor, United States Senator, or presidential electors. During the same period, the Democrats won no elections in the northern state of Vermont. In five more southern states and one northern state (Maine), the second party did not win more than one election out of every ten. In another nine states, the second party won fewer than one election out of four.[17]

Using elections for governor and for the members of each house of the legislature from 1946 to 1963, Austin Ranney classified the party systems of the fifty states by averaging:

> four basic figures: (1) the average per cent of the popular vote won by Democratic gubernatorial candidates; (2) the average per cent of the seats in the state senate held by the Democrats; (3) the average per cent of the seats in the state house of representatives held by the Democrats; and (4) the per cent of all terms for governor, senate, and house in which the Democrats had control.

His classification of the fifty states was as follows:
One-party Democratic (.90 or higher): 8 states.
Modified one-party Democratic (.70 to .8999): 9 states.
Two party (.30 to .6999): 25 states.
Modified one-party Republican (.10 to .2999): 8 states.
One-party Republican (less than .10): no states.[18]

17. The data are from Democracy and the American Party System, Austin Ranney and Willmoore Kendall, New York, 1956). Tables 2, 3, and 4, pp. 162–164. Ranney and Kendall classified 26 states as two-party systems, 10 as one-party states, and 12 as modified one-party states. Another classification will be found in Joseph A. Schlesinger, "A Two-Dimensional Scheme for Classifying the States According to Degree of Inter-Party Competition," American Political Science Review, Vol. 49 (1955) pp. 110–128.
18. "Parties in State Politics," in Jacob and Vines, op. cit., pp. 64–65.

FIGURE 7.4—PARTY COMPETITION: DEMOCRATIC PERCENTAGE
OF 1960 VOTE FOR PRESIDENT, BY STATES AND BY
CONGRESSIONAL DISTRICTS

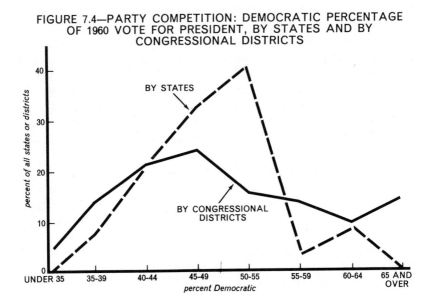

Not only is competition greater in the national arena than in state-wide contests; it is also greater in state-wide elections than in smaller units. Thus in the presidential election of 1960, the Democratic percentage of the vote for President was between 45-55 per cent in two out of three states but in only about one out of three congressional districts (Figure 7.4). Similarly, elections for U.S. Senator are more closely contested than elections for the House of Representatives (Figure 7.5).

In the towns, cities, counties, and state legislative districts, party competition is probably even weaker. Unfortunately, we lack good data with which to test this conjecture. But we do know that in a very high proportion of American cities elections are required by law to be nonpartisan:[19] The name of a political party cannot appear on the ballot. In two states, Minnesota and Nebraska, elections to the state legislature are

19.   In 1960, among three hundred and nine American cities with populations in excess of fifty thousand, 68 per cent used the nonpartisan ballot. Raymond E. Wolfinger and James Osgood Field, "Political Ethos and the Structure of City Government," *American Political Science Review*, 60 (June, 1966) 306–326, Table 5.

20.   Fred I. Greenstein, *The American Party System and the American People*, *op. cit.*, p. 56.

Table 7.7. *U.S. Regions Ranked by Proportion of Nonpartisan Cities, 1960*

REGION	NUMBER OF CITIES 25,000 AND OVER	PERCENTAGE NONPARTISAN
Plains	49	98.0
West	68	95.6
Mountain	12	83.3
South	96	75.0
Border	34	73.5
New England	71	62.0
Great Lakes	101	54.5
Middle Atlantic	97	23.7

SOURCE: Edward C. Banfield and James Q. Wilson, *City Politics*, Cambridge, Harvard University Press and the M.I.T. Press, 1963, p. 155. Calculated from the *Municipal Yearbook*, 1960.

legally non-partisan.[20] In some regions of the country, practically every city over twenty-five thousand requires non-partisan elections for local offices (Table 7.7). Even in cities where elections are formally and actually contested by both parties, the second party is often weak and rarely if ever wins the mayor's office or a majority of councilmen.

FIGURE 7.5—PARTY COMPETITION IN THE EIGHT MOST POPULOUS STATES: PERCENTAGE DEMOCRATIC FOR HOUSE CANDIDATES IN 1962 AND FOR ALL SENATE CANDIDATES, 1958-62 (INCLUDES NEW YORK, CALIFORNIA, PENNSYLVANIA, ILLINOIS, OHIO, TEXAS, MICHIGAN, AND NEW JERSEY)

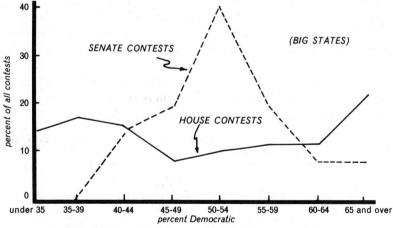

SOURCE: H. D. Price, The Congress and America's Future, — p. 44, Fig. 2.

All this does not mean, of course, that in these states and cities there is no active competition for public office. There is. Where the second party is weak, competition takes place *within* the dominant party. Yet even when intra-party conflict is sharp, it must necessarily occur not between highly organized parties but between individuals or loose factions. To be sure, in some one-party states, as in Louisiana over an extended period, two rival factions within the same party may perform many of the functions of political parties.[21] In general, however, the absence of sharp competition for office by organized political parties seems to accentuate the significance of personal qualities and to diminish emphasis on policies.[22]

If local governments fall somewhat short of the national government in the extent to which two or more organized parties compete vigorously to win elections and gain control over the policy-making machinery of government, they also seem to evoke less participation by citizens than the national government. In this respect, the local governments have disappointed the hopes of democratic ideologues like Jefferson who believed that the true centers of American democracy would be the local governments, which would attend to the problems of daily life of most interest and importance to the citizen, and, lying within easy reach, would be his most responsive and responsible instruments of self-government.

So far as one can judge from available data, citizens are less active in state and local elections than in national elections. Although the evidence is by no means all one-sided, one fact is clear: Presidential elections attract a larger number of voters (and probably much more attention) than most elections to state and local offices. Thus in the eighteen largest cities in the period 1948–1952, the vote in mayoralty elections ran from 10 to 30 per cent behind the vote in presidential elections (Table 7.8).

However, since all contests, including those for the House and Senate in midterm elections, fare badly in comparison with the presidential contest, it may be that participation in state and local elections is

21. Allan P. Sindler, "Bifactional Rivalry as an Alternative to Two-Party Competition in Louisiana," *American Political Science Review*, Vol. 49 (1955) pp. 641–62, and *Huey Long's Louisiana*, Baltimore, Johns Hopkins Press, 1956.

22. *Ibid.*; See also V. O. Key, Jr., *Southern Politics*, New York, Knopf, 1949. Charles R. Adrian, "Some General Characteristics of Nonpartisan Elections," *American Political Science Review*, Vol. 46 (1952) pp. 766–76; a revised version taking more recent data into account is found in Oliver P. Williams and Charles Press, *Democracy in Urban America*, Chicago, Rand McNally, 1961, pp. 251–63.

Table 7.8.   Average turnout in mayoralty and Presidential elections in large cities, 1948–1952

CITY	MAYORALTY	PRESI-DENTIAL	CITY	MAYORALTY	PRESI-DENTIAL
Chicago	51.5%	71.3%	New Orleans	40.5%	38.6%
Pittsburgh	50.5	61.3	Minneapolis	37.0	63.8
Philadelphia	49.8	63.5	Denver	36.7	66.1
Buffalo	49.1	64.2	Cleveland	34.8	53.0
Cincinnati	49.0	61.2	Detroit	33.8	58.0
Boston	47.0	62.6	Baltimore	31.5	46.2
San Francisco	46.3	60.6	Los Angeles	31.3	58.7
New York	42.3	57.7	St. Louis	30.4	59.2
Indianapolis	41.4	63.1	Kansas City	29.9	59.2

Note: Turnout is here measured as the percentage of all persons of 21 years of age or over who vote in general elections. The figure for the Presidential elections is the average of the 1948 and 1952 turnouts; that for the mayoralty elections is an average of the same period.

SOURCE: Banfield and Wilson, op. cit., Table 13, p. 225 from data furnished by Charles E. Gilbert.

————•◆•————

about as high as in off-year congressional elections.[23]

It is sometimes thought that participation in local governments was much higher in the good old days; that lower participation is entirely a modern phenomenon, resulting from the increased importance of national affairs. But such scattered evidence as we have does not seem to sustain this belief in a golden age of local democracy. For example, data on voting in New Haven, Connecticut, from 1820 to the present show conclusively that the proportion of citizens who have voted in elections for mayor has always been less than those who have voted in presidential contests (Figure 7.6).

It is difficult to say how common this pattern was in the nineteenth century. Turnout in state and national elections in the first half of the nineteenth century showed considerable variation from state to state. In Connecticut, turnout was invariably higher for national than for state elections; yet in the neighboring New England states, gubernatorial

23.   In the eighteen cities shown in Table 7.8, the median turnout for mayoralty elections was about 41 per cent of all persons of twenty-one years of age or over. In elections to the U.S. House of Representatives in 1950, when there was no presidential contest, the turnout was 41.6 per cent of the civilian population of voting age. Lester W. Milbrath, "Political Participation in the States," Table 2, p. 36, in Jacob and Vines, op. cit. Milbrath also states that "Turnout in state elections is closely comparable to turnout in Representative elections. If the state or Representative election occurs in a non-Presidential year, the turnout is likely to be significantly lower." (p. 37).

FIGURE 7.6—NEW HAVEN, CONN: PERCENTAGE OF CITIZENS
21 YEARS OLD AND OVER VOTING IN PRESIDENTIAL AND
MAYORALTY ELECTIONS, 1860-1950

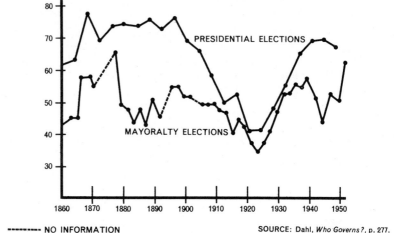

-------- NO INFORMATION   SOURCE: Dahl, *Who Governs?*, p. 277.

elections produced the higher turnout. New York and New Jersey were
like Connecticut; in Virginia, as elsewhere in the Old South, turnout was
higher in state elections than in national elections.[24]

Thus the evidence points to several conclusions, mainly negative. It
is not true, as an enthusiastic follower of Rousseau or Jefferson might
hold, that the smaller a political unit is, the more its citizens will participate in political affairs. To the extent that voting is a fair measure of
participation, the Rousseau-Jefferson hypothesis is definitely not true
today. Although there was probably greater variation in patterns of
electoral participation in the first part of the nineteenth century than
there is today, the Rousseau-Jefferson hypothesis was not confirmed by
experience even then. Nor is it true that participation in state and local
elections has fallen off as these units have grown in size and as the role of
the national government has expanded.

In short, local territorial governments in the United States are not,
and evidently never have been, distinctive sites for high levels of civic
participation.

24. Cf. Richard P. McCormick, *The Second American Party System, Party
     Formation in the Jacksonian Era*, Chapel Hill, the University of North
     Carolina Press, 1966, pp. 99, 123, 133, 186, 248, and *passim*.

The Case for Self-Government

There is no blinking the fact that local democracy—like national democracy—is highly defective. Yet, to right the balance, one needs to consider what democracy would be like in the United States if represent-ative governments did not exist in the states and localities. While one might argue persuasively that the best alternative to what we have now is more self-government, it would be hard to make a good case that, from a democratic point of view, we would be better off with less.

It may be worth asking, then, how the local governments in the United States compare with the national government as institutions of self-government. Are they markedly worse?

Although a precise answer is impossible, the evidence does support three propositions:

First, citizens seem to be about as concerned with local affairs as with national and international affairs.

Second, except by comparison with voting in presidential elections, citizens participate as much in local as in national politics, if not more.

Third, they probably have greater confidence in their capacity to act effectively at local levels.

CONCERN. It is possible that the state governments may fall into a kind of limbo, being neither so close to the citizen as the government of his town or city nor so conspicuously important as the national govern-ment; but there is some persuasive evidence that Americans are con-cerned with local affairs. Many of the problems that people regard as urgent and important require action by local governments: education, crime, poverty, racial discrimination, housing, parking, streets and high-ways, to name a few. In a survey conducted in 1956 in the Detroit area, "which is fairly typical of metropolitan publics . . . 19 per cent said they were very interested in foreign affairs, 32 per cent in national domestic affairs, and 44 per cent in local governmental affairs."[25]

In a survey of registered voters in New Haven, Connecticut in 1959, more people seemed to talk about, worry about, and be concerned with local affairs than with state, national or international affairs (Table 7.9).

In a national survey in the 1950s, the percentage of Americans who

25. Samuel J. Eldersveld, *Political Parties, A Behavioral Analysis*, Chicago, Rand McNally, 1964, p. 458.

Table 7.9. Interest in Local Affairs, New Haven, 1959

	TALK ABOUT	WORRY ABOUT	CONCERNED WITH
Personal matters	38%	53%	64%
Local affairs	30	19	12
State, national or international affairs	12	11	10
Other	9	3	3
Don't know, no answer	11	14	11
Totals	100%	100%	100%
	(525)	(525)	(525)

The questions were: "In your opinion what kinds of things do people around here talk about the most?"

"As nearly as you can tell what kinds of things do people around here worry about the most?"

"What about you—what things are you most concerned with these days?"

SOURCE: Unpublished data from a survey of 525 registered voters, New Haven, 1959.

felt that the local governments had some effect or great effect on their day-to-day lives was actually a shade larger than the percentage who felt this way about the national government. As one might expect, more people thought the national government had great effect; but more also thought that local government had some effect (Table 7.10). Similarly the percentage who felt that on the whole the activities of local government "tend to improve conditions in this area" was quite high, though a trifle short of the percentage who felt the same way about the activities of national government (Table 7.11).

PARTICIPATION: The relatively lower turnout in local elections than in presidential elections does not prove that Americans are less involved in local affairs. For one thing, the presidential contest is sui

Table 7.10. Estimated Degree of Impact of National and Local Governments on Daily Life

	NATIONAL GOVERNMENT	LOCAL GOVERNMENTS
Great effect	41%	35%
Some effect	44	53
No effect	11	10
Other, don't know, etc.	4	2
	100%	100%
Total number of cases	970	970

SOURCE: Almond and Verba, op. cit., pp. 80-81.

Table 7.11. "On the whole, do the activities of the national (local) government tend to improve conditions in this area, or would we be better off without them?"

	NATIONAL GOVERNMENT	LOCAL GOVERNMENT
Yes, tend to improve	74%	69%
Sometimes improve, sometimes not	18	23
Better off without them	3	4
Other, don't know, etc.	5	4
	100%	100%
Total number of cases	970	970

SOURCE: Almond and Verba survey, unpublished data.

generis. As I have already suggested, the turnout in elections for mayors and governors may be no lower than for U.S. Senators and Congressmen in midterm elections. In the second place, even if voters were as involved in local affairs as in national affairs, the lower frequency of sharp two-party competition would probably reduce the turnout at elections, partly because the contest itself would be less exciting, partly because the parties would work less vigorously to get out the vote. In elections for governor and U.S. Senator, for example, the turnout from 1956–1960 was considerably higher in the two-party states than in the modified one-party Democratic states; in the modified one-party Democratic states it was more than twice as high as in the one-party Democratic states.[26] In the third place, voting is only one form of participation; some of the other ways of participating in politics are more easily carried on at the local than at the national level: getting in touch with one's councilman about a torn-up street is a good deal easier than getting in touch with one's Congressman or Senator, or the President about the war in Vietnam.

CITIZEN EFFECTIVENESS.   Evidence does suggest that Americans look on their local governments as more accessible, more manageable, more responsive. In an exhaustive study of the political attitudes of fifteen lower-middle-class citizens in an Eastern city, Robert Lane found:

> . . . The fact is that these men were pretty discouraged by the idea of doing something about any big problem . . . Eastport's common men find themselves politically impotent on most

26. Ranney, "Parties in State Politics," op. cit., Table 3, p. 75. One anomaly is that in the modified one-party Republican states, turnout was only slightly lower than in the two-party states.

important specific issues, do not petition or write letters with any frequency, are dubious of the wisdom of the electorate on these issues, see elections as only partially successful instruments for imparting instructions to candidates, find themselves often confused by the complexity of public affairs, and tend to think of elected officials as better judges of policy than they themselves are.

Yet far from being alienated, most of these fifteen men felt that they were politically important. How, Lane asks,

. . . do they come to have this sense of political importance? One reason is that many of them have political connections and for local matters they have influence, can get close to somebody who may pretend to more authority than he has but who conveys to his circle of acquaintances the sense that they are in communication with important people when they speak to him.[27]

There are also other reasons, of course; but this sense of accessibility and responsiveness may be an important one. The national survey taken in the 1950s, mentioned a moment ago, tends to confirm the hunch that the closeness, accessibility, and comprehensibility of local government enhances the confidence of citizens that they can *do something* about local affairs. Almost two out of three respondents agreed and only a third disagreed with the statement that "politics and government are so complicated that the average man cannot really understand what is going on." Yet the number who said that they understood "local issues in this town or part of the country" very well was three times as large as the number who said they understood "the important national and international issues facing the country" very well. In fact, over half the respondents said that they did not understand national and international issues at all or not so well, compared with only a third who felt this way about local issues (Table 7.12).

Nor is it only a matter of being able to grasp local issues better; citizens also seem to think that they can act more effectively at the local level. To be sure, not many ever do act at either local or national levels. In fact, seven out of ten respondents in the survey just cited said they had never tried to influence a local decision, while eight out of ten said they had never tried to influence the Congress. Yet many were confident

27. Robert Lane, *Political Ideology*, op. cit., p. 165.

Table 7.12. *The Sense of Understanding of Issues*

	NATIONAL AND INTERNATIONAL	LOCAL ISSUES
Very well	7%	21%
Moderately well	38	44
Not so well	37	23
Not at all	14	10
Depends, other, don't know, etc.	4	2
	100%	100%
Total number of cases	970	970

SOURCE: Almond and Verba survey, unpublished data.

that, if the need arose, they would act and might even be successful. What did they think they could do, they were asked, if a law or regulation which they considered "very unjust or harmful" were being considered by the local government or by Congress? The number who said that it was very likely or moderately likely that they would do something about the law or regulation was slightly larger in the case of a local law (49 per cent) than for a national law (42 per cent). The number who said that it was not at all likely that they would do something about an unjust law or regulation was a little less for local laws (27 per cent) than for national laws (33 per cent). The percentages who expected that they could be successful in their efforts were somewhat higher in the case of the local law (Table 7.13).

Even if local governments fall a long way short of potential and ideal, they do provide channels through which citizens may express their views on local matters when they have an urge to do so. In the 1959 survey in New Haven, mentioned earlier, a sample of registered voters was asked: "Have you ever contacted any local public officials or politi-

Table 7.13. *If you made an effort to change a proposed law or regulation you considered very unjust or harmful, how likely is it that you would succeed?*

	LOCAL REGULATION	NATIONAL LAW
Very likely or moderately likely	28%	11%
Somewhat unlikely	15	18
Not at all likely, impossible	25	36
Likely only if others joined in	25	24
Other, don't know	6	9
	100%	100%
Total cases	970	970

SOURCE: Almond and Verba survey, unpublished data.

cians to let them know what you were interested in?" More than one out of every four registered voters said they had. Sixteen per cent said they had had some contact with political or governmental officials in New Haven in the past year. In fact, 8 per cent said they had been in touch with the Mayor at some time and 11 per cent with some other city official. Admittedly, these are not the high percentages one might hope for in a democratic polity, but to the extent that local channels do exist and are used by citizens, the domain of self government is enlarged.

8

THE POLITICAL PARTIES: ORIGINS AND CHARACTERISTICS

T HE PRESENCE OR ABSENCE of competing political parties can be used as a litmus paper test for the presence or absence of democracy in a country. No full-fledged modern democracy lacks parties that compete for votes and offices in national elections; no full-fledged dictatorship permits such competiton. The test is not infallible. Yet it is difficult to see how a democracy could operate at the national level without at least two parties, or why a dictator would permit a genuine opposition party to challenge him in free elections.

Yet it seems quite safe to say that of all the institutions of modern democracy, none was so badly understood, so poorly foreseen, or, paradoxically, so dreaded in the late eighteenth century as the emergence of organized, institutionalized, permanent political parties regularly competing with one another in national elections and continuing their antagonistic confrontation even between elections.

Nothing—not the uncertainty, nor the lack of foresight, nor the dread—about parties should be surprising. For, as late as the time of the Constitutional Convention, although political parties existed in embryo, they were very far from being developed, anywhere in the world, into mature organizations as we know them today. As for factions, were not their evils well-known? "In examining the history of nations, we discover examples of the pernicious tendency of faction," a New York jurist wrote in 1794. To prove his point he conjured up "the mortal conflict which existed between the houses of York and Lancaster," the disputes in France between Catholics and Huguenots, the fall of Athens and the decline of the Roman Republic.[1]

He had a point. Even as late as the end of the eighteenth century, it took extraordinary vision not to see political parties as destructive.

Factions: The Bane of Republics[2]

Of the three great milestones in the development of democratic institutions—the right to participate in governmental decisions by casting a vote, a system of representation, and the right of an organized opposition to appeal for votes against the government in elections and in parliament —the last is, in a highly developed form, so wholly modern that there are people now living who were born before it had appeared in most of Western Europe.

Throughout recorded history, it seems, stable institutions providing legal, orderly, peaceful modes of political opposition have been rare. If peaceful antagonism between factions is uncommon, peaceful competition among organized, permanent political parties is an even more exotic historical phenomenon. Legal party opposition is, in fact, a recent unplanned invention that has been confined for the most part to a handful of countries. Even more recent are organized political parties that compete peacefully in elections for the votes of the great bulk of the adult population able to exercise the franchise under nearly universal suffrage. Universal suffrage and enduring mass parties are, with few exceptions, products of the twentieth century; a hundred years ago they did not exist outside the United States.

Because some conflict of views seems to be unavoidable in human affairs, political societies have always had to deal somehow with the fact of opposition. Nevertheless, that there might legitimately exist an organized group within the political system to oppose, criticize, and if possible

1. William Wyche, "Party Spirit," in Noble E. Cunningham, Jr., ed., *The Making of the American Party System 1789 to 1809*, Englewood Cliffs, N.J., Prentice Hall, 1965, p. 13.
2. The first part of this section is adapted from my preface to *Political Oppositions in Western Democracies*, New Haven, Yale University Press, 1966.

oust the leading officials of government was until recently an unfamiliar and generally unacceptable notion. When the men at the American Constitutional Convention of 1787 expressed their fear of "factions" as the bane of republics, they spoke the traditional view. The most long-lived republic in history, the aristocratic republic of Venice, explicitly forbade the formation of enduring political organizations. Venice, like Rome before it, sought to provide in her constitution sufficient checks and balances among officials to prevent arbitrary decisions and to insure a large measure of consensus for the laws; thus organized opposition was seen as unnecessary and a danger to the stability of the Republic.[3] Not all the pre-modern democracies and republics went quite so far as Venice. Factions, coalitions, and alliances of one kind or another existed in and outside of the popular assemblies of Athens,[4] and in the late Roman Republic political alliances sought votes both for candidates and for laws in various popular assemblies. But evidently these groups were never highly organized, had no permanent structure, and even lacked definite names.[5] Moreover, like the Guelphs and the Ghibellines of medieval Italy or the Piagnoni and the Arrabbiati of Savanarola's Florence, factions typically settled their differences sooner or later, as they had come to do during the last century of the Roman Republic, by bloodshed.

3. All the more so because the aristocracy was acutely aware, particularly after the strife of the thirteenth century, that a split within the aristocracy would endanger its exclusive control over the constitutional machinery of the republic. For a thoroughgoing description of this constitution and the preoccupation of the aristocracy with the prevention of internal conflict see Giuseppe Maranini, *La Costituzione di Venezia*, Venice, La Nuova Italia Editrice, Vol. 1, *Dalle Origini alla Serrata del Maggior Consiglio* (1927), and Vol. 2, *Dopo La Serrata del Maggior Consiglio* (1931), particularly Vol. 1, pp. 168-171; the description of the highly complex method for electing the doge at pp. 187–190; and 324–350; also Vol. 2, pp. 99, 115–122.

4. "There were no parties in anything like the modern sense, either among the politicians or the general public. At the one end of the scale there were groups or cliques among the politicians. But such alliances were probably based on personalities rather than principles, and seem to have been temporary." A. H. M. Jones, *Athenian Democracy*, Oxford, Basil Blackwell, 1957, pp. 130–131. Jones concludes, however, "that Athenian policy was really determined by mass meetings of the citizens on the advice of anyone who could win the people's ear" (p. 132). See also Fustel de Coulanges, *The Ancient City*, Garden City, N.Y., Doubleday Anchor Books, n.d., pp. 340 ff.

5. Lily Ross Taylor, *Party Politics in the Age of Caesar*, University of California, Berkeley and Los Angeles, 1961. Also F. E. Adcock, *Roman Political Ideas and Practise*, Ann Arbor, University of Michigan, 1959, pp. 60–62.

The system of managing the major political conflicts of a society by allowing one or more opposition parties to compete with the governing parties for votes in elections and in parliament is not only modern, then; surely it is also one of the greatest and most unexpected social discoveries that man has ever stumbled onto. Up until two centuries ago, no one had accurately foreseen it. In Britain during the eighteenth century, rival groups had formed in Parliament, to which the names Whig and Tory were often applied. But

> ... Whig and Tories did not constitute political parties as they came to be in the late nineteenth and twentieth centuries. Those labels were often adopted by, or foisted upon, men who had little in common and few or no real ties. In 1714 and for many years thereafter, the basic political unit was the group or connexion, often called a party, formed under the leadership of a successful politician.[6]

In the parliament of Sweden during what came to be known as the Era of Liberty from 1718–1772, parliamentary factions "strongly reminiscent of the parallel groupings of Whigs and Tories in eighteenth century Britain" also developed.[7]

But these factional groups in Britain and Sweden were a long way from modern parties. There is little reason to suppose that in the late eighteenth century American political leaders knew anything about the Swedish system. As for Britain, the significance of the Whig and Tory factions in Parliament was quite unclear at the time, even in Britain; it was only much later that, looking backward, one could perceive in them the barest beginnings of a party system that has continued to develop and to change down to the present day.

The word 'party' itself did not have quite the same meaning to men like Washington, Madison, and Jefferson that it has today. Political party has come to signify an institution, a durable, organized force that outlasts the particular individuals who adhere to it at any moment. But when American political leaders used the term in the late eighteenth century— as they did more and more frequently from the Constitutional Conven-

6. Archibald S. Foord, *His Majesty's Opposition 1714–1830*, Oxford, the Clarendon Press, 1964, p. 20. See also Sir Ivor Jennings, *Party Politics*, Vol. II: *The Growth of Parties*, Cambridge, The University Press, 1961, pp. 24 ff. Sir Lewis Namier, *The Structure of Politics at the Accession of George III*, ed., New York, St. Martin's Press, 1961, ch. 2, "The Electoral Structure of England."

7. Dankwart A. Rustow, *The Politics of Compromise*, Princeton, Princeton University Press, 1955, pp. 11–12.

tion onward—they seem to have had in mind a *current of political opinion*, rather than an organized institution. Terms like party, faction, interest, sect, division, or group were used more or less interchangeably.[8]

Men at the Constitutional Convention and in public life during the first two decades were often confused as to the nature of party. No one, I imagine, thought that political conflict could be avoided entirely. But some important leaders seem to have believed that *persistent* cleavages of opinion could be avoided; perhaps men would come fresh to each question, ready to examine it with an open mind unclouded by attachments to any lasting faction or party. Leaders who held this view attacked "the spirit of party" for its baneful effects, as Washington did in his Farewell Address. When parties began to be organized, these men predicted terrible results: "Party spirit is the demon which engendered the factions that have destroyed most free governments," thundered the distinguished Senator Hillhouse of Connecticut in a Senate speech in 1808. "Regular, organized parties only, extending from the northern to the southern extremity of the United States, and from the Atlantic to the utmost western limits, threaten to shake this Union to its centre."[9] One difficulty with this view was that it was often—though not always—espoused by Federalists, who, so it appeared, did not object to the existence of their own party but only to that of their opponents, the opposition that Jefferson and Madison had the temerity to organize into a party.

It was in response to views like these that Federalist leaders sought to curb the nascent party of opposition; and it takes no great exercise of the imagination to conceive that the issue of a democratic versus an aristocratic republic hung in the balance during the years from 1794 to 1800. In 1794, President Washington himself took the occasion of the Whiskey Insurrection in western Pennsylvania to attack the Democratic Societies "as centers of sedition and resistance to government and requested the Senate and House to follow his lead. The Senate complied, but in the House Madison argued eloquently that it was unconstitutional

8. See for example Madison's "A Candid State of Parties" published in the Philadelphia *National Gazette* in 1792, reprinted in Cunningham, *op. cit.*, pp. 10 ff. Speaking of the time of the Revolution, Madison says that "those who espoused the cause of independence and those who adhered to the British claims, formed the parties of the first period." A moment later, he begins to speak of divisions: "The Federal Constitution . . . gave birth to the second and most interesting division of the people . . . those who embraced the constitution . . . those who opposed the constitution . . . This state of parties was terminated . . . in 1788."

9. Cunningham, *op. cit.*, p. 25.

for Congress to censure the clubs. Their members were simply exercising their right of free speech."[10] As Madison put it in a letter to Monroe, "The game was to connect the Democratic Societies with the odium of the insurrection, to connect the Republicans in Cong[ress] with those societies, to put the P[resident] ostensibly at the head of the other party, in opposition to both."[11]

The Alien and Sedition Acts passed by the Federalists in 1789 were animated by a similar hostility to criticism by opposition, and enforcement was a partisan matter. The Sedition Act in particular was used to bludgeon the opposition; twenty-five persons were prosecuted under the act, and ten of them, all Republican editors and printers, were convicted.[12]

As it turned out—fortunately for the future of the democratic republic—the actions of the Federalists did nothing to prevent and much to inflame the spirit of party they found so odious; consequently they along with the leading Republicans must be counted among the true, if unwitting, architects of modern parties. It was because of the views of Federalists—and because it was the Republicans, after all, who were being jailed for opposition—that Jefferson and Madison were so deeply alarmed by the Alien and Sedition Acts, which they saw as not only unconstitutional but also a despotic threat to republican government. They registered the strength of their objection by the Kentucky Resolution (drafted by Jefferson) and the Virginia Resolution (drafted by Madison) which denounced the Acts as unconstitutional and proposed as "the rightful remedy" a method that seventy years later, employed by other hands and in other circumstances, was to trip off the final round of events that culminated in secession and civil war. That remedy was for the states to "nullify" the allegedly unconstitutional acts of the national government.

Fortunately, the time of the Federalists was running out; the tide of republicanism was running in. When that tide swept Jefferson into office in the election of 1800, he pardoned the Republican editors and printers still in prison; the detestable Sedition Acts expired the day before he took the oath of office; he allowed the Alien Act to expire the following year. Thus the doctrine that political parties were constitutionally protected, an uncertain and even contested doctrine during the last decade

10. Page Smith, *John Adams*, Garden City, Doubleday and Company, 1962, 2 vols., Vol. II, p. 865.
11. Quoted in Cunningham, *The Jeffersonian Republicans, The Formation of Party Organization 1789–1801*, Chapel Hill, The University of North Carolina Press, 1957, p. 66.
12. Richard B. Morris, *Encyclopedia of American History*, New York, Harper and Bros., 1953, p. 129.

of the old century, came to rest on firmer ground during the first decade of the new.

Unlike many of their Federalist opponents, Jefferson and Madison held that opposing and persistent cleavages of opinion—parties in this sense—were inevitable in a free republic, even if, in some circumstances, their clashing ambitions might endanger the existence of the republic. In 1813, after four years away from Washington and the White House, Jefferson wrote his old friend John Adams that

> Men have differed in opinion, and been divided into parties by these opinions from the first origin of society; and in all governments where they have been permitted freely to think and to speak. The same political parties which now agitate the U.S. have existed thro' all time . . . To me then it appears that . . . these will continue thro' all future time: that every one takes his side in favor of the many, or of the few, according to his constitution, and the circumstances in which he is placed.[13]

Are Political Parties Inevitable in a Democratic Republic?

The fact that rival parties now exist in every national democracy and not in a single dictatorship hints at the possibility that parties may be inevitable in a democracy. If by party we mean organized, institutionalized parties, to leap to this conclusion would be going too far; small democratic organizations in which consensus is high sometimes get on without organized parties. But rival parties do seem inescapable in a democracy operating at the national level, whether that nation be as small as Iceland or as huge as the United States.

To begin with, the kinds of liberties required in an authentic democracy—freedom of speech, press, assembly, for example—make parties possible; or to put it in a slightly different way, it would be next to impossible both to prohibit all political parties and to allow full freedom of speech, press, and assembly. Stern and prolonged application of the Sedition Act might have curbed parties, but only by curbing freedom of speech, press, and peaceful assembly.

13. Cunningham, *The Making of the American Party System*, pp. 19–20.

The possibility of parties does not, however, mean that they are inevitable. What carves the actual out of the possible is in this case the ceaseless striving of political leaders for victory: their incessant efforts to win elections and marshall legislative majorities in support of particular persons, policies, or programs. The instrument invented in the United States between 1789 and about 1809 for winning elections and marshaling legislative majorities was the political party. If necessity is the mother of invention, then given the goals of ambitious men and the existing stock of knowledge, techniques, and institutions, the political party was as certain to be invented as the cotton gin, the steam engine, and interchangeable machine parts.

So that whatever the intentions of the Founding Fathers may have been, their Constitution, if it were kept to, made political parties not only possible but inevitable. With the Bill of Rights the Constitution made parties possible; with the institutions of representation and election designed in Articles I and II, it made parties inevitable.

We can see the parties struggling to be born in the early springtime of the new republic. In this country as elsewhere, parties were not spontaneous growths: They were created by the interaction of leaders and responsive followers. To be sure, in 1793 there was across the country a sudden and seemingly spontaneous flowering of popular associations that called themselves Democratic or Republican societies. These associations were uniformly on the side of what were coming to be called Republicans in distinction to Federalists. Yet as an historian has observed "they were partisans of the Republican interest, but they were not a party." For they did not nominate candidates, manage election campaigns, or seek to control legislatures.[14] They also lacked another characteristic of parties —durability. Within three years most of these societies had vanished.

It was not in these associations that the germ of party first appeared but, as in Britain and Sweden, in the national legislature. For, whatever Washington might have hoped, we can observe men like Hamilton, Madison, and Jefferson struggling to invent the political party.[15] The

14. Cunningham, The Jeffersonian Republicans, The Formation of Party Organization, p. 64.
15. See Cunningham, ibid., and also The Jeffersonian Republicans in Power, Party Operation 1801–1809. Chapel Hill, University of North Carolina Press, 1963; The Making of the American Party System 1789 to 1809 (documents) op. cit.; Joseph Charles, The Origins of the American Party System, New York, Harper Torchbooks, 1956, William N. Chambers, Political Parties in a New Nation, The American Experience 1776–1809, New York, Oxford University Press, 1963; Manning J. Dauer, The Adams Federalists, Baltimore, Johns Hopkins, 1953.

first Congress left few traces of party voting.[16] But Hamilton's economic program stimulated an opposition, led by Jefferson and Madison, that was to consolidate itself more and more fully in the succeeding Congresses. Probably nothing did more to foster this consolidation than the opposition in Congress to Jay's Treaty in 1795. The Republicans, as the congressional followers of Madison and Jefferson had begun to call themselves, held a caucus, the first in congressional history, to determine whether they would vote for the appropriations required to put the treaty into effect.[17] Under the stimulus of leadership, organization, and antagonism, both Federalists and Republicans became increasingly cohesive. When Jefferson became President, he had little difficulty in converting both the Republican party and the party caucus into efficient instruments for marshalling the votes of the Republican majorities in the Congress.

The institutions that have been used ever since to mobilize party support in Congress were well developed by the end of Jefferson's two terms in office: the caucus of the party faithful to determine the party line; the election of a partisan rather than a neutral Speaker of the House by the majority party; the development of recognized party leaders; close collaboration between the President and his party leaders in the Congress; and the judicious use of patronage by the President to solidify support.

Meanwhile, need had fostered additional party institutions. There was, above all, the problem of nominations. It was as obvious to Hamilton, Madison, Jefferson, and their peers as it is to us that unless they could marshall their forces in behalf of a single candidate, the opponents might win.[18] In 1796, both parties used an informal (and secret) con-

16. Cunningham, *The Jeffersonian Republicans*, p. 7.
17. *Ibid.*, p. 82.
18. In the case of the Presidency the problem was further complicated because as the Constitution then stood party leaders had to insure that their candidate for the Vice Presidency received fewer votes than their presidential candidate. As one might imagine this provided splendid opportunities for intrigue, as in 1796 when Hamilton conspired to secure *more* votes for the Federalist vice presidential candidate, Pinckney, than for the presidential candidate, Adams. In the end the maneuver failed, but Jefferson, the presidential candidate of the Republicans, received the second largest number of electoral votes after Adams, and thus became Vice President under Adams. In 1800, the Republicans failed to arrange properly for votes to be thrown away; as a result the Republican candidates for President and Vice President, Jefferson and Burr, ended in a tie. That was broken by Congress only after a lengthy crisis. The Constitutional defect, which by now was apparent to all, was eliminated in 1804 by the Twelfth Amendment.

gressional party caucus to gain agreement on the presidential candidate; thereafter, the device was regularly and openly used until 1824, when it fell into decay. (The present system of a national nominating convention began in 1831 with the new Anti-Masonic party, and in 1832 with the Jacksonian Democrats.)

Yet, unlike the factions and germinal parties in the eighteenth century parliaments of Britain and Sweden, incipient parties in the United States confronted still other needs, and it was these needs that added to the structure of the parliamentary, or legislative party, additional elements that made it recognizably modern—modern in the sense that the Model-T Ford, primitive though it may appear alongside one of the chrome-plated monsters of the present-day, nonetheless symbolizes the beginning of a radically new era in transportation. These needs were created because the United States was already a republic with broadly based suffrage, voters who had to be mobilized, won, persuaded, held firm. Thus there was an obvious need for party organization not only in the Congress but throughout the country, in every state and in every locality: to make nominations for numberless public offices from U. S. Senator to dog catcher, to skirmish in a variety of elected legislative bodies, to carry on the never-ending series of electoral campaigns, to mobilize voters. To intelligent and ambitious men who not only clearly perceived but enthusiastically embraced the institutions of a democratic republic—as many old Federalists were unable or unwilling to do— these needs were palpable, the means perhaps less obvious but by no means obscure to the eager and discerning eye. And so by the end of Jefferson's two terms in office the major parts of the modern machinery of the American party system had been invented.

Some of the instructions issued in 1805 to party workers by Alexander Wolcott, the Connecticut "State-manager" (as he signed himself) of the Republican party, would still be appropriate today:

> . . . I ask you . . . to appoint in each town of your county, an active, influential, republican manager . . .
> The duties of a TOWN-MANAGER will be,
> 1st. To appoint a district manager in each district or section of his town, obtaining from each an assurance that he will faithfully do his duty.
> 2d. To copy from the list of his town the names of all male inhabitants, who are taxed.
> 3d. To call together his district managers, and with their assistance to ascertain,

1st. The whole number of males, who are taxed [i.e. eligible to become voters],

2d. How many of the whole number are freemen [i.e. voters],

3d. How many of the freemen [voters] are decided republicans.

4th. How many — — — decided federalists.

5th. How many — — — doubtful.

6th. How many republicans who are not freemen, but who may be qualified [to vote] at the next proxies.

Wolcott went on with further instructions that would cheer the heart of any party leader today.[19]

Where the Republicans moved with amazing speed to construct the required machinery, the Federalists held back; their organization never came close to matching that of their opponents. Their lingering predilection for an aristocratic republic seems to have blinded them to their true place in a democratic republic, clouded their understanding of their real prospects, and thus perhaps contributed to their neglect of party machinery. In any case, this neglect was probably one cause of their decline.[20]

As Federalism began to disappear and the Republicans commanded ever wider support, the machinery of party was allowed to decay. But it never was totally lost, nor was the memory of it. There was no need to invent the political party a second time. During Jackson's Presidency, party machinery was quickly rebuilt. And it has endured ever since.

Eight Characteristics of the American Party System

The party systems of modern democracies are of great variety and complexity. Because the party system of each country is a particular combination of characteristics, every country can make a passable claim to the

19. The document is in Cunningham, The Making of the American Party System, pp. 115–118.
20. Shaw Livermore, Jr., The Twilight of Federalism, The Disintegration of the Federalist Party 1815–1830, Princeton, Princeton University Press, 1962, pp. 8–9, 29–30.

uniqueness of its party system. Among the democracies of the present day, multi-party systems are the most numerous; yet even they differ greatly. Only a few countries have followed the British two-party model; Britain herself does not always adhere to it, for sometimes a third party plays a critical role in British politics. The American version of the two-party model has not yet been copied in any other democracy.

Although one of the two contemporary parties did not emerge until the 1850s, the American party system took pretty much its present shape before the end of Jackson's Presidency.

A TWO-PARTY SYSTEM. The first and most obvious characteristic of the American party system is the fact that national elective offices—the Presidency and the Congress—are monopolized by two parties. In no other large democracy (and only a few smaller ones), do third parties have so slight a representation in national politics as in the United States. Since 1860 every presidential election has been won by either a Democrat or a Republican; in only four presidential elections during that period has a third party ever carried a single state. In American politics, rapid growth in third-party votes is a sure sign of an abnormal state of affairs, as in 1860 when the opposition to Lincoln was divided among three candidates, in 1892 when the Populist party was the vehicle of widespread discontent among farmers and urban workers, in 1912 when Theodore Roosevelt split the Republican party, and in 1948 when the States' Rights party fought another losing skirmish in the long battle for white supremacy. Since 1862, one of the two parties has always had a clear majority of seats in the House; in the Senate, independents or third-party members have prevented a clear majority during a total of ten

Table 8.1. Third-Party Seats Won in Elections to Congress 1862–1964

SEATS:	ELECTIONS:	
	HOUSE	SENATE
None	14	22
One	8	13
2–5	12	13
6–10	9	3
11–15	6	—
16–20	1	—
More than 20	1	—
Total elections	51	51

SOURCES: *Historical Statistics, op. cit.*, p. 691. *Congress and the Nation, op. cit.*, p. 63.

years. The number of seats held by third-party members is almost always extremely low (Table 8.1).

A moment ago, I offered some reasons why more than one party is likely to exist in a democracy. But, if the most frequent pattern is for democracies to have more than two important parties, why are there only two major parties in the United States? Because, to begin with, relatively few Americans disagree sharply on many essential matters that in other democracies help to create large followings for separate parties—Catholic parties in Italy, France, Germany and the Netherlands, for example, or Protestant parties in the Netherlands, or farmers' parties in the Scandinavian countries, or separate working-class parties throughout Europe.

In the second place, electoral mechanics have an impact. It hardly seems open to question that the introduction of any of the common systems of proportional representation for the election of Representatives to Congress would encourage splits in the major parties and serious competition from additional parties. Systems of proportional representation under which a party's share of seats in the legislative body is approximately equal to its share of votes in the country are used in most European democracies and contribute to (even if they do not completely explain) the existence of three or more sizeable parties.

In the United States, Representatives and Senators, like M.P.s in Britain, are elected in districts (or states) under the principle of winner-take-all. Notice how the two systems—proportional representation and winner-take-all—bear on the calculations of voters and politicians. Under P.R., voters and politicians can be sure that the proportion of seats won by a party will be very nearly the same as the party's nation-wide share of votes. Consequently, under P.R., voters know that they will not throw away their vote by voting for a minority party; and leaders of minority parties do not have much of an incentive to consolidate with other parties in order to win elections. Under the winner-take-all system, on the other hand, the share of seats a party wins ordinarily varies a good deal from its share of votes. It is easy to see why: If the voters for all the parties were spread evenly throughout the country, the largest party would win all the seats. Fortunately, party support is in fact unevenly distibuted around the country; a second party can therefore win victories in districts or regions where its votes are heavily concentrated. But the general effect—let us call it the snowballing effect—is to reward the winning party with a larger share of seats than votes, to penalize the second party by awarding it a share of seats smaller than its share of votes, and to handicap a third party still more or even to annihilate it (Table 8.2). This effect can be seen clearly if we examine the relation-

Table 8.2.   Percentage of Votes and Percentage of Seats, by Party, U.S. House of Representatives, 1920–1964.

	REPUBLICANS				DEMOCRATS		
	(1)	(2)	(3) Surplus (+) or Deficit (—) (Col. 2— Col. 1)		(4)	(5)	(6) Surplus (+) or Deficit (—) (Col. 5— Col. 4)
	Votes	Seats			Votes	Seats	
	%	%			%	%	
1964	42	32	−10	1964	58	68	+10
1962	48	40	− 8	1962	52	60	+ 8
1960	45	41	− 4	1960	55	59	+ 4
1958	44	36	− 8	1958	56	64	+ 8
1956	49	46	− 3	1956	51	54	+ 3
1954	47	47	0	1954	52	53	+ 1
1952*	49	51	+ 2	1952	49	49	0
1950	49	46	− 3	1950	49	54	+ 5
1948	46	39	− 7	1948	52	60	+ 8
1946	53	56	+ 3	1946	44	43	− 1
1944	47	43	− 4	1944	51	56	+ 5
1942	51*	48	− 3	1942	46	51	+ 5
1940	46	37	− 9	1940	51	62	+11
1938	47	38	− 9	1938	49	61	+12
1936	40	21	−19	1936	56	77	+21
1934	42	24	−18	1934	54	74	+20
1932	41	27	−14	1932	55	72	+17
1930	53*	49	− 4	1928	42	38	− 4
1926	57*	54	− 3	1926*	41	45	+ 4
1924	56	57	+ 1	1924*	40	42	+ 2
1922	52	52	0	1922*	45	47	+ 2
1920	59	70	+11	1920	36	30	− 6

Notes. Figures underscored are those of party winning largest percentage of votes.
*Years when minority party won larger percentage of seats than votes.

ship between the share of the votes cast for third parties in elections to the U.S. House of Representatives and the share of seats won by third parties (Table 8.3). In the election of 1920, for example, the third-party candidates for the House won 1.4 million votes, or 5.6 per cent of the total, and acquired exactly one seat out of 435, or slightly more than one fifth of 1 per cent!

The same principle operates in Senate elections. So, too, in presidential elections; because all the electoral votes of a state go to the presidential candidate with the largest share of popular votes in that state, the snowballing effect in presidential elections is even more visible. Because the Presidency is the most strategic post in the entire political system,

Table 8.3.   THIRD PARTIES: Votes and Seats, U.S. House of
Representatives,   1920–1964.

	(1) PERCENTAGE OF VOTES	(2) PERCENTAGE OF SEATS	SURPLUS OR DEFICIT
1964		0	
1962	0.3	0	−0.3
1960	0.4	0	−0.4
1958	0.2	0	−0.2
1956	0.6	0	−0.6
1954	0.7	0.2	−0.5
1952	1.5	0.2	−1.3
1950	2.0	0.2	−1.8
1948	2.6	0.2	−2.4
1946	2.2	0.2	−2.0
1944	2.2	0.5	−1.7
1942	3.3	0.9	−2.4
1940	3.1	1.1	−2.0
1938	4.3	0.9	−3.4
1936	4.5	3.0	−1.5
1934	4.1	2.3	−1.8
1932	4.1	1.2	−2.9
1930	2.8	0.2	−2.6
1928	1.1	0.2	−0.9
1926	2.5	0.7	−1.8
1924	4.1	0.9	−3.2
1922	3.6	1.1	−2.5
1920	5.6	0.2	−5.4

SOURCES: 1920–1956, Historical Statistics, op. cit., 1956–1962, Congressional District Data Book, Washington, U.S. Government Printing Office.

*Reporting of third-party votes is subject to considerable error. Different sources frequently disagree on totals.

and because it is completely indivisible, in a presidential contest the winner does indeed take all and leaves no crumbs to the loser. Consider what happens, then, in an election like that of 1912 when Taft and Theodore Roosevelt split the Republicans asunder. Taft won 23 per cent of the popular votes but only 1.5 per cent of the electoral votes; Theodore Roosevelt won 27 per cent of the popular votes and only 16.5 per cent of the electoral votes; while the victor, Woodrow Wilson, gained 82 per cent of the electoral votes by winning forty out of forty-eight states—yet he had only 42 per cent, less than a majority, of the popular votes. To a politician, the instructions contained in this kind of election are unambiguous: If you want to win a presidential election, don't split your party; don't back a third party; concentrate instead on building up the largest possible coalition of interests, no matter how heterogeneous, in support of the candidate of one of the two major parties.

A third reason why two parties, not three or more, monopolize national politics is the force of habit and tradition. The two parties have been dominant for a century; the invariable fate of third parties is to be overwhelmingly defeated and often to disappear after one election. Many people acquire their basic political orientations and loyalties early, when they are still strongly under the influence of parents and family. This is true also of attitudes toward the parties; hence party loyalties tend to be transmitted from parents to children. The mere fact then that the Republican and Democratic parties monopolize votes during one generation makes it very much easier for them to monopolize votes during the next generation. To break out of a minority position on the other hand, a third party must overcome the enormous inertia of habit.

VARIABILITY OF EFFECTIVE COMPETITION. The second characteristic of the American system is that the degree of effective competition between the two parties varies greatly throughout the country and, in general, declines with the size of the unit. As we saw in the last chapter, many towns and cities lack effective two-party competition either because party support is overwhelmingly one-sided or because the functions of parties have been curtailed by non-partisan elections—or both. Party competition is likely to be closer at the state level, as we saw; yet only about half the states can be regarded as having two-party systems. At the national level, however, the parties compete on a more even basis. To be sure, during long periods, one of the two parties may win the Presidency much more often than the other: the Republicans from 1896–1932, the Democrats from 1932–1964. But measured by the proportion of congressional seats and votes in presidential and congressional elections, neither party manages to hold a big lead for very long.

The degree of party competition also changes over time (Figure 8.1). A two-party system virtually vanished as the Federalists died out. During and after Jackson's Presidency, a new two-party system emerged. In fact, under this "second American party system," as one writer has called it, "the two new parties were balanced and competitive in every region. For a very brief period—between 1840 and 1852—the nation, for the only time in its history, had two parties that were both truly national in scope."[21] The disintegration of the Whigs, the rise of the Republicans as a strictly non-Southern party, which it has remained until recently, the

21. Richard P. McCormick, The Second American Party System, Party Formation in the Jacksonian Era, Chapel Hill, The University of North Carolina Press, 1966, p. 14.

creation of the one-party South—all led to a decline in two-party competition. Since about 1946, however, there has been rising competition between the two parties, with the Democrats increasing in strength in upper New England and the Midwest, and the Republicans growing throughout the South.

DIFFUSION AND DECENTRALIZATION OF CONTROL. Third, control over nominations and the policies of the parties is diffused and in many cases decentralized to state and local organizations. This is not to say that the parties are democratically controlled, for they are not; but neither is control as tightly centralized in the hands of a single set of leaders as in many parties in other democracies.

Even in the presidential nominating convention, one of the few methods by which American national parties act collectively, control is generally diffuse. Except for the party of a President at the end of his first term—when it is about as certain as anything can be in American politics that the President will completely dominate the convention that nominates him—control over a convention is usually spread so thin and the outcome so uncertain that millions of Americans, including the best informed ones in the midst of the convention, continue to speculate about the outcome of the winning ballot. Senatorial nominations are decentralized to state organizations; nominations of representatives to

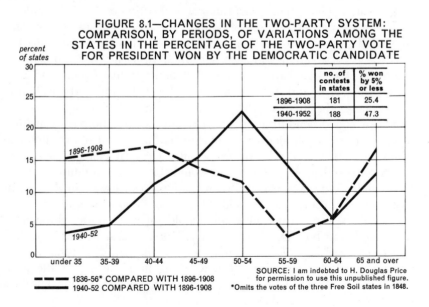

FIGURE 8.1—CHANGES IN THE TWO-PARTY SYSTEM: COMPARISON, BY PERIODS, OF VARIATIONS AMONG THE STATES IN THE PERCENTAGE OF THE TWO-PARTY VOTE FOR PRESIDENT WON BY THE DEMOCRATIC CANDIDATE

	no. of contests in states	% won by 5% or less
1896-1908	181	25.4
1940-1952	188	47.3

percent of states

- - - 1836-56* COMPARED WITH 1896-1908
——— 1940-52 COMPARED WITH 1896-1908

SOURCE: I am indebted to H. Douglas Price for permission to use this unpublished figure.
*Omits the votes of the three Free Soil states in 1848.

state and district organizations. Control over nominations of state and local officials is, of course, highly decentralized. And within states and localities, control is still further diffused by the direct primary.

Much the same diffusion and decentralization applies to policies; the incumbent President can largely determine presidential policy, and that, as we have seen, is a good deal; but control over the policies and votes of his party colleagues in Congress is comparatively modest—and in the states and localities negligible.

Why is control over party nominations and policies much more diffused and decentralized in the United States than in some of the important parties in other democracies? The most potent factor is probably the sheer force of federalism. Federalism insures that the states and localities are in a great many respects autonomous, independent of direct control by national officials. Strong state and local political organizations can be built without federal patronage or largesse and can survive electoral defeat at the national level; the innumerable nominations for state and local office, the never-ending cycle of state and local elections make it very much easier for the men on the spot to exert control than for national officials to do so. In addition, most of the laws controlling nominations, elections, party organization, and party finance, all highly strategic matters for party leaders, are passed and enforced by state governments. Another factor of considerable historical importance is the weight that urban machines have had within the two parties, particularly the Democratic Party. Then, too, American political attitudes seem to endorse diffusion and decentralization of power in all of our political institutions; it should not be too surprising if these attitudes carry over into the political parties. Among Americans, centralized parties seem to lack the legitimacy that they have in democratic countries, like Britain and Sweden, with ancient and strong traditions of hierarchy and centralization.

Finally, the past weighs heavily on the future simply because diffusion and decentralization of party control are thoroughly institutionalized. A party leader who sought to centralize control over nominations and policy would be throwing out a clear-cut challenge to thousands of party leaders whose power would thereby be diminished. Since men rarely yield power cheerfully, any national leader who sought to gain more control over his party would stir up fierce opposition from state and local leaders in the entrenched strongholds of party power throughout the length and breadth of the country. Diffused as it is, the individual power of these local leaders is not great on the national scene; united, they would be an awesome force. Knowing in advance that the most likely outcome would be their own disastrous defeat, national leaders never lay down the challenge.

LOW COHESION. Fourth, much the same factors that operate to prevent centralization of control in the parties also inhibit the development of parties which are highly united in support of particular policies. The most visible evidence of unity in a party is the extent to which members of a party vote the same way when they are confronted by bills and other measures in a legislature. If all the members of a party in a legislature always voted the same way, a party would of course display complete unity. In a two-party system, if each of the parties were perfectly unified, then on every legislative question over which the parties disagreed all the members of one party would vote one way while all the members of the other party would vote against them. Because total party unity is unusual, some studies of party cohesion define a 'party-vote' in a two-party system as one in which 90 per cent of the one party votes for and 90 per cent of the other against a question. Comparative studies using this measure show that while British and American parties may have been about equally low in cohesion in the nineteenth century,[22] in this century British parties display far greater unity in voting in the House of Commons than do our parties in the Congress (specifically the House) (Table 8.4).

High cohesion in the national legislature is not uncommon among

Table 8.4. Comparative Party Unity: Proportion of Party Votes Cast in Britain and United States, Selected 20th Century Sessions

BRITAIN, COMMONS[a]		UNITED STATES, HOUSE	
YEAR	PER CENT PARTY VOTES	YEAR	PER CENT PARTY VOTES
1924–25	94.4	1921	28.6
1926	94.8	1928	7.1
		1930–31	31.0
1927	96.4	1933	22.5
		1937	11.8
1928	93.6	1944	10.7
Average	94.9	1945	17.5
		1946	10.5
		1947	15.1
		1948	16.4
		Average	17.1

*Figures for Britain from Jones, "Party Voting in the English House of Commons," p. 40.

Source: Julius Turner, Party and Constituency, Baltimore, The Johns Hopkins Press, 1952, p. 24.

22. A. Lawrence Lowell, "The Influence of Party Upon Legislation in England and America," Annual Report of the American Historical Association for 1901, Washington, 1902, 2 vols., Vol. I, pp. 321–544.

the larger parties in many other democratic systems. To this extent the relatively low cohesiveness displayed by American parties is something of an anomaly, and—despite the beliefs of many Americans—not inherent in a democratic political system.

A word of caution is needed, however. Party unity is very far from being a negligible factor in the Congress. None of the other lines of cleavage in Congress—metropolitan-rural, North-South, liberal-conservative—seem to predict as well as party the way members will divide over a number of different issues and sessions. Thus the author of one statistical study of the question concluded that

> Quantitative analysis of roll call votes shows, contrary to majority opinion, that significant differences exist between our major parties. While it is true that American discipline falls short of that achieved in some European democracies, and is less effective than party discipline in the McKinley era in the United States, evidence of great party influence can still be found. Party pressure seems to be more effective than any other pressure on Congressional voting, and is discernible on nearly nine-tenths of the roll calls examined.[23]

And in some state legislatures—Connecticut, for example—the parties are about as cohesive as in any European parliament.[24]

IDEOLOGICAL SIMILARITY AND ISSUE CONFLICT. Fifth, although the parties frequently differ on specific issues, they are not markedly different in ideology. This does not mean, as is sometimes said, that American parties advocate no ideology at all. They do. But unlike parties in many European countries, both Republicans and Democrats in the United States advocate much the same ideology. Both parties express a commitment to democracy, to the Constitution, and to the key social and economic institutions of American life: privately owned business firms, universal free public education, separation of church and state, religious toleration, and the like. To a European accustomed to the sound and fury of clashing ideologies, American party battles seem tame and uninteresting.

In this case likeness is not identity, however. To a Buddhist the differences between Baptists and Episcopalians might seem negligible—but they are not so negligible to Baptists and Episcopalians. Although

---

23. Julius Turner, Party and Constituency: Pressure on Congress, Baltimore, the Johns Hopkins University Press, 1951, p. 23.
24. Cf. Duane Lockard, New England State Politics, op. cit. p. 279.

Republicans and Democrats profess to worship the same gods and endorse the same commandments, the rhetoric employed by the leaders of the two parties tends to annouce different emphasis. These differences in emphasis vary over time. To generalize from recent decades, one might say that where Democratic rhetoric emphasizes the equality of Americans in dignity, respect, and rights, Republican rhetoric emphasizes their liberties and differences in capacities; where Democratic rhetoric extolls the accomplishments of the federal government, Republican rhetoric extolls the benefits of action through state and local governments; where Democratic rhetoric emphasizes the virtues and possibilities of public action through government, Republican rhetoric emphasizes the virtues of business enterprise; where 'regulation of business' is often portrayed as desirable in Democratic rhetoric it is more often portrayed as evil in Republican rhetoric; where Democratic rhetoric declaims the needs and aspirations of the less well off—the poor, the underprivileged, the culturally deprived, the aged—Republican rhetoric declaims the needs and aspirations of the solid and successful strata. (Both, of course, unendingly praise the virtues of the average man, the middle class, the middle-of-the-road, the tax-payer, the American way.)

Despite differences like these in nuance and emphasis, the ideological commitments of leaders in both parties are usually so much alike that opponents find it tempting to distinguish themselves ideologically from one another by gross exaggerations, caricatures, and downright falsehoods typical of many American campaigns. Because it provided a firmer basis for ideological distinctions than usual, the 1964 presidential campaign was something of a deviant case. The Republican candidate, Senator Goldwater, unashamedly professed an extremely 'conservative' ideology that was intended to be, and was, at odds with the 'liberal' or 'liberal-conservative' ideology that most Republican and Democratic spokesmen had espoused for several decades. Even so the Senator's 'conservatism' was scarcely distinguishable from the prevailing ideology of both parties in the nineteenth century; and 'conservatives' found it difficult to formulate a coherent expression of abstract ideology that did not simply restate platitudes long since incorporated into the rhetoric of both parties.

The most marked difference between the parties is not in their ideologies but in their programs and policies. The differences are often much greater than a mere examination of rhetoric would lead one to expect—greater sometimes, in fact, than the difference between European parties that substitute rhetoric for concrete programs. It is very far from being the case that the parties adopt identical platforms at their national conventions. And although American parties are not as cohesive as parties often are in other countries, on many issues Democrats and Republicans divide quite sharply. The content of party conflict changes from one historical period to the next; but in every generation there are persistently divisive issues that distinguish Democrats and Republicans. Thus, in a study of the four sessions of 1921, 1931, 1937 and 1944, it was found that Democrats and Republicans in the House disagreed markedly on measures pertaining to tariff; patronage; government (as opposed to private) action on electric power, crop insurance, and other matters; the size of the federal bureaucracy; public works; social, welfare, and labor matters; and farm policy.[25] (A list of key measures on which a majority of Democrats have opposed a majority of Republicans in the House from 1945–1965 is shown in the Appendix to this chapter.)

When the President lines up on one side and the leaders of the opposition party on the other, the chances are particularly good that a high proportion of Democrats will vote one way and Republicans another. From 1961–1965, for example, the Democrats in House and Senate gave much more support to the measures of the Democratic Administration than did the Republicans (Figure 8.2).

The explanation for this combination of ideological similarity and conflict over issues goes to the very heart of the American political system. An overwhelming proportion of American voters do not sharply divide on norms that in other countries generate followings for ideologically divergent parties. A party that preaches anti-democratic doctrines, revolutionary aims, hostility to the Constitution or constitutional processes, religious, racial, or ethnic conflict, the repression or favoring of a particular religion, or nationalization of the means of production at best appeals to a small part of the electorate. The two major parties do not diverge very much ideologically; and the major parties direct their appeal to the great bulk of the electorate. For reasons we have already explored, the effect of the election machinery is to reduce even further the prospects of success for an ideologically divergent party. Hence, paradoxically, party conflict in campaigns, elections, and policy-making constantly reinforces the prevailing ideology and weakens the impact of political movements with rival ideologies. A similarity of ideological perspectives among most Americans has insured the success of ideologically similar parties; and the domination of American politics by ideolog-

25. The difference between the percentage of Democrats and the percentage of Republicans who voted for a given measure on a roll call was on the average more than 50 per cent. On tariff measures, the average difference was almost 80 per cent. Turner, op. cit., pp. 36–38.

FIGURE 8.2—PRESIDENTIAL SUPPORT SCORES 1961-1965

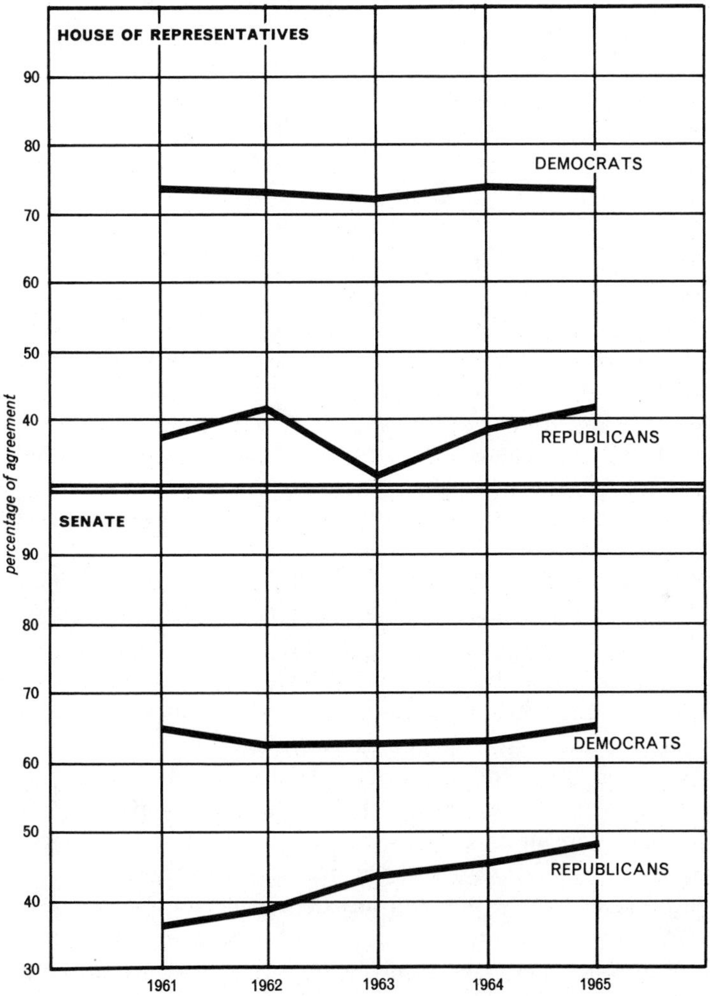

SOURCE: Presidential Support Scores from The Congressional Quarterly Service. Number of roll calls used to determine Presidential support scores were: for House, 1961—65; 1962—60; 1963—71; 1964—52; 1965—112. For Senate: 1961—124; 1962—125; 1963—115; 1964—97; 1965—162.

ically similar parties has in turn reinforced the similarity of ideological perspectives among the American people.

Yet, because these ideological perspectives are not identical but vary in strength, emphasis, and to some extent even in content, they allow for considerable—at times extensive—divergence on matters of policy. The strategy of the parties, then, is to seek support among voters not only by proclaiming their own ideological purity and the horrendous deviation of the other party from ideological orthodoxy, but also by advocating policies they expect to appeal to voters. But, it might be asked, if both parties want to win the largest number of votes, why don't they both advocate the same policies? Often, of course, they do. But there are several important reasons why they do not. For one thing, like other people politicians also lack perfect information about voters' attitudes; in the absence of perfect information there is considerable uncertainty as to what strategy will have the greatest appeal and will maximize votes in the coming election. Like other people, politicians fill in areas of ignorance by making guesses. And, like other people, the hunches of politicians are shaped by their own experiences, prejudices, wishes, and fantasies; by the views of people on whom they depend for information and advice; by their conceptions of what their most loyal and deserving supporters actually want; and even by their views as to what is 'best for the country.'

DIFFERENCES IN PARTY FOLLOWINGS. The sixth characteristic of American parties has a double aspect: (a) With few exceptions, each of the parties draws votes in significant numbers from every stratum of the population; but (b) many strata consistently vote more heavily for one party than the other. In general, then, neither party has a monopoly of the votes within any category of Americans. Yet the hard core of undeviating supporters for each party is located in different strata. Nothing is static, of course, including the composition of party followings. But the hard core of each party is particularly slow to change.

Figure 8.3 displays some of the important differences in the way people in different groups voted in presidential elections in the 1950s and early 1960s. The groups most favorable to the Republicans were people of higher incomes and social status, with college educations and professional and managerial occupations, people in medium-sized towns and cities, and Protestants. Groups most favorable to the Democrats were people of lower incomes and social status, with grade school and high school education, working in skilled or unskilled manual occupations, trade union members and their families, residents of metropolitan areas, Catholics, and Negroes.

FIGURE 8.3—THE AMERICAN ELECTORATE, 1948-1960:
PERCENTAGE OF THE TWO PARTY VOTE WON BY DEMOCRATIC
PRESIDENTIAL CANDIDATES IN VARIOUS CATEGORIES OF VOTERS

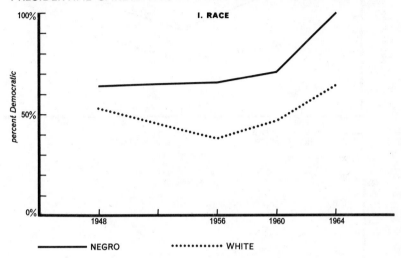

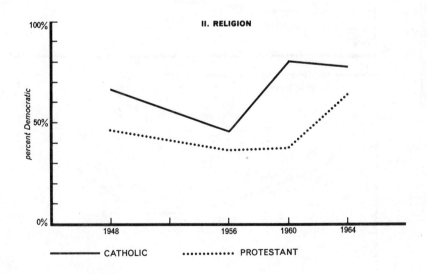

III. TRADE UNION MEMBERSHIP

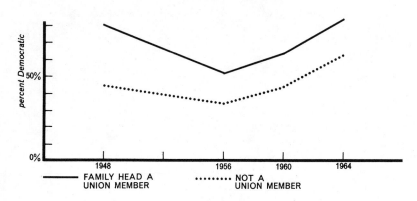

FAMILY HEAD A UNION MEMBER   .... NOT A UNION MEMBER

IV. EDUCATION

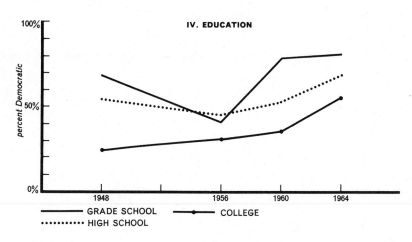

GRADE SCHOOL   COLLEGE
.... HIGH SCHOOL

V. RESIDENCE

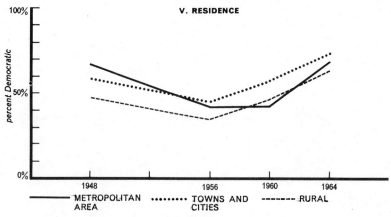

METROPOLITAN AREA   .... TOWNS AND CITIES   -------- RURAL

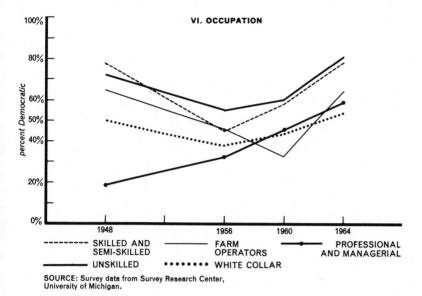

VI. OCCUPATION

- - - - - - SKILLED AND
SEMI-SKILLED
——— UNSKILLED
——— FARM
OPERATORS
• • • • • • • WHITE COLLAR
—•— PROFESSIONAL
AND MANAGERIAL

SOURCE: Survey data from Survey Research Center,
University of Michigan.

The followings, the policies, and the ideological emphases of each party usually reinforce one another. Democrats use rhetoric and advocate policies designed to appeal to their followers in working-class occupations and the big cities; Republicans use rhetoric and advocate policies designed to appeal to their followers in the business community and small towns. When the Democrats place more emphasis on equality and the virtues of the underprivileged, and Republicans on opportunity and the virtues of the more privileged, they are appealing to their respective hard cores of loyal followers. Yet neither party wishes to ignore potential votes in other social strata; hence each party designs its rhetoric and its program not only to retain the loyalty and enthusiasm of its hard core of zealous adherents but at the same time to win over less committed voters in all the major categories of the population.

DURABILITY. The seventh characteristic of American parties is their extraordinary durability. The life of the Democratic Party can be traced as far back as President Jackson in 1830 with no historical cavils; and a good claim can be made that the present party is the direct institutional descendant of Jefferson's party. The Republican Party has contested every national election since 1856. The two parties have thus dominated national politics for a century. No other party system in the world is so old.[26]

Why have American parties endured so long? First, by assiduously seeking to advance and protect the interests of the social groups from which they draw their most dependable support, the parties retain a hard core of loyal followers even in greatest adversity. These social groups endure; their loyalty helps the parties to endure. For the Democrats, the two low-points in this century were the presidential elections of 1920, when they received 34 per cent of the popular votes, and 1924, when their share plummeted to 29 per cent. The low points for the Republicans were 1936 (36.5 per cent) and 1964 (38.5 per cent) (Figure 8.4).

Thanks to their hard core of loyalists, neither party has ever come close to being wiped out. Second, with an extraordinary number of people, party loyalties are acquired early in life, under the influence of family and friends, and thereafter remain unaltered except under the impact of a major trauma like the Great Depression. Third, the parties have been skillful enough to adjust their programs and even their rhetoric to changing times and popular attitudes, though ever since the 1930s, the Republicans have found it difficult to adapt to the transformations brought on by the Depression and the New Deal. Combined with all of these factors, the electoral system and the ideological cohesion of the great bulk of the electorate have, as we saw earlier, made it exceptionally difficult—in fact impossible so far—for a third party to win over enough voters to displace either of the two major parties.

THE VARIABILITY IN PARTY SUPPORT. It would be misleading, however, to forget what is the most obvious—and in some ways the most important—characteristic of American parties: the variation in the extent to which the parties are effective in winning loyalty and support. The history of American parties shows how rapidly the electoral fortunes of a party may change. No politician is likely to forget this lesson. As a consequence the typical party politician works zealously to discover what voters want. When he knows or thinks he knows what voters want, he tries to shape the political strategies of his party in order to win their votes on election day.

In a loose way, American national elections—or, more precisely, a brief series of several elections—can be classified into two broad catego-

26. In Britain, the Conservatives trace their lineage back to the late-eighteenth-century Tories led by the younger Pitt; the Liberals to the Whigs led by Charles James Fox; but Labour dates back only to 1905.

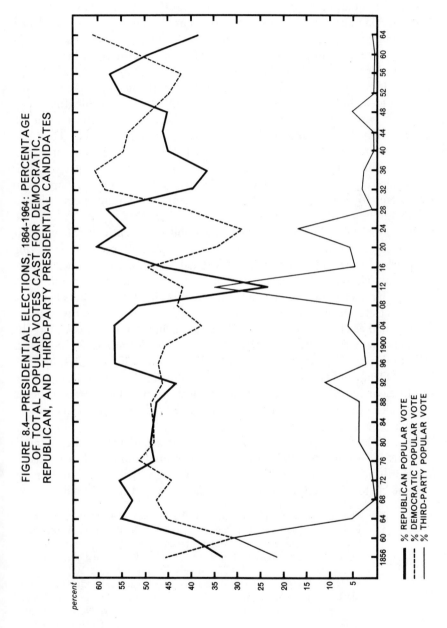

FIGURE 8.4—PRESIDENTIAL ELECTIONS, 1864-1964: PERCENTAGE OF TOTAL POPULAR VOTES CAST FOR DEMOCRATIC, REPUBLICAN, AND THIRD-PARTY PRESIDENTIAL CANDIDATES

% REPUBLICAN POPULAR VOTE
% DEMOCRATIC POPULAR VOTE
% THIRD-PARTY POPULAR VOTE

ries: maintaining elections and re-aligning elections.[27]

Maintaining elections are normal; re-aligning elections are abnormal. Maintaining elections seem to occur during periods of moderate conflict; re-aligning elections are more likely during periods of severe conflict. The most important re-aligning elections in American history were probably these: 1796–1800, 1856–1860, 1892–1896, and 1932–1936.

In maintaining elections, pre-existing party loyalties predominate. The great bulk of the electorate consists of people who identify themselves with one of the two major parties. Between elections and during the campaigns their party loyalties are not severely strained. They perceive no serious conflict between their habitual loyalty to a party, and the candidates, policies, programs, and actions of that party. Their loyalty and the absence of highly divisive issues within the party tend in fact to soften or eliminate their perceptions of differences between themselves and their party.

Maintaining elections, then, are stabilizing elections. They reflect and even reinforce party loyalties and perpetuate pre-existing voting patterns in the electorate with only small changes. In a series of maintaining elections, the parties may be quite evenly matched or one party may have a significant advantage. In the first situation, a small change in the electorate may reduce the previous majority to a minority. All the national elections from 1874 to 1894 were maintaining elections, but the elections were remarkably close. In 1880, the Republican presidential candidate (Garfield) won with a plurality less than 40,000 votes; in 1884, the Democrat (Cleveland) won with a plurality less than 30,000 votes. In eight out of the ten congressional elections, the Democrats gained a majority in the House; in only two elections did they gain a majority in the Senate.

Where one party acquires a significant advantage, as the Republicans did from 1896–1932, the other party loses more or less regularly. Until there is a major realignment in voters' loyalties, the minority party is likely to win the Presidency only if there is a split in the majority party

27. The following discussion draws on V. O. Key, "A Theory of Critical Elections," *The Journal of Politics*, Vol. 27 (Feb. 1955) pp. 3–18. Campbell, et al., *The American Voter, op. cit.*, pp. 531 ff. Angus Campbell, "Voters and Elections: Past and Present," *The Journal of Politics*, Vol. 64 (November, 1964) pp 745–757. Angus Campbell, "Surge and Decline: A Study of Electoral Change" and "A Classification of the Presidential Elections" in Angus Campbell, Philip E. Converse, Warren E. Miller, and Donald E. Stokes, *Elections and the Political Order*, New York, John Wiley and Sons, 1966; Campbell et al., "Stability and Change in 1960: A Reinstating Election," *Ibid.*, ch. 5, pp. 78–95.

as in 1912 when Wilson won the Presidency with 42 per cent of the popular vote, or if they have the good fortune to nominate a candidate of extraordinary popularity, like General Eisenhower in 1952 and 1956, who manages to win votes for *himself* even though he cannot win voters for his *party.*

As these examples suggest, even during a long series of maintaining elections, political attitudes and loyalties are never completely frozen. Even maintaining elections may reflect changes of four kinds:

¶ Slow, *long-run* shifts may occur throughout practically the entire electorate, as in the period 1896–1928 when there seems to have been a long-run shift toward the Republicans throughout the North, or from 1936–1964 when a massive glacial shift toward the Democrats took place.

¶ Superimposed on the slow, secular shifts in the electorate as a whole, *long-run* changes also take place within specific groups at much slower or faster rates; for example from 1936–1964, the proportion of Negroes voting Democratic increased much more rapidly than among any other group.

¶ *Short-run* fluctuations usually occur from presidential to mid-term congressional elections; typically there is a drop-off in the percentage of the vote cast for candidates of the President's party.

¶ *Short-run* surges may also occur in presidential elections, as in 1952–1956 when, despite the long-run increase in the percentage of voters who identified themselves with the Democrats, General Eisenhower nonetheless won enormous personal victories.

The best explanation for these last two short-run changes has been furnished by Angus Campbell.[28] His explanation rests upon four characteristics of elections:

1. *The size of the turnout in national elections depends on a combination of intrinsic political interest and the impact of short-term political forces. People with a high level of intrinsic interest vote in most or all national elections; people with little intrinsic interest vote only when additionally stimulated by impelling short-term forces. The weaker the total impact of*

28. "Voters and Elections: Past and Present," *The Journal of Politics,* 26, 4 (November, 1964), 745–757.

the short-term forces, the smaller will be the total turnout.

2. *The smaller the turnout in a national election, the greater the proportion of the vote which is contributed by people of established party loyalties and the more closely the partisan division of the vote will approach the basic underlying division of standing commitments to the two parties, what Lord Bryce referred to years ago as the "normal voting strength."*

3. *The larger the turnout, the greater the proportion of the vote which is made up of marginal voters, people who have relatively weak party identification, relatively little intrinsic political interest, and relatively little political information.*

4. *If the sum of the short-term forces is approximately balanced in its partisan impact, the total vote will not vary from the vote division to be expected from the underlying "normal party strength." If the sum of the short-term forces favors one candidate-party alternative over the other it will swing the vote division toward that alternative, with the greatest movement occurring among the marginal voters. The greater the total impact of the short-term forces, the greater will be the potential deflection from the "normal party strength."*[29]

In presidential elections, turnout is invariably higher than in mid-term elections. This helps to explain both the mid-term decline of the party in power and the occasional surge of votes toward one presidential candidate during periods of moderate conflict, when the shift clearly cannot be attributed to the de-stabilizing effects of severe conflict. Angus Campbell suggests

> . . . *that the familiar off-year loss does not depend on an inevitable cooling of the public ardor for the President's party, although this undoubtedly occurs in particular years. It depends rather on a pattern of circulation of votes which is characteristic of presidential and off-year elections. In the relatively stimulating circumstances of a presidential election the turnout is high. As we have just noted, the regular voters whose intrinsic political interest is high enough to take them to the polls even under less stimulating conditions are joined by marginal voters who are less concerned with politics but may be activated if the stakes seem high. Ordinarily one of the two candidates*

29. Ibid., p. 748.

standing for the presidency will be benefited by the political circumstances of the moment more clearly than the other, either because of embarrassments of the party in power, the personal qualities of the candidates, domestic or international conditions, or for other reasons. The advantaged candidate will draw to him the votes of a majority of the marginal voters, who have relatively little party attachment and are responsive to such short-term influences. He will also profit from some defections by regular voters from the opposition party who are sufficiently tempted to break away from their usual party vote at least temporarily. In moving toward the advantaged candidate both the regular and the marginal voters, especially the latter, tend to support both the candidate and his party ticket. In the off-year election which follows, two movements occur. The regular voters who moved across party lines to support a presidential candidate they preferred are likely to move back to their usual party vote when that candidate is no longer on the ticket. The marginal voters who had given the winning candidate a majority of their votes in the presidential election do not vote in the election which follows. Both of these movements hurt the party of the candidate who benefited from the votes of the two groups in the presidential election. The loss of congressional seats is the result.[30]

Thus a series of maintaining elections can be likened to a rather stable sanddune on the edge of the ocean in the absence of great storms. Occasional winds change the shape of the dune somewhat. A steady wind from one direction may gradually displace the center of the entire dune to the left or to the right. Not all parts of the dune change at the same rate. Nonetheless, its shape and position remain substantially unchanged from one year to the next.

A series of re-aligning elections are better symbolized by a dune subject to the pressure of a storm. Disorganized by the storm, its structure momentarily destroyed, it undergoes violent changes in form and position. After the storm, one who had long regarded it with affection might find it impossible to recognize the old dune.

In a series of re-aligning elections, then, the party loyalties of a great mass of voters are first torn loose and then re-attached either to a new party or to the opposite party. After a series of re-aligning elections has run its course, party alignments are decisively different. The balance of

30. *Ibid.*, pp. 750–751.

support may be tilted significantly away from one party toward another. A party may even be destroyed. Severe political conflicts precede and accompany re-aligning elections. The issues of politics are too visible to enable many voters to remain loyal to a party that holds a position in the conflict markedly different from their own.

The elections of 1796–1800 were re-aligning elections—though if we consider that the parties were still in their infancy, perhaps a more appropriate term would be *aligning* elections. In any case, conflicts disrupted the coalition that had made the Constitution, weakened the Federalists, and crystallized so much support for the Democratic-Republicans that after their victory in 1800 they were never defeated by the Federalists.

The elections of 1856–1860 were re-aligning elections. The Whigs disintegrated in the North. Northern Whigs, Free Soilers, and even many northern and border-state Democrats turned toward the Republican Party. While Reconstruction temporarily created Republican governments in the South, as quickly as it was permitted to do so the South became the Solid South; and it remained so until the 1950s and 1960s.

The national elections from 1892 to 1896 were re-aligning elections. From 1876 to 1892, the Democrats and Republicans had been running neck-and-neck in presidential races. In four of these elections, the Democratic candidate had outpolled the Republican in popular votes; in the fifth (1880), the Republican, Garfield, had won with a margin of less than ten thousand votes over his Democratic rival—a difference of less than one half of one per cent of the total popular vote! In the late 1880s, agrarian discontent fanned into flame the most important third-party movement since the rise of the Republicans: the People's Party. In 1896, Populists and Democrats jointly endorsed William Jennings Bryan as their candidate for President. But the Republicans, led by William McKinley, turned back the agrarian challenge. For the first time since 1872, the Republican candidate won a majority of popular votes. The Middle West, where the Democrats had developed strength, became a Republican strong-hold. No Democratic candidate again won a majority of popular votes until Franklin Roosevelt's election of 1932; and except in 1912 and 1916, Democratic candidates lost by huge margins. From 1900 to 1932, the Democrats polled fewer votes than the Republicans in all congressional elections save three; not once did they win a majority of all popular votes.

The presidential elections from 1932 to 1936 were also re-aligning elections, for they marked a shift away from the Republican party toward the Democrats that continued for the next three decades. In the nine presidential elections from 1932 to 1964, the Republicans won only twice

Table 8.5. *"In politics as of today, do you consider yourself a Republican, Democrat, or Independent?"*

	1940	1950	1960	1964
Democratic	42%	45%	47%	53%
Republican	38	33	30	25
Independent	20	22	23	22

SOURCE: American Institute of Public Opinion, July 5, 1964.

—with General Eisenhower in 1952 and 1956. In that thirty-four year period. Republicans had majorities in the House of Representatives for only four years. The extent to which deeper underlying tides were running against the Republican Party was strikingly visible in the midst of its greatest triumph, the 'surge' election of 1956 in which General Eisenhower was swept into office by a crushing majority: For the second time since the election of 1876, the party that won the Presidency did not win a majority of seats in the House.

For the past quarter century, the Gallup poll has been asking its samples: "In politics, as of today, do you consider yourself a Republican, Democrat, or Independent?" The responses from 1940 to 1964 reveal the steady shift away from the Republicans (Table 8.5).

These, then, are the most important characteristics of the American parties. For all practical purposes there are only two parties. The amount of competition between them varies both in time and in place, though in general it diminishes with the size of the unit and hence declines from presidential elections to statewide elections and thence to elections in House districts, cities, towns, and state legislative districts. Control over nominations and policies is diffused and decentralized. They display rather low cohesion as compared with European parties. They are distinguished less by ideological differences than by differences in rhetorical nuance and often important differences in programs and policies. They have marked differences in the social, economic and other characteristics of their followings. They are extraordinarily durable. And yet there is a great deal of variation in the support the voters give to each party from one election to the next, and even more markedly over a series of elections.

But what of the dangers of faction that were so much on the minds of the Founders? Do political parties exacerbate conflict and thereby endanger republics? Do they help to tame conflict and thereby help republics to survive? Or do they sometimes intensify and sometimes inflame conflicts? Do the passions of party increase the irrationality of voters?

In short: for better or worse, what do political parties contribute to a democracy? This is the question I propose to deal with in the next chapter.

Appendix

Some Issues on Which a Majority of Democrats have Opposed a Majority of Republicans in the House of Representatives, 1945–1965.

DATE	BILL	DEMOCRATS FOR–AGAINST	REPUBLICANS FOR–AGAINST
1945	Make House Un-American Activities Committee permanent	70–150	138–34
	Extend Foreign Trade Agreements Act, and authorize President to reduce tariffs up to 50%.	205–12	33–140
	Full Employment Act	195–21	58–105
1946	$3.7 loan to Britain	157–32	61–122
	Labor Disputes Act	109–120	149–33
	Labor Disputes Act, passage over President Truman's veto.	96–118	159–15
1947	Amend the U.S. Constitution to limit to two terms the tenure of the President.	47–120	238–0
	Passage of Labor Management Relations Act over the President's veto.	106–71	225–11
	Extend rent controls, but allow 15 per cent increases under specified conditions.	63–110	142–71
	Reduce individual income tax rates	63–105	236–2
	Admission of Hawaii as 49th State	54–77	141–56
1949	National Housing Act	192–55	34–131
	Agricultural Act extending for one year existing rigid supports.	79–165	160–4
	Trade Agreements Extension Act of 1949	7–235	144–5
	Defense Assistance Act	187–27	51–94
	Korea Aid Act	170–61	21–130

Some Issues (continued)

DATE	BILL	DEMOCRATS FOR–AGAINST	REPUBLICANS FOR–AGAINST
1950	Fair Employment Practice Act	116–134	124–42
	Foreign Economic Assistance Act motion to recommit bill with instructions to delete $25-million authorization to initiate President Truman's Point Four program of technical aid to under-developed countries.	31–191	118–29
	Amend the Natural Gas Act of 1938 to exempt sales of independent producers to interstate pipelines from price regulation	97–116	79–57
1951	Trade Agreements Extension Act. Simpson (R Pa.) amendment to restore "peril points" provision	42–163	183–4
	Mutual Security Act—motion to recommit with instructions to cut economic aid to Europe	37–162	149–14
1952	Bill to establish a Universal Military Training Program	81–131	155–30
	Defense Production Act amendments to request the President to invoke injunction provisions of the Taft-Hartley Act to halt steel strike	82–117	145–47
	Bill to maintain support prices for cotton, wheat, corn, rice, tobacco, and peanuts at 90 per cent of parity through 1954	133–35	74–85
1953	Hawaii Statehood	97–100	177–37
	Establish a special House committee to investigate and study educational, philanthropic and other organizations exempt from federal taxation	69–113	140–49
	Authorize issuance of 217,000 special quota immigration visas.	88–111	132–74
1954	Housing Redevelopment	127–61	48–150
	Omnibus Farm Bill; amendment to support five basic commodities on a flexible scale	45–147	182–23
	Unemployment Compensation; to increase benefits	92–68	17–173
	Atomic Energy; to permit exchange of atomic information with U.S. allies and develop peace-time uses of atomic energy with the aid of private industry.	36–146	195–7

Some Issues (continued)

DATE	BILL	DEMOCRATS FOR—AGAINST	REPUBLICANS FOR—AGAINST
1955	Reciprocal Trade Extension; motion to recommit with instructions to amend Farm Price Supports.	80–140	119–66
	Amend Agricultural Act of 1949 to provide high, rigid farm price supports for basic commodities.	185–29	21–172
	Alaskan-Hawaiian Statehood	105–107	113–63
	Amend the Natural Gas Act to exempt producers from public utility regulation and protect consumers from excessive rate increases.	86–136	123–67
	Housing Act. Omnibus measure, amendment eliminating public housing.	66–152	151–36
1956	Agricultural Act of 1956—90 per cent mandatory supports	189–35	48–146
	School construction; aid for local school construction	119–105	75–119
1957	Amendment to appropriation for Dept. of Agriculture to bar use of funds for a soil bank acreage reserve program on 1958 crops.	154–46	38–141
	School Construction Assistance Act; motion to strike the enacting clause (kill the bill)	97–126	111–77
1958	Temporary Unemployment Compensation Act; a bill embodying most of the Administration proposals	60–148	163–17
	Trade Agreements Extension Act; motion to recommit bill	61–160	85–108
	Preemption Doctrine; bill to provide that no act of Congress should be construed as nullifying state laws on the same subject	100–109	141–46
	National Defense Education Act authorizing approximately $900 million in federal grants; motion to recommit the bill.	45–147	95–86
	Labor-Management Reporting and Disclosure Act	149–61	41–137
1959	Public Works Appropriation Bill making an across-the-board cut of 2½ per cent of the funds provided in a vetoed bill, but retaining 67 projects that were not in the President's budget. Passage of the bill over the President's veto required.	260–5	20–116

Some *Issues* (continued)

DATE	BILL	DEMOCRATS FOR–AGAINST	REPUBLICANS FOR–AGAINST
1959	A bill to provide a new wheat program for the 1960 and 1961 crops.	195–71	7–143
	A bill to permit federal courts to strike down state laws under the federal preemption doctrine only if Congress had specified its intention to preempt the field of legislation involved or if a state and a federal law were in irreconcilable conflict, and to permit state enforcement of laws barring subversive activities against the Federal Government.	111–162	114–30
	Labor-Management Reporting and Disclosure Act; amendment to substitute for the commitee bill the language of their bill containing curbs on secondary boycotts and organizational and recognition picketing, and giving the states power to handle "no man's land" labor disputes.	95–184	134–17
1960	School Construction Assistance Act of 1960	162–97	44–92
	Increase minimum wage protection—substitute amendment; no overtime protection to employees of interstate retail chains.	90–176	121–27
1961	Administration's emergency feed grains program, providing for a rise in price supports for feed grains.	205–41	4–161
	Fair Labor Standards Amendments raising the minimum wage from $1 to $1.25; amendment substituting a new text raising the minimum to $1.15 an hour.	74–177	142–26
	Housing Act	210–38	25–140
	Motion to instruct House conferees not to agree to a Senate amendment authorizing $95 million to add electric generating facilities to the Hanford, Wash. plutonium producing reactor.	81–155	154–9
	Emergency Educational Act	164–82	6–160
1962	Resolution disapproving President Kennedy's Reorganization Plan No. 1 of 1962, to create an Urban Affairs and Housing Department	111–137	153–13

Some Issues (continued)

DATE	BILL	DEMOCRATS FOR–AGAINST	REPUBLICANS FOR–AGAINST
1962	Motion to recommit (kill) the bill which provided a system of supply-management controls for wheat, corn, and other feed grains.	48–204	167–1
	Trade Expansion Act; motion to recommit the bill.	44–210	127–43
	Foreign Assistance Act	178–68	72–96
	Authorize President to match up to $100 million in purchases of United Nations bonds by other UN members.	191–46	257–134
1963	Supplemental Appropriations amendment to add $450 million for accelerated public works program.	208–33	20–151
	Area Redevelopment Act Amendments	189–57	15–152
	Revenue Act lowering corporate and personal income taxes and making other changes	223–29	48–126
1964	Foreign Aid appropriation bill; motion to recommit the bill and insert an amendment designed to bar the Export-Import Bank from guaranteeing credits to Communist countries or their nationals for the purchase of U.S. commodities.	66–162	152–7
	Authorize $312 million as the U.S. contribution to an increase in the financial resources of the International Development Ass'n.	70–161	138–28
	Urban Mass Transportation Act	173–61	39–128
	Appropriate $3.7 billion for foreign assistance and related agencies; motion to recommit the bill with instructions to reduce economic aid funds by $247.8 million	55–185	143–23
	Economic Opportunity Act; a variety of programs to combat poverty.	204–40	22–145
	Bar the Supreme Court and lower federal courts jurisdiction over matters dealing with state legislative reapportionment.	96–140	122–35

SOURCE: "Key Votes, 1945-64," *Congress and the Nation,* op. cit. Part II, 38a-96a.

9

POLITICAL PARTIES:
CONTRIBUTIONS TO
DEMOCRACY

I N THE LIGHT OF LONG EXPERIENCE, not only in the United States but in
all other democracies, there is no longer any substantial ground for
doubting that political parties make substantial contributions to the
operation of a democracy—at any rate to a large democracy. To most
democrats who reflect on the problem, the positive contributions of
parties far outweigh their negative aspects. But in many democracies, not
least the United States, the negative aspects stimulate a lively interest in
the possibility of reforming the parties or the party system.

The principal contributions of parties, it might be suggested, are
three:

¶ They facilitate popular control over elected officials.
¶ They help voters to make more rational choices.
¶ They help in the peaceful management of conflicts.

Yet each of these propositions must be qualified. To explore ade-
quately the contributions and defects of parties, even American parties,
would require a volume in itself. The essays, monographs, and full-scale
books that appraise political parties and advance or criticize proposals
for reform would form a sizeable library.

A brief discussion can nonetheless open up some of the major questions.

Parties and Popular Control

One of the strongest claims made for political parties is that they assist the electorate in gaining some degree of control over elected officials and, thus, over the decisions of government.

For one thing, they carry on much of the organizing that makes a large-scale system of elections, representation, and legislation workable. The ambitions that induce party politicians to carry on these organizing tasks may repel democratic purists who would prefer motives closer to those invoked in the noble rhetoric with which men good and bad usually cloak their deepest purposes. Yet, whatever one may think of the motives of party politicians, these men (and women) perform some functions that are essential if democracy is not to dwindle into flatulent ineffectuality: Nominations, for example. In the absence of concerted effort, an election in which a candidate satisfactory to a majority *might* have emerged victorious may be won instead by a candidate who is satisfactory only to a minority. Surely, it is no virtue if a majority of like-minded voters are presented with three satisfactory candidates to run against a fourth candidate they agree is worse; for if they distribute their votes over the three they like, the fourth may win even though he be the most objectionable. Once like-minded voters see that it is worthwhile to organize themselves around a single candidate they have already acquiesced in the beginnings of a party.

The organization furnished by party is particularly necessary if an opposition is to exist. The dominant forces have somewhat less need of party organization; a President might, for example, operate with a sort of non-party coalition. This is no doubt why party machinery fell into decay when opposition temporarily became merely an exercise in futility during the long death-agonies of the Federalists and before the re-appearance of new cleavages around which an opposition could form. When there was no opposition, there were no effective parties. One could also put it the other way round. When there is no party, there is not likely to be an effective opposition. To displace the incumbents, who have the resources of government at hand, an opposition needs to organize, focus its forces, keep up the pressure, draw in every possible ally—all of which spells party. It is, thus, no accident that in Europe it was usually the Labour or Socialist opposition parties that first developed modern party organization—during the lengthy period they dwelt in opposition before assuming office.

Then, too, the sheer efficiency of party organization for winning political victories means that a single party, unchecked by another, would be a danger in a republic. One party needs to be counterbalanced by another. Let there either be no parties, or at least two parties, but never only one party, the citizens of a republic might well resolve. For if there is only one party, those among us who disagree with it will surely be outweighed, even though we be more numerous than our opponents. Since we cannot prevent at least one party from forming, lest by doing so we destroy our republican liberties, let there always be two parties or more. In this way we shall insure another kind of separation of powers and create additional checks and balances to sustain our liberties.

A fourth way in which parties assist popular control is to enable the many to pool their resources to offset the advantages of the few. This is doubtless one reason why Federalists looked upon parties with less enthusiasm than did Republicans. The chief resources of the many are their numbers and their votes; unorganized and leaderless they are no match for smaller numbers with wealth, skills, information, and informal organizational networks. Even when parties are internally oligarchical, as they generally are, a party competing for the votes of the otherwise unorganized many gives them more power than they would have if there were no parties at all.

Despite these contributions, parties have been subjected to a barrage of criticism on the ground that they are internally undemocratic and are ruled by oligarchies.[1] The charge is in considerable measure true. That the nominations and policies of political parties tend to be controlled by leaders, rather than the rank and file of members or registered supporters, seems undeniable. There is, as we saw, more decentralization and diffusion of control in the two American parties than in many European parties; even so, both the Democratic and Republican parties would be more accurately described as coalitions of oligarchies than as democratic organizations.

Given the democratic ideology prevailing among Americans, it was to be expected that efforts would be made to 'democratize' control over nominations in American parties; these efforts have diffused power, but

1. Among the most famous and most influential criticisms of this kind were those of M. Ostrogorski, *Democracy and the Organization of Political Parties* (1902), recently edited and abridged by S. M. Lipset, 2 vols., Garden City, New York, Anchor Books, 1964; and Robert Michels, *Political Parties* (1915), New York, Collier Books, 1962. For an appraisal of Ostrogorski, see Austin Ranney, *The Doctrine of Responsible Party Government*, Urbana, University of Illinois Press, 1962. For a critique of Michels, see John D. May, "Democracy, Organization, Michels," *American Political Science Review* (June, 1965), pp. 417–429.

they have not by any means turned the parties into democratic systems. As we saw, presidential candidates were first nominated by the Federalist and Republican caucuses in Congress. While the caucus continued to be used for several decades for presidential and vice presidential nominations, an alternative system began to develop for nominating candidates to other offices, national, state, and local. This was the nominating *convention*, which, being a representative system, seemed more appropriate than the caucus to the spirit of democracy. The caucus fell into even worse repute because it sometimes dramatized for all to see the fact that nominations were made by unrepresentative cliques. One such episode, in 1824, killed the congressional caucus as a device for nominating presidential candidates. Of two hundred sixteen Republicans in Congress who were invited to attend the nominating caucus that year, only sixty-six attended. This small minority proceeded to nominate for President of the United States a minor league politician, W. H. Crawford. In the election Crawford ran well behind Andrew Jackson, who led the other candidates in popular and electoral votes, and also behind John Quincy Adams, who trailed Jackson but ultimately won the Presidency when the House of Representatives had to decide the election. The convention made its first appearance for a presidential nomination in September, 1831, when the brief-lived Anti-Masonic party nominated candidates for President and Vice President at a convention in Baltimore. Henry Clay's National Republicans (soon to become the Whigs) followed suit in December, also in Baltimore. Jackson's followers, the Democratic Republicans, met in the same city in May, 1832, to nominate Jackson and Van Buren.[2] Ever since then, the national convention has been used for nominating presidential and vice presidential candidates.

Although national nominating conventions are representative in form, probably no one who knows how they work would argue that they are in any genuine sense democratic. At most, the convention is a contest among coalitions of state and local oligarchs. Because representative democracy seemed to have failed, advocates of democratic control over nominations turned to direct democracy: party members or supporters would themselves choose the candidate of their party. This was the direct primary.

Toward the end of the last century the convention began to be displaced by the direct primary, which is now almost universally employed for party nominations to executive offices other than the Presidency and the Vice Presidency. Yet even the direct primary has not

2. These events are described in Ostrogorski, *op. cit.*, Vol. II, *The United States*, pp. 17–39.

democratized the parties—in part, of course, simply because most people do not participate in crucial day-to-day decisions or, for that matter, even in the primaries. In examining fifteen non-Southern states over the period 1932–1952, the late V. O. Key discovered that "in three out of four primaries . . . the total Democratic primary vote plus the total Republican primary vote did not exceed 35% of the number of citizens 21 years of age or over . . . At the extreme of high participation in only one out of twelve primaries did more than 50% of the potential vote turn up at the polls"[3] (Table 9.1).

Running a party, like operating any other complex institution, is a full-time business; and as in other institutions, power tends to accrue to

Table 9.1. *Gubernatorial Primaries in Selected States According to Percentage of Potential Electorate Voting in Republican or Democratic Primary, 1926–1952*[a]

PARTICIPATION PERCENTAGE	NUMBER OF PRIMARIES[b]	PERCENTAGE OF PRIMARIES	PERCENTAGE OF GENERAL ELECTIONS
10–14	9	5.1	0.0
15–19	22	12.5	0.0
20–24	23	13.1	0.0
25–29	37	21.0	1.1
30–34	39	22.2	2.8
35–39	15	8.5	5.7
40–44	5	2.8	4.5
45–49	10	5.7	9.7
50–54	9	5.1	13.1
55–59	4	2.3	8.0
60–64	2	1.1	13.6
65–69	1	0.6	14.2
70 and over	0	0.0	27.3
	176	100.0	100.0

[a]The states included in this tabulation are Vermont, North Dakota, Maine, Wisconsin, Michigan, New Hampshire, Pennsylvania, Kansas, Massachusetts, Illinois, Wyoming, Ohio, Colorado, West Virginia, and Missouri. The selection of states for inclusion in this table was dictated chiefly by the availability for the period covered of the types of data needed for the analyses made in [V. O. Key] Table 16 and Figure 14.
[b]In the enumerations of this column one primary equals a pair of simultaneous primaries, Republican and Democratic. Thus in nine primaries, so defined, between 10 and 15 per cent of the potential electorate voted for either Democratic or Republican aspirants for the gubernatorial nomination.
SOURCE: V. O. Key, Jr. *American State Politics*, New York, A. A. Knopf, 1956, p. 135.

3. Key, *American State Politics*, p. 134.

those who make it a full-time business. Consequently, neither American political parties nor those of any other country are likely to be very democratic in their internal operations. But how much does internal party democracy really matter? Political parties are sometimes likened to business firms competing for customers—the customers being in this case the voters. And just as business firms are driven by competition to satisfy consumers, even if they are *internally* not governed by consumers in the way that a consumers' cooperative is, so, it is sometimes argued, competitive parties will fulfill all of the essential functions of democratic control listed a few pages earlier, even though each party is internally controlled by its leaders.[4]

Seen from this perspective, the most important question is not who runs the parties but to whom are the parties responsive? To the leaders themselves, to the rank-and-file registered party member, or to the voters? If the main function of competing parties is to insure that the views of voters are translated into government policies then it is less important that parties be internally democratic than that they be responsive to the views of the voters.

In actual practice, American parties seem to respond to all three forces: to the party leaders, to the rank-and-file, and to the voters. What happens if a party responds more to its leaders than to the voters? The answer seems obvious: It will probably be defeated in elections—if the other party is closer to the views of the electorate.

There is some interesting evidence bearing on this point. In 1957–1958, three social scientists surveyed about half the delegates and alternates to preceding presidential nominating conventions and compared the views of these party 'leaders' with a national survey of voters. The results revealed that on five major categories of issues—public ownership of resources, government regulation of the economy, equality and welfare, taxes and foreign policy—the differences in views were as follows:

¶ The greatest difference in views was between Democratic and Republican leaders.

¶ Almost equally great was the difference between Republican leaders and Democratic followers.

¶ Democratic followers and Republican followers showed the slightest—and indeed often negligible—differences in their views.

4. An interesting and important theoretical analysis bearing on this subject will be found in Anthony Downs, *An Economic Theory of Democracy*, New York, Harper & Brothers, 1957.

¶ There were relatively small differences in views between Democratic leaders and Democratic followers.

¶ But—the most startling finding—the differences between Republican leaders and Republican followers were almost as great as the difference between Republican leaders and Democratic followers.

¶ And there was actually a greater difference between Republican leaders and Republican followers than between Democratic leaders and Republican followers![5]

What these findings strongly suggest, then, is that by the late 1950s the Republican leaders big and small around the country, the activists who exercise dominant influence over nominations and policy, no longer represented their Republican followers, nor—and this is even more important—did they represent the great bulk of the voters, Republicans or Democrats.

During this period, as we have seen, voters continued their steady shift in allegiance toward the Democratic Party. Then, in 1964, the most ideologically conservative activists in the Republican Party, whose views probably represented only a minority among Republican voters and an even smaller minority in the electorate as a whole, seized control of the nominating convention from the Republican 'establishment,' nominated Senator Goldwater, and suffered one of the three or four worst defeats in the entire history of the party.[6]

The lesson seems fairly clear: When the policies of party leaders get too far out of line with those desired by the voters, support for the party will erode, and the party is likely to get beaten in elections.

5. Herbert McClosky, Paul J. Hoffman, and Rosemary O'Hara, "Issue Conflict and Consensus among Party Leaders and Followers," *American Political Science Review*, Vol. 54, (June, 1960) 406–427, Table 1, p. 410, and *passim*.

6. For an analysis, see P. E. Converse, A. R. Clausen, and W. E. Miller, "Electoral Myth and Reality: The 1964 Election," *American Political Science Review*, Vol. 59 (June, 1965) 321–336. The percentages of the total popular vote received by the Republican presidential candidate in their four great defeats were:

    1964, Senator Goldwater, 38.5%
    1936, Alfred M. Landon, 36.5
    1912, William H. Taft, 23.2*
    1856, John C. Fremont, 33.1

   *In 1912 Theodore Roosevelt, the Progressive candidate, received 34.9 per cent of the votes, many of them from Republicans; Woodrow Wilson, the Democratic candidate, received only 41.9 per cent of the votes.

In sum: The main contributions that parties make to democracy are not to be found in their internal operations but in their external effects—in competing for votes, organizing elections and legislatures, strengthening the opposition, providing offsetting checks to one another, and helping the many to overcome the otherwise superior resources of the few.

Parties and Rationality

Of what value is popular control, however, if voters are simply duped by party leaders or mindlessly vote for their parties without weighing the candidates and the issues? It might be argued that even if parties do help the electorate to gain some degree of control over elected officials, the control of the voters is in large measure spurious because it is irrational. Do parties reduce the irrationality of politics—or do they actually increase it?

It would be absurd to attribute to political parties all the forms of irrational and non-rational behavior that have ever been commonplace in human affairs and that exist in political systems of all sorts. The relevant question is whether parties change the amount and kinds of 'irrational' behavior from what would exist in the absence of parties.

Unhappily, the question is all but unanswerable. 'Levels' or 'amounts' of irrationality are terms that at best have only metaphorical meaning. No one has been able to measure changes in 'the amount of rationality' in political systems. The most extreme cases of collective irrationality in modern times have occurred in dictatorships, I believe, where whole populations have fallen under the absolute domination of paranoid leaders like Stalin and Hitler. By comparison, the stable democracies appear to be models of rational action. The question is, then, whether democracies would be more—or less—rational without competing parties.

One could theorize endlessly in response to this question without arriving at a conclusive answer. Let me therefore confine my conjecturing —for this it must be—to two aspects that everyone would agree do characterize political parties: (1) Parties present to voters a very small number of alternatives out of the total number theoretically available. This effect is particularly strong in a two-party system with single-member districts; for at elections the voter is usually confronted with only two rival candidates. (2) Each party develops a core of followers whose loyalty is fortified by non-rational factors like sentiment, pride, jealousy, combativeness, gamesmanship, and habit.

REDUCING ALTERNATIVES. Consider the first point. A voter presented with two rival candidates, might prefer neither of them so much as a third possible candidate who failed to win a nomination by either party. Similarly, on some matter of policy a voter may like the policy proposed by both parties less than some other alternative neither party is willing to advance. Reasoning along these lines, one might conclude that multi-party systems would offer voters a more rational choice than two-party systems. Yet, if four parties are better than two, are eight parties better than four? And sixteen parties better than eight? Or, for that matter, why not a separate candidate for every point of view held by any citizen in the country? But suppose the voter were confronted with a choice among twenty parties and twenty candidates. Might he not then reason as follows: These are too many alternatives; I cannot possibly appraise them all. Anyway, what do I gain if the man I vote for wins? If there are twenty parties in the parliament, my representative and all the others will have to make many compromises by the time they reach the final decision. How do I know what compromises they will make? Would it not be much better if most of the compromises had been made already, so that I could then choose between two possible coalitions, knowing roughly the direction in which each would go if it won a majority of seats . . . ?

Evidence does, in fact, suggest that the need to choose among a large number of parties is, for all except a small minority of voters, highly confusing and may lead, as in France, to seriously discrediting the whole party system.[7]

Such reasoning might cause a voter to oscillate between two poles At one pole, accepting the need for eliminating alternatives in order to arrive at a decision, he would enjoy the advantage of being confronted at elections by only two major alternatives. At the other pole, accepting the need to have his favorite alternative presented to him in order to have full freedom of choice, he would enjoy the advantage of being confronted at elections by a wide array of alternatives. Carried to an extreme, the first would result in a plebiscite, like those under the French Fifth Republic, where the only choices were to vote yes or no to a simple propo-

7. Philip Converse and Georges Dupeux, "Politicization of the Electorate in France and the United States," in *Elections and the Political Order*, op. cit., Ch. 14, esp. pp. 277–278.

sition. In this case, the voter might feel badly cheated and powerless because the choices were too narrow. The second solution, carried to the other extreme, would result in an array of choices so great that no voter could possibly estimate the effect of his vote on the ultimate outcome of the election and parliamentary bargaining. In this case, he might feel badly cheated and powerless because the choices were far too many.

The fact remains, then, that whenever a diversity of viewpoints and desired alternatives exists among the citizens of a democracy, the citizens must, sooner or later, by one process or another, reject all but one alternative (even if the final choice is, in effect, the null alternative of inaction). There is no escaping this process; it is the essence of 'rationality;' the only question is where and how it takes place. Much of the process of winnowing out alternatives could take place *before* an election, or *in* the election itself, or in negotiations *after* the election. All party systems do some winnowing *before* an election, making the *election* itself more decisive by reducing the alternatives, thus leaving less winnowing to be done *after* the election by bargaining and negotiation among members of different parties. The contrast is most marked between the British two-party system and a multi-party system like that of Italy, or France under the Third and Fourth Republics. The American party system, like the multi-party systems of the Scandinavian countries or the Netherlands, stands somewhere in between.

The notion, then, that parties increase irrationality in making choices by reducing the alternatives is based upon too simple a picture of the processes by which collective political decisions can be made, for all such processes necessarily involve a drastic reduction in the alternatives. Although the question is obviously exceedingly complex, it seems much more reasonable to conclude (as most students of party do) that on the whole the parties play a beneficial role in this process.

CONSEQUENCES OF PARTY LOYALTY. Consider now the second aspect of parties, the fact that they develop a core of followers loyal to the point of blind, nonrational support. The more the parties succeed in their efforts, it might be said, the more the weight of reason in politics is bound to decline. Parties may be the backbone of democracy; but all bone and no brain makes for a dull system. Does party loyalty insure the rationality of voters?

There are four markedly divergent answers.

The first and oldest, traceable to Rousseau, was the dominant theme of one of the earliest systematic analyses of British and American parties, that by M. Ostrogorski in 1902.[8] "Ostrogorski's conception of democracy," a modern critic has said, "was essentially atomistic. He thought of a democratic society as one in which isolated individuals engage in the rational discussion of public affairs, freely combining with other individuals on the basis of identity of views on particular issues."[9] To Ostrogorski all permanent parties are bad. Party loyalty turns into a kind of religious dogma:

> . . . To prevent the great mass of adherents on whom rests the power of the party from escaping it, their minds and their wills must be inveigled by every kind of device, . . . [Ostrogorski wrote] They unite their contingents in superstitious respect for pure forms, in a fetish-like worship of the "party," inculcate a loyalty to its name and style, and thus establish a moral mortmain over men's minds . . . They stereotype opinion in creeds which enforce on it a rigid discipline, they conceal the divergences of views that arise by composite programmes in which the most varied problems are jumbled together, which promise everything to everybody.[10]

Ostrogorski's solution was simple. It consisted

> in discarding the use of permanent parties . . . and reserving to party its essential character of a combination of citizens formed specially for a particular political issue . . . Party holding its members, once they have joined it, in a viselike grasp would give place to combinations forming and reforming spontaneously, according to the changing problems of life and the play of opinions brought about thereby. Citizens who part company on one question would join forces in another.[11]

Although in the United States, as we shall see, the parties approximate the condition described in the last sentence more closely than Ostrogorski could have known, in this country as in every other democracy his specific solution has been decisively rejected in favor of permanent parties. A second view, seemingly more in keeping with reality, became

8. M. Ostrogorski, Democracy and the Organization of Political Parties (1902), edited and abridged by S. M. Lipset, 2 vols., Garden City, New York, Anchor Books, 1964.
9. Ranney, op. cit., p. 115.
10. Ostrogorski, op. cit., Vol. II, p. 354.
11. Ibid., p. 356 (emphasis added).

much more widely accepted than Ostrogorski's. This is the view that while the great bulk of the voters are party loyalists who act not so much in pursuit of rational aims as from nonrational loyalties, a considerable body of independents stands outside the two parties. It is the votes of these independents, the argument runs, that essentially determine elections. And independents, it is said, are relatively rational and reflective: It is they who give genuine consideration to the candidates and programs of the two parties and then make their choices. Consequently, so long as the number of these thoughtful independents is sufficiently large and the number of loyalists on each side is less than a majority, the independents determine the outcome. Hence party competition places the decisive voice in elections exactly where it belongs, with the more thoughtful, judicious, and reflective citizens committed to neither party. Unlike Ostrogorski's appraisal, this view is on the whole favorable to the role of parties: They are useful, at any rate, as long as they do not gain so many partisans that they no longer need to contest for the votes of the independents.

Alas for this optimistic view, it was based almost exclusively on data available within easy reach of the armchair. Beginning with the presidential election of 1940, social scientists used the new techniques of opinion surveys in a series of studies that have revolutionized our knowledge about American voters.[12] From these studies, based upon lengthy and carefully analyzed interviews with a scientifically selected sample of the electorate, a new picture emerged—based for the first time, it seemed, on hard fact. In this new group portrait, the face of the rational voter is all

12. The principal studies for the following elections are:
1940: Paul F. Lazarsfeld, Bernard Berelson, and Hazel Gaudet, *The People's Choice*, 2nd. ed., New York, Columbia University Press, 1948.
1944: Sheldon J. Korchin, "Psychological Variables in the Behavior of Voters," Doctoral dissertation, Harvard University, 1946.
1948: Bernard R. Berelson, Paul F. Lazarsfeld, and William N. McPhee, *Voting*, Chicago, University of Chicago Press, 1954.
1952: Angus Campbell, Gerald Gurin, and Warren E. Miller, with the assistance of Sylvia Eberhart and Robert O. McWilliams, *The Voter Decides*, Chicago, Row-Peterson, 1954.
1954: Angus Campbell and Homer C. Cooper, *Group Differences in Attitudes and Votes, A Study of the 1954 Congressional Elections*, Ann Arbor, University of Michigan, 1956.
1956: Angus Campbell, Philip E. Converse, Warren E. Miller, Donald E. Stokes, *The American Voter*, New York, John Wiley & Sons, 1960.
1960: Angus Campbell, Philip E. Converse, Warren E. Miller, Donald E. Stokes, *Elections and The Political Order*, New York, John Wiley and Sons, 1966; Ithiel de Sola Pool, Robert P. Abelson, and Samuel P. Popkin, *Candidates, Issues and Strategies, A Computer Simulation of the 1960 Presidential Election*, Cambridge, M. I. T. Press, 1964.

but invisible. For social scientists have learned what was plausible enough all along: People who are most interested and most informed about politics are also likely to be the most partisan, and the least partisan voters are likely to be uninterested and uninformed about issues, personalities, and other aspects of a campaign. Unfortunately for the older portrayal of the independent as the ideal voter, it now became clear that the less partisan or more 'independent' of party loyalties a voter is, the less likely he is to be interested in politics, to be informed about candidates and issues, to go to the polls, or, if he does, to make up his mind judiciously after carefully reflecting on the alternatives. The portrait of the voter painted by these studies is, then, rather gloomy. On the one hand, it appears, most voters are party loyalists who vote less out of an intelligent concern for policy than from sheer loyalty, habit, and inertia. On the other hand, the reflective independent, once honored for his contribution, scarcely exists in real life. A voter who is not interested enough in politics to be partisan is unlikely to be interested enough to have an intelligent judgment on the election.

In the light of the evidence from these recent studies, campaigns and elections began to seem rather meaningless. The overwhelming number of interested voters, these surveys revealed, make up their minds even before the campaign starts. In fact, the more interested a voter is the more likely he is to make up his mind even before the candidates are nominated! To be sure, some voters are open-minded. Those who have 'open' minds during the campaign and do not decide how they will vote until the polling day draws near are very likely to have minds so open, it seems, as to be downright vacant. An election, looked at in the bleakest light shed by the data, seemed to be little more than sound and fury, signifying nothing . . . a tale told by an idiot.

Combined with a measure of healthy iconoclasm endemic among social scientists, the hard facts of election studies helped to give wide credence to this perspective among social scientists engaged in studying elections. Yet there is some reason for thinking that, as is often the case, a plausible view had been pushed too far. In a book which he was unable to complete before his death, the late and highly distinguished political scientist V. O. Key had moved to a counterattack with an impressive array of evidence drawn from opinion surveys covering every presidential election from 1936 to 1960.[13] According to Key's evidence, even if not many voters change their minds as a result of a campaign, many more

13. V. O. Key, Jr., with the assistance of Milton C. Cummings, Jr., *The Responsible Electorate, Rationality in Presidential Voting 1936–1940*, Cambridge, Mass., Harvard University Press, 1966.

Table 9.2. Percentages of Those Who Voted in Preceding Presidential Election Shifting in Preference and in Reported Vote from
One Major Party to the Other

PERIOD OF SHIFT	IN PRE-ELECTION PREFERENCE	N*	IN POST-ELECTION REPORT OF VOTE	N*
1936–40	17%	(12,031)	16%	(4319)
1940–44	14	(12,086)	11	(1673)
1944–48	18	(5,223)	13	(1795)
1948-52	17	(6,120)	20	(1795)
1952–56	13	(2,789)	(not given)	
1956–60	21	(4,295)	22	(1857)

*N is the total number of persons in the sample or in the combined samples from several surveys.

SOURCE: V. O. Key, The Responsible Electorate, Cambridge, Harvard University Press, 1966, Table 22, p. 19.

decide from one presidential election to the next to shift their vote from the presidential candidate of one party to that of the other party. The proportion of voters who shift between one presidential election and the next probably fluctuates somewhere in the neighborhood of 15-20 per cent. (Table 9.2). If we add to these 'shifters' the new voters (i.e., who have not voted in a previous election), then the rest, the 'standpatters' who do not change from one election to the next are in the neighborhood of 60-70 per cent of the electorate (Table 9.3). More important, Key also found a moderately close connection between one's views on policy and one's chances of shifting or standing pat. Far from being will-less partisans, the standpatters tend to be voters whose views are closer to those of the party they support than to the other party. The shifters tend to be people who, by shifting, give support to the party that is closer to their views than the party they had supported in the preceding elections, the portrait that emerges from Key's analysis is, on the whole, a benign one: " . . . voters are not fools. To be sure, many individual voters act in odd ways indeed; yet in the large the electorate behaves about as rationally and responsibly as we should expect, given the clarity of the alternatives presented to it and the character of the information available to it."[14]

Whatever the experts may have thought, on Key's showing the American voter appears to cast his vote with a reasonably intelligent judgment as to which party is the more likely to pursue the kinds of policies he prefers.

14. Ibid., p. 7.

Table 9.3. Percentages of New Voters, Shifters, and Standpatters
in Presidential Elections, 1940–1960

ELECTION	NEW VOTERS	SHIFTERS	STANDPATTERS	
1940				
Pre-election preference	16%	14%	70%	100%
Post-election report	16	13	71	100
1944				
Pre-election preference	15	13	72	100
Post-election report	13	10	77	100
1948				
Pre-election preference	23	14	63	100
Post-election report	16	11	73	100
1952				
Pre-election preference	30	12	58	100
Post-election report	20	16	64	100
1956				
Pre-election preference	27	10	63	100
Post-election report				
1960				
Pre-election preference	27	15	58	100
Post-election report	14	19	67	100

SOURCE: Key, *The Responsible Electorate*, Table 23, p. 20.

Parties and Conflict

What of the possible third contribution of American parties, the contribution they make to the peaceful management of political conflicts? Do they not actually intensify conflict—and, at times, endanger the prospect for a peaceful settlement of disputes by democratic means?

The answer to these questions forms a large and complex topic. To gain some grasp of the way the American political system handles conflict, we can no longer continue to examine the major political institutions separately, one by one. Instead, we need to begin to see how these institutions interact with one another and with the forces of conflict and conciliation. This is the subject of the next part of this book.

Part Three

How a Pluralist Democracy behaves in the midst of cleavages and conflicts

10

CONFLICT AND
CONCILIATION

Stability and Change

NOT SO VERY LONG AGO democracy was viewed almost everywhere as a radical, even revolutionary, system of government. A political system in which the national government is chosen by means of free elections in which most adult male citizens are entitled to vote and where political parties are actively competing for votes—this kind of system is a twentieth-century achievement. In most of the constitutional democracies of the present day—Britain and Sweden, for examples—manhood suffrage was significantly restricted until the time of the First World War. (Women were excluded from voting in national elections in the United States, as nearly everywhere else, until 1919; in Switzerland, that paragon of stable democracy, women still have no right of suffrage under the federal constitution, though some cantons have granted it.) During most or all of the nineteenth century, many countries that are now constitutional democracies were oligarchies in which power was constitutionally lodged in the hands of a few—for example, Germany, Italy, Austria, and until the advent of the Third Republic in 1874, France.

In the period between the world wars, as the constitutional democracies were endangered by new revolutionary movements—Communism, Fascism, Nazism—the view that democracy is a radical or revolutionary system began to wane. While revolutionary dictatorship, not democracy, came to be widely looked upon—and in many democracies feared—as the wave of the future, advocates of democracy went over to the defensive. In the quarter century after the onset of the Great Depression in 1929-30, the very survival of the constitutional democracies was desperately challenged by the newer forms of revolutionary dictatorship in a series of contests where the outcome was highly uncertain. After the end of the Second World War, the contest extended to the developing parts of the world. There, where democratic political habits and traditions are lacking and human misery is greatest, revolutionary dictatorships frequently blend nationalism, Marxism, and opportunism with much of the rhetoric and some of the ultimate aims, but few of the practices, of constitutional democracy.

As the democracies assumed the posture of defense, their intellectuals frequently displayed a mood of pessimism and even a kind of desperate masochistic satisfaction in announcing the obsolescence of constitutional and pluralistic democratic systems. Perhaps because totalitarian change was so great a danger, political theorists, sociologists, and many other students of democratic life began to place heavier stress on the conditions necessary for a *stable* democracy. Perhaps because internal conflict had grown so menacing, they also focused on *consensus*. Thus stability and consensus each became a sort of fetish, particularly among American political scientists and social theorists. By contrast, conflict and change were perceived not so much as offering the possibility of a better future (as democratic ideologues a century earlier would have said), but as menacing the foundations of existing democracy itself.

Quite possibly this intellectual mood reached a peak in the 1950s and has since been waning. However that may be, what is astonishing in retrospect is how much conflict many stable democracies have managed to absorb in the twentieth century, and how much change they have sponsored. In Britain, Sweden, Denmark, Belgium, and the Netherlands, to name a few cases, the extension of the suffrage and the democratization of political life were themselves profound yet ultimately peaceful changes. In almost every democracy, including the United States, twentieth-century leaders have carried through extensive—one might almost say revolutionary—programs of social reconstruction in order to mitigate the inequalities, the insecurities, and the injustices that industrialization and urbanization perpetuated, intensified, generated, or rendered more obviously unnecessary and capable of being eliminated. The heartening fact is that countries that already had achieved or were well advanced on the road to constitutional democracy before the First World War have nearly everywhere won and kept the loyalty of their people to democracy: for example, Switzerland, Britain, Norway, Sweden, Denmark, Iceland, Finland, Holland, Belgium, Canada, Australia, New Zealand—and, of course, the United States. In these countries, the working classes— once a source of internal danger because they were excluded from political life—have been integrated peacefully into the political system; in most of these countries, socialist and labor parties, drawing their strength mainly from skilled and unskilled workers, have participated extensively in government. Nor, in these countries, have the older elite groups, the aristocratic strata or the middle classes, been seriously alienated by democratization. In short, in these countries, extensive social and political changes have not prevented, but even have encouraged, conciliation among different social groups and the pacification of many ancient internal hostilities.

The United States, too, has undergone changes that half a century ago no one foresaw: the expansion of welfare measures and government intervention in the economy; the almost overnight assumption by the United States of its role as a major, *the* major, world power; and since the early 1950s huge steps toward the ultimate political, economic, and social liberation of Negroes.

To look upon constitutional pluralist democracies as incapable of significant change is, then, to misread the evidence of this century. In fact, perhaps only in the relatively small number of countries where democracy is quite firmly rooted can *extensive change* be reconciled with *extensive consent*. For there is a great deal of evidence to show that more profound changes can be made in the attitudes of people when they *participate* in changes (as they must if their consent is needed) than when they are *coerced*. Coercive change is more likely to produce speedy and outwardly dramatic yet superficial changes in attitudes. With participation, changes may seem to be taking place more slowly because consent is not won instantly, yet changes with consent are likely to be deeper and more longlasting.[1]

Nonetheless, it would be a false gloss on reality to say that change is easy in democracies, or to contend that change and stability pose no problems. For change almost always entails conflict between conservative social forces who gain or believe they gain from preserving the existing state of affairs or the direction in which things are moving, and their challengers whose aspirations require changes in the status quo or in the general direction of historical movement.

It is the set of problems involved in change and conflict, in stability and consensus that I now propose to explore. Before focusing explicitly

1. Sidney Verba, *Small Groups and Political Behavior*, Princeton, Princeton University Press, 1961, chs. 9, 10, "The Participation Hypothesis."

on the American political system, however, it will help if we first try to sort out some of the key problems and possibilities.

Change: Incremental, Comprehensive, Revolutionary

One of the commonest characteristics of literary utopias is that nothing ever changes. Yet it is a central fact of life that no living system is ever static. What is true of living organisms is also true of systems consisting of live human beings—economic systems, social systems, political systems.

Since change is ubiquitous, it is possible to examine it from a thousand different perspectives and to classify it in a thousand different ways. Let us focus our attention on *political* change and the *sources* or *causes* of political change.

Political change may be distinguished as to location and magnitude. As to location, change may take place in:

1. The operating *structure* of government, as when a democratic republic replaces an oligarchy, a dictatorship replaces a democracy, a presidential system replaces a parliamentary system, or direct election of Senators replaces election by state legislatures.
2. The *policies* adopted and enforced by the government, as when Congress passed civil rights acts in 1964 and 1965, or Medicare in 1965.
3. The *relative influence* of different strata and groups on the policies and decisions of government, as after the election of 1800 when small farmers and southern planters clearly gained greater influence while New England commercial interests lost.
4. The social, ethnic, religious, psychological, or other significant *characteristics of political leaders*. (In what follows I propose to ignore this last kind of political change and concentrate on the others.)

Political change may be small or great with respect to each of these locations or dimensions. For the sake of simplicity, however, let me reduce change to three magnitudes.[2]

1. Incremental, or marginal, when
   a. The operating structure is unaltered, except perhaps in matters of detail.
   b. Changes in policies are gradual and incremental rather than sweeping innovations or reversals of established policies. And,
   c. These changes result from negotiating and bargaining among spokesmen for groups whose relative influence remains more or less stable or subject only to gradual changes.
2. Comprehensive, when
   a. The operating structure is unaltered, except in matters of detail.
   b. Sweeping innovations or decisive reversals of established policies occur. And,
   c. These policy changes result from significant shifts in the relative influence of different groups.
3. Revolutionary, when comprehensive change in policies and relative influence (2b and 2c) is also combined with profound alterations in the operating structure of government.

Incremental change is the normal pattern in American political life. Although incremental change often seems depressingly slow and is rejected by revolutionaries as inadequate, a few examples will show how much can be achieved by means of a series of small but steady changes. Anything that grows at the rate of 3 per cent a year will double in size about every twenty-three years; at 5 per cent a year it will double in fourteen years. The United States achieved its extraordinarily high gross national product by growing at a rate of about 3 2/3 per cent a year from the 1840s onwards. The population increased from seventeen million in 1840 to 184 million in 1960 by growing at an average rate of about 2 per cent a year. Gross national product per capita during this period grew at the rate of about 1 2/3 per cent a year; personal consumption at about 1

---

2. The reader who enjoys playing with typologies—a somewhat barren enterprise to which social scientists are strongly addicted—may wish to construct for himself the eight possible combinations of 'small' versus 'large' changes in structures, policies, and group influence.

3/4 per cent a year. The world population explosion that has caused so much concern in recent years is produced by annual increments of only 2–4 per cent. The highest rate of growth in per capita gross national product in the 1950s in any industrial country, Communist or non-Communist, was less than 7 per cent. The average annual increase in the population of cities over twenty thousand in the United States from 1920-1950 was less than one-fifth of one per cent. Sixty-two per cent of the American population of voting age cast votes in the presidential election of 1964; if the percentage of the population voting were to grow by only 3 per cent a year, more than 95 per cent of the potential electorate would vote in the election of 1980. If output per man hour in the United States increases by 5 per cent annually, in fifty years each worker would produce eleven times as much as he does now.[3]

Incremental change, then, can be a powerful means for transforming a society—and has been so in the United States. However, comprehensive changes also occur at times; in fact, comprehensive changes are, as we shall see in later chapters, associated with some of the most dramatic events in American political history.

What of revolutionary political changes? The war between the American colonies and Britain is properly called a revolution, for it resulted in a profound change in the structure of government, in the relative influence of Americans and British officials, and in the policies pursued by the government. Making and adopting the Constitution might also be regarded as revolutionary in the sense employed here, even though that revolution, unlike the preceding one, was free of violence. For the Constitution clearly represented a decisive change in governmental structure; the policies of the new government, particularly Hamilton's economic policies, were sweeping innovations; and (the point is more debatable) the new government was associated, even if briefly, with a significant increase in the influence of men of commerce and finance. The Hartford Convention in 1814 and the South Carolina legislature in 1832 (of which more in the next chapter) might be said to have *sought*

3. The data on which the calculations in the paragraph are based were drawn from the following sources: Bruce M. Russett, ed., *World Handbook of Political and Social Indicators*, New Haven, Yale University Press, 1964, Tables 1, 7, 10, 45; Hearings Before the Joint Economic Committee, Congress of the United States, April 7–10, 1959, Part 2, Table 1, p. 271; Abram Bergson and Simon Kuznets, *Economic Trends in the Soviet Union*, Cambridge, Harvard University Press, 1963, Tables VIII. 2, VIII. 3, and VIII. 4, pp. 337–340; *Congress and the Nation*, op. cit., p. 1532. Louis J. Walinsky, "Keynes Isn't Enough," *The New Republic*, Vol. 154 (April 16, 1966), pp. 14–16.

revolutionary change, unsuccessfully. The Civil War was one part revolution, one part the failure of a revolution. The Secessionists failed to revolutionize the structure of government by seceding and establishing an independent confederacy. Yet if the North defeated the South's revolution, Lincoln and the Republicans represented a decisive shift of influence away from southern planters to free farmers, commerce, industry, and northern labor; and the legislation and constitutional amendments enacted during and after the Civil War constituted sweeping, indeed revolutionary shifts in long-established policies. The challenge of the Confederacy was, however, the last large-scale appeal to a revolutionary change of regime that has been made in American politics; since that time, proposals for revolutionary change have been the exclusive monopoly of tiny political movements on the extreme fringes.

Sources of Political Change

Why do political changes come about? What generates the forces that lead to political changes?

To seek satisfactory answers to these questions would take us far beyond the confines of this book and into a domain where knowledge is rather speculative. Processes of change are obviously of critical importance to understanding the past, acting in the present, and shaping the future; they have been much studied, yet they are not at all well understood.

However, it is possible to distinguish some of the important factors that trigger political changes. One is changes in technique or technology. A new technique, instrument, or machine is introduced. Because it outperforms the old, practical men acting from practical motives replace the old with the new. As the new technique spreads, it alters opportunities, advantages, handicaps, relations among people, groups, regions. There are changes in access to resources of power, changes in perspectives, ideas, ideologies, changes in demands, changes in patterns of conflict and agreement. And so political change occurs.

The introduction of gunpowder into Europe ended the military superiority of the mailed and mounted knight; it heralded the day of the musket and foot-soldier. And so it helped to bring feudalism to an end. The mariner's compass vastly expanded the possibilities of navigation; it facilitated the discovery of the New World and the creation of overseas empires; it was to one of these that Englishmen fled and created a new social, economic, and political order. Eli Whitney's invention of the cotton gin, as every American schoolchild is taught, made cotton a highly profitable crop; the profitability of cotton stimulated the spread of slavery and the domination of the South by a planter class. Thus, in the endless, complex, and little-understood chain of causes of which Whitney's invention is an early link, there is also the Civil War, the Ku Klux Klan, the "separate but equal" doctrine, the Supreme Court decision of 1954, and the Civil Rights Acts of 1964 and 1965.

Changes in social and economic institutions may also precipitate political changes. Institutional changes may of course be triggered by technological changes; the relationships are extraordinarily complex. The modern, privately owned, limited-liability business corporation was an institutional change that swept away most other forms of business in the nineteenth century. The competitive price system and the free market were institutional innovations of the late eighteenth and early nineteenth century. They responded to but they also generated technological changes; they created a new business class, a new middle class, a new urban proletariat, and a new set of problems, conflicts, and political changes that have not come to an end. In England, the same dense network of causes, one historian has argued, connects an innovation in 1795 by well-meaning justices of the peace trying to cope with rural unemployment and poverty to the triumph of the ideas of Adam Smith, the scrapping of all governmental controls over the price of labor, land, goods, and capital, and thence, in reaction and self-defense, to English socialism and the welfare state.[4] Why did the United States become a land of small free farmers in the nineteenth century, while Brazil did not? Both had a great supply of land. But the Englishmen who settled America did not bring feudal institutions here, whereas the Portuguese and Spanish in Latin America did.

There are, in the third place, ideas and beliefs. Simple mechanistic interpretations of history treat ideas in the minds of men as mere reflections of technology and institutions. Ideas are not, certainly, completely autonomous; but neither are technology and institutions. The relationships are too complex to try to sort out here. Yet ideas, beliefs, perspectives, and ideologies do change, and it is obvious that these changes often precipitate political changes. As Tocqueville pointed out in his introduction to *Democracy in America*, equality had long been spreading throughout Europe before the Americans founded their republic. Equality was spreading—ineluctably, so it seemed to him—as an idea and as a fact. If a growing equality in the actual conditions of life helps to sustain the idea of equality, may not the idea of equality help to sustain the fact of equality? Or, to take a more specific example, argu

4. Polanyi, *The Great Transformation*, New York, Rinehart and Co., 1944.

ments over the virtues and vices of balanced budgets—an issue over which a number of Americans have displayed considerable passion—are above all a question of ideas and beliefs, indeed of abstract theories and models (even if often exceedingly primitive ones) of the relations between budgetary deficits and surpluses and such matters as full employment and foreign trade. Differences in ideas about these matters have steadily led to conflict between academic economists and conservative bankers.

Ideas, institutions, and techniques are intertwined in ways too complex to unravel. During Andrew Jackson's great conflicts over the Bank of the United States, why did none of the protagonists give serious consideration to a solution that would probably be one of the first to occur to a presidential adviser or a member of Congress today: a government regulatory commission to keep the Bank in check? In large part, it seems, because the regulatory commission as an institution had really not yet been invented and its possibilities were not yet understood. The perceptions, ideas, ideology, if you will, that have developed with the growth of the regulatory state of the twentieth century were for all practical purposes not present in 1830. Jackson did not reject the idea of a regulatory commission in the sense that a critic of regulation might reject it today; nor could he have adopted the idea of a regulatory commission. For he simply did not perceive the idea as we do today, nor did anyone else in his time.

Thus perspectives change, social and economic institutions change, technology changes. And these changes trigger political changes. But government and politics are not necessarily mere by-products of changes. Government policy may trigger changes in ideas, in social and economic institutions, in technology. The policies and practice of the New Deal surely helped to change the perspectives of Americans about the proper role of government. It was government action that created a new institution in the Tennessee Valley Authority. It was government action that produced the institutions of modern social security (action in this country was long antedated by the innovation in Europe). And it was government action that led directly to the most awesome technological innovation in history, the unleashing of nuclear power.

The Depth of Change and Conflict

When one reads about some great revolution, one is inclined to suppose that sooner or later everyone in the society was, surely, drawn into the orbit of the revolution. Yet it might be far more realistic to assume—as some theorists have—that rapid historical changes and political conflicts of all kinds, even great revolutions, directly involve only the tiniest and most visible minorities, the activists and elites, in spheres political, social, economic, cultural, religious. Probably the truth usually lies somewhere between these extreme views. Unfortunately it is impossible to specify precisely where the truth does lie, for our knowledge is severely limited.

The unhappy fact is that until the late 1930s, when systematic opinion surveys first began to be used, no means existed for measuring the spread of views and opinions in a population. As a result, we may never recapture the data needed for estimating in any except a very crude way how views were distributed in the past; we cannot therefore know much about detailed or rapid changes in views. We cannot go back to the eve of the Civil War and conduct a survey of the opinions of a properly selected sample of Americans and follow it up with one in 1865 to see what changes had occurred. Hence historical generalizations about the way opinions were distributed among Americans (or any other population) before about 1936 must be treated with great caution. Yet we cannot hope to understand past changes and conflicts without making some assumptions as to attitudes in the general population—among voters, for example.

It is useful, I think, to take as a central hypothesis that certain general characteristics of political life which have been found to hold since the 1930s were also true of American citizens before the 1930s. There are, certainly, no plausible grounds for thinking otherwise, and there is a good deal of indirect evidence in support of the hypothesis.

What is striking from modern evidence is how many Americans there are to whom political life is totally foreign. A substantial proportion of American adults—probably not less than one out of four nor more than one out of two—are for all practical purposes a-political. Politics is so remote from their lives as to lack much meaning: They rarely vote or otherwise participate in politics, and their views on political matters are uninformed and shallow. These people constitute what might be called the a-political strata. They seem to constitute a significant proportion of every citizen body in all historical periods. And there is not much doubt that in the United States the a-political strata have always constituted a sizeable group.

It is highly reasonable to suppose, then, that during all periods of American history the 'burning issues of the day,' the 'great debates,' the 'fierce conflicts' of politics have scarcely engaged the attention of the a-political strata at all; perhaps a quarter to a half of the adults have always been so wholly involved in the events of their daily lives—worries over jobs, income, health, family, and friends—that they have barely followed what later generations regard as great historical events. Ordinary voters who do at least bother to vote are no doubt more engaged. But it is the minority of politically active citizens who are highly active politically—and most of all the tiny minority of leaders—who have always been most fully engaged in political conflicts. No matter how important historians might regard it today, to most Americans in 1854, the passage of the Kansas-Nebraska Act was doubtless very much less interesting and important than the marriage of a daughter, a son moving West, a death in the family, the baby's croupe, the bad harvest, the local scandal.

But of course when the leaders and the politically active citizens fail to resolve their differences, as they did in 1860, the cost in lives is levied on the whole people.

Conflict: Moderate and Severe

Utopias are not only marked by the absence of change. They are also unflawed by conflict. Most Utopias are pervaded by the deathly stillness of the graveyard. Yet in every political system there is perpetual and unceasing conflict.

In a republic, conflict is particularly visible because it is permitted; it is not all driven underground; it is protected, even institutionalized.

Now it is true that conflict can be dangerous to a political system. And citizens take a certain gamble when they opt for a republic. For the citizens of a republic may react to severe political conflict in ways that endanger or destroy the survival of their republic: by violence, suppressing one's opponents, civil war, secession, disloyalty, even by widespread demoralization, apathy, and indifference.

Yet to say that severe political conflict is undesirable is not to say that all political conflict is undesirable. So long as men have different views and the liberty to express their views, conflicts will exist. To condemn all political conflict as evil is to condemn diversity and liberty as evils. If you believe that some diversity is inevitable, and that liberty is desirable, then you must hold, logically, that political conflict is not only inevitable but desirable.

This is therefore the dilemma: In a democracy moderate political conflict is both inevitable and desirable. Yet severe political conflict is undesirable, for it endangers any political system, and not least a democracy. A democratic republic can escape from this dilemma only if conflict is somehow kept within bounds. But how is this possible? How can conflict, like atomic energy, be tamed and put to peaceful purposes?

It is not easy to say precisely what one means by the severity or intensity of a conflict, but the essential criterion appears to be this: Within a particular political system the more that the people on each side see the other side as enemies to be destroyed by whatever measures may be necessary, the more severe a conflict is. Evidence that a conflict is increasing in severity would therefore be an increasing harshness of language in which one's opponents were portrayed as implacable enemies to be annihilated; an increasing stress on or actual employment of violence against opponents; or an increasing use of means to victory that previously were regarded as impermissible, illegitimate, perhaps even illegal or unconstitutional.

What circumstances, then, are likely to lend moderation to a dispute or, conversely, to inflame it into a conflict of great severity?

To begin with the most obvious point, how severe a conflict is depends on how much is at stake. The more at stake, the harder a question is to settle.

But how severe a conflict is also depends on whether the people engaged in the dispute can discover mutually beneficial solutions. The ideal outcome, naturally, would be one in which all the contestants were not only better off than before but better off than under any alternative solution. To be sure, if solutions of this kind were common, conflict would rarely occur. Nonetheless, there is a clear difference between a dispute in which no contestants can come out ahead except by making others worse off ('If you win, I lose,' or what mathematicians call a 'zero-sum game'); and a dispute in which there is a solution under which no one will be worse off than before, and some may even be better off. If two people are faced with a deal in which every dollar A gains will make B worse off than he is now, neither of them has much incentive to negotiate. If the best solution for both is identical—if each stands to gain most by one solution—then negotiation is hardly necessary. If, on the other hand, A's best solution is different from B's, but there appear to be compromise solutions under which one or both might be better off than they are now, and neither worse off, both have every reason to negotiate in order to arrive at a mutually acceptable decision.

The worst possible conflict, then, is one involving very high stakes and no solutions other than the mutually incompatible kind, 'If you win, I lose.' Consequently, conflicts involving two mutually incompatible ways of life among different citizens are bound to place an exceedingly

FIGURE 10.1—AGREEMENT PILES UP HEAVILY ON ONE SIDE: THE J-CURVE

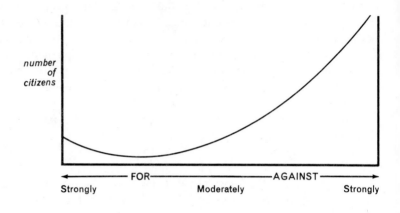

serious strain on a republic. Here the term 'way of life' means the rights, privileges, and human relationships a group most highly prizes—their families and friends, economic position, social standing, respect, religious beliefs, and political powers. Any group that sees its way of life at stake in a dispute will, obviously, be reluctant to compromise. If the whole society is divided and if no compromise is possible—if the conflict is over two completely incompatible ways of life—then a democracy is likely to break down. There are no cases, I think, in which a democratic republic has managed to settle conflicts of this kind peacefully.

So far we have been concerned with the characteristics of the conflict itself. But the severity of a conflict also depends on the people who are engaged in it, particularly their numbers and their location in the political system.

In a republic, elections mean that sheer numbers are often important. Hence how severe a conflict is depends in part on how many citizens hold similar or moderate views and how many hold extreme views. The greater the relative number of citizens who hold extreme (and opposing) views, the greater the danger that a conflict will be disruptive. Conversely, the greater the proportion of citizens who hold views that differ only slightly—that is, moderate views—the less the danger. In a

FIGURE 10.2—DISAGREEMENT IS MODERATE: THE BELL CURVE

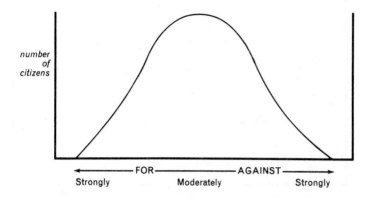

number of citizens

◄——————— FOR——————— AGAINST ———————►

Strongly   Moderately   Strongly

stable republic, the great bulk of citizens will, presumably, more or less agree on many questions. In some cases, the agreement would pile up so heavily on one side of an issue that the matter would cease to produce much controversy. A graph of such a distribution would assume the shape that statisticians call, for obvious reasons, a J-curve[5] (Figure 10.1). A vast number of questions that might be of abstract interest to philosophers, moralists, theologians, or others who specialize in posing difficult and troublesome questions are, in any stable political system, irrelevant

5. For theory and data bearing on the discussion in this section, see particularly V. O. Key, Jr., *Public Opinion and American Democracy*, New York, A. A. Knopf, 1961, Ch. 2 and *passim;* and Robert A. Dahl, ed., *Political Oppositions in Western Democracies*, New Haven, Yale University Press, 1966. Discussions of relationships between the behavior of political parties and various distributions of political opinions may be found in Anthony Downs, *An Economic Interpretation of Democracy*, New York, Harper and Bros., 1957; and Gerald Garvey "The Theory of Party Equilibrium," *American Political Science Review*, Vol. 60 (March, 1966) pp. 29–38. A useful critique of some of the assumptions involved will be found in Donald E. Stokes "Spatial Models of Party Competition," in Angus Campbell, Philip E. Converse, Warren E. Miller, and Donald E. Stokes, *Elections and the Political Order*, New York, John Wiley and Sons, 1966, ch. 9.

FIGURE 10.3—DISAGREEMENT IS SEVERE AND EXTREME: THE U-CURVE

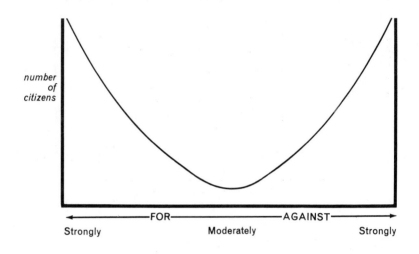

to politics because practically everyone is agreed and no one can stir up much of a controversy. If a controversy does arise because of the persistence of a tiny dissenting minority, in a republic the chances are overwhelming that it will soon be settled in a way that corresponds with the view of the preponderant majority.

Sometimes people may disagree more markedly and yet hold moderate opinions. A distribution of this kind, which is sometimes called a bell-shaped or a double J-curve, is illustrated in Figure 10.2. When a conflict of views takes this shape, the chances are that it will be solved rather easily. Democratic systems with two major parties manage conflicts of this kind with special ease, because both parties tend to converge toward the center. Since an overwhelming number of voters are clustered at the center, and only a few at the extremes, the two major parties not only may ignore the extremes with impunity, they must do so if they want to win elections. The costs of making an appeal to voters with extreme attitudes is to lose the much more numerous support of the moderates near the center.

In cases of the first two kinds, where opinion is strongly one-sided or overwhelmingly moderate, the conflict is not likely to be severe. If the extremes predominate, however, conflicts of great severity are likely

FIGURE 10.4—MODERATION AMONG LEADERS, EXTREMISM AMONG ORDINARY CITIZENS

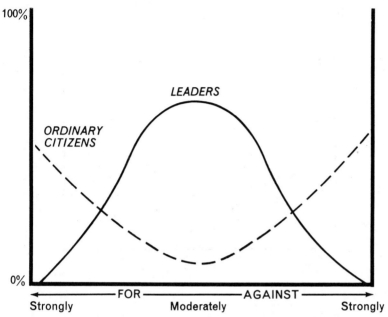

(Figure 10.3). Whenever extreme opinions grow at the expense of moderate opinions or one-sided agreement, obviously conflict becomes much more dangerous, for it is much harder to find a basis for mutually profitable compromises. Moreover, in these circumstances the political parties find it profitable to adapt their appeals to the views of citizens at the extremes. While extreme parties flourish, center parties grow weak. Sooner or later, one of the extreme parties or coalitions is likely to begin considering ways by which it may suppress or destroy the other, and violence is on the way.

The severity of a conflict depends, however, not only on the sheer numbers of people who hold divergent views, but also on their positions in the political system. Officials and other political leaders may be more moderate or more extreme in their views than ordinary citizens. Thus leaders may exaggerate or minimize the cleavages of opinion among the general population. The more they minimize cleavages, the less severe the political conflict; the more they emphasize and exaggerate differences of opinion, the more severe the conflict is likely to be. In Figure 10.4, leadership opinion is moderate, while rank-and-file opinion is sharply divided. In Figure 10.5, the situation is reversed; ordinary citizens are not as badly split as leaders. We would expect a situation like that suggested

FIGURE 10.5—EXTREMISM AMONG LEADERS, MODERATION AMONG
ORDINARY CITIZENS

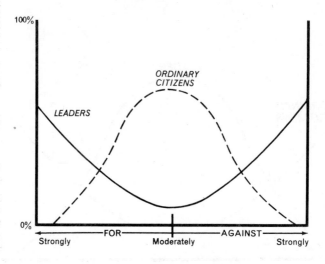

by Figure 10.5 to produce more severe political conflict and greater danger to a republic than the situation represented by Figure 10.4.

In a republic, what could produce differences between the attitudes of ordinary citizens and the attitudes of political leaders? If political leaders were chosen at random from the general population, then significant differences would be most unlikely. But the selection of political leaders is, as we know, very far from a random process. Even in a republic, some kinds of people are more likely to gain public office and power than others.

Citizens who are the most interested and active in politics are more likely to rise to the top than citizens who find politics uninteresting or otherwise unattractive. People who are interested and active in politics often differ in important respects from people who are less interested, less active, less effective, in short less influential. In the United States, for example, citizens who are most interested and active in politics and most confident that they can be effective tend also to have more education, higher incomes, and jobs of higher status. Because these conclusions are drawn from surveys made only since the 1930s, one cannot be certain that the differences of the last several decades existed earlier. But since much the same differences show up in other democratic countries, there is good reason to think that the social-psychological factors so evident now were also present in earlier years in the United States. In any case, if the more active, interested, and influential strata of citizens tend to differ from the rest of the population in education, income, and occupations, is it not likely that they will also differ in political views? Hence instead of mirroring the political views of the rest of the population, leaders might be either more moderate or more antagonistic, and this may increase or decrease the severity of the conflict.

The way in which attitudes are distributed geographically is also relevant, particularly in countries where legislators are not chosen under some system of proportional representation. If a country is divided into election districts or states in which the office goes to the candidate with the most votes, and all other candidates with fewer votes are defeated, the intensity of a political conflict may depend on where different views are located in the country. An opposition minority that is concentrated in a particular region will find it easier to gain representation in the legislature than one that is dispersed more or less evenly throughout the nation. Moreover, even without extra representation because of the election system, a regional minority is in a relatively strong position to keep its views alive, to command conformity to its views within the region, to punish dissenters, and to portray their opponents as outsiders, aliens, foreigners.

The special effects of regionalism on conflict call attention to a broader observation—namely, that the severity of a conflict depends on the way in which one conflict is related to another. A society offers a number of different lines along which cleavages in a conflict can take place; differences in geography, ethnic identification, religion, and economic position, for example, all present potential lines of cleavages in conflicts. If all the cleavages occur along the same lines, if the same people hold opposing positions in one dispute after another, then the severity of conflicts is likely to increase. The man on the other side is not just an opponent; he soon becomes an enemy. But if (as Madison foresaw) the cleavages occur along different lines, if the same persons are sometimes opponents and sometimes allies, then conflicts are likely to be less severe. If you know that some of your present opponents were allies in the past and may be needed as allies again in the future, you have some reason to search for a solution to the dispute at hand that will satisfy both sides. The people on the other side may be your opponents today; but they are not your enemies, and tomorrow they may be your allies.

There is still one more factor to consider. Political institutions themselves may exacerbate conflicts, or make it easier to settle them. It is striking how in the hands of the English, the eighteenth-century Parliament became an institution for settling disputes that up until then—and in most other countries afterward—threatened the regime itself.[6] This development within Parliament does not wholly explain, of course, why Britain has not had a civil war since the seventeenth century; a fuller answer would require, among other things, an explanation of the path of parliamentary development itself. Nonetheless, the presence in Britain since the end of the seventeenth century of an institution that elaborated a set of conventions, devices, practices, and mechanisms for settling disputes has surely helped Britain to make changes and to negotiate internal conflicts peacefully for the past three hundred years.

It would take no great imagination to conceive of political institutions that would have the opposite effect, that would intensify rather than reduce conflict. Suppose, for example, that the American Constitution automatically awarded the Presidency and a majority on the Supreme Court to the party with the most numerous votes in an election, and awarded Congress to the party with the next largest number of votes. Conflict would then be built squarely into the constitutional system. (The attentive reader, remembering at this point that the Founding Fathers deliberately sought to build conflict into the constitutional structure, may wonder about the effects of their design on political conflicts in the United States. We shall come to that problem in due time.)

Although the extent to which political institutions intensify or soften conflicts is a highly complex matter, one might hope to distinguish political mechanisms according to whether they facilitate gaining *consent* through negotiation, or facilitate making *decisions* with or without much consent, or facilitate both *consent and decisions*.

A system that required extensive consent but made it difficult to reach a decision—for example, a system in which all decisions had to be made by unanimous vote—would so greatly prolong negotiations and impede decisions that the prospect of mounting a revolution in order to get something done might become increasingly attractive. On the other hand, in a system where it was easy for leaders to make decisions without seeking the consent of others, minor questions could be settled with dispatch. But when ordinary citizens seriously disagreed with one another or with their leaders in such a system, decisions could be imposed without their consent; to secure obedience many citizens would have to

6. Archibald S. Foord. *His Majesty's Opposition 1714–1830*, London, Oxford University Press, 1964.

be coerced by the government. By embittering and alienating the citizens who were coerced, a system like this might ripen disputes into resistance and revolution. Thus a system that could somehow facilitate both negotiation of consent and arriving at decisions might serve best to keep conflicts from becoming so severe as to generate a revolution.

Conflict: A Paradigm

Let me now draw together the threads of this discussion on conflict into a paradigm or model that will be helpful in understanding the next four chapters.

The intensity or severity of a political conflict in a republic is indicated by the extent to which people on each side see the other as an enemy to be destroyed; evidence that political disagreements are becoming severe is an increase in threats or actual use of violence, suppression of opponents, civil war, secession, disloyalty, or a marked increase in demoralization, apathy, indifference, or alienation.

The intensity or severity of a political conflict depends on at least four sets of factors:

1. The way in which politically relevant attitudes are distributed among the citizens and leaders.
   a. The greater the number of citizens who hold extreme (and opposing) views the more severe a conflict is likely to be. Conversely, the greater the number who hold moderate views, the less severe a conflict is likely to be.
   b. The more extreme the views of political leaders and activists in comparison with the views of ordinary citizens, the more severe the conflict; conversely, the more moderate the views of leaders and activists in comparison with other citizens, the less severe the conflict is likely to be.

2. The patterns of cleavage.
   The more conflicts accumulate along the same lines of cleavage, the more severe they are likely to be; conversely,

Table 10.1. *A Paradigm: Some Factors that Moderate or Intensify Political Conflicts*

	conflict is more likely to be	
	MODERATE if:	SEVERE if:
1. The distribution of attitudes is	convergent	divergent
a. Attitudes of citizens are	convergent	divergent
b. Attitudes of political leaders and activists are	convergent	divergent
2. Lines of cleavage are	overlapping (cross-cutting)	non-overlapping (cumulative)
3. Threats to ways of life are	absent	present
a. Privileged groups feel	secure	seriously threatened
b. Aspiring groups feel	successful	frustrated
4. Political institutions provide		
a. Negotiations for consent but not decisions	no	yes
b. Decisions without consent	no	yes
Agreed processes for negotiating consent and arriving at decisions	yes	no

the more conflicts intersect along different lines of cleavage, the less severe they are.

3. How much is at stake.
   a. The more at stake, the more severe a conflict is likely to be.
   b. A conflict in which no contestant can possibly make himself better off except by making other contestants worse off is likely to be more severe than a conflict in which there is a possibility that no contestant need be worse off than before, and some may be better off.
   c. Conflicts involving incompatible 'ways of life' are bound to be particularly severe.

4. The political institutions.

    a. Political institutions and processes are likely to intensify conflicts if they require the groups involved to negotiate but do not provide any acceptable way by which leaders can terminate negotiations and arrive at a decision.

    b. Political institutions and processes are likely to intensify conflicts if they make it possible for leaders to make decisions without engaging in negotiations to obtain the consent of the persons, groups, or parties involved.

    c. Political institutions and processes are most likely to reduce the intensity of conflicts if they embody widespread agreement on procedures, *both* for negotiating in order to gain consent and for terminating the negotiations and arriving at a decision.

These propositions are summarized in Table 10.1.

I I

COMPREHENSIVE CHANGE
AND SEVERE CONFLICT

I T IS OFTEN SUPPOSED, not only by foreigners but by Americans themselves, that except for the one Civil War the American political
system has managed to avoid severe conflicts. Americans, it is often
said, are a moderate people; they display their moderation even in their
conflicts, most of all in their political conflicts. How much truth does
this view contain?

The last chapter suggested that we define the severity of conflict
along these lines: The more one side looks upon the other as an enemy
to be destroyed by any means available, the more severe the conflict is.
Unfortunately it is not easy to translate this definition into a precise and
satisfactory way of measuring the relative severity of different conflicts.
However, if one accepts as signs of the severity of a conflict such indicators as threats or moves to disrupt the constitutional system, or threatened or actual violence against or on behalf of national policies, or expressions by sober and informed observers or participants that a given
conflict will lead to disruption, revolution, or civil war—if one accepts
these as portents, then the weight of historical evidence does seem to offer
solid support to this proposition: From the very first years under the new
Constitution, American political life has undergone *about once every
generation* a conflict over national politics of *extreme severity.*

The Recurrence of Intense Conflict[1]

To suggest the evidence for this proposition, let me review some familiar historical episodes.

¶ Before the Constitution had completed its first decade, the Alien and Sedition Acts (1798)—which threatened the very existence of any organized political opposition—were challenged by the legislatures of Kentucky (1798) and Virginia (1799) in resolutions that hinted for the first time (but definitely not the last) that a state government might deliberately refuse to enforce a federal law which its legislators held to be unconstitutional. The specters raised by the Alien and Sedition Acts on the one side, and by the Kentucky and Virginia resolutions on the other, were temporarily banished by what Jefferson called "the Revolution of 1800."

¶ Within hardly more than another decade, New England Federalists, driven to desperation by the embargo policies enforced by the Republicans, assembled at Hartford (December, 1814) in a convention that not only adopted a set of resolutions calling for extensive constitutional changes but issued a report asserting among other things that "in cases of deliberate, dangerous, and palpable infraction of the Constitution, affecting the sovereignty of a State and liberties of the people; it is not only the right but the duty of such a State to interpose its authority for their protection, in the manner best calculated to secure that end."[2]

¶ Less than another score of years went by before the United States approached civil war over the tariff. In 1828, the legislature of South Carolina adopted a set of eight resolutions holding the newly passed "Tariff of Abominations," which ultimately hit cotton exporters with what seemed to them undue harshness, unconstitutional, oppressive, and unjust; in an accompanying document written by John C. Calhoun the legislature espoused the view that in such cases a single state might "nullify" an unconstitutional law (1828). Four years later when the South Carolinians were still chafing under the protective tariff, a conven-

1. This section draws heavily on my essay "The American Oppositions: Affirmation and Denial," in Political Oppositions in Western Democracies, New Haven, Yale University Press, 1966.
2. Richard B. Morris, ed., Encyclopedia of American History, New York, Harper & Bros., 1953, p. 153.

tion called by the state legislature adopted an ordinance that 'nullified' the tariff acts of 1828 and 1832, prohibited the collection of duties within the state, and asserted that the use of force by the federal government could be cause for secession. The state legislature passed laws to enforce the ordinance, to raise a military force, and to appropriate funds for arms. President Jackson thereupon sought and gained from Congress the legal authority to enforce the tariff laws, by military means, if necessary. A compromise tariff was worked out in Congress, South Carolina rescinded her Ordinance of Nullification, and civil war was avoided—or rather postponed for thirty years.

¶ Thereafter, the middle years of the century were occupied with various aspects of the controversy over slavery, particularly whether slavery should be permitted in the great unsettled areas of the West, a question that touched the most sensitive interests of Northerners and Southerners. Finally, as everyone knows, the issue no longer could be contained; and for four terrible years men died of wounds and disease to settle the question—or so it was supposed.

¶ Although it does not quite fit in our list of severe conflicts, there occurred in the decade before the Civil War a curious political phenomenon that is worth remarking. In the 1840s European immigration, chiefly from Ireland and Germany, greatly increased. A nativistic, anti-foreign, anti-Catholic, super-patriotic reaction began to set in. In the early fifties, political tickets consisting of anti-foreign candidates appeared in New York, Pennsylvania, and New Jersey. Soon a party began organizing secretly; it called itself the American party; because its members refused to divulge their secrets, their enemies called them Know Nothings. The party showed some promise of replacing the Whig Party. As it turned out, however, the life of the American party was brief and unsuccessful, for it was consumed in the struggle over slavery. Had it prospered, the whole course of American history would have been different.

¶ The issue of slavery was settled only in part by the Civil War: slavery was abolished, to be sure, but the freed Negroes were not long permitted to enjoy equal political rights—to say nothing of economic, educational, or social privileges. Ten years after Appomattox, the election of 1876 brought the country to the verge of civil war, but as so often before and after, the outcome was compromise rather than war; yet a compromise that tacitly allowed the restoration of White Supremacy throughout the South and thus adjourned the whole problem of effective citizenship for Negroes until the middle of the present century.

¶ This adjournment allowed economic questions to take over. During the last third of the century, discontented farmers and urban workers formed a pool of recurring opposition to the policies of a national govenment which responded less and less to their demands than to those of the new men of business, industry, and finance. Out of economic dissatisfaction, radical and reformist movements developed: Socialist Labor, the Greenbackers, the Farmers' Alliance, Populism, the Socialist Party, the IWW. The trade union movement also had its turbulent beginnings: the Knights of Labor, the AFL, the railway unions. Strikes, lockouts, and protest meetings frequently led to severe violence.[3]

¶ In the presidential elections of 1896, William Jennings Bryan, a man of primitive intellect and beguiling eloquence, whom Democrats and Populists had jointly nominated as their candidate, and who in his simple and confused protests against the "domination of Eastern Capital," evidently evoked support among a considerable number of farmers and some urban workers, was defeated by McKinley after a campaign period of unusually high tension.[4]

¶ Sixteen years later, a new Democratic President, the second since the Civil War, was elected; under Wilson's leadership many of the specific reforms that had been demanded earlier by Populists and Socialists were carried out. Although these reforms were sharply opposed, the conflicts seem to have lacked some of the earlier intensity; the country was not widely viewed as approaching another civil war.

¶ The next generation witnessed the Great Depression, mass unemployment, extensive discontent, the election of the third Democratic President since the Civil War, new outbreaks of violence, the rise of quasi-democratic or anti-democratic political movements on both right

3. For example, in 1886 during a demonstration near the McCormick Reaper Works in Chicago, six strikers were killed by the police and many more were wounded. The next day two thousand persons attended a protest meeting in Haymarket Square; policemen ordered the meeting to disperse; a bomb was thrown, killing a policeman; in the ensuing battle, seven more policemen and four workers were killed, sixty policemen and fifty workers were wounded. Six men who had addressed the meeting were sentenced to death; four were hanged the following year. In 1894, Grover Cleveland, the first Democrat elected to the Presidency since 1856, now in his second term as President, called out Federal troops in order to break a great nationwide strike of railway workers against the Pullman Company.

4. Bryan won 47 per cent of the two-party vote and carried twenty one states —all of them, however, agricultural states of the South, Midwest, and West.

and left, and extensive changes in national policies, changes that from 1935 onward were fought with increasing bitterness. Driven to extreme measures by a Supreme Court dominated by conservatives who steadily rejected the major items of the New Deal as unconstitutional, President Roosevelt in 1937 even tried to 'pack' the Court. It was his first important move to prove unpopular, and he was defeated. From about 1937 until the bombing of Pearl Harbor in 1941, political leaders were bitterly divided over the question whether it was better to meet threats of military aggression by 'isolation' or 'intervention.'

¶ Less than thirty years later, the unsolved problem of equal rights and opportunities for Negroes produced a new eruption of demonstrations, discontent, and violence—not only in the South but also in the Negro ghettos of the large Northern cities. And in 1964 the long-frustrated opposition of the radical right, capitalizing on white reactions to Negro discontent, temporarily captured the Republican Party and at last found national spokesmen in the Republican nominees for President and Vice President, Senator Goldwater and Representative Miller.

Whoever supposes, then, that American politics has been nothing more than a moving consensus, a sort of national Rotary Club luncheon, has not sufficiently reflected on the regularity of intense conflict, crisis, and violence in American history.

The Pattern of Severe Conflict

Like massive hurricanes that sweep in from the Atlantic, brief, violent, and devastating tornadoes of the Middle West, or earthquakes along the West Coast, great conflicts in American political life are long remembered by the survivors, much discussed, and imperfectly understood. Yet it is possible to discern some elements in the pattern.

If we take as our point of departure a period of moderate conflict that adheres to the pattern described in the last chapter, then the development of a severe conflict is marked by the kinds of shifts suggested in the paradigm presented on page 280.

DIVERGENCE OF ATTITUDES. Leaders of rival coalitions diverge more and more in their attitudes on key political questions. This growing divergence may come about in a variety of ways:

[286]

¶ Older leaders may change their original views. This is probably the least likely development.

¶ Questions that would have divided leaders had they arisen
earlier—and perhaps did divide them at times—may
become much more salient and urgent than before.

¶ New issues emerge on which the views of leaders had not
previously crystallized.

¶ Older leaders may be replaced by newer leaders with different
views. For example, the generation of the Revolution
and the Constitutional Convention virtually disappeared from active political life after Madison's second term, and a whole new generation—John Quincy
Adams, Clay, Calhoun, Jackson, Van Buren, Webster
—took its place. This new generation had in turn
largely disappeared by the 1850s, when still another
generation, that of Lincoln and Douglas, took over.

As we saw in the last chapter, even when the views of political
leaders are known, it is difficult to speak with confidence about the development of 'public opinion' in a severe conflict. The most reasonable
assumption is, however, that the 'public' responds to the divisive issue
slowly and in diverse ways. At one extreme the a-politicals remain untouched even at the peak of tension (or right up to the time when political conflict turns into organized slaughter from which even the a-politicals cannot escape—as happened in 1861). Thus a recent examination of
"letters from the 1850s and 1860s, which had been preserved by old
families in the various attics of a small Ohio community" revealed that
"no references to abolition were ever found in any of the letters"![5]

At the other extreme, the political actives are heavily involved.
Indeed, it is mainly the actives who determine the course of the conflict;
severe conflict means a growing intensity of conflicting views among the
actives; it is they who settle or fail to settle a dispute.

What of the in-between group, the ordinary voters? For the most
part they intervene only in one way: by voting. But that one way can be
important. Although most voters continue to vote their traditional party
loyalties, without regard to the course of a dispute that seems to be
polarizing the country, some do change. Ironically, they may change for
reasons that have nothing to do with the conflict: A farmer in 1860

5. Philip E. Converse, "The Nature of Belief Systems in Mass Politics" in
David E. Apter, ed., *Ideology and Discontent*, Glencoe, Ill., The Free
Press, 1964, pp. 206–261, p. 251.

might have voted against the Democrats because his crops were poor or his prices were low and he felt that the Democrats were responsible because they had held the Presidency. The perception the ordinary voter has of what is at stake when *he* votes need not have much to do with what political leaders think is at stake. Nonetheless, political leaders do interpret the election returns; they must perforce interpret an election in terms of their own perspectives, which may not be those of the voter. Hence political leaders often interpret an election as favoring or dis-approving this or that policy. As a result their own enthusiasm for one alternative may wax or wane. In politics nothing succeeds like success.

Moreover, whatever the voters may intend, an election has conse-quences for the balance of power among the contesting groups. One party, for example, may sweep the Congress and the Presidency, while the other is reduced to a legislative minority. Probably we shall never know much about what was in the minds of voters when they went to the polls in 1860. But the consequence of their votes was to reduce the spokesmen for Southern slaveholders to a clear minority in Congress, and to confront that minority with a President who would not yield on the key issue of whether slavery was to be allowed in the territories. The message of the election was, then, that slaveowners were a political minority without enough safe allies in the rest of the country; that they would remain forever a minority; more, that they would henceforth be a diminishing minority. Thus, though most voters North and South al-most certainly did not intend it, the indirect consequence of the election was to encourage Southern leaders to embark on the fatal course that led to secession and civil war.

FROM CROSS-CUTTING TO CUMULATIVE CLEAVAGES. As a conflict intensifies, ties which have held the politically active strata together and made it relatively easy for them to negotiate disputes begin to snap; their views have less and less in common. The snapping of social and ideological ties, the diminution of overlapping cleavages, polariza-tion into two hostile camps, the appearance of a single, dominant fault line separating the country (or at any rate the most active and articulate elements in the political life of the country) into two parts—in short, the change from overlapping or cross-cutting cleavages to non-overlap-ping or cumulative cleavages—may be both a cause of growing conflict and a consequence.

In most of the severe conflicts listed earlier, the process did not go very far: if it had, the Revolution of 1776 might not have been our last revolution, nor the Convention of 1787 our last full overhauling of the

Constitution, nor the Civil War our last civil war. But in the years just before the Civil War the process of polarization into two camps went much further than at any other time in history. Here is how the ties snapped in three major kinds of nationwide institutions:

> Several major religious groups split into separate Northern and Southern churches over the issue of slavery:[6]
> 1844: the Methodist Episcopal Church
> 1845: the Baptist Church
>
> The political parties fell apart or split:
> 1850-1856: disintegration of the Whigs
> 1854-1860: formation and rise of the Republican Party as a sectional party with no southern wing.
>
> Splitting of the Democrats in 1860:
> Northern Democrats nominate Douglas
> Southern Democrats nominate Breckenridge
>
> The Federal Union split:
> 1860, Dec.: South Carolina secedes
> 1861, Jan.: Florida, Alabama, Mississippi, Georgia, Louisiana
> Feb.: Texas
> April: Virginia
> May: Arkansas, Tennessee, North Carolina

HIGH STAKES.   In all the conflicts described at the beginning of this chapter, the stakes were high (or, what amounts to the same thing, seemed to be) for one side or both. Often a conflict was interpreted by one side or the other as allowing no satisfactory compromise because gains by one side entailed losses by the other; this was the case, for example, in the tariff dispute of 1828-32 when Southern leaders argued that any protective tariff imposed for the benefit of Northern industry caused a corresponding loss to Southern exporters of cotton. In fact, in each of the severe conflicts mentioned above, leaders on one side—and sometimes on both sides—believed that the way of life to which they and their constituents were attached was seriously threatened by the goals pursued by their opponents. Whether or not their views were 'rational' or

6.   After the outbreak of war in 1861, the Presbyterian Church and the Protestant Episcopal Church also split.

[289]

even factually correct is irrelevant: People hate and fight no less if what they believe to be true happens to be false.

Each of these severe conflicts could also be interpreted as a situation in which leaders of strata whose way of life was supported by the status quo now saw themselves threatened at the foundations by the aspirations and policies of other groups whose expanding influence, if unchecked,

Table 11.1. The Stakes of Conflict: Ways of Life

SPOKESMEN FOR THE FOLLOWING GROUPS OR STRATA:	WERE PERCEIVED BY SPOKESMEN FOR THE FOLLOWING GROUPS OR STRATA AS THREATENING THEIR WAY OF LIFE:	THUS PRODUCING SEVERE POLITICAL CONFLICT AND THESE CRISES:
Small farmers, Southern planters, Democratic-Republicans	New England commercial interests, Federalist 'aristocracy.'	1798–9: Alien and Sedition Acts; Va. and Ky. Resolutions.
Northern and Western Whites; manufacturers; Western farmers; abolitionists.	Southern Whites	1828–32: Tariff, So. Car. Nullification. 1840–60: Slavery in the territories. 1860–77: Civil War and Reconstruction.
Immigrants, Catholics, Irish, Germans.	Native Protestants	1850–60: Know-Nothingism
Farmers and urban laborers	Businessmen, bankers	1880–1900: new parties, Greenback, Socialist, etc.; strikes, violence. 1892–1896: Populism as major force. 1933–37: New Deal
Southern Negroes	Southern Whites	1865–75: Reconstruction 1954–present: integration, civil rights, violence.
Northern Negroes	Northern urban Whites	1960s: integration: violence—Harlem, Rochester, Chicago, Los Angeles, etc.

would destroy or at the very least seriously impair their way of life. At the outset of a conflict, the 'conservative' strata may have enjoyed enough influence with national policy-makers—the President, the Congress, and the Supreme Court—to insure their own protection, even if insurance against defeat required vigilance and unremitting struggle. But as leaders of the 'conservative' strata began to believe that their influence was diminishing and that soon they might be unable to stem the tide, they more and more perceived their opponents as implacable enemies who must be destroyed lest they be destroyers.

How the conflicts described a moment ago fit this interpretation is shown in Table 11.1.

American Political Institutions
as Managers of Conflict

What of the fourth factor in our paradigm of conflict, political institutions? In times of moderate conflict, American political institutions encourage compromise, consensual decisions, and incremental changes. But what is the effect of the political institutions when proposals for more comprehensive changes inspire severe conflicts? Political institutions continue to provide stubborn and well organized groups numerous opportunities to veto, modify, or delay the passage or enforcement of policies that would entail comprehensive change. Hence even in the face of proposals for more far-reaching changes, and even in the presence of increasingly severe conflict, the tendency of the political institutions is to handle severe conflicts along the same lines as moderate conflicts. American political institutions, then, encourage political leaders to respond to severe conflicts in three ways:

1. By forming a new political coalition that can overpower the opposition. But this, as we shall see, is a difficult solution.
2. By incremental measures that postpone comprehensive change.
3. By enduring compromises that remove the issue from serious political conflict.

OVERPOWERING THE OPPOSITION. A severe conflict is sometimes moderated or even terminated when one political coalition gains enough power to overcome the resistance of its opponents. Instead of compromising, the winning coalition enacts its policies despite the opposition of the defeated coalition. If the opposition fights back, as it is likely to do, it finds itself too weak to prevail. Unable to reverse the main direction of policy imposed by the winning coalition, the opposition may in time accept the major policies enacted by the winners and settle down to bargaining for incremental adjustments; thus severe conflict gives way to a period of moderate conflict.

Probably the only effective way in American politics for one coalition significantly to reduce the bargaining power of an enemy coalition is to turn it into a visible and even isolated political minority by defeating it in national elections. However, because of the large number of positions where an embattled minority, unable to win the Presidency or a majority in either house of Congress, can dig in and successfully continue to challenge the policies of the majority coalition, a single electoral victory is ordinarily not necessarily enough, particularly if the contest is close. The victories of the winning coalition may have to be large, thus visibly demonstrating the weakness of the opposition, and repeated in a series of presidential and congressional elections, thus demonstrating for all to see that the minority coalition has little chance of regaining its power and must come to terms with the victors.

In at least three instances, severe conflicts seem to have been moderated or terminated in this way:

1. After Republicans overwhelmed Federalists in the elections of 1800 and continued to do so for a generation. By 1814 when the Federalists at the Hartford Convention talked disunion, their leaders gained little national support. After 1814 Federalism disappeared as an effective political movement, though old Federalist leaders constituted a kind of feeble opposition until they died or despaired.[7]

2. From the mid-term elections of 1894 onward, and particularly after the presidential election of 1896 when Republicans overwhelmed the coalition of Democrats and Populists that supported William Jennings Bryan and thereby moderated (and postponed) a severe conflict over economic policies. The defeat of the Populists meant that neither of the two major parties would develop into a farmer-labor

7. Shaw Livermore, Jr., *The Twilight of Federalism, The Disintegration of the Federalist Party 1815–1830*, Princeton, Princeton University Press, 1962.

coalition with an ideology and program comparable to those of the British and European Labor and Socialist parties. A major challenge to unregulated capitalism was turned back and a socialist alternative was effectively removed from American political competition (Chapter 15).

3. After 1932 when elections temporarily destroyed the power of the Republican coalition centered on the policies of business and thereby made it possible for most of the New Deal proposals of FDR to be enacted. By the time the Republican opposition was able to regroup, it could no longer undo the New Deal except in minor ways. However, it entered into a coalition with Southern Democrats, which by bargaining in Congress impeded or prevented further reforms until the power of both the Republicans and the Southern Democrats was temporarily smashed by the presidential and congressional elections of 1964.

Yet elections are often indecisive; neither Truman's re-election in 1948 nor Kennedy's election in 1960 enabled the victorious President to enact the major policies he and his party had advocated in the campaign, despite the fact that both Presidents had Democratic majorities in Congress. Truman presented to Congress an extensive Fair Deal program involving a number of social reforms. But only a few of these had been enacted when he went out of office.[8] Why are elections so infrequently decisive? Why, people often ask, don't elections settle things one way or the other? Why is it so difficult for a President and Congress ostensibly of the same party to terminate a severe conflict by over-riding the objections of their opponents, carrying through their legislative program, and letting the country decide at the next election whether it likes the changes or disapproves of them?

By now it must be clear to the reader that American political institutions were never designed to operate in this fashion; nor do they. But in addition to the institutions themselves, several aspects of American beliefs, sentiments, or loyalties reduce still further the likelihood that

8. Congress passed legislation providing for housing and slum clearance, and an expansion of Social Security coverage. It failed to pass "Fair Deal" proposals for federal aid to education, health insurance, a new Department of Health, Education, and Security, repeal of the Taft–Hartley Act, a reorganized farm plan providing direct production payments to farmers, a fair employment practises commission, and eliminating the poll tax. Most of these proposals have since been enacted, mainly under President Johnson.

elections can be decisive. For one thing, party loyalties are, as we have seen, incredibly persistent. It is uncomfortably close to being true that either of the two major parties could probably win twenty million votes for its presidential candidate even if it nominated Ed the Talking Horse. The overwhelming electoral sweeps in the presidential elections of 1936, 1952, and 1964 left the defeated minority with a substantial share of popular votes (37 per cent in 1936, 44 per cent in 1952, 39 per cent in 1964). In the twenty-six presidential elections from 1864-1964, the defeated party received less than 40 per cent only seven times; it received 45 per cent or more in twelve elections, and from 40-45 per cent seven times. A party overwhelmed by a landslide is far indeed from being in a hopeless situation.

Then, too, the votes of a winning coalition are not uniformly distributed throughout the country; there are sizeable regional variations. A political minority in the nation may be a political majority in a region, as with the New England Federalists in 1800 or the Democrats in the South in every election won by a Republican President from 1860 onward. A defeated minority with a powerful regional base stands a good chance not only of surviving but of keeping most of its senior political leaders in Congress.

Finally, Americans are not agreed on a single, definite, generally accepted rule for legitimate decision-making in government.[9] Although the legitimacy of rule by majorities is frequently invoked, the majority principle is not, among Americans, a clear-cut rule of decision-making. This principle invoked to support 'national' majorities (i.e., as revealed in national elections) is also used to support local, state, or regional majorities. This conflict over the legitimacy of 'national' versus 'local' majorities, as we saw in Chapter 2, goes all the way back to the Constitutional Convention.

Another widely held American doctrine, expressed at the Convention, implied in the Declaration of Independence, and traceable to Locke, holds that majorities lose their legitimacy if they infringe on natural rights or other absolute standards of political right or justice. Because there is always much dispute as to what these natural rights or absolute standards are and how far they extend, the boundary between majority rule and individual rights has been continually disputed throughout America's national history. Yet the doctrine that the right of a majority to govern is properly restricted by 'unalterable' rights is not widely challenged among Americans.

Since the earliest times, doctrines of unalterable rights and of states

9. See above, Chapter 1, pp. 34–42, and below, Chapter 13, pp. 325–326.

rights have both been invoked by defeated minorities to challenge the legitimacy or constitutionality of laws enacted or proposed by President and Congress. Attacks on national law in the name of the rights of individuals or states or both were expressed in the Virginia and Kentucky Resolutions of 1798-99, the declaration of the Hartford Convention in 1814, the South Carolina Resolutions in 1828, the "Exposition and Protest" accompanying them, the Ordinance of Nullification in 1832, and South Carolina's "Declaration of the Cause of Secession" in December, 1860. These principles were revived in the South from 1954 onward as the doctrine of 'interposition' to justify resistance to the Supreme Court's decisions on integration.

American political institutions, then, do not ordinarily endow the candidates or parties who receive a majority of votes in an election with enough power to carry out their policies over the opposition of the defeated minority. And American political beliefs do not endow the winning majority with over-arching and unambiguous legitimacy; nor do they deprive the defeated minority of grounds on which to argue that its policies and not those of the majority must be allowed to prevail.

Consequently, while a severe conflict is sometimes terminated by an overwhelming victory for one side in a congressional and presidential election, the American political system and American beliefs make this solution somewhat difficult and uncommon.

POSTPONING COMPREHENSIVE CHANGES. American political institutions are excellently designed for making incremental changes. But they also foster delay in coming to grips with questions that threaten severe conflict. It is true that delay may provide precious time during which a seemingly severe problem may change its shape, become more manageable, even disappear. But postponement may also inhibit leaders from facing a problem squarely and searching for decisive solutions—solutions that may be forced upon them many years later when they can no longer delay.

Policies of economic reform which were barely more than marginal have sometimes taken decades or even generations to accomplish. When the Democrats won the Presidency and majorities in the Congress in 1892 that enabled them to pass an income tax law, the Supreme Court, rightly forseeing that the income tax could be the foundation for redistribution at the expense of the rich, struck it down; it required sixteen years and the Sixteenth Amendment to make it possible for Congress to enact an income tax again. The regulation of child labor, as we saw, was held up for a generation by a Supreme Court unwilling to yield to Congress and President. In 1948, President Truman, acting on recommendations from his advisory Committee on Civil Rights, recommended federal legislation against lynching, the poll-tax, segregation in public transportation, and discrimination in employment. Although mild civil rights legislation was passed in 1957 and 1960, no major legislation on civil rights cleared Congress until 1964, almost two decades after President Truman's recommendations.[10] Passage of American welfare and social security laws has followed the enactment of comparable laws in most European democracies by one to several generations. A national medical care program has been advocated for generations. In 1945, President Truman proposed to a Congress a comprehensive medical insurance program for persons of all ages. The first law establishing a national system of medical insurance, though only for the elderly, was not enacted until 1965.

COMPROMISE. The existence of innumerable fortified positions from which an embattled but well organized minority can fight off and wear down an attack, combined with the absence of any *single* rule for making legitimate decisions on which the political activists are agreed, means that it is difficult to terminate a conflict by the clear-cut victory of one side over another. Hence severe conflicts are sometimes handled by reaching a compromise. Occasionally the result is a long-lasting compromise. Two of the most enduring compromises of this kind in American history both involved the Negro; both sought to eliminate the Negro as a source of severe conflict among Whites; both succeeded in doing so for long periods; both were at the expense of the Negro; and by present-day standards in all civilized countries, both were unjust. One dealt with the Negro as slave, the other with the Negro as freed slave.

The first was the Missouri Compromise of 1820 which, by providing that slavery would be permitted south but not north of the line 36°30' across the vast territory acquired in the Louisiana Purchase, promised to maintain a balance between the numbers of free and slave states and thereby preserve to each side a veto over future national policies. This compromise kept the problem of slavery in the territories and the future of slavery itself within manageable bounds for thirty years. Then the new land acquired as a result of the Mexican war added territories not covered by the old compromise and, as we shall see in the next chapter, triggered off the decade of severe conflict that eventuated in the Civil War.

The second great compromise was arrived at in 1877, after the long crisis produced by the contested presidential election of 1876. We shall

10.   For further details, see below, ch. 16, pp. 416–428.

return to it in the next chapter. Briefly, however, the effect of this settlement was to bury Reconstruction and to permit white Southerners to restore White Supremacy. Once again the fate of the Negro was removed as a source of severe conflict—once again by Whites at Negro expense. This shameful compromise endured for seventy years. The beginning of the end for the compromise of 1877 was legislation mentioned a moment ago on civil rights and employment introduced by President Truman. His proposals split the Democratic Party and strengthened the coalition of Southern Democrats and Northern Republicans in Congress; hence it was not until the passage of the Civil Rights Acts of 1964 and 1965 that the Compromise of 1877 came finally to an end.

These two experiences say something about the limits of compromise. First, there are moral limits; by the standards of the contemporary civilized world, both of our great national compromises went beyond these limits. Second, it is obvious that one necessary condition for any such compromise is that the contestants can somehow discover an alternative that vastly reduces the threat from the other side, particularly by eliminating or markedly decreasing the dangers to the way of life defended by one or more contestants. Such a solution may not exist, or—what amounts to pretty much the same thing—it may not be discovered. The Compromises of 1820 and 1877 were possible only because Negroes had no voice in arranging them. If spokesmen for the slaves had enjoyed the same veto power over national policies that spokesmen for slaveholders possessed until 1860, the Compromise of 1820 would have been impossible. If the freedman had been as influential in 1877 as white Southerners that compromise too would have been impossible.

A TENTATIVE CONCLUSION.   One effect of all these factors is to impede decisive action through the ordinary processes of presidential leadership and congressional law-making. The consequences of this are two-fold and not lacking in paradox. The system encourages Presidents who wish to be decisive to draw on their reservoir of powers that lie outside the control of Congress or Courts; hence in these domains, most visibly in foreign policy, the President is more and more his own master and the normal processes are more and more displaced by executive decision. Yet side by side with presidential decisiveness in areas where he cannot be closely controlled, the system operates to inhibit decisive action. Thus while incremental changes can be bargained for, large reforms that elsewhere have been enacted in a single session of parliament hard on the heels of a single election must in the United States await many elections and many sessions of Congress. To make the point once more, the system encourages incremental change; it discourages comprehensive change. It facilitates the negotiation of moderate conflicts.

But what is the effect of American political institutions on severe conflict? Do they intensify conflict by preventing early if drastic changes in policies? Do they prolong and exacerbate severe conflict? Although the evidence we have examined in this chapter lends itself to this interpretation, one must confess that the evidence is murky and allows a different argument. Yet it would be hard to deny that the danger is there.

Political Integration, Conflict, and Change

The Constitutional Convention, we saw, did not decide whether the United States was to be an aristocratic or a democratic republic. That decision was made by the Americans who came after, who affirmed their commitments to a democratic rather than an aristocratic republic.

A democratic outcome depended upon widespread acceptance among Americans of the legitimacy of a democratic republic as a system of government for Americans, and on the legitimacy of certain procedures for arriving at political decisions—procedures, in the case of Americans, largely but not wholly fixed by the Constitution.

Severe and prolonged conflict may cause one or another of the antagonists to reject the system itself. If rejecting the system produces nothing more than apathy, the structure may nonetheless survive. But if rejection leads to revolution or civil war, the structure may be destroyed. The twentieth century has seen this happen: in Italy between 1919-1924, in Germany between 1929-1934, in Spain between 1935-1938. In each of these cases the costs of conflict, rejection, and revolution were staggering.

Each of the conflicts mentioned at the beginning of this chapter and recapitulated in Table 11.1 (p. 290) endangered the solution that Americans had arrived at by about 1800: a democratic republic operating within the institutional and procedural limits set by the Constitution. If leaders and citizens in the conflicting groups were to reject this solution, then the American democratic republic very likely could not survive.

As it turned out, some alienation, some rejection of the American republic did occur side by side with political integration. In the early years, the victory of the small farmers doubtless sped their political integration and strengthened their loyalty to the Republic. Yet the other side of the coin is that many of the defeated New England Federalists rejected it; the importance of their rejection was mitigated only by the fact that they were few in numbers. Many of them remained alienated from the emerging democratic republic, hostile to the very idea of democracy and wide sharing of power. From his conversations in the United States (May, 1831–February, 1832), Tocqueville observed that

> . . . when the democratic party got the upper hand, it took exclusive possession of the conduct of affairs, and from that time the laws and the customs of society have been adapted to its caprices. At the present day the more affluent classes of society have no influence in political affairs; and wealth, far from conferring a right, is rather a cause for unpopularity than a means of attaining power. The rich abandon the lists, through unwillingness to contend, and frequently to contend in vain, against the poorer classes of their fellow citizens. As they cannot occupy in public a position equivalent to what they hold in private life, they abandon the former and give themselves up to the latter; and they constitute a private society in the state which has its own tastes and pleasures. They submit to this state of things as an irremediable evil, but they are careful not to show that they are galled by its continuance; one often hears them laud the advantages of a republican government and democratic institutions when they are in public. Next to hating their enemies, men are most inclined to flatter them. . .
>
> But beneath this artificial enthusiasm and these obsequious attentions to the preponderating power, it is easy to perceive that the rich have a hearty dislike of the democratic institutions of their country. The people form a power which they at once fear and despise. If the maladministration of the democracy ever brings about a revolutionary crisis and monarchical institutions ever become practicable in the United States, the truth of what I advance will become obvious.[11]

The old Federalists did not change by much; rather they died out and were replaced by a younger generation with more flexible notions.

The conflict between Northerners and Westerners on the one side,

11. Alexis de Tocqueville, *Democracy in America*, Vol. 1, pp. 186, 187.

and Southern slaveholders on the other, was accompanied in its last stages by an increasing rejection of the American democratic republic by spokesmen for the slavocracy. The rejection was long-lasting: the full political integration of the South into a democratic political system was retarded for a century after the Civil War by the refusal of Southern Whites to concede political equality to Negro citizens. Only now, and painfully, is that long alienation from democracy crumbling.

The conflict between immigrants and native Protestants never expanded politically beyond the limits of Know-Nothingism. Hostilities remained and often had political consequences. For one hundred seventy years no person not of Anglo-Saxon Protestant stock was elected President. The parties feared even to nominate presidential candidates of immigrant origins or Catholic faith. In 1928 the Catholicism of Alfred E. Smith was a factor in the election. No Catholic was elected President until 1960. Despite all this, the immigrants and their children, who could easily have remained a large politically unintegrated element in the population, were quickly absorbed into the political system and soon came to accept the ideology and institutions of American democracy. Indeed, in few countries in the world have so many people been so fully integrated into a democratic system in so short a time. Thus the conflict between imigrants and native Protestants never erupted on a nation-wide scale; though it persisted, it was contained.

In many other countries, the conflict between labor and capital—to use two vague labels—has led to the alienation of one stratum or the other. Nearly everywhere in Europe the rapid expansion of the working classes posed a severe problem of political integration. For if the spokesmen of capitalism had their way, the revolutionary spirit was likely to spread among working-class groups and organizations. And if the spokesmen of the working class appeared on the verge of gaining power, then the defenders of the economic status quo might be alienated and withdraw their support for democratic institutions. Unlike every European democracy, in the United States workers did not develop a separate working-class political movement. Unlike many of the most stable and highly developed European democracies, in the United States a labor-socialist party did not gain office, introduce extensive reforms, consolidate the commitment of workers to the notion of peaceful change by means of democratic procedures and institutions. Yet in following another route, the American working classes were politically integrated into the American Republic: and in the process their economic antagonists, businessmen, were not permanently alienated. The development was long, however, and often disturbed by sharp conflict. We shall return to it in Chapter 17.

The failure of white Americans to provide equal political, economic, educational and social opportunities for Negroes produced among many Negroes a kind of rejection that took the form of political apathy, hopelessness, and indifference. Then as Negroes began to exchange apathy for new forms of political action, and as they gained federal protection for their rights, many whites, especially in the South, fell back on the old, anti-democratic, aristocratic ideology and constitutional doctrines to justify resistance to equality. Perhaps at no time since the years just before the Civil War was conflict more intense than in the declining decade of Southern white power from 1954–1964. Meanwhile, in the depressed Negro ghettos of the great Northern cities, where slum dwellers were moved by a spirit of alienation and despair, violence began to erupt. Some Northern Whites now began to feel threatened. The peaceful political, social and economic integration of the American Negro remains perhaps the greatest internal problem of our time.

Thus conflicts and rejection of the democratic republic ebb and flow in American political life. For a time moderate conflicts prevail. Then the tides of antagonism begin to surge, and political conflict grows more deadly. Yet even during severe conflicts, the pattern of moderation is never totally transformed into the pattern of severe conflict. When by one means or another the antagonisms diminish, the pattern of moderate conflict reappears. But it too is impermanent. The high tide of conflict has almost always risen within the life of about one generation.

12

POLITICAL POLARIZATION
AND CIVIL WAR

I N THE DISPUTES that thrust this country into civil war, American
experience offers a compelling and tragic illustration of severe
conflict. It is the course of this conflict, the greatest failure in the
history of the American democratic republic, that we examine in this
chapter.

Whether any republic could have arrived at a peaceful solution to
any issue as monumental as slavery had become in the United States, no
one can say with confidence. What we do know—what no American can
forget—is that the American political system was unequal to the task of
negotiating a peaceful settlement to the problem of slavery. Violence was
substituted for politics. Yet even civil war, the supreme mark of political
failure, did not solve the issue, which was now transformed from slavery
to the question of whether Negroes were to acquire full and effective
citizenship.

The Civil War did not answer this question. Nor did Reconstruction. The unresolved issue was passed down from one generation to the
next, until it exploded for all the world to see, a century after the outbreak of the Civil War.

Symptoms of Rising Conflict

In May, 1856, John Brown and a small   party of anti-slavery Kansans
massacred five pro-slavery men in the Pottawatomie region of Kansas.

Over the next few years, violence frequently broke out between pro- and anti-slavery forces in Bleeding, Kansas. At almost the same time as the Pottawatomie Massacre, Senator Charles Sumner of Massachusetts delivered a vehement attack on slavery in the Senate; his speech was not free of personal invective; shortly afterward a Southern Congressman entered the Senate and beat Sumner furiously over the head with a heavy cane. In both houses of Congress there were other outbursts of violence involving antagonisms over slavery. In the course of a debate about Kansas in 1858, proceedings in the House became riotous. On other occasions, too, the House and Senate verged on open physical violence.[1]

At a time when intemperate language was commonplace, public figures frequently invoked threats of secession, disruption of the Union, violence, civil war. In letters, in the press, even in Congress, the more radical Southerners began to speak of secession as the only alternative if the North could not be brought to terms. As the election of 1860 approached, Southerners frequently reiterated the threat that the South would secede if a Republican were elected President. Seward stoked the fires of controversy by his famous statement in Rochester in October, 1858: "It is an irrepressible conflict between opposing and enduring forces, and it means that the United States must and will, sooner or later, become either entirely a slaveholding nation or entirely a free-labor nation." Just one year later, John Brown staged his futile raid at Harpers Ferry in a vain, ill organized, and half-insane attempt to free the slaves of Virginia. On the heels of the news of Harpers Ferry, the legislature of Alabama met and authorized the governor to call a state convention if a Republican should be elected President in 1860. In the summer of 1860, a number of conservative South Carolina Democrats, hitherto opposed to the 'fireeaters' who advocated secession, declared that if the Republicans were to win the election in November, South Carolina would secede. If this was Southern bluster and bravado, in November the bluff was called. It was not a bluff. On December 20, 1860, the state of South

1. For historical details this chapter relies most heavily on the following works: Roy Nichols' exceptionally important study of the Democratic Party from 1856–1860, *The Disruption of American Democracy*, New York, Mac-Millan Book Company, 1948. Also his *The Stakes of Power, 1845–1877*, New York, Hill and Wang, 1961. C. Vann Woodward, *Reunion and Reaction: The Compromise of 1877 and the End of Reconstruction*, Boston, Little Brown and Company, 1951; Also his *The Burden of Southern History*, New York, Vintage Books, 1960, *The Strange Career of Jim Crow*, New York, Oxford University Press, 1957, and "Seeds of Failure in Radical Race Policy," *Proceedings of the American Philosophical Society*, V. 110, no. 1 (Feb. 1966), 1–9.

Carolina seceded from the Union. Within six months ten other Southern states had followed. Lincoln, backed by a substantial share of articulate Northern opinion, refused to permit the Southern states to secede and thereby disrupt the Union. The result was civil war.

'Explanations' of the 'causes' of the Civil War abound. Yet in the best of circumstances—under laboratory conditions—causal analysis is not easy. Causal interpretations of complex, multi-faceted, and almost certainly multi-causal historical events are particularly uncertain and vulnerable. It would therefore be absurd in this brief chapter to introduce another causal theory about the origins of the Civil War. All the following analysis is intended to show is that the events of 1850–1861 closely conform to the expected pattern indicated by the paradigm on page 280. Conditions which encourage moderation gave way to conditions that would be expected to eventuate in a more severe conflict. Probably never before or since in American history has the pattern of moderate conflict been so fully transformed into the pattern of severe conflict.

FIRST CONDITION: DIVERGENCE OF VIEWS. During the course of the 1850s, events and new perspectives posed the issue of slavery in the territories in such a way that compromise became increasingly difficult. As the decade wore on, the issue of slavery was more and more bound up with a second major question—union or secession.

At the start of the decade, there was an exact balance in the Senate between the slave states and free states. Slavery already existed in fifteen Southern States and it was prohibited in fifteen Northern states. The balance in the Senate could be maintained or disrupted by what happened in the Western territories. Should slavery be protected in the territories, or prohibited? If it were protected, would there not be, in due course, more slave states than free states? If it were prohibited in the territories, could there ever again be an additional slave state? Would not the South become an ever smaller minority in the nation, and in the Senate, finally perhaps too small to prevent the free states from abolishing slavery by constitutional amendment and, if need be, by coercion?

In principle, the policies adhered to by the federal government on slavery required an answer to a single question applied to three different regions. The question was this: Should slavery be prohibited or protected? The regions were these: the existing free states of the North and Northwest, the slave states of the South, and the territories of the West.

Consider the alternatives. An abolitionist would prohibit slavery in all three regions. His position demanded a revolution in Southern life and institutions. If enough Americans had supported the abolitionist position in 1800, the attempt to perpetuate slavery and the tragedies caused by that evil anachronism might never have occurred. Although we shall never know how many Americans held the abolitionist position before the Civil War, the membership of the Anti-Slavery Society amounted to only 3 or 4 per cent of the adult population outside the South.[2] Discrimination against Negroes was commonplace in the North; Northerners who were prepared to accept the Negro as their equal were evidently a minority, and probably a very small minority.[3] It is clear that until the outbreak of war the abolitionists remained a tiny opposition whose views were widely thought to be extreme—as revolutionary views generally are.

A less revolutionary position, though in the perspectives of the 1850s a radical one nonetheless, was taken by Lincoln, Seward, and the Republican Party. Like all the other major protagonists to the great controversies of the 1850s, with the exception of the abolitionists, Lincoln and most leading Republicans assumed that although the free states would continue to prohibit slavery, slavery might be left intact in the South. In fact, as the price of Union, the South might even be given additional guarantees that its peculiar institution would be protected from the abolitionists. In this view, the institution was so deeply rooted in the South that it could not be abolished in the near future; hence Southern slavery would be protected until such time as the South itself would peacefully yield it up. What was immediately at stake, however, was not slavery in the South or the prohibition of slavery in the North; it was the question of whether slavery was to be permitted in any of the Western territories.

As early as 1846, David Wilmot, a Democrat from Pennsylvania, had introduced a resolution that would have barred slavery in all the territories. Although the Wilmot Proviso was never adopted, it became a rally-

2. Philip Converse, "The Nature of Belief Systems in Mass Publics" in David Apter, ed., *Ideology and Discontent*, New York, the Free Press, 1964, p. 250. "This figure is for 1840, and it undoubtedly advanced further in the next decade or two, although one deduces that the expansion of membership slowed down after 1840. Our estimates do not take into account, however, the standard inflation of membership (intentional or unintentional) that seems to characterize movements of this sort." p. 260, fn. 46.

3. "The fact was that the constituency on which the Republican congressmen relied in the North was a race-conscious, segregated society devoted to the doctrine of white supremacy and Negro inferiority . . . Ninety-three percent of the 225 thousand Northern Negroes in 1860 lived in states that denied them the ballot, and seven percent lived in the five New England states that permitted them to vote." Woodward, "Seeds of Failure in Radical Race Policy," *op. cit.*, p. 1.

ing point for a number of northern Congressmen. The view of Lincoln and some of his fellow Republicans was essentially that of the Wilmot Proviso: The federal government should prohibit slavery throughout the length and breadth of the territories; hence it would be all but certain that when these territories finally came into the Union, they would enter as free states, not slave states. Although Lincoln and Seward were willing to compromise on many points in order to reassure the Southern slavocracy—compromises often thought to be serious blemishes on Lincoln's over-blown reputation as the Great Emancipator—on this issue they never budged. And the frantic efforts to forge another great compromise during the tense months as the year 1860 closed and the new year began all failed because neither Lincoln nor the leaders of the South would alter their positions on the crucial issue of slavery in the territories.

A considerably more limited opposition to slavery provided better grounds for compromise in the early 1850s than was offered by the Wilmot Proviso. This was the policy of 'popular sovereignty' embodied in the famous Compromises of 1850 and 1854. The solution was outwardly democratic and simple: Let the people of the territories choose whether they wish to protect or to prohibit slavery.

Confronted by the problem of providing government for the territories acquired from Mexico (land to which the old Missouri Compromise of 1820 did not apply), the aging veteran Henry Clay and the new Senator from Illinois, Stephen Douglas, had in 1850 engineered the solution of popular sovereignty for California, New Mexico, and Utah. Then in 1854, when the vast unorganized remnants of the Louisiana purchase were given territorial government, Douglas piloted through Congress another compromise on the same basis; but under pressure from Southerners to put slavery on an equal footing, the venerable Missouri Compromise was repealed outright. At its national convention in Cincinnati in 1856, the Democratic Party proclaimed popular sovereignty as its official doctrine.

Douglas's solution suffered from two disadvantages common to compromise proposals in times of profound controversy. First, it was ambiguous, since it did not specify clearly when the people of a territory were to decide about slavery. (Opponents of slavery favored an early decision; spokesmen for the slavocracy wanted it as late as possible, only when the territory was ready for admission as a state. Presumably, both were operating on the assumption that slaveowners would move into a territory much more slowly than free farmers.)

Second, and more important, popular sovereignty became increasingly less acceptable to the major antagonists. Lincoln, Seward, and a

Table 12.1.   Principal Positions on the Question of Slavery,
1850–61

| | | TYPE OF ACTION PROPOSED FOR | | |
STAND ON SLAVERY	FREE STATES	TERRITORIES	SOUTHERN STATES	SPOKESMEN AND PROPOSALS
Revolutionary Opposition	Prohibit	Prohibit	Prohibit	Abolitionists
Radical Opposition	Prohibit	Prohibit	Protect	Wilmot Proviso, Lincoln, Seward, Republicans
Limited Opposition	Prohibit	Protect or Prohibit: People decide	Protect	Advocates of Pop. Svty.: Clay, Douglas—Compromise of 1850, 1854, Cincinnati Platform of Dem. Party
Limited Defense	Prohibit	Protect and Prohibit: Congress decides		Advocates of extending Mo. compromise; Crittenden
Radical Defense	Prohibit	Protect	Protect	Taney: Dred Scott, Calhoun, Constitutional Democrats, Breckenridge

sizeable number of other leaders rejected popular sovereignty because they favored the total exclusion of slavery in the territories. Spokesmen for Southern slaveholders also found it more and more unacceptable. Many of them came to espouse a view that was, in its own way, as radical a break with the past as Lincoln's policy. This was the view that only the people of a *state* had the power to prohibit slavery. Hence the federal government had no constitutional power to prohibit slavery in the territories, nor did the people of the territories, until (or just prior to) their admission as a state. It was the duty of the federal government, then, to protect the rights of slaveholders throughout all the territories. Between this position and Lincoln's there was no room for compromise.

Although numerous minor variations on these main themes can be detected, they did not change the alternatives in any significant way. The five principal alternatives are summarized in Table 12.1.

As the decade wore on, the question of slavery in the territories (and with it the ultimate future of slavery in the South) more and more required an answer to a second question: Was the Union to be preserved at all costs, or was secession a permissible solution? Is one particular combination of human beings into a single polity more right than any other combination? If so, why? If one of the main ends of a democratic republic is to secure the consent of all citizens, should not citizens who no longer consent to the basic principles of their government be allowed to depart in peace? Why must the integrity of the Union not be broken by secession? Although the Civil War settled the matter by establishing the principle that secession from the United States is impermissible, the questions themselves are among the most troublesome in the whole domain of political theory.

Lincoln's answer, as everyone knows, was a profound commitment to the Union. In part, his view reflected the nonrational and almost unanalysable nationalism that forms a vital prerequisite for the modern nation-state all over the world. Nationalists may disagree about boundaries; but they do not doubt that, once the nation has been defined, that nation must be preserved. In addition to Lincoln's nationalism, which was doubtless widely shared in the North (and in the South as well), there was also his deep commitment to the importance of the American democratic republic, founded on principles of liberty and equality, as an example for all mankind. If the South should secede, then the greatest living evidence for the proposition that a democratic republic could survive the challenge of dissident minorities would no longer serve as "proof of the impossible." "If the minority will not acquiesce, the majority must, or the government must cease," Lincoln said in his first inaugural address. ". . . If a minority in such case will secede rather than acquiesce, they make a precedent which in turn will divide and ruin them. . . . Rejecting the majority principle, anarchy or despotism in some form is all that is left." As he said at Gettysburg, the Civil War was a testing of whether any nation conceived in liberty and dedicated to the proposition that all men are created equal could long endure.

Nearly every one of the groups listed in Table 12.1 contained both Unionists and those who advocated or accepted secession. Some abolitionists who despaired of developing a free society as long as the South was in the Union were not unhappy at the prospect of a separation. There were even Republicans who took this pragmatic view of the matter and did not share Lincoln's passionate belief that the Union must be preserved. At the other extreme, some Southerners who advocated radical defense of slavery were, throughout most of the decade, opposed to secession; many of these fell in line only during the last months before

Table 12.2. *Slavery and Secession, 1850–61*

| | STAND ON SECESSION | |
STAND ON SLAVERY	PRO-UNION	PRO-SECESSION
Revolutionary Opposition	Most abolitionists, Radical Republicans	Some abolitionists
Radical Opposition	Lincoln, Seward, most Republicans	Some Republicans
Limited Opposition	Clay, Douglas	—
Limited Defense	Crittenden, Buchanan, Alexander Stephens	—
Radical Defense	Taney—Dred Scott	Calhoun, Yancey, Jefferson Davis

Fort Sumter. In the election of 1860 the Constitutional Union Party, which had only two planks—support for the Constitution and loyalty to the Union—gained much of its support from Southern Whigs. Its presidential candidate, Senator John Bell of Tennessee, together with the pro-Union candidate of the Democratic Party, Senator Douglas, carried eight of the fifteen slave states against Breckenridge, the candidate of the secessionist Democrats. In the fourteen slave states where presidential electors were chosen by the voters (characteristically, the anachronism of choosing electors in the state legislature still existed in South Carolina), Breckenridge received only 570,000 votes to his opponent's 705,000.

If we put the two dimensions of policy together—slavery and secession—a new pattern emerges (Table 12.2).

Among the spokesmen and leaders who helped form public opinion, discussed and debated the alternatives, and made the decisions, the events of the 1850s thinned out the center and pushed leaders more and more toward the northwest and southwest corners of Table 12.2. The Presidental election of 1860, in which no advocate of any of the principal positions won a majority of popular votes, provided the final polarizing thrust that gave Lincoln and the Republicans in Congress enough control to insure that their views would prevail, and encouraged Southern leaders to unite upon the view that only secession would protect slavery in the South. Between these two radically opposed alternatives, it proved impossible to find any compromise.

SECOND CONDITION: A ZERO-SUM CONTEST WITH HIGH STAKES. By the spring of 1861, leaders had exhausted the major possibilities of compromise between the two radical positions. No compromise could be acceptable so long as Republicans and Southerners

[309]

held to their positions. Yet neither would yield, for in the 1850s the issue of slavery was converted into a zero-sum contest in which the stakes were different ways of life.

In the perspectives of the principal contestants, either slavery had to be prohibited in all the territories or it had to be allowed in all the territories. And the stakes in the contest (if we interpret them as the contestants claimed to see them) had come to be nothing less than this: a society based on slavery or a society based on free farmers and free labor.

These alternatives were most sharply visible in the perspectives of Southern leaders. From the Constitutional Convention onward, it had been reasonably obvious that the South could maintain slavery only under a Constitution that insured protection for the rights of slaveholders in the Southern states; the South had, in fact, gained such a Constitution in 1787; and the South could maintain it as long as slave states had enough power to veto a change in the Constitution. If the time were to come, however, when the growth of population and free states permitted the North and West to override the opposition of the South and to alter the Constitution, then the institution of slavery, and with it the whole structure of the planter society, would be imperiled.

This was the shape of the future which Southern leaders insisted more and more vehemently they saw in every solution not guaranteeing a full opportunity for slaveholders to implant their institutions in the territories; hence not only in the Wilmot Proviso and the Republican commitment to free territories but even in popular sovereignty. Quite possibly even an outright Constitutional guaranty would not insure that slavery would in fact be exported to the Western Territories. If not, then surely the only solution was secession. If slavery could be introduced in the West, however, then another solution might be acceptable to Southerners: this was nothing less than the principle announced by Taney in the Dred Scott case, that Congress had no power to prohibit slavery in the territories.

The alternatives may have seemed less stark in the free states than in the South. Nonetheless, from 1856 onwards, Northern politicians who were unwilling to commit themselves to halting the expansion of slavery by federal legislation were to an increasing degree challenged and defeated by opponents who were prepared to put a definite and permanent end to the spread of slavery beyond its existing boundaries. Not only were individuals voted out; whole parties were defeated. The Whigs disintegrated; the Democrats split; the Republicans surged.

The evidence suggests, then, that even if the perspectives on the future were not so grim in the North as in the South, among Northerners a variety of views helped to crystallize the belief that the territories should be preserved exclusively for free farmers. Among these precipitating factors was a loathing for slavery that went far beyond the abolitionists; many people who were not ready to accept Negroes as their equals nor willing to bear the costs of abolishing slavery where it was already entrenched were, like Lincoln, sickened by all proposals, even those in the name of compromise, that would let slavery expand one inch beyond its existing limits. Then, too, the states of the North and Northwest were still populated predominantly by farmers—free farmers—some of whom had themselves wrested land out of the wilderness; of the others many, perhaps most, must have shared the deeply ingrained expectation, now well over a century old, that the great rich lands to the West were open to them, their neighbors, their sons, or other white farmers like themselves. The spread of slavery would violate that interest, destroy that dream. (It is relevant as a symbol that the first act of the Republicans after secession began was to admit Kansas as a free state.) There were also economic issues on which the veto of the Southern slaveholders prevented solutions favored by many Northerners: the admission of Kansas, the tariff, federal expenditures for internal improvements, railroads to the West. Early in 1861, as soon as enough Southern states had seceded to make the Republicans a majority in Congress, Republicans together with a handful of northern Democrats rushed bills through Congress that admitted Kansas, raised the tariff, and by ending a mail subsidy for steamships to the Pacific Coast eased the way for the construction of a railroad to California.[4] Within a few years, other major policies were enacted that the South had long opposed: the Homestead Law, land-grants for agricultural colleges, subsidies for two trans-continental railroads, a Contract Labor Law permitting agents to contract abroad for labor, and, under the pressure of war, even an income tax.

Thus slavery in the territories was no narrow issue. In the waning years of the 1850s, it was interpreted by more and more leaders (and presumably by many involved citizens) as a matter that posed two alternative ways of life, two kinds of society, two visions of man's fate and man's hope.

THIRD CONDITION: DECLINE OF OVERLAPPING CLEAVAGES. In the course of the 1850s, the issue of slavery in the territories was like a wall rising between neighbors. At the beginning of the decade the wall could still be climbed; but as it grew higher, it

4. Nichols, The Disruption of American Democracy, pp. 476–ff.

Table 12.3.   Election of 1860: Votes Won

	N (000)	%
Republicans: Lincoln	1,866	40
Democrats: Douglas	1,383	30
Southern Democrats: Breckenridge	848	18
Constitutional Union: Bell	593	12
Total	4,690	100%

SOURCE: W. Dean Burnham, Presidential Ballots, 1836-1892, Baltimore, Johns Hopkins Press, 1955, p. 246.

became more and more impassable to traffic of all kinds. A pattern of cross-cutting cleavages which had prevailed through the Compromise of 1854 was transformed into a pattern of non-overlapping or cumulative cleavages.

To be sure, total polarization was never reached. But, like Mercutio's wound, it was enough.

Between 1850–60, the Whig Party, one of the two national parties which had leaders and constituents in both North and South, disintegrated into a weak rump party in the South, and thereafter vanished.

Between 1854 and 1860, a new party took the place of the Whigs. The Republican Party was exclusively a Northern and Western party. If we discount the Federalists in their declining years, for the first time in the history of American parties one of the two major parties did not spread across both sides of the Mason and Dixon line. In the election of 1860, Lincoln won only 1.4 per cent of the total vote in the fifteen slave states (Table 12.3). In ten slave states Lincoln did not gain so much as a single vote!

In 1860, the Democratic Party, which for more than sixty years had been the great nationwide party, whose leaders had worked with unflagging zeal to knit the sections together, split apart on the issue of slavery in the territories. One wing, the Constitutional Democrats, became a predominantly Southern party. The other, Douglas's party, barely retained any Southern following at all in the elections of 1860 (Table 12.3). Southern Whigs and other unionists organized a new party, the Constitutional Union Party; its platform was "The Constitution of the Country, the Union of the States, and the enforcement of the laws." But it, too, proved to be a sectional party.

Thus in 1860, for the first (and so far last) time in American history, four, not two, major parties sought the Presidency. No party came close to winning a majority of popular votes (Table 12.3) and each was

Table 12.4.   Election of 1860: Percentage of Votes Won,
by Major Regions

	NORTH AND WEST	SOUTH	TOTAL
Lincoln	98.6%	1.4%	100%
Douglas	88	12	100
Breckenridge	33	67	100
Bell	13	87	100

SOURCE: Computed from data in Burnham, op. cit., pp. 78, 246.

wholly or almost wholly either a Southern or non-Southern party (Table 12.4).

Congress, hitherto the forum of compromise, became in the late 1850s a battle ground where almost every issue split the membership into the same two camps. In 1858–1859, Congress had lengthy deadlocks on almost every issue: the admission of Kansas, transcontinental railroads, rivers and harbors appropriations, a homestead bill, the tariff. Deadlock and conflict so much dominated the session that the Congress was not even able to agree on the annual appropriation for the Post Office, and at the end of the session the Post Office Department was left without funds. In the Congress that met in the winter of 1859–60, no party had a majority in the House; it took two months and more than forty ballots simply to elect a Speaker. During all this time the legislative business of the House was at a complete standstill.

In the 1840s and early 1850s, political leaders who might have quarrelled over slavery agreed on so many other key questions that they were impelled toward a compromise on slavery. In Congress, in politics generally, and, it seems, in the country, attitudes North and South of the Mason Dixon line were not so distinct as to prevent coalition, agreement, mutual concession, and compromise on many issues. An opponent on one issue was not necessarily an opponent on all issues. By the late 1850s, however, the chances were that a Northerner and a Southerner not only disagreed about slavery; they disagreed about a great many other key questions as well. The political leaders of the country were increasingly polarized into two opposing sides. More and more, then, one's enemies today would be one's enemies tomorrow and the day after. The North-South fault line split the country not only on slavery in the territories and the admission of Kansas, but on the tariff, government aid for roads, harbors, and other internal improvements, the need for and the route of transcontinental railways, federal land grants for educational institutions, homestead laws, banking laws, constitutional theory, ideological views on aristocracy and democracy. By the spring of 1860, a year

[313]

before Sumter, a Senator from South Carolina privately observed: "There are no relations, not absolutely indispensable in the conduct of the joint business, between the North and South in either House. No two nations on earth are or ever were more distinctly separate and hostile than we are here."[5]

It would be easy, nonetheless, to exaggerate the point. Among political leaders the cleavage was never total. As to the views of the people themselves, one cannot be certain how much they ever became polarized. Then as now the views of ordinary citizens must have been more fragmented, less coherent, less clearly formed than the views of men whose daily lives were wrapped up in the great public controversies. To many citizens, perhaps to most (though one cannot be sure), the issues of slavery probably seemed more remote, less distinct, perhaps even less important that the preoccupations of daily life.

Perhaps the North-South fault line was weakest on the very issue that moved to the forefront in 1860–1861: Union or secession. Not all those who supported or were willing to go along with secession were Southerners; and by no means all Southerners supported secession. Without question the secessionists were a minority in the nation. Very likely they were a minority even in the South. Of the four candidates in the presidential election of 1860, none advocated outright and immediate secession. Three were flatly opposed to secession. Although Breckenridge was the candidate of the secessionists, he said he did not favor it as a solution. Breckenridge won only 18 per cent of the national vote (Table 12.3) and he won considerably less than a majority—38 per cent—of the votes in the South. In fact, Breckenridge received absolute majorities in only eight of the fifteen slave states. Moreover, it appears that even in these states a considerable number of his supporters were opponents of secession who were loyal southern Democrats, supporting, as they thought, the candidate of their party. Later, in voting on candidates for the conventions called in the seven states that seceded before Fort Sumter fell, the issue of union or secession was made clearer. In these elections many of the counties that had voted for Breckenridge voted against secessionists in favor of Union candidates. Support for secession was concentrated most heavily in the counties with large numbers of slaves, where the vote was about 7–3 for secessionist candidates. In counties where slaves were few, the proportions were reversed: voters supported pro-Union candidates by about 2–1.[6] Even in the states that led the

5. Nichols, *The Stakes of Power, 1845–1877*, p. 287.
6. S. M. Lipset, "The Emergence of the One-Party South," in *Political Man*, Garden City, N.Y., Doubleday and Company, 1960, pp. 344–356, Table II, p. 349.

movement to secede, the secessionists barely outnumbered their Union-
ist opponents; in Mississippi in the election of candidates for the convention that was to vote on secession, the ratio of votes cast for secession
versus cooperation was 4–3; in Alabama, 9–7; in Georgia, 5–4. As late as
March, North Carolina voted decisively against secession.[7] Tennessee
and Arkansas did not vote to secede until after the outbreak of war. Four
other slave states remained in the Union; Maryland, Delaware, Kentucky, Missouri; and West Virginia split off from Virginia rather than
secede.

Thus it is probably no exaggeration to say that it was a small minority of slaveholders who, together with their retainers, followers, and
spokesmen, engineered secession and thereby precipitated civil war.[8] It
seems altogether possible that if a plebiscite had been held during the
week before Fort Sumter, and perhaps after, it would have revealed the
secessionists to be a minority in the South. Yet with skill, energy, and
luck, secessionist leaders gained control in seven states in the deep South,
and in the end brought four additional but more reluctant slave states
along.

FOURTH CONDITION: NEGOTIATION WITHOUT DECI-
SION?   How, if at all, did the operation of American political institutions affect the course of the controversy over slavery?

That the institutions and the ways of thinking which men brought
to these institutions provided powerful inducements for negotiation and
compromise on the issue of slavery is hardly open to question. In the first
half of the century, the issue which was to tear the country apart during
the second half was handled by one compromise after another: 1820,
1850, 1854. The inertial forces of the system continued to operate until
May of 1861. During the final year of peace, or cold war, there were
frantic and unceasing efforts to arrive at a compromise that would head
off the event that so many saw and feared: the Conference Convention;
the Crittenden Compromise; the Committee of Thirty-three in the
House; the Committee of Thirteen in the Senate; proposals by Toombs,
Jefferson Davis, Stephen Douglas, and countless other political leaders;
the constitutional amendment proposed by the House and backed by
Seward and Lincoln which would have preserved slavery in the states
where it already existed. (The amendment, incidentally, passed both
House and Senate as—height of irony—the *Thirteenth* Amendment, but
its ratification was consumed by war.)

7. See Nichols, *Disruption*, pp. 418, 435, 499.
8. Cf. Burnham's comment, "...it was probably a rather small minority which
    engineered secession in a good many Southern states," *op. cit.*, p. 83.

By 1860, however, events were too advanced for these compromises. Did the political institutions encourage compromise too much and too long? Did they inhibit political leaders and citizens from squarely confronting the alternatives?

It is impossible to provide a confident answer. Human rationality has distinct limits. Because history has unfolded its answer to us, we can now discern those who in 1820 already divined correctly the shape of the future. But wrong guesses about 1860 could not be proved wrong in 1820.

Nonetheless, it seems clear that the political institutions provided both Southerners and Northerners with sound reasons for believing that slaveholders—or the political representatives of the South—could prevent national laws directed to the peaceful abolition of slavery. So long as the South was in the Union, then, the alternatives were either revolution or some sort of compromise, for no decision on slavery could be reached without the assent of the South.

The power of the South was protected by federalism and the Constitution, for slavery could not be abolished in Southern states except by amending the Constitution. The power of the South was further protected by the Senate, where numbers of states counted, not numbers of people. The South might also seek protection from the Supreme Court, as it did in the case of Dred Scott.[9] The South gained further political

9. *Dred Scott v Sandford*, 19 How. 393 (1857). The Court, incidentally, has never been more knowingly and deliberately a political and legislative body than in that case. One of the Justices, Catron, kept his old friend Buchanan, the incoming President, closely informed of what was happening; Buchanan was thus able to compose his Inaugural Address in the confident expectation that Taney and four other members of the Court would relieve Buchanan of the need for making a statement in his Inaugural on the controversial matter of slavery in the territories. On March 4, Buchanan announced in his Inaugural that the forthcoming decision of the Court had made the question of slavery in the territories "happily, a matter of but little practical importance." Rather disingenuously, since he knew what the decision was to be, he also pledged: "To their decision, in common with all good citizens I shall cheerfully submit, whatever this may be." Within a few days, the Supreme Court, as Buchanan expected, announced its decision. A bare majority of five members of the Court—four of whom were Southerners— declared the Missouri Compromise unconstitutional; four, all Southerners, declared that Congress could not prohibit slavery in the territories. Although their lack of foresight is scarcely credible, Buchanan and Taney evidently believed that the Dred Scott decision would actually solve the most burning issue of contemporary politics by judicial declaration. Never has the fragile basis of the Court's power over political questions been made so obvious. (For these details, see Nichols, *Disruption*, pp. 60–73.)

advantage, as it was to do for the century following the Civil War, by the professionalization of politics and the long continuity in leadership that enhanced the influence of her spokesmen. An historian has written:

> The control of the Federal government by the South during the fifties had been almost complete. While the Presidents were of Northern origin they had been nominated by national conventions dominated by Southern leaders. The Cabinets had generally had four of the seven members from the South. In Congress the most important committees were chaired by Southerners. At one time the President pro tempore of the Senate and the chairmen of the Foreign Relations, Finance, and Judiciary committees were experienced representatives from the South. When the Democrats were in control, the Speakers of the House were Southern. Five of the nine members of the Supreme Court were from that section. These men controlled both legislation and the fortunes of statesmen. . . .[10]

Finally, the very merits of the political parties as instruments for settling moderate conflict may have disabled them during severe conflicts. The parties, both Democratic and Whig, were unideological, conglomerate, nationwide, cross-cutting parties avid for compromise on an issue that their leaders accurately foresaw would, if inflamed, destroy them. The small parties, like Free Soil, that tried to pose the issue of slavery clearly were crushed by the great giants. For many years, the efforts of the parties succeeded; they were able to compromise the issue and thereby keep the peace. In 1836 they had even pushed through a 'Gag Rule' in the House, which prevented the House from taking up "petitions, memorials, resolutions, propositions or papers relating in any way or to any extent whatsoever to the subject of slavery or the abolition of slavery."[11] The rule or others even stricter endured until 1844. By these and other means the oldest, largest, and most clearly national party—the American Democracy as it called itself—managed to maintain a compromise between Northern and Southern wings until 1860.

Yet the hypothesis—it can be no more than that—is defensible: If the American system had been based more fully on the principle of majority rule at the national level, and if the parties had been more concerned with ideological issues, they might have presented a clearer

10. Nichols. *The Stakes of Power, 1845–1877*, p. 76.
11. Morris, *Encyclopedia, op. cit.*, p. 179.

picture of the alternatives much earlier than they did. Southern slave-holders would have seen quite early that slavery was subject to a decision by the representatives of a majority of voters. As a distinct minority in the nation, their bargaining power would not have been amplified as it was by the innumerable devices of the American Constitution that rein-force minorities against majorities.

If slavery had been ended earlier, without disrupting the country, the gains would have been incalculable; for a problem would have been solved while it was still manageable in the ways of peace. But would a political system less responsive to minority power only have led to seces-sion earlier, when the republic was still young? If the Republic had split earlier, what would have been the fate of Southern and Northern Ne-groes? Compared with what actually transpired, would their lot have been worse—or better?

This much seems clear: The political institutions encouraged com-promises that preserved in the South a system based on slavery for so long that this peculiar and anachronistic but deeply entrenched way of life was not likely to be revolutionized by peaceful negotiations.

Change, Compromise, Reconciliation

Only the immediate question was settled by Civil War: Slavery was forever barred not only in the territories but in the old slave states as well.

Unimpeded by the political opposition of the Southern slavocracy, the Republican coalition of North and West carried through a program of comprehensive changes that insured the expansion of industry, com-merce, and free farming. I have already mentioned the main items. Instead of a Thirteenth Amendment that would have preserved slavery, another Thirteenth Amendment abolished it. Instead of the policies of economic laissez faire that the slavocracy had demanded (side by side with a rigid and meticulous governmental intervention to protect slavery), the Republicans substituted the doctrine that the federal government would provide assistance for business, industry, and farm-ing: the protective tariff, homesteads, land subsidies for agricultural colleges, transcontinental railways and other internal improvements, national banks. When the defeated South came back into the Union, it had to accept the comprehensive alteration in government policy and economic institutions that the historian Charles A. Beard was later to name the Second American Revolution.

Yet the revolution in the South that might have liberated the freed Negro slave, a revolution sought by some abolitionists and Radical Republicans, was never carried out. The only hope that Negroes might commence their march to full equality depended upon the prospects for a social, economic, and political revolution. But the freed Negro was securely provided with neither land nor education nor civic rights.

How could the domination of politics by a small white oligarchy be ended? For this was the central pattern of political life in the South in the pre-Civil War period. As in many developing nations of the world today, one hopeful possibility lay in land reform. If a large body of prosperous, independent, free farmers (as in the North) could be created by redistributing land holdings, then political power might come to rest with coalitions of free farmers, white and black, and the dominance of the great landowner might be destroyed. Education and civil rights would also be required. In time, the system would be able to sustain itself without protection from the outside.

It was some such strategy that a few Radical Republicans such as Thaddeus Stevens seem to have had in mind during Reconstruction. Even if hesitantly and from a variety of motives, the Radical Republicans in Congress took steps to reorganize the Southern economy, society, and polity. In 1866 they passed the Southern Homestead Act; although it was weak and never implemented, it provided that in five Southern states where federal lands remained, all public lands (constituting one third of the total area of these five states) were reserved exclusively for homesteaders. Like many whites, most Negroes needed education; this was a major aim of Reconstruction government in creating public school systems in the Southern states. Above all, Negroes needed political influence, which first of all meant the ballot. Neither the Civil Rights Act of 1866 nor the Fourteenth Amendment, which the Southern states were required to accept before being readmitted to Congress, provided for Negro suffrage. However, the Military Reconstruction Act of 1867 organized the South into five military districts and instructed the commanding general of each to register Negro voters and to protect their right to vote by stationing soldiers at polls and registration places. By the end of 1867, 703 thousand Negroes (and only 627 thousand whites) had been registered.

Yet the revolution so boldly envisioned by a few was never completed. As we have seen during the present century, it is extraordinarily difficult for outsiders to impose a lasting revolution on a country. Without support from people inside a country, policies imposed entirely from outside are likely to produce only shallow changes.

Freed slaves could not make a revoluton unaided. They were a black minority amidst a national and even a regional majority of whites. In its awful destruction of pride, self-reliance, and family—that tiny island of human solidarity which has sometimes withstood, elsewhere, a thousand years of oppression—slavery left its scars.[12] If there was to be a revolution after the Civil War, it had to be made by white citizens for black citizens. But the North was too irresolute, too infirm, and too divided in its aims to persist in the revolutionary reconstruction of Southern institutions that might have liberated the freed man. The white South and its traditional leaders were much more easily mobilized to resist that revolution.

How many Northern citizens, or even Northern leaders, ever eagerly embraced the idea of making a revolution in Southern society remains uncertain. There is strong evidence that few Northerners who supported Reconstruction in the South were ready to accept Northern Negroes as their equals. After the Civil War, as before, Northerners remained notably unenthusiastic about extending civil rights to the Negroes in their midst. Except for Minnesota and Iowa—neither of which had many Negroes—no Northern state in the post-war period voluntarily granted the suffrage to Negroes; efforts to do so were steadily defeated.[13] As the obstacles to reconstruction in the South became more evident, support dwindled in the North. The reforming spirit flagged. "One is driven by the evidence," C. Vann Woodward has written, "to the conclusion that the radicals committed the country to a guarantee of equality that popu-

12. A lively debate goes on among historians as to whether American slavery was the most—or least—inhuman in the Western hemisphere. The most devastating interpretation is by Stanley M. Elkins, *Slavery*, New York, Grosset's Universal Library, 1959–1963. See also Kenneth M. Stampp, *The Peculiar Institution*, New York, Vintage Books, 1956. For a different interpretation, see Marvin Harris, *Patterns of Race in the Americas*, New York, Walker & Co., 1964.

13. By 1869, nine northern states permitted Negroes to vote. In addition to the five New England States, Minnesota, and Iowa, these included "Nebraska, which entered the Union with Negro suffrage as a congressional requirement, and Wisconsin by decision of her Supreme Court". Woodward, "Seeds of Failure in Radical Race Policy," *op. cit.*, p. 7. The Republican platform of 1868 proclaimed: "The guaranty by Congress of equal suffrage to all loyal men at the South was demanded by every consideration of public safety, of gratitude, and of justice, and must be maintained; while the question of suffrage in all loyal (i.e., northern) States properly belongs to the people of those states." *Ibid.*, p. 6

lar convictions were not prepared to sustain."[14] Their leaders also wearied. Men like Charles A. Dana, editor of the influential *New York Sun* and once a Radical, used his newspaper to proclaim throughout Grant's second term; "No force bill! No Negro domination!" Old anti-slavery men like William Cullen Bryant, editor of the *New York Evening Post*, James Russell Lowell, and Robert Ingersoll all foreswore Radicalism and Reconstruction. Edwin L. Godkin in the columns of the *Nation* (a journal that had been in the vanguard in opposing the subjugation of the Negro) now steadily attacked the notion that the evils of the South could be cured by outsiders.[15]

Neither the people nor their leaders were prepared to commit themselves to the long, persistent, and often disagreeable tasks of reconstructing an alien society—nor, for that matter, their own. The old and often decent impulse to compromise and conciliate was strong. Equality of the Negro had little to attract white citizens other than the weak appeal of abstract justice—and, for a time, the prospect so alluring to the Radical politicians, a Republican South founded upon Negro votes. A policy of reconciliation (at the expense of the Negro) made a strong appeal not only to the spirit of compromise so deeply ingrained in Americans, but to history, tradition, identity, race, and economic interest, North and South. Revolution was tiresome; in any case by 1876 all the signs showed that the revolution was failing.

In the defeated states where Negroes were a minority, whites used a mixture of votes and intimidation to restore their control. In states like Mississippi where Negroes were a majority, for whites to win elections required an even stronger dose of intimidation and Ku Klux Klan. In one state after another, reconstruction governments that fully protected the rights of Negro voters in the old slave states were displaced by 'conservative' governments: Tennessee in 1869, Virginia and North Carolina in 1870, Georgia in 1872, Alabama and Arkansas in 1874, Mississippi in 1876. By the time of the elections of 1876, Republican governments controlled only three Southern states, South Carolina, Louisiana, and Florida. Two sets of actions symbolized what was happening and foreshadowed the full restoration of white supremacy. In 1873 a minority, and in 1876 a majority, of the Supreme Court announced in language plain enough for all to understand that it was stripping the Negro of the protections he was presumed to have under the Fourteenth Amendment;

14. Woodward, *The Burden of Southern History*, p. 83; see also his comments at pp. 79–83, 90–93.
15. Paul H. Buck, *The Road to Reunion*, 1865–1900, New York, Vintage Books, 1959, p. 101.

instead, the Court would use the Amendment to protect business enterprise from government regulation.[16] In July, 1876, Southern Congressmen won enough support among their Northern colleagues to gut the Southern Homestead Act of 1866: land reform, half-hearted at best, was ended.

In November, 1876, the presidential contest led to a disputed outcome in which both candidates, backed by their parties, claimed victory. The bitter and inflamatory dispute went on through the fall of 1876 and the winter of 1877 and was finally settled only a few days before the date for the new President's inaugural (March 4). This compromise permitted the Republican candidate to take office and marked the end of Reconstruction in the South.

The leading historian of that episode has summed it up:

The Compromise of 1877 marked the abandonment of principles and of force and a return to the traditional ways of expediency and concession. The compromise laid the political foundation for re-union. It established a new sectional truce that proved more enduring than any previous one and provided a settlement for an issue that had troubled American politics for more than a generation. It wrote an end to Reconstruction and recognized a new regime in the South. More profoundly than Constitutional amendments and wordy statutes it shaped the future of four million freedmen and their progeny for generations to come. It preserved one part of the fruits of the "Second American Revolution"—the pragmatic and economic part—at the expense of the the the other part—the idealistic and humanitarian part. . . .

The Compromise of 1877 did not restore the old order to the South, nor did it restore the South to parity with other sections. It did assure the dominant whites political autonomy and nonintervention in matters of race policy and promised them a share in the blessings of the new economic order. So long as the Conservative Redeemers held control they scotched any tendency of the South to combine forces with the internal enemies of the new economy—laborites, Western agrarians, reformers. Under the regime of the Redeemers the South became a bulwark instead of a menace to the new order.[17]

16. In The Slaughter House Cases (1873); United States v Reese (1876); United States v Cruikshank (1876).
17. Woodward, Reunion and Reaction: The Compromise of 1877 and the End of Reconstruction, Boston, Little, Brown, pp. 245–246.

After the compromise, troops were withdrawn in the states where they still remained. All serious efforts at reconstruction ceased. The attempt to create an independent yeomanry of white and Negro farmers failed utterly:

> In spite of the low price of land and the small acreage in which it could be acquired, few Negroes or white farmers were financially capable of purchasing farms and becoming actual owners. The split-up of the plantation did not result in a land-owning, independent and sturdy yeomanry. A system of tenancy, in which the laborer worked assigned tracts and shared the produce with the owner, developed and became permanent. It can be demonstrated that the increase in the number of small farms was a barometer for measuring the increase in tenantry. By 1880 forty-five per cent of all the farms of Georgia were operated by tenants. . . .
>
> The abounding poverty depressed the tenant into a status approximating peonage. Lacking sufficient savings to live through a season of growing crops without borrowing, he discovered that credit was an expensive luxury. Banking facilities in rural areas fell sadly short of the demand. Even where they existed, the only security the tenant had to offer the bank was a lien placed on his share of the anticipated crop. The village merchant with whom he traded for food, clothing, and other supplies perforce became his banker, giving credit in return for a crop lien. By 1880 approximately three fourths of the agricultural classes in the South were chronic debtors, and the merchants through their control of credit were the dominant factor in the new economic structure.[18]

White supremacy was restored. The South became the one-party region it remained for almost a century. For white Southerners not only abhorred the Republican Party as responsible for inflicting civil war on their soil, freeing the slaves, and attempting to push through the policies of Reconstruction; they also saw that whites could unite to maintain white supremacy in a single party, whereas they would be dangerously weakened if they divided into two competing and conflicting parties.

The Supreme Court of the United States, as it must do sooner or later, adhered to the terms of the compromise: It undertook the long and sordid process of whittling down the meaning of the Fourteenth and Fifteenth Amendments—and converting the Fourteenth into a protec-

18. Buck, op. cit., pp. 151, 152.

tion for business enterprise against state regulation. As the Court and federal government stood aside, Negroes were, in time, disfranchised throughout the South. In 1896 in *Plessy* v. *Ferguson* the Court wrapped the Constitution around the doctrine of segregation.

"Capitulation to racism," as Woodward has called it, now became complete. During the years that followed *Plessy* v. *Ferguson* a new wave of segregationism fastened the yoke of Jim Crow and Negro disfranchisement firmly upon the South,[19] a system into which most white (and many Negro) Southerners were to be so thoroughly inducted by indoctrination and overwhelming social pressure backed by violence that they received it as a precious and unalterable way of life to be protected against all change and all interference. It was not until after the middle of the present century that this way of life—one of the greatest anachronisms, surely, of the twentieth century—finally came under an attack from outside and from within so powerful and so steady that the hallowed ways began to yield, at last, to new ways that for the first time in the nation's history might be reconciled with the promises of American democracy.

19. Woodward, *The Strange Career of Jim Crow, op. cit.*

13

THE CONDITIONS OF
MODERATE CONFLICT

Periods of Moderate Conflict

IF YOU WERE TO PICK at random any year in American history since the Constitutional Convention to illustrate the workings of the political system, you would stand a rather good chance of being able to describe American politics during that year as follows:

> ¶ Important government policies would be arrived at through negotiation, bargaining, persuasion, and pressure at a considerable number of different sites in the political system—the White House, the bureaucracies, the labyrinth of committees in Congress, the federal and state courts, the state legislatures and executives, the local governments. No single organized political interest, party, class, region, or ethnic group would control all of these sites.
>
> ¶ Different individuals and groups would not all exert an equal influence on decisions about government policies. The extent of influence individuals or groups exerted would depend on a complex set of factors: their political skills, how aroused and active they were, their numbers, and their access to such political resources as organization, money, connections, propaganda, etc. People who lacked even suffrage and had no other resources—slaves, for example—would of course be virtually powerless. But because *almost* every group has some political resources—

at a minimum, the vote—most people who felt that their interests were significantly affected by a proposed change in policy would have some influence in negotiations.

¶ All the important political forces—particularly all the candidates and elected officials of the two major parties—would accept (or at any rate would not challenge) the legitimacy of the basic social, economic, and political structures of the United States. Organized opposition to these basic structures would be confined to minority movements too feeble to win representation in Congress or a single electoral vote for their presidential candidate.

¶ Political conflict would be moderate.

¶ Changes in policies would be marginal.

As we saw in the last chapters, these characteristics do not always fit American politics. But most of the time the American political system does display these characteristics.

Why should this be so? Our paradigm of conflict in Chapter 10 suggests four reasons:

The political institutions reward moderation and marginal change, and discourage deviant policies and comprehensive changes.

In the United States there is a massive convergence of attitudes on a number of key issues that divide citizens in other countries.

As one result, ways of life are not seriously threatened by the policies of opponents.

On issues over which Americans disagree, overlapping cleavages stimulate conciliation and compromise.

A Multiplicity of Check-Points

Because the first part of this book describes American political institutions in some detail, it will suffice at this point to consider briefly some of the consequences of the institutions as a whole. When one looks at American political institutions in their entirety and compares them with institutions in other democracies, what stands out as a salient feature is the extraordinary variety of opportunities these institutions provide for an organized minority to block, modify, or delay a policy which the minority opposes. Consequently, it is a rarity for any coalition to carry out its policies without having to bargain, negotiate, and compromise with its opponents; often, indeed, it wins a victory in one institution only to suffer defeat in another.

The multiplicity of check-points that American political institutions provide organized minorities result from three inter-related factors. First, there is a great diversity of political institutions. Second, among these institutions there is no clear-cut hierarchy of legal and constitutional authority. Third, there is no de facto hierarchy of power.

The President, the House, and the Senate are separate institutions. Each reposes on a separate and different system of elections with different terms of office and different electorates. Groups weighty in a presidential election may be much weaker in House and Senate elections. The policies of a particular group or coalition may be supported in one institution and opposed in another. In many areas of policy, each of these major institutions has a veto over the others. Each has a reservoir of legal, constitutional, and de facto power.

Neither the Executive, the House, nor the Senate is monolithic. A group may be strong in one executive agency, weak in another; strong in a particular House or Senate committee, weak elsewhere. A group may have individual spokesmen and opponents located at various places in the executive agencies, the regulatory commissions, the House, the Senate, the standing committees, a conference committee.

The political parties are themselves coalitions. Nominations are not centrally controlled. National party leaders have limited resources for influencing their members in Congress. A minority may be defeated at the presidential nominating convention, yet retain its strength in state and local party organizations; it cannot be pushed aside.

Again and again in the history of the Supreme Court, a minority coalition that could not win the Presidency or majorities in Congress has preserved a majority within the Supreme Court to fight a rear-guard delaying action. Chief Justice John Marshall fought Thomas Jefferson. In the Dred Scott case, Chief Justice Roger B. Taney, fearing what future majorities might do, fought to preserve dead or dying ones. Embattled minorities entrenched in the Court knocked out the income tax in 1894, child labor laws in 1918 and 1922, New Deal reforms from 1935 to 1937. In its epochal decision on school integration in 1954, the Court pronounced policy that could not possibly have passed through Congress at that time. Even if they rarely win their wars in the Congress, minorities well represented on the Court can win some impressive battles.

Even when minorities lose in national politics, they still may win in the states. Although defeated in Civil War, the white South nonetheless forced the North to concede white supremacy, thanks in considerable measure to the institutions of federalism. In the North, trade unions and advocates of factory reform, abolition of child labor, workmen's compensation, shorter hours, protection of women workers won in the state legislatures what they could not win nationally without the agreement of President, Congress, and Court. The principle holds even within the states, where legislative, executive, and judicial institutions follow the pattern of the national government, though often with greater fragmentation. Local governments provide still other check-points.

Neither the Constitution, constitutional doctrine, nor American ideology have ever treated all these institutions, national and federal, as components of an ordered hierarchy in which some constitutional units are invariably subordinate to others. Constitutionally speaking, the President does not dominate Congress; nor, on the other hand, is the President a mere agent of Congress; the Senate is not constitutionally superior to the House, nor Congress and President to the Judiciary, nor the governors and state legislatures to the President and Congress.

Nor do Americans agree, as we have already seen, on any single principle of legitimate decision-making that would provide a way of ordering these institutions into a lawful hierarchy.[1] Majority-rule? Yes, but which majority? Operating in what institution? By what means? And anyway what of minority rights? Given varying interpretations of political legitimacy possible within the American tradition, the extent to which a particular principle or institution is upheld often depends on whose ox is being gored. In the 1930s, liberals attacked the Supreme Court and defended majority rule; in the 1950s and 1960s, the prestige of the Court among liberals had never been higher. During the early years of the New Deal, conservatives saw the Court as a bastion of freedom; in the 1950s some of them came to view it as rather tyrannical. During the New Deal and the Fair Deal, liberal Democracts frequently extolled the virtues (and political legitimacy) of a strong President; with the election of a Republican President in 1952 they began to discover new virtues in Congress; but that theme was quickly muted after 1960. Many conservatives insist that 'power must be kept close to the people'; they praise the legitimacy of 'states' rights'; but they oppose attempts to bring power 'closer to the people' by re-apportioning state legislatures or allowing Negroes to vote.

To be sure, there is the belief in the final legitimacy of rule by the people: that "this country, with its institutions, belongs to the people who inhabit it," as Lincoln said. "Whenever they shall grow weary of the existing government, they can exercise their constitutional right of amending it, or their revolutionary right to dismember or overthrow it." Yet the 'people' have not chosen to amend the Constitution in order

1. Cf. Chapter 1, pp. 39–42, and Chapter 11, pp. 294–295.

to establish a single hierarchy of authority in our political institutions. Quite the contrary: 'The people' have never shown the slightest interest in any of the schemes for doing so that are sometimes propounded by eager constitution-makers. Moreover, a *majority* of the people is not constitutionally sovereign even in amending the Constitution, unless that majority happens also to constitute a majority in three fourths of the states. Indeed, a unanimity of opinion in three fourths of the states does not make 'the people' constitutionally sovereign even in its power to amend the Constitution in at least one respect; for the final words of Article V of the Constitution read as follows: ". . . no state, without its consent, shall be deprived of its equal suffrage in the Senate."

To anyone searching for a single principle of legitimate decision-making, it is of little value to say that 'the people' may exercise "their revolutionary right to dismember or overthrow" the political institutions. Perhaps if Americans converged on a single principle it would be this: Unanimity, though unattainable, is best; institutions must therefore be so contrived that they will compel a constant search for the highest attainable degree of consent.

If in constitutional theory there is no hierarchy of legitimate authorities, then fact, as we have seen, conforms with theory. That the President is no mere agent of the Congress; that the Congress is not subordinate to the President; that neither the federal government nor a state is subordinate to the other on all matters—these are facts of political life, facts doubly resistant to change because fact corresponds to constitutional doctrine and American ideology.

The institutions, then, offer organized minorities innumerable sites in which to fight, perhaps to defeat, at any rate to damage an opposing coalition. Consequently, the institutions place a high premium on strategies of compromise and conciliation, on a search for consensus. They inhibit and delay change until there is wide support; they render comprehensive change unlikely; they foster incremental adjustments. They generate politicians who learn how to deal gently with opponents, who struggle endlessly in building and holding coalitions together, who doubt the possibilities of great change, who seek compromises.

Consensus

Americans ordinarily agree on a great many questions that in some countries have polarized the citizenry into antagonistic camps. One consequence of this massive convergence of attitudes is that political contests do not usually involve serious threats to the way of life of significant strata in the community. Thus, two of the four conditions mentioned a moment ago typically exist in American political life.

One word of warning may be useful at this point: It is easy to exaggerate, as foreigners often do after visiting this country, the extent to which Americans agree. As we saw in the preceding chapter, Americans do disagree among themselves; sometimes these disagreements lead to severe conflict; in one case they led to civil war.

Keeping in mind the fact that once a generation or thereabouts Americans engage in severe conflicts, it is nonetheless true that ordinarily there is a fairly high degree of unity among Americans.[2]

The evidence from surveys[3] indicates that:

¶ It is very nearly impossible to find an American who says that he is opposed to democracy or favors some alternative—at least for the United States. On the contrary, nearly everyone professes to believe that democracy is the best form of government.[4]

¶ Although substantial numbers of citizens approve of proposals for specific constitutional changes, the broad elements of the system are widely endorsed.[5]

2. The rest of this section and the following section are taken from my chapter "The American Oppositions; Affirmation and Denial," in *Political Oppositions in Western Democracies*, New Haven, Yale University Press, 1966.

3. For analyses of greater breadth or depth than space permits here, the reader should consult: Clyde Kluckhohn, "The Evolution of Contemporary American Values" *Daedalus*, Vol. 87, No. 2 (Spring, 1958) 78–109; Robert Lane, *Political Ideology, Why the American Common Man Believes What He Does*, New York, The Free Press, 1962; Gabriel A. Almond and Sidney Verba, *The Civic Culture, Political Attitudes and Democracy in Five Nations*, Princeton, Princeton University Press, 1963; V. O. Key, Jr., *Public Opinion and American Democracy*, New York, Knopf, 1961; Herbert McCloskey, "Consensus and Ideology in American Politics," *American Political Science Review*, 58, No. 2 (June, 1964), pp. 361–382.

4. James W. Prothro and C. W. Grigg, "Fundamental Principles of Democracy: Bases of Agreement and Disagreement," *Journal of Politics*, Vol. 22 (Spring, 1960), 276–294.

5. Thus 61 per cent said they would favor changing the terms of members of the House of Representatives from 2 years to 4 years; 24 per cent were opposed; 15 per cent expressed no opinion. There was little difference by region or party. AIPO release, Jan. 14, 1966. 50 per cent said they would favor limiting U.S. Senators to two 6-year terms; 38 per cent were opposed; 12 percent had no opinion. AIPO release, Jan. 26, 1966. The evidence

¶ There is substantial agreement that if defects exist in the laws and the Constitution they should be cured by traditional legal and political processes of change.[6]

¶ Most Americans also display complacency about their economic institutions. Proposals for extensive reconstruction do not enjoy much support. The great corporations, it appears, have gained rather wide acceptance. A minority holds that corporations should be more severely regulated; a smaller minority holds that they should be nationalized. The trade unions are somewhat more unpopular than the corporations; many would like to see them more severely regulated by the government; but few say that they would like to see trade unions done away with altogether.[7]

¶ Although a majority of Americans seem willing to place

for wide support for the main elements in the Constitution is indirect, e.g., "Should the Constitution be made easier to amend?" No, 69 per cent, AIPO, March 1, 1937, in Hadley Cantril, *Public Opinion 1935–1946*, Princeton, Princeton University Press, 1951, p. 939. "Do you think the Constitution of the United States should ever be changed in any way?" No, 54 per cent; Yes, 34 per cent; Don't know, 12 per cent; NORC, Nov., 1943, in *Ibid., loc. cit.*

6. One study provides as evidence for the point the percentages of "political influentials" (N=3020) and "general electorate" (N=1484) agreeing to the following statement: "There are times when it almost seems better for the people to take the law into their own hands than wait for the machinery of government to act." Political influentials 13 per cent; general electorate 27 per cent, in McCloskey, *op. cit.*, p. 365. In 1965 only 10 per cent of a national sample said that they had "ever felt the urge to organize or join a public demonstration about something." AIPO release, Nov. 17, 1965.

7. On business, see the Survey Research Center, Institute for Social Research, University of Michigan, *Big Business from the Viewpoint of the Public*, Ann Arbor, 1951, pp. 18, 20, 26, 44, 56. In the midst of the Great Depression, responses to the question "Should the government attempt to break up large business organizations?" were: No, 69 per cent; Yes, 31 per cent (=100 per cent), no opinion, 10 per cent. (AIPO, July 19, 1937, in Cantril, *op. cit.*, p. 345) On government ownership, see polls #14 and 16, p. 345; #53, 54, 59, p. 349; and #73, p. 351. The percentages of Americans who say they approve of labor unions has varied from 60 to 76 per cent for three decades; Gallup figures are: 1936, 72 per cent; 1941, 64 per cent; 1953, 75 per cent; 1961, 63 per cent; 1965, 71 per cent. However, in recent years more people have said that the laws regulating labor unions were not strict enough than have said they were right or too strict. AIPO release, Feb. 14, 1965.

themselves in the 'working class,' their sense of 'class' is obviously weak. The key word seems to be 'working,' not 'class.' Few believe that 'class lines' divide Americans into hostile camps.[8]

¶ Most Americans continue to profess a strong confidence in the possibilities of personal achievement in the American milieu. A great many continue to believe that personal success is attainable by hard work and skill.[9]

¶ Thus Americans tend to express satisfaction rather than discontent with their lot. Most Americans claim that life in the United States is the best they could attain anywhere in the world; almost no one wants to emigrate. They expect that their own material conditions will improve, and that for their children life will be much better, provided there is no war.[10]

These propositions concerning American attitudes suggest two questions: (1) How deeply are these attitudes sustained? and (2) How did such an astonishing unity of views ever come about?

DEPTH AND DISTRIBUTION. How deeply these attitudes run, how firmly they are held, and how they are shared among Americans are questions on which historical data shed almost no direct light, and modern survey data only a little more. Survey data do, however, lend some support for the following hypotheses:

8. See V. O. Key's analysis, "Occupation and Class," ch. 6 in Public Opinion and American Democracy, op. cit. Also Robert R. Alford, Party and Society, Chicago, Rand-McNally, 1963, ch. 8.
9. The hypothesis that there has been a decline in the motivations for personal achievement is highly dubious. See Lipset's discussion of "A Changing American Character?" ch. 3 in The First New Nation, op. cit. The data cited in Key, op. cit., in fn. 2 and 4, p. 47 and fn. 5, p. 48. And Fred I. Greenstein, "New Light on Changing American Values: A Forgotten Body of Survey Data," Social Forces, Vol. 42 (1964), 441–450.
10. In 1965, white persons in a national survey said overwhelmingly that they were satisfied with their family income (69 per cent); housing (77 per cent), the work they did (87 per cent), the education their children were getting (77 per cent). Among non-whites, however, the proportions who were dissatisfied were: on income, 64 per cent; housing, 66 per cent; on the work they did, 38 per cent; and on the education their children were getting, 46 per cent. AIPO release, Sept. 1, 1965. See also William Buchanan and Hadley Cantril, How Nations See Each Other, Urbana, University of Illinois Press, 1953, p. 53.

1. If Americans are agreed on abstract general propositions about popular government, majority rule, the Constitution, the virtues of individual liberty, and so on, an attempt to apply these generalities to concrete problems is likely to produce extensive disagreements.[11]
2. Statistically speaking, the more formal education an American has, the more likely he is to express support for the general views just described. The greater his income, the more likely his support—though we cannot be sure about the very rich, who are too small a group to show up in surveys. Support also increases with the status or social prestige of one's occupation; it is higher among professional people, for example, than among skilled workers. Again, it is not possible to be sure about small categories—corporate executives, or Wall Street brokers, for example. Finally, the more active and involved one is in political affairs, the more likely he is to support these views.[12]
3. The connection between the word and the deed is rather uncertain. In particular, to express disagreement with widely prevailing views does not at all mean that one will actually do anything more to act out his dissent. Many— perhaps most—Americans who express disagreement do not, it seems, try to change the attitudes of others by discussion, or bring about changes by joining dissident political movements or trying to secure the nomination and election of candidates favorable to their views. The reasons for inaction include political apathy and indifference, lack of strong feeling, pessimism over the prospects of success, ignorance, and so on.[13]

11. The best evidence is found in Prothro and Grigg, *op. cit.*; McCloskey, *op. cit.*; and Samuel A. Stouffer, *Communism, Conformity and Civil Liberties*, Garden City, New York, Doubleday, 1955.
12. See the survey data reported and analyzed in Fred I. Greenstein, *The American Party System and the American People*, Englewood Cliffs, N.J., Prentice-Hall, Inc., 1963, ch. 3, pp. 18–36; S. M. Lipset, *Political Man*, Garden City, New York, Doubleday, 1960, ch. IV, "Working Class Authoritarianism," pp. 97–130. See also Stouffer, *op. cit.*, *passim*.
13. The evidence is indirect but strong. See Herbert McCloskey, "Conservatism and Personality," *American Political Science Review*, vol. 52 (March, 1958), 27–45. Robert Lane, *Political Life*, Glencoe, Ill. The Free Press, 1959, ch. 5, pp. 63–79 and ch. 12, pp. 163–181. A. Campbell, P. E. Converse, W. E. Miller, D. E. Stokes, *The American Voter*, New York, John Wiley & Sons, 1960, ch. 5, pp. 89–115.

Thus the patterns of support, disagreement and apathy help to sustain the prevailing views and weaken the effectiveness of opposition to them. Since support tends to increase with education, income, occupational status, and political activity; and since political influence is also to a considerable extent a function of these same factors, the influence of supportive attitudes tends to be disproportionately increased, while opposition tends to be politically ineffectual.

Factors Sustaining Consensus

Chapter 3 explained how a political consensus developed among Americans in the nineteenth century. Yet it is one thing to show how a certain unity of views happened to arise, and quite another to explain how it continued to exist when the United States ceased to be a nation of small independent farmers. By 1880 workers in non-farm occupations exceeded those in farming. Thereafter the farmers were an ever smaller minority; by 1957 less than one out of ten persons in the labor force was in agriculture, and of these only about half owned their own farms.[14]

Probably the sheer inertia of an already venerable tradition helped the United States through periods of crisis. But the crises themselves may have helped even more. The inertial force of the traditional attitudes must have increased as each great challenge to the liberal democratic, privatistic, success-oriented ideology was turned back. Each challenge offered the possibility of a rival ideology—aristocracy, slavocracy, socialism, plutocracy. Yet in each case these potential rivals for the minds of Americans were defeated, and the older victorious ideology then became thoroughly intertwined with traditionalism. To attack the conventional ideas meant more and more to attack the whole course of American national history, to show that Americans had failed, long ago, to take the right path.

Yet these challenges might not have been successfully overcome if the "equality of condition" which Tocqueville had observed had vanished; if, in short, blatant contradictions had developed between the lives led by ordinary Americans and the aspirations offered in the dominant ideology. Despite increasing economic inequalities that accompanied industrialization, particularly in its early stages after the Civil War, evi-

14. *Historical Statistics*, Series 1–12 and K 8–52.

dently enough of the old "equality of condition" survived—if not in reality, at least in expectations—so that the old ideas won converts even among the very people who were worst off under industrial capitalism.[15]

Two additional elements have helped to sustain the dominant traditional ideology in the twentieth century. One of these is the educational system, which from the primary grades through high school, and even in the universities, emphasizes the values and institutions expressed in the dominant liberal-democratic ideology. While the relationship between formal education and ideas is complex, most of all with any specific person, one simple and imposing statistical fact is that in survey after survey of political attitudes and ideas among Americans, the amount of formal education appears as a highly significant variable; more often than any other, indeed, education shows up as the most significant variable, even when the effects of socio-economic status and occupation are cancelled out.[16] As we have already observed (and this is the important point) the greater one's formal education, the more likely he is to endorse the key propositions in the prevailing ideology.

The other influence, that of the mass media—radio, television, newspapers, and mass circulation magazines—is harder to assess. Concrete data are few. Critics on the left argue that the great bulk of Americans are lulled by the mass media into a complacent acceptance of the values in the prevailing ideology—chiefly the emphasis on private property and personal success, and that these beliefs in turn protect the position of certain important elite groups, business leaders, men of wealth, and so on. Critics among the ranks of the radical right tend to view the mass media in much the same way; they see the mass media as major instruments (along with the educational system) by which the liberal

---

15. Comparative studies of rates of social mobility are still too few for confident conclusions. The view of S. M. Lipset and Reinhard Bendix that "the overall pattern of social mobility appears to be much the same in industrial societies of various Western countries (*Social Mobility in Industrial Society*, Berkeley and Los Angeles, University of California Press, 1960, p. 13) appears, in the light of later studies, to be doubtful. Perhaps the most that one can say at this point is that social mobility is or has been relatively high in the United States, as compared with such European countries as Britain and the Netherlands, in some but not in all respects. See S. M. Miller, "Comparative Social Mobility: A Trend Report," *Current Sociology*, IX, 1 (1960), 1–5. Also Thomas Fox and S. M. Miller, in Merritt and Rokkan, eds., *Comparing Nations*, New Haven, Yale University Press, 1966, pp. 217–238.

16. Key, *op. cit.*, ch. 13, "The Educational System," pp. 315–343.

'establishment' acquires and retains its dominance over American institutions and attitudes.[17]

Both views, I think, exaggerate the direct, manipulative influence of the mass media on American attitudes. The opposition of three quarters of the daily newspapers of the United States may have reduced the amount of support for Franklin D. Roosevelt, but it did not prevent him from being re-elected three times. Or, to take a more recent example, differences in attitudes toward a highly controversial issue like medical care were in 1956 related in a very weak way to the amount of exposure to the mass media. Moreover, some of the differences were the opposite of what one might expect from simple theories of the influence of the media on 'mass man.' Thus among persons with only a grade school education, both support for (76 per cent) and opposition to (15 per cent) a government program of medical care was higher among those *most* exposed to the mass media.[18]

The explanation is not mysterious. There is a good deal of evidence that the individuals and groups who might be most susceptible to positive influences from the media because of weak social, psychological, and political ties—'mass man'—also pay much less attention to the media; whereas the individuals who are most 'exposed' to the mass media are in general those with the strongest social, psychological, and political barriers between them and manipulative efforts.[19] The views of left and right

17. The following quotation could as easily have come from a source on the Left as on the Right: "...the mass circulation media in this country have virtually closed their columns to opposition articles. For this they can hardly be blamed; their business is to sell paper at so much a pound and advertising space at so much a line. They must give the masses what they believe the masses want, if they are to maintain their mass circulation business; and there is no doubt that the promises...reiterated by the propaganda machine of the government, have made it popular and dulled the public mind to the verities of freedom." The source is, in fact, an editorial note in a rightwing publication, *The Freeman*, June, 1955, cited in Daniel Bell, "Interpretations of American Politics" in *The New American Right*, Daniel Bell, ed., New York, Anchor Books, 1964, p. 68, fn. 23. The editorial was attacking the mass media for lulling the public into socialism. The best known criticism from the Left, sounding many of the same themes, is in the late C. Wright Mills, *The Power Elite*, New York, Oxford University Press, 1956, ch. 13, "The Mass Society," pp. 298–324.

18. V. O. Key, *op. cit.*, p. 398.

19. A sophisticated and skeptical attempt to access the influence of the mass media is V. O. Key, *op. cit.*, chs. 14 and 15, "Media: Specter and Reality," and "Media: Structure and Impact," pp. 344–410. On the general problem of manipulating attitudes, see also R. E. Lane and D. O. Sears, *Public Opinion*, Englewood Cliffs, N.J.: Prentice-Hall, Inc., 1964, ch. 5, "Leaders' Influence on Public Opinion." See also Elihu Katz and Paul F. Lazarsfeld, *Personal Influence*, Glencoe, Ill., Free Press, 1955.

also underestimate, I think, the extent to which the mass media themselves reflect stable values in the American culture; for better or worse, culture and media reinforce one another.

What is essentially correct, however, is that the amount of time and space devoted by the mass media to views openly hostile to the prevailing ideology is negligible.[20] An American who wishes to find criticism of the basic social, economic, and political structures can indeed find them; but he will have to search outside the mass media. And, naturally, the number who are strongly motivated enough to do so is relatively small. Hence the general effect of the mass media is to reinforce the existing institutions and ideology.[21]

To sum up: The moderate character of political conflict, the tendency for changes to be marginal rather than comprehensive, the weakness of structural and revolutionary oppositions, the importance of bargaining and negotiation—these aspects of the 'normal' pattern of moderate conflict in the United States can be accounted for in considerable part by the three factors discussed in this chapter: the effects of the political institutions, the convergence of attitudes, and the resulting lack of serious threats to ways of life. But the fourth factor in the paradigm of conflict in Chapter 10—overlapping cleavages—is also important. This is the pattern to be explored in the next chapter.

20. "Extraordinarily few (American) journals, either daily newspapers or magazines, act as agencies of political criticism. They may dig to find the facts about individual acts of corruption, but the grand problems of the political system by and large escape their critical attention," Key, *op. cit.*, p. 381.
21. For a similar conclusion, see Key, *op. cit.*, p. 396.

14

OVERLAPPING CLEAVAGES—
LOW POLARIZATION

LTHOUGH AMERICANS tend to agree on a great many questions,
there are some over which they disagree. Over the course of
American history, certain types of issues have recurred as subjects of conflict: the nature and extent of democratic processes, foreign
policy, the role of the government in the regulation and control of the
economy, the place of the Negro in American life.

Yet these issues do not ordinarily polarize Americans into two
exclusive and antagonistic camps. Indeed, the pattern of disagreements
in political attitudes and loyalties may itself actually inhibit polarization
and encourage conciliation. In particular, two characteristics of the
pattern of cleavages stimulate efforts toward conciliation and compromise and weaken pressures toward polarization.

First, differences in political attitudes, actions, and loyalties are not
highly related to differences in region, social standing, occupation, and
other socio-economic characteristics. Of course there often is *some*
relation; but it is usually rather weak. People in the same region, in the
same status group, or in the same occupation do not tend to form distinct homogeneous political blocs. Consequently, *polarization of politics
along social, economic, or regional lines is inhibited.*

Second, differences in political attitudes and loyalties are not highly
inter-related among themselves. Two people who hold the same attitudes on one question frequently hold different attitudes on other questions. To overstate the point, every ally is sometimes an enemy and every

enemy is sometimes an ally. Consequently, *polarization of politics along ideological lines is inhibited.*

Regional Differences

Consider geography: American politics has often been described as a conflict between different sections or regions. And it is true, of course, that with respect to the place of the Negro in American life the cleavage between North and South has been persistent and sometimes bitter. As we saw in Chapter 12, from 1850 to about 1877 the bundle of issues associated with slavery and the Negro polarized American politics to an unprecedented degree.

With this single exception, however, regional conflicts have never polarized Americans into distinct camps. Like the other major sources of conflict in American politics, the importance of regional factors varies greatly from one issue to another: Although powerful on any issue touching the role of Negroes in American life, regional differences are only moderately important on other issues and even negligible on a great many questions. Moreover, regionalism in politics is probably declining. Finally, regional conflicts follow a pattern of overlapping cleavages, not polarization.

Evidence for these propositions is readily available from the arena where regional conflicts might be expected to show up most clearly, in Congress.

Southern Democrats have displayed more unity in the way they vote in Congress than any other regional group. Yet even Southern regionalism is quite limited. The distinctiveness of Southern Democrats tends to be confined to a few issues, mainly those involving the Negro.[1] From 1937 onward, it is true, a majority of Southern Democrats allied themselves on a number of occasions with a majority of Northern Republicans

1. See Raymond E. Wolfinger and Joan Heifetz, "Safe Seats, Seniority, and Power in Congress," *American Political Science Review,* 59 (June 1965), 337–349. H. Douglas Price, "Are Southern Democrats Different?" in Polsby, Dentler, and Smith, eds., *Politics and Social Life,* Boston, Houghton-Mifflin, 1963, pp. 740–756; Julius Turner, *Party and Constituency: Pressures on Congress,* Baltimore, The Johns Hopkins Press, 1951, p. 130 fn., and see also the conclusion of V. O. Key on examining Senate roll calls for seven Senate sessions from 1933 through 1945: ". . . it is primarily on the race issue that the South presents a united front against the rest of the United States," *Politics, Parties, and Pressure Groups,* 3rd. ed., New York, Thomas Y. Crowell Co., 1952, p. 265. See also his *Southern Politics,* New York, Knopf, 1949, chs. 16 and 17.

in voting against a majority of Northern Democrats. This conservative coalition was particularly noticeable during John F. Kennedy's Presidency when it defeated a number of his legislative proposals. Yet even during this period, the coalition appeared on only 28 per cent of the votes in the House and Senate in 1961, 14 per cent in 1962, and 17 per cent in 1963.[2]

Aside from Southern Democrats, it is difficult to find any persistent regional patterns in congressional voting. Among Republicans in Congress there is, in fact, no equivalent to Southern Democrats. One study of four sessions of Congress found that

analysis of the party loyalty of Republicans from various sections reveals shifting alliances from session to session. In 1921 and 1931, West Central and Border Republicans rebelled against majorities from other areas. In 1937 the West rebelled against the East. In 1944 Central states were in control of the party, and insurgency was strongest on the Pacific Coast, and to a lesser extent in the Northeast and Rockies.[3]

In the population at large, it is difficult nowadays to discover distinctive regional clusters of attitudes. Attitudes change, of course, and like other aspects of life, regional differences in attitudes are probably in decline. Thus the South is not, despite its reputation, more 'conservative'

Table 14.1. Opinion, South and Non-South, on Job Guarantee, Big Business Influence, Union Influence, and Power and Housing (1956)

OPINION	JOB GUARANTEE		BIG BUSINESS		UNION		POWER AND HOUSING	
	S	N	S	N	S	N	S	N
Agree strongly	53%	46%	55%	52%	50%	51%	43%	43%
Agree but not very strongly	16	14	16	18	16	16	13	16
Not sure: depends	9	7	9	7	8	7	11	9
Disagree but not very strongly	9	13	9	11	13	11	11	11
Disagree strongly	13	20	11	12	13	15	22	21
	100%	100%	100%	100%	100%	100%	100%	100%
Number	456	1131	348	924	341	976	332	917

SOURCE: V. O. Key, Public Opinion and American Democracy, p. 104.

2. Congressional Quarterly Weekly Report (April 17, 1964), p. 737.
3. Turner, op. cit., p. 146.

on most questions than the rest of the country—and perhaps never has been.[4] Table 14.1, for example, shows how Southerners compared in 1956 with other Americans in their responses to four questions on which conservatives and liberals are usually thought to be divided. The respondents were asked whether they agreed or disagreed with the following statements:

> The government in Washington ought to see to it that everybody who wants to work can find a job.

> The government ought to see to it that big business corporations don't have much to say about how the government is run.

> The government should leave things like electric power and housing for private business men to handle.

> The government ought to see to it that labor unions don't have much to say about how the government is run.[5]

The differences between South and North were not very great. In fact, Southerners were somewhat more favorably disposed than Northerners toward government job guarantees and keeping down the influences of big business on the government (Table 14.1).

The Midwest was once thought to be the stronghold of isolationism. It may once have been. Yet opinion surveys over almost three decades have not revealed large differences between the opinions of Midwesterners and the rest of the country on international affairs.[6]

4. It is worth recalling that during the period of unrest from the 1870s to about 1896, the South seemed to be more 'radical' than the rest of the country. See Hannah G. Roach, "Sectionalism in Congress (1870 to 1890)," *American Political Science Review*, 19 (Aug. 1925), 500–526, and C. Vann Woodward, *The Burden of Southern History*, New York, Vintage Books, 1960, pp. 149 ff.

5. Key, *Public Opinion and American Democracy*, op. cit., p. 560.

6. Since this statement runs contrary to a widespread impression, the reader may wish to satisfy himself by looking at some surveys. During the two years preceding the entry of the United States into World War II, surveys showed that opinion in the East Central and West Central states was only slightly more 'isolationist' than in the other regions outside the South: the South was consistently less 'isolationist' and more 'interventionist.' Cf. the surveys reported in Hadley Cantril, ed., *Public Opinion 1935–1946*, Princeton, Princeton University Press, 1951, pp. 966–978. After America's entry into the war, opinion in favor of joining a world organization was as high in the Midwest as elsewhere, and may have been higher than in some other regions. (*Ibid.*, #7, p. 906; #35, p. 910.) A 1956 survey that distributed

(continued on next page)

Indeed, evidence from surveys in the 1950s suggests that by then the South had replaced the Midwest as the least "internationalist region" (Table 14.3). Yet as the table also shows, the differences among regions on these issues were small.

The reputation of the Midwest as the center of isolationism may have been built upon the conduct of a number of militant isolationists in Congress from Midwestern states. Yet a careful study of voting on foreign aid measures from 1939–58 in the House of Representatives shows that

Mid-western isolationism, to the extent that it did exist, was peculiar to the Republican party. G.O.P. Congressmen from the central regions were more isolationist than those from the East and Pacific coasts in each Congress. On the other side of the aisle, however, Democrats from the Midwest were consistently more internationalist than those from the Southern and Mountain states, particularly after the 77th Congress. (1941–42)[7]

(continued from preceding page)

    responses along a scale measuring attitudes "toward American involvement in foreign affairs"* revealed the following:

Table 14.2. Region in Relation to Distribution Along Scale Measuring Attitudes Toward American Involvement in Foreign Affairs*

INTER-NATIONALISM	MIDWEST	NORTHEAST	FAR WEST	SOUTH
High	53%	59%	58%	56%
Medium	27	25	24	26
Low	20	16	18	18
	100%	100%	100%	100%
Number	372	469	177	398

*Respondents were asked whether they agreed or disagreed with the following statements:

"This country would be better off if we just stayed home and did not concern ourselves with problems in other parts of the world."

"The United States should give economic help to the poorer countries of the world even if they can't pay for it."

"The United States should keep soldiers overseas where they can help countries that are against communism."

"The United States should give help to foreign countries even if they are not as much against communism as we are."

SOURCE: V. O. Key, *op. cit.*, p. 107, 562.

7. Leroy N. Rieselbach, "The Demography of the Congressional Vote on Foreign Aid, 1939–1958," *American Political Science Review*, 58 (September, 1964) 577–588, at pp. 582–3. See also Table IV, p. 582.

Table 14.3. Regional Distribution of Foreign Policy Attitudes in
the 1950s

ISSUE	SOUTH	BORDER	EAST	MIDWEST	WEST
Pro-Negotiations	37%	38%	43%	44%	45%
Show Foreign-Policy Knowledge	52	59	71	69	73
Sophistication on Foreign Policy	42	37	55	50	53
Favor Committing Troops Abroad	42	45	53	45	51
Defend Europe	25	26	31	34	31
Sympathetic to Europe	31	28	46	36	41
Soft Policy to Red China	20	24	26	26	28
Favorable to Asian Neutrals	40	30	50	49	43
Disarm H-Bomb	28	24	33	32	31
Pro-Preparedness	31	36	39	34	39
Pro-United Nations	60	61	67	67	67

SOURCE: Ithiel de Sola Pool, Robert P. Abelson, Samuel L. Popkin, *Candidates,
Issues, and Strategies,* Cambridge: The M.I.T. Press, 1964, Table 2.5, p. 93.

————•◦•————

How then can we account for the fact that, if we exclude the question of the Negro, regional conflict is ordinarily moderate and does not split the country into persistently antagonistic divisions?

In the first place, outside of the Old South, genuinely regional ways of life in sharp contradiction to one another have never developed in the United States. To be sure, there were and still are regional differences— in speech, in manners, in bearing, even to some extent in styles of life; and typically an American has some loyalties, of a sort, to his region. But (putting the South and the special problem of the Negro to one side) these moderately differing regional cultures have never, as such, constituted much of a threat to one another, at least not in a politically relevant way. The fact that a man from Maine speaks in a fashion which someone from Oklahoma may find puzzling or amusing, or that a New Englander is more formal and less easy-going in his ways than a Westerner, hardly constitutes the materials for sharp and enduring political controversies. Regional differences in this sense have always been the source less of political conflicts than of superficial and usually good-natured rivalries, a standing opportunity for any speaker to flatter his audience by sounding the virtues of the region, and a justification for the belief, illusory but highly prized among Americans, that they are a people of incredible diversity.

In the second place, Americans have never stayed long enough in one place to permit regional loyalties to gain the power these might have if people were more content with life in the old home town. That Americans are a restless people, a nation not only of immigrants but also of migrants, has become a national and international cliché; but it happens to be true. One American in four is now living in a state different from the one in which he was born. Of these migrant Americans, about half have moved from a state next to the present one, and the other half from some more distant state. About one person in seven was born in some other region. And what is true now, we learn from the census, has been true for at least a hundred years. The percentages for 1850 vary only slightly from those for 1950.[8] With an expanding frontier, Americans have always been on the move. In 1850, in the region consisting of Ohio, Indiana, Illinois, Michigan, and Wisconsin, one white resident out of three had been born in some other region; further west in the seven states bounded by Minnesota and North Dakota on the north and by Missouri and Kansas on the south, more than one half of the native white population had migrated from other regions; in Arkansas, Louisiana, Oklahoma, and Texas, slightly less than one half were from outside that region. A century later, the frontier was the Pacific Coast, where more than half of the 1950 population had been born elsewhere—a quarter, in fact, in the Midwest; nearly half the people in the Mountain States came from a different region; even in the South Atlantic states about one white person in seven was not, by birth, a Southerner.[9]

Third, the various regions of the United States are internally very heterogeneous. So much so, in fact, that it is exceedingly difficult to decide how to draw regional boundaries: One must choose one set of states for one purpose, another set for a different purpose. The U.S. Census, the Federal Reserve Board, the Department of Agriculture, the student of electoral politics—all use rather different regions. Are there four regions in the United States—or fourteen?

New England and the South are, for historical reasons, the easiest to identify as distinct regions. Yet neither New England nor the South has ever been a political monolith. Both have been split internally along many different lines of cleavage. Socio-economic conflicts have been as bitter among white Southerners as anywhere in the United States; indeed, it is not much of an exaggeration to say that the only question on which the white people of the South have ever been able to unite is on maintaining the subordination of the Negro—and even on this question there has generally been a dissenting minority. New England, unlike the South, has never had even this incentive to provide it with enduring political unity. As for other regions, they are even more heterogeneous politically.

8. *Historical Statistics*, Series C 1–14, p. 41.
9. *Ibid.*, Series C 15–24, pp. 41, 43.

Fourth, what has passed for 'regional' conflict in the past has usually been no more than a special case of socio-economic conflict. The 'regional' conflicts that occupy attention in history books generally occurred when the occupations or incomes of some people in one section of the country were thought to be threatened in some way by people in another section. Even slavery might be interpreted in this fashion. To some extent, the American economy has always been based upon regional specialization; different regions have somewhat different specialties.[10] Hence the economic needs, opportunities, and goals of some of the people in one region may come into conflict with those of another. When the country was predominantly agricultural, climate and soil influenced the kinds of crops produced; and the availability of markets was affected by location, transportation facilities, and tariffs. All of these factors created opportunities for conflict. But they were at base socio-economic conflicts. If regional differences have rarely been great enough to polarize American society along regional lines, what then of socio-economic difference?

Socio-economic Differences: Occupations

Alas for simplicity, socio-economic differences in the United States also tend to produce many intersecting lines of cleavage rather than one big dividing line, or even two or three of them.

The way in which a citizen makes his living, his occupation, his property, the source, amount, and security of his income, all these economic factors have been highly important in shaping the way different citizens appraise the stakes involved in political issues. Because Americans differ in their economic positions, and because differences in economic positions foster differing political views, political controversies can often—though by no means always—be traced to ways in which citizens differ from one another economically. Although economic explanations of American politics do not explain everything, they do explain a good deal.

Yet when we try to explain American politics by looking for economic factors, the resulting cleavages are more significant for their

10. Cf. H. S. Perloff, E. J. Dunn, Jr., E. E. Lampard, and R. F. Muth, *Regions, Resources and Economic Growth*, Baltimore, The Johns Hopkins Press, 1960.

variety and complexity than for their simplicity. In fact, one soon makes two discoveries. You find that no matter how you classify Americans, whether in economic categories or any others, the groups invariably turn out to be politically heterogeneous; that is, on most questions any category of Americans is internally divided in its views in somewhat the same way the rest of the population is divided. You also find that even when individuals or groups agree on one issue, they are likely to be split on another. This seems always to have been the case.

Before the Civil War when most Americans were farmers, differences in crops, markets, problems of transportation and competition, and effects of credit, mortgages, and the supply of currency all helped to produce political conflict. Conflicts over the tariff, national expenditures for canals and roads, banks, the control of the Mississippi— all can be partly explained by economic differences. Yet so far as one can now tell from rather inadequate data, the same economic groups were not always allied. Coalitions both in the electorate and in Congress were somewhat fluid. Even after the Civil War, as industrial capitalism began to displace agriculture in the American economy, the cleavage between businessmen and urban proletariat did not come to dominate politics as it did in a number of European countries and as one might reasonably have expected it would in the United States.[11] Labor and socialist parties failed to gain much ground. The two major parties remained, as they had been before, conglomerate parties with catch-all programs. It is true that the Republicans and Democrats often seemed to have different centers of gravity. The Republican center of gravity was business; in the Democratic Party it was the White South and increasingly the great urban political machines based on the immigrants and the poor. But because businessmen were in a minority, as they always are, the Republicans could not win elections without the support of farmers and even of urban workers. White Southerners were, as had been obvious to their sorrow for generations, also in a minority; hence Democrats could not win presidential elections without support in the North and West, that is, among farmers and urban workers.

In the twentieth century political conflicts have not been fought across any single and constant socio-economic boundary. For example, it is virtually impossible to find any sizeable economic stratum in the United States whose opinions on political questions are violently at odds with those of the rest of the population. Thus if we classify Americans according to whether the head of the household is a professional man, a businessman, a clerical worker, a skilled worker, an unskilled worker, or a

11. Cf. Chapter 16.

farmer, we invariably find that whenever Americans in general disagree on some question, then people within each of these occupational groups will also disagree among themselves. This is not to say that opinion is uniform among all occupational groups; it is not, and the differences are of great importance. What is striking is not how much variation there is from one group to another, but how little.

For example, in 1956, to the question whether the national government should do more, or less, in trying to deal with unemployment, education, housing, and the like, in all the occupational categories, the largest percentage felt that what the government was then doing was about right; the percentage who felt this way varied from 40 per cent among professional men to 68 per cent among unskilled laborers. But clearly every major occupational group had a sizeable minority in disagreement with any position a majority would agree to (Figure 14.1).

In 1956 respondents from the same occupational groups were asked whether they agreed or disagreed with these two statements: (1) the government ought to help people get doctors and hospital care at low cost, and (2) the government ought to see to it that big business corporations don't have much to say about how the government is run. The results are shown in Table 14.4.

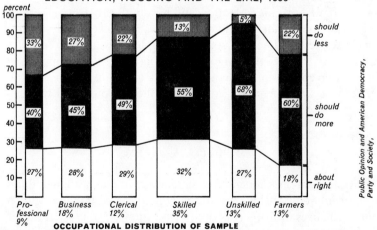

FIGURE 14.1—ATTITUDES TOWARD INTERVENTION BY THE NATIONAL GOVERNMENT IN MATTERS OF UNEMPLOYMENT, EDUCATION, HOUSING AND THE LIKE, 1956

Responses to the Question: "Some people think the national government should do more in trying to deal with such problems as unemployment, education, housing and so on. Others think that the government is doing too much. On the whole, would you say that what the government has done has been about right, too much, or not enough?" Data Source: Survey Research Center, University of Michigan, 1952.

FROM: V.O. Key, *Public Opinion and American Democracy*, Fig. 6.1, p. 124

Table 14.4. Relation of Occupation to Opinions on Medical Care and on Restraint of Big Business Influence

	PROFES-SIONAL	BUSINESS	CLERICAL	SKILLED	UNSKILLED	FARMERS
	MEDICAL CARE					
Agree	38%	45%	49%	56%	65%	61%
Depends	15	9	7	9	8	5
Disagree	41	37	31	23	13	24
No opinion	6	9	13	12	14	10
	100%	100%	100%	100%	100%	100%
	RESTRAIN BIG BUSINESS INFLUENCE					
Agree	53%	48%	52%	56%	42%	54%
Depends	8	8	5	6	3	5
Disagree	23	24	20	13	10	14
No opinion	16	20	23	25	45	27
	100%	100%	100%	100%	100%	100%
Number	163	242	169	487	235	180

SOURCE: V. O. Key, *Public Opinion and American Democracy*, New York, Alfred A. Knopf, 1961, p. 126.

These differences of opinion within occupational groups, and the similarities of opinion from one group to another, mean that conflict rarely if ever occurs along clear-cut occupational lines of cleavage. A political leader who favors active government intervention in the economy will draw both his supporters and his opponents from all occupational groups. He cannot therefore make his appeal exclusively to the laboring classes, lest he lose his support among business and professional men and farmers. And by the same token, a conservative who opposes government intervention in economic life will gain supporters from a great variety of economic groups, including skilled laborers and farmers.

Social Classes

Social classes are not much more significant. In fact, although differences in status unquestionably exist in the United States and are highly important in the lives of many Americans, class lines are so blurred that it taxes the ingenuity of social scientists to provide justifiable methods for classifying Americans according to their social class. In sample surveys, the problem is generally solved in two ways. The individual respondent himself may tell the interviewer what class he thinks he belongs to; social scientists often call this his 'subjective' status or 'class' identification.

Alternatively, the social scientist may himself assign an individual to some set of classes—two, three, five, six, or whatnot—according to so-called objective criteria, such as the amount of education he has, his occupation, and his income. The product of this method is often called his 'objective' status or class.

Following the first tack, in 1956 the Survey Research Center of the University of Michigan put the following question to a national sample of Americans: "There's quite a bit of talk these days about different social classes. Most people say they belong to the middle class or to the working class. Do you ever think of yourself as being in one of these classes?" One out of every three respondents said no. These people who did not spontaneously put themselves in any class were then asked, "Well, if you had to make a choice, would you call yourself middle class or working class?" With the aid of still another question, all the respondents were ultimately sorted out as follows:[12]

Middle Classes		
Upper	7%	
Average	29%	36%
Working Classes		
Upper	9%	
Average	52%	61%
Don't Know		3%
		100%

Thus, Americans are not, as is sometimes thought, a people who all think of themselves as belonging to the middle classes.[13]

12. Key, op. cit., p. 140. Similar results were found by Richard Centers. The Psychology of Social Classes, Princeton, Princeton University Press, 1949, p. 77.

13. Earlier surveys in which respondents were asked to choose between the upper, middle or lower class resulted in nearly everyone placing himself in the middle class and thereby encouraged the illusion that few Americans identified themselves with the working class. Once the option of 'working class' was offered in addition to 'lower class,' the proportion in the 'middle class' declined to a minority. In fact, in a study of nine nations undertaken in 1948, the proportion who identified themselves with the working class was higher among Americans than among Australians, Frenchmen, Germans, Italians, and Norwegians:

"If you were asked to use a name for your social class, would you say you belong to the middle class, working class, or upper class?"

	Aust.	Brit.	Fr.	Ger.	Ital.	Mex.	Neth.	Nor.	U.S.
Middle	50%	35%	45%	52%	54%	45%	33%	43%	42%
Working	47	60	46	41	42	51	60	45	51
Upper	2	2	6	3	4	2	4	1	1
Don't Know	1	3	4	4	0	2	3	11	3

Source: William Buchanan and Hadley Cantril, How Nations See Each Other, Urbana, Univ. of Illinois Press, 1963, p. 13.

The two principle methods we use to assign Americans to social classes seem to show several things. In the first place, class identity seems to be very weak. One adult American out of three, as we have seen, says that he does not ever think of himself as being in the middle class or the working class. Even among those who identify themselves with one or the other, class feelings seem to be tepid. It is illuminating, in fact, to look beyond the bare statistics to the kinds of things the respondents say to the interviewers who ask them what 'class' they belong to. Happily, some of the responses made to a survey in 1956 have been summarized by V. O. Key, and reveal, as he says, "the tenuous quality of class identification":

    . . . . *A Nebraska farm housewife on class: "I suppose it would be working class as that is about all we do." A North Carolina gift shop proprietress when asked if she had to make a choice: "That's a new one to me. I just want to say I'm as good as any of them." An Ohio skilled worker when faced by the choice problem: "I wouldn't say. (Why?) Well, what is the middle class and working class?" A South Carolina housewife: "I think middle class and working class come under the same heading." A Los Angeles housewife: "I can't say. I just wouldn't know." The wife of a New Mexico miner: "I don't quite understand the difference. I guess we work so we must belong to the working class. I don't quite see it." An Idaho lady: "I'm retired but used to be working class." A Pennsylvania steelworker: "When you're in a mill you're workin'." A North Carolina retail grocer had never thought of herself as being of a class: "I think that class talk is just political talk. Here the Republicans are called the rich man's party, and they run a man who came up from just plain people, and the Democrats say they are the little man's party and they run a millionaire." Wirer in California radio factory: "Well I work for a living so I guess I'm in the working class." Retired Ohio worker: (Ever thought of yourself as being in one of these classes?) "Never gave that a thought, missus." The wife of a Kentucky brewery salesman: (Ever thought of self in class?) "I never thought of that." An interviewer noted: "I've had more trouble with R's (respondents) in regard to this class thing. Where the distinction is, no one seems to know."*

    The schedule also contained a question whether the respondent's family when he was growing up was working class or middle class. A Connecticut respondent: "Middle class after '29. Upper class before '29." An Iowa farmer: "I've always been just average—no upper class stuff for me or my family." A Texas widow reported that her family had been upper middle: "We didn't have a college education but we tried to keep ourselves with good characters and things like that." The wife of an Ohio skilled worker: "No, just average people; don't know if we came in any class." A retired hospital orderly said his father had been middle class: "Upper part. My father owned a saloon." A Texas lady: "We always had plenty but what class I don't know."[14]

In a study of nine nations in 1948, few Americans seemed to see people in other classes than their own as implacable enemies. In response to the question, "Do you think you have anything in common with fellow countrymen not in the working class?" seven out of ten Americans who had identified themselves with the working class answered yes.[15]

Despite its weakness as a divisive factor, status or social class does of course provide some basis for political cleavages in the United States. "The extensive modern literature on social class and political behavior has shown persistently that individuals of higher status (subjectively or objectively) tend to give 'conservative' responses on questions of economic policy and tend as well to vote Republican; individuals of lower status respond more 'radically' and vote Democratic."[16] The relation-

14. Key, op. cit., p. 141, fn.
15. In most of the countries, the percentages were considerably higher among middle class and upper class respondents than among working class respondents. Appendix D, *Reports of Survey Agencies*, p. 125 et seq. Among working class respondents only, the percentage answering yes to the following questions were:
"Do you think you have anything in common with fellow countrymen not of your class?"

(Working class respondents only)

	Yes
United States	70%
Australia	70
Norway	66
Great Britain	60
France	58
Germany (British zone of occupation)	53
Mexico	46
Netherlands	45
Italy	37

SOURCE: Buchanan and Cantril, op. cit., pp. 17, 18.
16. Angus Campbell et al., op. cit., p. 346.

[351]

ship is, however, not very strong. That is, we find once again that a sizeable proportion of people with higher status are not conservative whereas a large fraction of voters in the lower status group are. The relationship is particularly weak if we simply and arbitrarily divide the population into two classes—a working class and a middle class, or, if you like, into a lower class and an upper class, or people in blue collar and white collar occupations. In most countries, manual workers tend to vote for Leftist parties more heavily than people in nonmanual occupations. We would expect, therefore, that in the United States manual workers would vote more heavily Democratic than nonmanual workers. And they do. But a comparison of public opinion surveys over more than a decade shows that the difference in party preference between people in manual and nonmanual occupations is markedly less in the United States than in Britain or Australia (though higher than in Canada, where class-voting is almost negligible). (Figure 14.2).

In the United States in recent decades, a third to nearly a half of the non-manual strata have voted Democratic. And, with the exception of 1948, from a third to nearly a half of the manual strata have voted Republican (Figure 14.3).

As Figure 14.2 shows, the relationship is also not very steady. That is, the extent to which one's status seems to have a bearing on one's political views seems to fluctuate. In the presidential election on 1944,

FIGURE 14.2—CLASS VOTING IN THE ANGLO-AMERICAN
COUNTRIES, 1936-1962

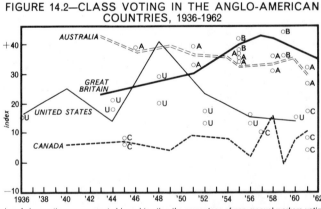

*The index of class voting was computed by subtracting the percentage of non-manual workers voting for "Left" parties from the percentage of manual workers voting for "Left" parties. For Great Britain, the Labour party was used; for Australia, the Australian Labor party; for the United States, the Democratic party; for Canada, the CCF (or NDP) and Liberal parties. Where two parties were classified as "Left," their votes among each strata were combined. For a discussion of the index, see Chapter 4. See Appendix B for the exact questions asked in each survey the occupational divisions used, the dates of polls, and the numbers of cases in manual and non-manual occupations. The surveys were taken at various times between 1952 and 1962. All questions referred to voting intention or past vote in a national election.

SOURCE: Robert R. Alford, *Party and Society*, Chicago, Rand McNally & Co., 1963, pp. 102-103.

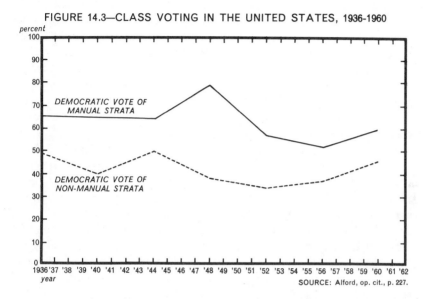

FIGURE 14.3—CLASS VOTING IN THE UNITED STATES, 1936-1960

SOURCE: Alford, op. cit., p. 227.

which took place in the midst of a great war of survival, the relationship between one's status or class and the way one voted in the election was quite weak. Franklin Roosevelt, the wartime President, drew his support from all social strata. After the war, however, economic questions again became highly controversial, as they had been before the war. Seizing upon economic discontents in his 1948 campaign, President Truman employed much of the New Deal ideology of the 1930s, attacked the Republicans as the party of wealth and business, challenged his opponent with an ambitious reform program, his Fair Deal, and castigated the Republican-dominated Congress for rejecting his proposals. In that election, the relationship between status and presidential vote rose to a postwar peak. From that high point it receded in subsequent elections. General Eisenhower's appeal transcended class; like FDR in 1944, Eisenhower in 1952 and 1956 attracted support among all segments of the population.[17]

Finally, to confuse the role of social class even further, there are persistent discrepancies between 'subjective' status—the class with which a voter identifies himself—and 'objective' status defined by occupation or other measures. Some blue-collar workers say they belong to the middle

17. See also Campbell et al., *The American Voter*, New York, Wiley, 1960, op. cit., p. 347.

class; a considerable number of white collar workers say they are in the working class. Given the vagueness of class boundaries in the United States, these anomalies are scarcely surprising. But what is highly significant is that if two people whom an observer would put in the same social class nonetheless put themselves in different social classes, they are likely to make rather different judgments about political matters. A skilled worker who tells you that he belongs to the middle class is also likely to look at political questions with the kinds of values, biases, and aspirations that tend to prevail among people with distinctly middle-class occupations—business and professional men, for example. A skilled worker who says that he belongs to the working class, on the other hand, is likely to consider political choices more nearly from the same viewpoint as other workers. To be specific, if we take a group of citizens from the same broad occupational category, those who identify themselves as pertaining to the working classes are much more likely to have a 'liberal' outlook on economic issues than those who say they belong to the middle classes. Among white-color workers, for example, in a 1956 survey there were nearly twice as many ultra-liberals among those who identified themselves with the working class as among those who identified themselves with the middle class (Table 14.5).

Table 14.5. Occupation and Class Identification in Relation to Position on Domestic Liberalism Scale[a] (1956)

HEAD'S OCCUPATION	RESPONDENT'S CLASS IDENTIFICATION	
	WORKING	MIDDLE
White-collar	40%	22%
Blue-collar	50	35
Farm operator	41	32

[a]Entries are percentages of each cell ranking high on domestic liberalism scale. The percentage base excludes those in each cell with too few opinions on the component issues to permit placement on the scale.
SOURCE: Key, op. cit., p. 143.

Ethnic and Religious Cleavages

The common belief that distinctive ethnic and religious identifications are weakening in the United States as the descendants of the various immigrants become assimilated into American life has been recently challenged in a study of ethnic groups in New York; the authors conclude:

Religion and race seem to define the major groups into which American society is evolving as the specifically national aspect of ethnicity [i.e., the specific nation from which one's ancestors came] declines. In our large American cities, four major groups emerge: Catholics, Jews, white Protestants, and Negroes.[18]

Yet, ethnic and religious loyalties—like region, status, occupation, and economic position—do not as such produce sharp political cleavages. Voting patterns are very much more distinctive than political attitudes. Jews and Catholics vote more heavily Democratic than Protestants; Negroes vote more heavily Democratic than Whites; and voters of Irish, Italian, Polish, German and Scandinavian descent often seem to have somewhat distinctive voting patterns. The differences may be more apparent in local elections than in national elections, more important in the Northeast than in the West, and most distinctive when a representative of their own ethnic group—or an enemy of their ethnic group—has a leading place on one ticket.[19]

The extent to which religious differences cut across 'class' differences is revealed in a very general way by data on voting.[20] In national elections over the past generation, among both manual workers and nonmanual workers, Catholics have voted Democratic in considerably higher proportions than Protestants. The differences between Catholics and Protestants were least in the elections of 1952 and 1956, when general Eisenhower was the Republican candidate, and, as might be expected, greatest in 1960 when John F. Kennedy, a Catholic, was the Democratic candidate. The biggest discrepancy in 1960, incidentally, was between 'middle class' (nonmanual) Catholics and Protestants; many Catholics who had moved into nonmanual occupations maintained their traditional loyalties as Democratic voters.

18. Nathan Glazer and Daniel Patrick Moynihan, *Beyond the Melting Pot*, Cambridge, Mass., the MIT Press and Harvard University Press, 1963, p. 314.
19. See the evidence in Raymond E. Wolfinger, "The Development and Persistence of Ethnic Voting," *American Political Science Review*, 59 (Dec. 1965) 896–908; Louis Harris, *Is There a Republican Majority, Political Trends, 1952–1956*, New York, Harper and Brothers, 1954, ch. 6; Angus Campbell and Homer C. Cooper, *Group Differences in Attitudes and Votes, A Study of the 1954 Congressional Election*, Ann Arbor, Survey Research Center, 1956, ch. 3; Alford, *Party and Society*, pp. 241 ff.; Campbell et al., *The American Voter*, pp. 319 ff. In the 1964 presidential election the fears aroused among Negroes by the candidacy of Senator Goldwater amplified their predisposition to vote Democratic to near unanimity.
20. See Figure 8.3, *supra*, p. 227.

To look at the same data in another way, Protestants split most sharply along class lines in 1936 in the midst of the Great Depression, when Franklin Roosevelt was running for a second term. Catholics split most sharply in 1952 when many middle-class Catholics succumbed to the appeal of Eisenhower; in 1960, on the other hand, Kennedy all but obliterated the appeal of class among Catholics by his appeal as a fellow Catholic.[21]

Thus religion or ethnic identity may either amplify the effects of class and status on voting, as in the case of Negroes or working-class Catholics; or conversely, religion or ethnic identity may depress the significance of class and status by providing a cross-cutting cleavage, as in the case of middle-class Catholics and Jews or white working-class Protestants. Moreover, just as the impact of occupation and economic position on voting may vary, depending on the state of the economy, so the impact of religion and ethnic identity is not a constant but a varying factor, depending on current issues and on the candidates themselves.

More important, differences in voting and partisan loyalties among ethnic and religious groups do not seem to reflect significant differences in ideology or attitudes about policy. This is not to say that there are no discernible differences in political predispositions and beliefs among the different groups. Nonetheless, differences in attitudes and beliefs often reflect other factors like education and economic position; or else the differences are highly specific and depend on some particular issue that impinges directly on the group, as in the case of Catholic views on governmental aid to parochial schools or the views of Negroes on civil rights. On the whole, when these factors are removed, except for party loyalties it is difficult to find much distinctiveness in the political attitudes of the various ethnic and religious groups.

Ideology: Democracy, Liberalism, Conservatism

Americans are frequently portrayed by foreigners and by themselves as a supremely pragmatic and un-ideological people. This is, at best, a half-truth.

21. See Table 11, pp. 92–94, in Seymour M. Lipset, "Religion and Politics in the American Past and Present," in Robert Lee and Martin Marty, eds., *Religion and Social Conflict*, New York, Oxford University Press, 1964.

For Americans are a highly ideological people. It is only that one does not ordinarily notice their ideology because they are, to an astounding extent, all agreed on the same ideology.

As we have already seen, perhaps more than any other people in the world, Americans are united in expressing faith in a democratic ideology, even if they often do not act on what they claim to believe. Since their ideology is a source of unity rather than cleavage, the moment in which to observe the American as an ideologist is not when he talks about domestic politics but when he talks about international politics and especially when he talks about America in relation to the rest of the world. Here we find the ordinary American looking at political problems in a distinct ideological framework.

In a world conference of average citizens, who could fail to guess what the American would say? He would tend to see all changes as movement toward democracy or away from it. He would have no difficulty judging which systems were the best, which should be praised, which should be emulated; for the best would be democratic, and the democratic would be the best.

An American with an 'internationalist' perspective is likely to see the United States as the leader of a 'free world' and her task as helping the rest of the world develop democratic institutions. His American critic holds, like as not, that one important reason why Americans should not extend economic and military aid to other countries is that to convert them to the ways of democracy is a hopeless illusion. It is no accident that for many decades the champions of isolation, like Senator Borah of Idaho and Senator LaFollette of Wisconsin, were also old Progressives nurtured on the optimistic democratic vision of the American Midwest and Far West. Nor is it an accident that when Woodrow Wilson in his message to Congress on April 2, 1917, asked the Congress to declare war against the Central Powers, he coined the famous sentence that was to sound so ironic to later generations: "The world must be made safe for democracy." Robbed of the touchstone of democracy, an American would find it anguishing, perhaps impossible, to distinguish the good from the bad on the world scene.

The ideology of democracy, then, tends to unite Americans; it does not sharply divide them. Nonetheless, Americans have often disagreed as to what democracy means both as an idea and in practise. They have disagreed as to how far democracy and equality should be extended, how widely the advantages enjoyed by elite groups should be distributed throughout the general population, how much equality of opportunity and of power is desirable. The controversy among the Founders between those who wanted an aristocratic republic and those who wanted a democratic republic was just such an ideological cleavage. Further, these two ideological viewpoints have reappeared in various guises ever since the Constitutional Convention. It will do no great harm if, for the moment, we call the one that stresses equality and democracy 'liberalism' and the other 'conservatism.' Most of the time, no doubt, people of wealth, property, and high status have tended to be 'conservative,' while the less well-to-do have tended to be 'liberal.' Moreover, throughout long periods liberals have probably been more numerous in one party while conservatives have been more often drawn to the other. Thus the Federalists, the Whigs, and the Republicans were more attractive to well-to-do conservatives, while the Democratic-Republicans and the Democrats gained the loyalties of the liberals of more modest circumstances.

Of course one must be exceedingly cautious in placing too much confidence in these historical hypotheses, for the data with which one could test them properly are almost entirely lacking except for recent years. Fortunately, however, for the most recent period, from the 1930s, survey data have demonstrated beyond any reasonable doubt that, as we saw a moment ago, voters of higher status tend to be conservative in ideology and are likely to vote Republican, while voters of lower status tend to be more liberal in ideology and are more likely to vote for Democratic candidates.[22]

Conceivably, a three-way relationship between status, ideology, and party might divide Americans into two rather sharply polarized groups. A single line of cleavage might separate people according to status, ideology, and party, as follows:

	Camp I	Camp II
Status	Upper	Lower
Ideology	Conservative	Liberal
Party	Pro-Republican	Pro-Democratic

But the tendency in this direction is restrained by numerous exceptions. Each of the tendencies is important; yet none is strong enough to exert a dominant pull on American political life.

As our discussion of occupations and social class has already shown,

22. "...This triangle of relationships (has been) replicated in dozens of empirical studies.... Obviously, the facts presented by these relationships cannot be soberly questioned," Campbell et al., op. cit., p. 203.

the connection between status and party is highly imperfect. Likewise (as we saw, for example, in Figure 14.1) in every large occupational or status group a significant minority hold opinions ideologically diverse from the prevalent views; a considerable number of manual workers are as conservative as nonmanual workers, and many nonmanual workers are as liberal as the majority of nonmanual workers.[23] Even the link between ideology and party is not overwhelmingly powerful. Both parties have been supported by conservatives and liberals. Finally, one relationship often dilutes the purity of another: For example, low-status Republicans are evidently about as likely to be highly liberal on domestic issues as are low-status Democrats. Conversely, high-status Democrats tend, like high-status Republicans, to be conservative.[24]

Why, you might ask at this point, aren't liberalism and conservativism more powerful in stimulating a clear-cut cleavage? There are at least three reasons: these two ideologies are vague; they consist of several different dimensions; and in any case coherent ideological thinking is highly uncommon among American voters.

VAGUENESS. Neither liberalism nor conservatism is a clear-cut, thoroughly worked out statement of principles and programs so much as a hodge-podge of ideas, ideals, and policies. Because of their generality and vagueness, liberal and conservative ideologies do not provide a clear-cut guide for a citizen who has to make up his mind on a single issue. On concrete questions liberals disagree among themselves, and so do conservatives. For example, many liberals who support welfare measures such as federal aid to education, which unquestionably requires federal expenditures, nonetheless want to cut taxes. Indeed, the Survey Research Center uncovered the paradox that in 1956 among voters who favored school aid, more were in favor of lower taxes than among those who opposed federal aid. One's attitudes toward tax cuts seemed to be only remotely connected to one's liberal or conservative ideology. Whether a voter wants taxes cut evidently depends more on the size of his income than on his general economic ideology. It will be astounding to some and perfectly reasonable to others to learn that "even among persons of equal education or with similar occupations, it is the high income people who are relatively more willing to pay taxes than have the government post-

23. See also Key, *Public Opinion and American Democracy*, Table 6.10, p. 143; and Herbert McCloskey et al., "Issue Conflict and Consensus Among Party Leaders and Followers," *American Political Science Review*, 54 (June, 1960), 406–427.
24. Campbell et al., *op. cit.*, pp. 207–208, including fns. 7 and 8 and fig. 9.1.

pone doing things that need to be done. It is the low-income group that demands a tax reduction even at the expense of such postponement."[25]

Dimensions of Liberal and Conservative Ideologies

In truth, the terms 'liberal' and 'conservative,' which we have been using without apology up to this point, cover a wide assortment of views. What we have been calling 'liberalism,' no doubt to the irritation of some people who think of themselves as 'true' liberals, is a favorable view of government intervention in economic and social problems to aid citizens who suffer from the effects of an unregulated economy and unequal distribution of incomes and opportunities. Yet there is another aspect to historical liberalism—the emphasis on individual liberty.

A person who is concerned about reforming the economic institutions that were created by industrial capitalism need not be particularly concerned about political and civil liberties. These two concerns, which in America are often put together under the label of liberalism, are logically and ideologically distinct. Indeed, the proof, if one were needed, is the classic nineteenth-century English liberal who combined his belief in political liberty with an equally fervent belief in the virtues of a laissez-faire economy; in twentieth-century continental Europe, those who call themselves Liberals often have had more in common with their nineteenth-century counterparts than with the present-day liberals of the English-speaking countries. It would serve no good purpose to argue here over the meaning of the terms 'liberal' and 'conservative.' What is important is to recognize that these loose ideologies comprise several different dimensions; political libertarianism and economic reformism may go together, but they equally well may not.

Now it is an exceedingly important fact that, in the United States, people who are in favor of economic reforms are frequently anti-libertarian on questions of civil and political rights.[26] Conversely, some citizens who oppose government intervention in the economy nonetheless support government intervention on behalf of civil and political rights. As a

25. *Ibid.*, p. 196.
26. S. M. Lipset, *Political Man*, Garden City, New York, Doubleday, 1960, ch. IV, "Working Class Authoritarianism," pp. 97–130.

good example, we may take the questions of medical care and racial integration. Do people who believe that the government ought to help people get doctors and hospital care at low cost also believe that the government should intervene in the question of whether white and colored children go to the same school? Not necessarily. In the South, in 1956 about 61 per cent of the people in one sample survey endorsed the idea of government help for doctors and hospital care. But more than half of these Southerners who favored a government medical care program opposed government intervention in behalf of racial integration in the schools. Of course we are not too surprised to find this result in the South, even though it confirms in a quite striking way the fact that support for economic reform and for political and civil rights are two very different things.

What is even more noteworthy, however, is that a similar splitting occurred in the North. There, 51 per cent of the sample supported a federal medical care program in 1956. Yet of these 'economic liberals,' only half supported federal intervention to enforce the rights of Negro children to go to schools with white children. On the other hand, 27 per cent of the Northerners in this sample were opposed outright to a federal medical care program. Yet of these 'economic conservatives' almost as many favored federal intervention in the matter of school integration as opposed it (see Table 14.6). Thus a coalition of 'economic liberals' is necessarily a very different thing from a coalition of 'civil-rights liberals.'

Let me cite one more example. In 1956, people were also asked whether they agreed or disagreed with the statement that "The government ought to fire any government worker who is accused of being a Communist even though they don't prove it." Fortunately for American self-respect, the overwhelming majority of people in the sample rejected this denial of the elementary notions of Anglo-American justice; fortunately, too, there were virtually no differences as between Democrats and Republicans. Yet it is a highly significant fact that while 70 per cent of those who were most conservative on economic issues rejected the idea, among those who were most 'liberal' on economic matters only 56 per cent rejected it.

In addition to the two dimensions of economic reform and personal liberties, still a third dimension needs to be considered: foreign affairs. Historically, the philosophy of liberalism has been associated with internationalism; conservatives are often more nationalistic than liberals. Among Americans, then, does economic reformism go with internationalism and economic conservatism with isolationism? Not at all. In 1956 the proportion of internationalists was nearly as high among economic

[361]

Table 14.6. Combinations of Opinion on Medical Care and School Integration, North and South

| SCHOOL INTEGRATION | MEDICAL CARE[a] | | | | |
	PRO	DEPENDS	CON	DON'T KNOW	TOTAL
North:					
Pro[b]	25%[c]	4%	11%	4%	44%
Depends	3	1	1	1	6
Con	18	3	13	3	37
Don't Know	5	1	2	5	13
	51%	9%	27%	13%	100%
South:					
Pro	17	2	6	2	27
Depends	4	1	1	1	7
Con	35	5	14	4	58
Don't Know	5	—	—	3	8
	61%	8%	21%	10%	100%

[a]"The government ought to help people get doctors and hospital care at low cost."
[b]That is, those who disagreed with the proposition "The government in Washington should stay out of the question of whether white and colored children go to the same school."
[c]Entries are percentages of the sample holding the specified combinations of opinion.
SOURCE: Key, op. cit., p. 170.

conservatives (50 per cent) as among economic liberals (58 per cent); likewise the proportions of isolationists were about the same among economic liberals and conservatives—in fact, in this particular survey there were a few more isolationists among the liberals.

Table 14.7. Relation of Position on Domestic Liberalism Scale to Position on Internationalism

| INTER- NATIONALISM | ECONOMIC LIBERALISM | | |
	LOW (ECONOMIC CONSERVATIVES)	MEDIUM	HIGH (ECONOMIC LIBERALS)
High (Internationalists)	50%	59%	58%
Medium	32	28	21
Low (Isolationists)	18	13	21
	100%	100%	100%
Number	226	598	491

SOURCE: Key, op. cit., p. 158.

It follows, then, that the foreign policies forged after the Second World War commanded the support of both liberal voters and conservative voters, and at the same time these policies were opposed by both liberals and conservatives. Or to put the matter in another way, a relatively liberal leader like President Truman could generally count on support for his foreign policies from citizens who opposed his domestic policies, while some citizens who supported his domestic policies were lukewarm or hostile to his foreign policies. The same thing held true with a more conservative President like Eisenhower: he drew support for an internationalist foreign policy from liberals who opposed him on domestic issues.

There is still another dimension to liberalism and conservatism, or so at least it is commonly supposed. This dimension (or set of dimensions) consists of attitudes toward change, innovation, tradition, custom, and conventional morality. Considered along this dimension, we might say that conservatives tend to resist change as undesirable and often unnecessary, while liberals accept it more sympathetically as inevitable and desirable. Drawing upon the writings of political philosophers like Edmund Burke, Herbert McCloskey has devised a scale for "conservatism" in this broad sense.[27] Yet curiously enough, in 1956 among the general population there was no significant relationship between this sort of conservatism and the political party with which people identified themselves, even outside the South. Moreover, this species of conservatism seemed to be almost unrelated to the economic policies a voter would support.[28]

The ideologies of conservatism and liberalism, then, are made up of a number of different dimensions. We have examined four: economic reform, political and civil liberties, foreign policy, and attitudes toward change. There may be—and very likely are—still others. Consequently, two people who find themselves close together along one dimension of liberalism-conservatism are likely to find themselves very far apart along another dimension. Thus the different dimensions of liberalism and conservatism divide Americans one way on one kind of issue but quite another way on another kind of issue.

The Limits of Ideological Thinking

Most Americans (like most people everywhere) simply do not possess an elaborate ideology. It is difficult for political philosophers accustomed to

27. See his article "Conservatism and Personality," *American Political Science Review*, 52 (March, 1958), 27–45.
28. Campbell et al., *op. cit.*, p. 211.

manipulating abstract ideas to realize how slight and fragmentary is the analytical framework most people bring to bear on political problems. There is some evidence on this subject from surveys in 1956 and 1960 that is of unusual interest, for these two surveys represent the first serious attempt to use survey methods to examine the level of ideological thinking among a national sample of American voters. In 1956 the respondents were asked whether there was "anything in particular that you like about the Democratic Party," or anything "that you don't like." The same questions were asked about the Republican Party. They were also asked whether there was "anything in particular about Eisenhower (Stevenson) that would make you want to vote for him," or "against him." The answers some people gave indicated that they thought in terms of a liberal-conservative continuum of some sort, even if an exceedingly vague one. In fact, this continuum was almost the only dimension that could be discovered in the data.[29] Others responded by citing possible benefits or dangers to this or that group—to farmers, workers, doctors, big business. A third group simply made comments about the goodness or badness of the times—peace or war, prosperity or recession. A fourth group made no comments at all on any political issues under debate (see Table 14.8). Even though the liberal-conservative dimension was about the only one that seemed to exist at all, less than one voter in six seemed to appraise the 1956 election in terms of liberal or conservative ideologies. An example of an 'Ideologue' might be the woman residing in a Chicago suburb who responded to the question of what in particular she didn't like about the Democratic Party:

Table 14.8.   Ideologues and Non-ideologues Among
American Voters

	TOTAL SAMPLE	VOTERS
I. Ideologues	2½%	3½%
II. Near-ideologues	9	12
III. Group interest	42	45
IV. Nature of the times	24	22
V. No issue content	22½	17½
	100%	100%

Source: Campbell et al., *The American Voter*, p. 249.

———•◆•———

29.   Philip E. Converse, "The Nature of Belief Systems in Mass Politics," in *Ideology and Discontent*, David E. Apter, ed., New York, The Free Press, 1964, pp. 206–261.

*Well, the Democratic party tends to favor socialized medicine—
and I'm being influenced in that because I came from a doc-
tor's family.*
(Like about Republicans) *Well, I think they're more middle-
of-the road—more conservative.* (How do you mean, "conservative"?) *They are not so subject to radical change.* (Is there
anything else in particular that you like about the Republican
Party?) *Oh, I like their foreign policy—and the segregation
business, that's a middle-of-the-road policy. You can't push it too
fast. You can instigate things, but you have to let them take
their course slowly.* (Is there anything else?) *I don't like Mr.
Hodge.* (Is there anything else?) *The labor unions telling
workers how to vote—they know which side their bread is
buttered on so they have to vote the way they are told to!*
(Dislike about the Republicans?) *Mr. Hodge!* (Is there anything else?) *I can't think of anything.*

A 'Near-Ideologue' is represented by a man in upstate New York:

(Like about Democrats?) *Well, I like their liberalness over the
years. They certainly have passed beneficial legislation like social security and unemployment insurance, which the average
man needs today.*
(Dislike about Democrats?) *The Communists linked to Roosevelt and Truman. Corruption. Tax scandals. I don't like any of
those things.*
(Like about Republicans?) *I also like the conservative element
in the Republican Party.* (Anything else?) *No.*
(Dislike about Republicans?) *No, not at present.*

Slightly under half the voters seemed to evaluate the two parties
and the two candidates according to the benefits or harm they might
confer on particular groups, as with the Ohio farm woman who said:

(Like about Democrats?) *I think they have always helped the
farmers. To tell you the truth, I don't see how any farmer could
vote for Mr. Eisenhower.* (Is there anything else you like about
the Democratic Party?) *We have always had good times under
their Administration. They are more for the working class of
people. Any farmer would be a fool to vote for Eisenhower.*
(Dislike about Democrats?) *No, I can't say there is.*

[365]

(Like about Republicans?) *No.*
(Dislike about Republicans?) *About everything.* (What are you thinking of?) *They promise so much but they don't do anything.* (Anything else?) *I think the Republicans favor the richer folks. I never did think much of the Republicans for putting into office a military man.*
(Like about Stevenson?) *I think he is a very smart man.* (Is there anything else?) *I think he will do what he says, will help the farmer. We will have higher prices.* (Anything else?) *No.*
(Dislike about Stevenson?) *No. But I have this against Stevenson, but I wouldn't vote against him. In the Illinois National Guards he had Negroes and Whites together. They ate and slept together. I don't like that. I think Negroes should have their own place. I don't see why they would want to mix.*
(Like about Eisenhower?) *No.*
(Dislike about Eisenhower?) *Yes. He favors Wall Street. I don't think he is physically able, and he will step aside and that Richard Nixon will be president.* (Anything else?) *To tell the truth, I never thought he knew enough about politics to be a President. He is a military man. He takes too many vacations and I don't see how he can do the job.*

One quarter of the people explained their preferences and dislikes, as a woman in Louisville did, by referring in one way or another to good times or bad times:

(Like about Democrats?) *Well, I really don't know enough about politics to speak. I never did have no dealings with it. I thought politics was more for men anyway.* (Well, is there anything you like about the Democratic Party?) *I like the good wages my husband makes.* (It is the Republicans who are in now.) *I know, and it's sort of begun to tighten up since the Republicans got in.* (Is there anything else you like about the Democratic Party?) *No.*
(Dislike about Democrats?) *No, I couldn't think of a thing.*
(Like about Republicans?) *Well, truthfully, the Republican Party just doesn't interest me at all.* (There isn't anything you like about it?)
No—I just am not particularly interested in either one.

About one in six said nothing at all about political issues; they simply preferred one party to the other, or one candidate to the other, or virtually could not respond at all. Thus a Massachusetts man replied:

(Like about Democrats?) *I haven't heard too much. I don't get any great likes or dislikes.*
(Dislikes about Democrats?) *I hate the darn backbiting.*
(Like about Republicans) *No.*
(Dislike about Republicans?) *No.*
(Like about Stevenson?) *No, I don't like him at all.*
(Dislike about Stevenson?) *I have no use for Stevenson whatsoever. I had enough of him at the last election. I don't like the cut-throat business—condemn another man and then shake hands with him five minutes later.*
(Like about Eisenhower?) *As a man I like Eisenhower better. Not particularly for the job of President, but he is not so apt to cut your throat.*
(Dislike about Eisenhower?) *No.*[30]

In 1960 the people in the sample classified in Table 14.8 were reinterviewed. This time they were asked: "Would you say that either one of the parties is more *conservative* or more *liberal* than the other?" Respondents who said yes were asked which party seemed the more conservative and, then, "What do you have in mind when you say that the Republicans (Democrats) are more conservative than the Democrats (Republicans)?" Thirty-seven per cent of the respondents "could supply no meaning for the liberal-conservative distinction." Slightly more than 50 per cent of the respondents furnished evidence that they could identify the meaning of these terms correctly, more or less. To a majority of these people, however, liberalism was simply equated with government spending and conservatism with economy.[31]

Obviously then, a great many people have only weak traces of a liberal or conservative ideological framework within which to judge political issues, candidates, and parties. This does not mean that they are necessarily making foolish or uninformed choices. It does mean that they have to find some framework for judgment, other than a liberal or conservative ideology. What seems to happen in a great many cases is that as a voter moves from indecision to decision, he by-passes his ideology and takes a much more direct route. Somehow ideology is short-circuited. In some cases it is short-circuited by immediate consideration of self-interest or group interest that do not require ideological analysis and that

30.   These quotations are from Campbell, et al., op. cit., pp. 228–248.
31.   Converse, op. cit., pp. 219–222.

may, in fact, lead to support for policies that a full-blown ideologue would oppose. The fact that the less well-to-do segments of the population favor tax cuts, for example, has very little or nothing to do with their other economic policies: here primitive self-interest short-circuits ideology. Party loyalties also short-circuit ideology. Once a voter has developed a firm attachment to a party, he can by-pass the painful task of appraising policies and candidates according to ideological criteria. Having concluded long ago that the Democratic Party or the Republican Party was better for him, for his group, or for the nation, he now supports the party's candidates and the party's general policies (so far as he is familiar with them) without much further thought. Attraction or hostility toward a candidate because of his personal qualities also helps to short-circuit the more complex route of ideological thinking. It has been estimated that in 1956 the personal appeal of Eisenhower in comparison to Stevenson gave the Republicans a net advantage of nearly 8 per cent of the votes. In 1964, on the other hand, highly adverse reactions to Goldwater's personal attributes combined with a more favorable view of Johnson among the electorate is estimated to have given the Democrats a net advantage of 5 per cent of the votes. Thus, the difference between Eisenhower in 1956 and Goldwater in 1964 probably cost the Republicans in the neighborhood of 13 per cent of the vote.[32]

Are we then to conclude that liberal and conservative ideologies in their various manifestations and multiple dimensions are unimportant in American politics? Such a conclusion is surely unwarranted for two reasons. First, while the great bulk of the people can often by-pass ideological considerations, they cannot always do so. In a complex world, even the connection between self-interest and national policies is often so obscure that it cannot be traced out by an uninformed mind; ideology, however vague it may be, may sometimes help to establish the connection. On international policies in particular, the commitment of Americans to democracy and political self-determination perhaps serves as a guide, even if a vague one, to some citizens.

Second, some people are much more ideologically-minded than others. As might be expected, the more active a person is in political life, the more likely he is to think in ideological terms.[33] In all that we have been saying so far, we have been describing ordinary voters, the rank and

32. Donald E. Stokes, "Some Dynamic Elements of Contests for the Presidency," *American Political Science Review*, 60 (March, 1966), pp. 19–28, esp. pp. 22–23; fig. 4, p. 23.
33. Key, *op. cit.*, p. 440; Campbell et al., *op. cit.*, p. 258; Converse, *op. cit.*, pp. 226–231.

file citizens. But ideologies have always been the special property of political activists. In American political life, as elsewhere, political activists are very much more ideological than the great bulk of the population. Thus liberal-conservative differences that are absent, blurred, confused, or contradictory among ordinary citizens, and particularly among citizens who are least involved in politics, are much sharper among the politically active strata.

The greater salience of ideology among activists and leaders produces the paradox that while activists are in greater agreement than ordinary citizens in their adherence to a democratic and libertarian ideology, they are more divided ideologically on questions of government policy.[34] The explanation for both the greater ideological unity and greater ideological disagreement among the activists and leaders is evidently the same: Ideological considerations are much more salient among activists than among ordinary citizens. Hence, to the extent that the perspectives of the general American democratic and libertarian ideology is salient among activists, they are united by their common ideology; but to the extent that liberal and conservative ideologies are salient, they are divided by their differing ideological perspectives. And since it is these very people, the activists and leaders, who more than any others shape not only policies, party platforms, and nominations but constitutional and political norms, democratic, liberal, and conservative ideological perspectives do have a significant effect on American political life.

Summary

The pattern of ideological divergencies in the United States is roughly the pattern that ordinarily prevails with respect to geographical, socio-economic, ethnic, and religious differences. Conflicts do not accumulate along the same lines of cleavage. On the contrary, different conflicts seem to involve rather different lines of cleavage. As a result, citizens who hold similar views on one issue are likely to hold divergent views on another—or no views at all. How this general pattern bears on the way party coalitions are formed during elections and in Congress is not only complex but rather obscure; it is reasonable to suppose, however, that the general effect is to attenuate the severity of any particular electoral

34. As we have already seen above, Ch. 8, pp. 214 ff. and Ch. 13, pp. 332–334.

and legislative conflict. If you think that among your opponents in today's contest are some potential allies for tomorrow's, you are likely to be conciliatory and unlikely to press extreme demands that could eliminate the possibility of winning recruits from the other side for a new contest another day.

Obviously, unless attitudes are highly polarized, it is impossible to divide a population into two like-minded collections of people. No matter what criterion is used for dividing people, within each of any two categories there will be many conflicting views. Given the existence of a two-party system, it follows that unless attitudes are highly polarized, each of the two parties can hope to win only by constructing an electoral coalition made up of people whose views coincide on some questions but diverge on others. This is exactly what happens most of the time in the United States. As long as (1) political attitudes are not polarized and, (2) only two major parties exist, there can be no escape from two parties with heterogeneous followings.

Although we have surveys and election studies for only the past quarter century, there is substantial reason for thinking that low polarization has been the usual condition of American politics, and that the reasons for low polarization have been about the same in the past as they are now: Large socio-economic groups have generally been heterogeneous in political attitudes, and persons who agree on one question disagree on others.[35]

There have been historical fluctuations; undoubtedly the tide of polarization ebbs and flows. Probably polarization rose to high points during each of the major crises described in Chapters 11 and 12, and afterward it again receded. But extreme polarization is rare in American politics, and it never persists over long periods. Most of the time political life displays the characteristics of moderate conflict that have been examined in the last two chapters.

35. Although it covers only a limited period, a recent study of Jacksonian Democracy lends support to this interpretation. See Lee Benson, *The Concept of Jacksonian Democracy: New York as a Test Case*, Princeton, Princeton University Press, 1961, particularly ch. 12, "Outline for a Theory of American Voting Behavior."

Part Four

How political activists can exert influence in a pluralist democracy

15

INFLUENCING THE CONDUCT
OF GOVERNMENT

W HETHER HE IS AWARE of it or not, the daily life and the long-
run chances, opportunities, advantages, and handicaps of each
citizen are powerfully shaped by the actions and inactions of
American governments. If you doubt it, perform any one of the following mental experiments: imagine that the American governments abolish
public education; triple the tax rate; equalize incomes; abolish police and
judiciary; prohibit divorce on any grounds; repeal all laws having to do
with property; prohibit strikes and trade unions; nationalize all private
businesses; suppress all political parties except one; sell all highways to
private owners; make it a criminal offense to go to church. That these are
extreme possibilities is irrelevant; that these are *possible* emphasizes what
American governments actually do by showing what they might do.

American governments, then, like most other governments exercise
great influence over the lives of their citizens. Only governments can
legally punish a citizen who refuses to send his children to school, to
treat them humanely, to have them vaccinated against smallpox. Only
governments can lawfully seize a citizen's property without his consent
and compel him to pay taxes. Governments have the legal authority to
coerce; they can fine, imprison, or even kill citizens who disobey their
rules. American governments add to their legal powers a very large measure of legitimacy: Most citizens feel that it is not only dangerous to
disobey the laws but also wrong to do so. Armed with legality and legitimacy, American governments can and do acquire vast resources. They

can and do use these resources not only to punish but also to reward; they allocate jobs, salaries, grants, contracts, payments, and other benefits in infinite variety. Cash expenditures by the federal government alone amount to about 20 per cent of the gross national product, state and local expenditures, more than 10 per cent; thus government spending is equal to about one third of the gross national product.[1]

Because governments are extraordinarily influential, they are inevitably the objects of influence. To influence the conduct of government is to influence the way it uses its powers of compulsion, coercion, punishment; its capacity to render actions legal or illegal, legitimate or illegitimate; its ability to allocate rewards, benefits, privileges, handicaps, wealth, incomes, influence, and power itself. It is easy to see, then, why few things are fought over with more persistence, vigor, and bloodshed than the conduct of government. But how, specifically, can and do Americans influence the conduct of their governments? This is the question that will concern us in this chapter and the next two chapters. To answer it will require, first, drawing together a number of matters that have already been treated in previous chapters.

Prospects for Success

All societies regulate the ways in which people may attempt to influence the government. Only in a Hobbesian state of nature is everything permissible; and a state of nature in which everything is permissible would surely be as unbearable as Hobbes insisted it must be.

Like other systems, democracies regulate attempts to influence government. Thus they try to rule out efforts to gain influence and power over government officials by coercion, violence, and corruption. More than other systems, they also try to disperse influence widely to their citizens by means of the suffrage, elections, freedom of speech, press, and assembly, the right of opponents to criticize the conduct of government, the right to organize political parties, and in other ways.

Even so, it is obvious that citizens do not enjoy perfectly equal chances of getting the government to do what they want it to do. Why

1. See "Federal cash expenditures as a percentage of Gross National Product, 1869–1964" in D. J. Ott and A. F. Ott, *Federal Budget Policy*. Washington, The Brookings Institution, 1965, 42, fig. VI. For state and local expenditures, see James A. Maxwell, *Financing State and Local Governments*, Washington, the Brookings Institution, 1965, 22.

not? At least four kinds of factors affect the chances that a citizen or a group of citizens can secure favorable action from the government. These are: one's own situation, the situation of one's allies, the situations of one's opponents or potential opponents, and the amount of change one seeks.

If one reflects on his own chances of influencing the government, he will readily see that his chances depend on his own situation, that is, his political resources, his political skills, and his incentives. Your political resources consist of all the means available to you for influencing the behavior of other people. In this culture, your political resources include your access to money, hence your wealth, your income, and your credit; they also include your control over jobs; your vote; your popularity, friendships, reputation, and esteem in the eyes of others; your knowledge or access to knowledge; your control over mass media and other means of communication; and many other things.

One important political resource easily lost sight of is *time*. If you have no time left over from your other affairs to try to change the conduct of government, you are unlikely to be in a position to exercise much influence over it. Conversely, the more time you have available, the better your chances. Time is one of the most critical resources that professional politicians have; by hook or crook they manage to spend almost full time at the game of politics, while most of us devote only a few hours out of the year.

Still another resource which is unevenly distributed—inevitably so— is *officiality*. Constitutional rules, law, and practise allow officials to do things that ordinary citizens cannot. A major difference between the policeman and the man he arrests is that the office of the policeman entitles him to make arrests, using force if necessary. Official position invariably allocates to officials some resources that are denied to others; thus only judges can decide legal cases and only legislators can pass laws. By conferring officiality on the winner and denying it to the loser, elections award extra resources to the winner. In 1876, one electoral vote—a rather dubious one at that—was enough to confer the Presidency on Rutherford B. Hayes rather than on Samuel J. Tilden; even in that age of weak Presidents, the Presidency gave important legal authority to Hayes, such as the veto, that was denied to Tilden.

Allied to officiality as a resource, but not identical with it, is *legitimate authority*: the widespread view that an individual or an office *ought* to be obeyed. Thus the President is powerful not only because of what the Constitution authorizes him to do but also because of what history and tradition authorize him to do.

Except for the ballot, all these resources are unequally distributed among American citizens. Hence it should not be too surprising if various citizens exert unequal influence on the conduct of government.

Yet, even if two individuals had practically identical resources, they might nonetheless be unable to exercise equal influence over the conduct of government if one of them were politically more *skillful*. Political skill might be considered, of course, as a special kind of resource, but it seems more illuminating to think of it as a capacity for using one's resources efficiently. There have been many attempts to describe political skills but none more eloquent nor more repellent than Machiavelli's portrayal of *The Prince*. Although almost all political observers agree with Machiavelli that differences in political skills exist and are important, political skills, like military, entrepreneurial, artistic, and scientific skills, are hard to pin down and not well understood. Thus *The Prince* is still widely held to be a fount of wisdom about political skill, even though it is an extremely one-sided treatment of the matter.

Even if two individuals had identical resources and skills, one might exercise more influence over government than another simply because he *wanted* to influence the government and the other did not. If you do not care what the government is doing, you probably won't use your resources and skills to influence it; the more you care, the more of your resources you will be willing to invest and the harder you will try to acquire the necessary skills. Thus, your influence is partly dependent on your goals and estimates of the best strategies for obtaining them. We might call this third factor *incentives* for acquiring political skills and for employing resources to influence the conduct of government.

Because no one is alone in a political system, chances of success will also depend upon the situation of one's allies and opponents. All that has been said about resources, skills, and incentives applies equally to them. Allies may enable you to multiply resources and skills and hence improve your chances of success. Conversely, the greater the resources, skills, and incentives of your opponents, the worse your prospects are. Indeed, one of the characteristics of political systems is the frequency of *mutual escalation*: If you and your allies begin to invest your skills and resources in order to change the conduct of government, your political activity activates your opponents. They too mobilize their skills and resources; they seek allies. In response, you now mobilize more skills and resources and search for additional allies. Yet your reaction once again provokes your opponents to respond. Fortunately, legal limits and accepted norms vastly reduce the likelihood that mutual escalation will finally proceed to the level of violence, although that possibility is never wholly out of the question—as the American Civil War illustrates. Another restraint on mutual escalation results from its *anticipation*. If you are quite sure your opponents will respond by escalating, you may decide that the potential gain from political action is not worth the cost. People sometimes think that politics is a cheap game to buy into; but it can be a costly game to win. This is one reason why many people with sizeable resources nonetheless remain aloof from politics or confine their actions to some specific aspect of the conduct of government that they care most about— schools, or taxes, or foreign policy, or civil liberties, or racial integration, or agricultural subsidies, or one of a thousand other possibilities.

In addition to the resources, skills, and incentives of you, your allies, and your opponents, your chances of gaining a favorable action from the government depend on still another factor: *how much change you re-quire in the behavior of other people in order for the government to do what you want it to do.* The greater the amount of change required, the less your chances of success—other things being equal, of course. What is the amount of change required? If there were time to explore it here, the concept would prove to be a highly complex one of many dimensions; but it is convenient, and sufficient for the purpose of this chapter, to think of the amount of change required as having two dimensions: the number of persons who must change their minds, and the difficulty involved in getting them to change their minds. Obviously, chances of success are much better if it involves persuading only one key member of a congressional committee rather than all the members; winning over a majority of only one committee rather than a majority of a whole chamber; or 10 per cent of the electorate rather than 51 per cent, etc. In Southern states, a Republican candidate for office would ordinarily have to change the minds of many more voters than his Democratic opponent in order to win. In presidential elections, the two major parties each begin with a hard core of millions of supporters; to win, a candidate needs to change the minds of only a minority of the electorate. But third party candidates, who begin with only a tiny hard core of support, might have to change the minds of almost half the electorate in order to win.

As we all know, changing one's mind may be very easy or extraordinarily difficult. If you reflect a moment, you will probably agree that you find it easier to change your mind when you see only small differences between the alternatives than when you see large differences; thus if you are a Republican it is ordinarily easier for you to switch to another Republican when your preferred candidate fails to gain the Republican nomination than to switch to the Democratic candidate. It is easier to change your mind on matters you consider unimportant than on important matters. It is easier to change recently acquired or superficial views than long-standing, deeply rooted views. It is easier to change consciously held opinions than unconscious attitudes, easier to change your opinions than your personality, loyalties, identifications—in short, yourself.

Now if you want to get other people to change their views, it appears that the greater the amount of change in other people's behavior you require for success, the more resources and skills you will need to use, the greater your incentives will have to be, and the more you need allies. The easier it will be for your opponents, on the other hand, to block the change. Conversely, the less the amount of change in other people you require, the less resources and skills you need, the lower your incentives may be, and the less you may have to depend on allies. These elements are summarized in Figure 15.1.

What conclusions can be drawn from this somewhat general and abstract discussion? Let me list some conjectures—most of them rather obvious—suggested by the discussion so far:

℈ Other things being equal, a full-time professional politician is more likely to influence the conduct of government than a part-time amateur, a rich man than a poor man, an

FIGURE 15.1—SUCCESSFUL EFFORTS TO INFLUENCE GOVERNMENT

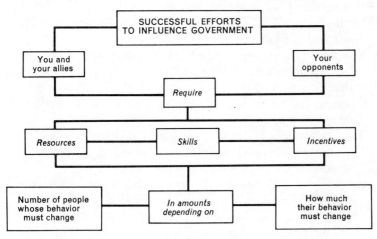

educated person than an uneducated person, a newspaper editor than a newspaper reader, a celebrity than an obscure citizen, etc.

⁋ Other things are rarely equal, however, and a citizen who has less of one resource than another citizen may nonetheless gain greater influence because he has other resources. Though he has less money, he may have more time, more energy, greater popularity, stronger ethnic ties.

⁋ A citizen who is weak in resources may gain allies and thereby increase the total resources, skills, and incentives mobilized for his policies.

⁋ Probably no resource is uniformly most effective in American politics. A variety of resources therefore is generally a greater political asset than a very large amount of only one kind of resource.

⁋ It is generally easier to maintain old programs than to initiate new government policies. To maintain an existing program usually requires less change in the behavior and views of the people. What is more, once a program exists the program itself is likely to generate resources—time, money, organization, information—that can be used to win support for it; and the people employed in the program will ordinarily have strong incentives to preserve it. Nothing is harder to create than a new institution, nothing harder to destroy than an established one.

⁋ Modifying a law is easier than changing the attitudes that give rise to a law.

⁋ You have more chance of gaining favorable action if you have to influence only one segment of government rather than several. The greater the number of obstacles on the course, the better the chance that you will fall on your face.

⁋ The less a proposal deviates from prevailing ideas and ideology, the better its chance of success. Hence marginal changes stand a better chance than comprehensive changes.

⁋ Advocates of a change usually try to make it appear smaller than it is; opponents try to make it appear larger. Advocates portray their proposal as conforming with the prevailing practises, ideas, and institutions; opponents are more likely to portray it as an attack on prevailing practises, ideas, and institutions. If opponents succeed in portraying it as un-American, they have won more than half the battle.

¶ In general, it is easier to veto a change than to initiate one, easier to preserve the status quo than to change it, easier to make technical changes than ideological changes, easier to make incremental changes than comprehensive or revolutionary changes.

¶ It follows that suporters of the status quo usually need fewer resources, less skill, and lower political incentives to prevent changes than opponents of the status quo need in order to make changes. Reformers and radicals, then, require more resources, skills, and incentives than conservatives. Revolutionaries require even more.

In a very general way, these observations seem valid. But one must be cautious in drawing further conclusions that would be invalid. Since people who benefit most from the status quo and thus have the greatest resources of wealth, income, and social standing are likely to support the status quo most strongly, it might appear that conservatives who defend the status quo would always be in an impregnable position. Not only is this conclusion historically incorrect; it does not follow from what we have said. For those who benefit most from the status quo are often fewer *in numbers* than those who expect to benefit by a change; moreover, well-to-do defenders of the status quo may be more out of touch with other citizens and hence lack political skills and popularity. Critics of the status quo may greatly outnumber defenders; by combining and organizing they may mobilize greater total resources; they may possess greater skills; they may even have stronger incentives and a greater willingness to use what resources they have to bring about change. Thus if the defenders of the status quo often win a great many skirmishes, critics of the status quo sometimes win the big battles.

The Key Governmental Actor

Because the American governments are highly influential, they are also objects of attempts to influence them. Concretely, governments are made up of officials. Because officials exercise the authority of government, they are inevitably the objects of attempts by others to influence the way they exercise this authority.

[379]

In all the American governments, no single official is so often a target of influence as the President, because no other single official exercises such great control over the conduct of the national government as the President. The President's extraordinary influence follows from his extraordinary resources, skills, and incentives.

As we have already seen, among the President's resources, unmatched by any other official, are:

¶ His pre-eminence in legal authority, the duties, privileges and powers which by law and constitution no one else can legally perform: e.g., his veto, the need for his signature on laws, his right to act as commander-in-chief of the armed forces.

¶ The extraordinary legitimacy, respect, and deference endowed on his office during the course of its historical evolution.

¶ His widespread popularity, partly resulting from the factor just mentioned, partly a result of his election, partly a prerequisite to being elected.

¶ His command of public attention, and thus his influence on the content of the mass media.

¶ His influence over appointments and promotions to key posts in the national government.

¶ His unparalleled access to expertness, knowledge, secret information.

¶ His influence over the executive and administrative agencies of the national government, and hence the way they allocate rewards and punishments.

Not only does the President have exceptional resources; any man who wins that office is likely to have acquired exceptional political skills before he enters the White House, skills that will be further refined by the manifold challenges of the Presidency. Then, too, the President has stronger incentives than most people for using his skills and resources as effectively as possible, for few people can see more clearly than the man in the White House how much hangs on his success and failure.

Because the Presidency is the repository of more influence than any other office, the President becomes the most important object of political influence. All politically active groups tend to gravitate toward the White House. It is difficult and often impossible for any group to affect the conduct of the national government over continued and active presidential opposition. Even with presidential support, a group may fail to secure favorable action from the government; without it, their chances are much worse. Those who most need the President's aid are those who seek the greatest changes, who advocate comprehensive alterations, innovations, radical departures from existing policies. But even for conservatives, it is comforting to have an ally in the White House who can be counted on to oppose attempts to change the status quo.

How then does a group gain presidential support? Most commonly, by supporting the President. Probably the most effective way to gain the President's support is to be in on the process of choosing him: by helping him to be nominated or by helping him to get elected or re-elected. One may win the support of the President by giving him support in other ways: by supporting his policies, for example, particularly when he is in trouble and badly needs help. Allies of the President may also win his present gratitude and his future support by refraining from criticizing policies they disagree with: in the metal of politics, silence can be golden. Groups may cultivate his friendship or the friendship of his friends and associates. They may even seek to win him over by persuasion. Rational persuasion—or at any rate semi-rational persuasion—may be more important in winning Presidents over to proposed policies than is commonly supposed. Failing these and other friendly ways of winning presidential support, one may turn to the public, the citizen body, the voters, in the hopes that if one can write the handwriting on the wall in letters large enough, the President will read it.

Even if a group has access to the President, it may also need to influence the Congress or some part of Congress. A group that lacks presidential backing may need to cultivate support in Congress all the more. The techniques that are used to win presidential support are also used to acquire support among Senators and Representatives. But Senators and Representatives are ordinarily closer and more accessible; it is easier to approach one's Congressman than to gain a hearing from the President.

An individual, a group, an organization, a movement that seeks comprehensive change or a major innovation in government policies must turn toward the White House, then, for leadership. But groups with less ambitious goals may gain all they seek with little more than the cooperation of a handful of Congressmen. They may use Congress to veto, delay, or amend a hostile measure advanced by the President. Strategically placed support in Congress may be enough to provide the marginal changes in existing policies that a group considers critical: a loophole opened up, an appropriation increased or cut, standards weak-

ened or tightened, an agency rebuked by an appropriations subcommittee, an investigation launched, a speech on the Senate floor. One's Senator or Representative can also serve as an ambassador to one of the administrative agencies.

A persistent organization may—and sooner or later probably will—
establish a Washington representative to lobby for its interests in Congress. Retired Senators and Representatives—retired, usually, by the
voters—are available. Between 1946–1965, twenty former Senators and
seventy-six former Representatives registered themselves as lobbyists
under the Federal Regulation of Lobbying Act passed in 1946.[2] Each
year several hundred groups report a total of about four million dollars
for lobbying in Congress; unreported lobbying would doubtless swell the
totals to figures considerably larger. Some grasp of the range and variety
of interests represented by lobbying in Washington may be gained from

Table 15.1.   Lobby Spending by Categories, 1960–1963

	1961		1962		1963	
	GROUPS REPORTING	AMOUNT SPENT	GROUPS REPORTING	AMOUNT SPENT	GROUPS REPORTING	AMOUNT SPENT
Business	171	$1,672,259	170	$1,836,126	153	$1,521,600
Citizens	52	494,175	50	531,002	51	707,333
Employee & Labor	40	892,569	37	945,206	36	1,130,124
Farm	22	367,238	22	412,524	21	405,849
Military & Veterans	10	133,735	6	141,991	5	140,180
Professional	17	426,120	19	344,455	20	318,519
Total	312	$3,986,096	304	$4,211,304	286	$4,223,605

SOURCE: Congress and the Nation, p. 1593.

Table 15.2.   Top Lobby Spenders, 1949[3]

American Medical Assn.	$1,522,683
Committee for Constitutional Government	620,632
Townsend Plan — $200,646* ⎱	
Townsend National Weekly — $231,465 ⎰	432,111
National Assn. of Electric Companies	388,883
Transportation Assn. of America	319,765

(continued)

2. Congress and the Nation, pp. 1572-1576.

Table 15.2. Top Lobby Spenders, 1949 (continued)

United World Federalists	291,672
Citizens Committee on Displaced Persons	222,809
Assn. of American Railroads	194,159
National Small Business Men's Assn.	192,070
National Milk Producers Federation	178,161
National Assn. of Real Estate Boards	138,600
National Physicians Committee for Extension of Medical Service	130,969
General Electric Co.	128,563
National Assn. of Manufacturers	117,230
AFL—$74,300 ⎱ CIO—$42,034 ⎰	116,335
Colorado River Assn., Los Angeles	115,120
National Assn. of Margarine Manufacturers	101,037
National Coal Assn.	99,560
Committee for the Nation's Health	98,244
Central Arizona Project Assn., Phoenix	97,301
The Producers' Council	96,007
National Council of Farmer Cooperatives	95,489
Southern States Industrial Council	94,873
Southern Pine Industry Committee	93,746
Chamber of Commerce of the U.S.	90,945
Unemployment Benefit Advisors Inc.	86,175
National Federation of American Shipping	84,196
National Assn. of Stevedores Inc., New York City	75,089
American Hotel Assn., New York City	74,966
National Tax Equality Assn., Chicago	74,028
National Assn. of Home Builders	71,942
American Legion	71,769
National Rural Electric Cooperative Assn.	65,014
American Farm Bureau Federation	60,134
American Civil Liberties Union	56,618
Council of State Chambers of Commerce	56,300
National Grain Trade Council	55,807
American Tariff League	55,775
U.S. Savings and Loan League, Chicago	54,824
National Postal Committee for Books, New York City	54,598
American Hospital Assn.	53,726
Conference of American Small Business Organizations	49,609

*Includes certain unreimbursed donations to the Townsend National Weekly.

SOURCE: *Congress and the Nation*, p. 1587.

3. Although figures are available for recent years, 1949 is used here because it represents a wider range; in the 1950s a number of organizations, including the National Association of Manufacturers and the Chamber of Commerce of the U.S. "decided that they were not actually covered by the 1946 law, and therefore ceased reporting that any funds had been spent for lobbying activities." *Congress and the Nation*, p. 1585.

an examination of Table 15.2, which lists the groups who spent most for lobbying in 1949. (For an explanation of why this early year was chosen, see footnote 3.)

With or without the aid of lobbyists, groups may also seek to gain their ends directly through the administrative agencies themselves. Among the groups listed in Table 15.2, the American Medical Association doubtless seeks to maintain good working relations with the Department of Health, Education, and Welfare; the National Association of Electric Companies with the Federal Power Commission; the Transportation Association and the Association of American Railroads with the Interstate Commerce Commission; the National Small Business Men's Association with the Department of Commerce and the Small Business Administration; the National Milk Producers Federation, the National Association of Farmer Cooperatives, and the American Farm Bureau with the Department of Agriculture; the AFL-CIO with the Labor Department; and so on. These relationships are sometimes antagonistic ones; occasionally, on the other hand, the private group may virtually capture the government agency. Thus a student of interest groups describes the relationships between the Farm Bureau Federation (a private association of farmers) and the federal agricultural agencies under the New Deal as follows:

> In addition to the advantages which accrued to the Farm Bureau by reason of the policy of the Agricultural Adjustment Administration, a tightly drawn web between the administrative structure of the government agency and that of the private association produced a coalition of monopolistic proportions. The source of the Farm Bureau foothold in administering the Agriculture Adjustment Act lay in its long standing affiliation with the Extension Service. The county farmers association, having the responsibility of assigning quotas and insuring compliance was a basic part of the AAA program. Since the Extension Service was already operating in the field, it was the logical agency to administer the program. While the AAA machinery was being established, the Farm Bureau, working through the Extension Service, actually supervised the establishment of local units. Farm Bureau representatives performed the task of delivering benefit checks to farmers, which symbolized the organization as a dispenser of the public largess and, on occasion, deducted organizational dues before final transmittal. After the initial organizational phase of the AAA, the Farm

Bureau-Extension administration continued to be the center of reliance for the farmer. The parent organization confined its operation to central review in Washington.[4]

An individual or a group may also turn to the Supreme Court for help. Sometimes the Court will extend the protection of the Constitution to an otherwise defenseless person: The next chapter examines a dramatic example. However, for reasons already explored in Chapter 6, a group in outright opposition to the dominant national coalition of the day is unlikely in the long run to secure striking success in the Court. Even such an opposition group may nonetheless win delaying actions—and sometimes the delay can go on for a very long time, as in the defeat by business interests of child-labor legislation. A group stands a better chance of winning the Court's support and protection if the national coalition is divided, or if the group itself represents one segment of the national coalition; or, in some cases, if the group stands outside the national coalition, neglected or overlooked. The Court is an awkward, uncertain, unreliable and rarely used instrument for bringing about major changes in national policies; it is better for veto than for positive innovation. Yet as we have seen, it was neither the President nor the Congress but the Supreme Court, responding not to outside pressures but to the sense of justice and ideological commitments of the Justices themselves, that launched the United States on the road to integration and civil rights. It was the Court, as we have seen, that altered the existing balance of political power among cities, suburban, small town, and rural areas by forcing the states to reapportion their legislatures. In both these cases, however, the action of the Court was directed to state governments; particularly in the case of civil rights, the Court's action was not particularly effective until the Executive branch, and ultimately Congress, backed it up with new and positive policies to replace those struck down by the Court.

The states and local governments are in many ways duplicates of the national government on a local scale. Individuals and organizations may succeed in achieving at these lower levels what they could not gain at the national level. They may even use the states to defy the national government. Within the state itself, the same process goes on. Groups who lack influence with city governments may turn to the state legislature; urban groups unable to gain what they want at the state level may concentrate on the city administration, and city administrations themselves may

4. Harmon Zeigler, *Interest Groups in American Society*, Englewood Cliffs, New Jersey, Prentice-Hall Inc., 1964, p. 191.

by-pass the state government and acquire allies, funds, and legal backing in Washington.

The patterns of political activity and influence in the United States are incredibly complex. Perhaps the best way to gain an appreciation of that bewildering complexity is to look at some concrete cases, as I propose to do in the next chapter. Many people, it seems, find it uncomfortable to accept the complexities of reality. Simplistic theories of power abound, tempting precisely because they convert bewildering variety to simple, tidy, easily understandable order.

Any simple theory about how American citizens influence the conduct of their government is bound to be misleading; any brief statement is even more inadequate. Nonetheless, two general conclusions seem scarcely contestable. First, differences among citizens in their resources, their skills, their incentives, their allies, and their opponents have prevented, and perhaps in some degree always will prevent, a close approximation to perfect equality among citizens in their influence on the conduct of government. Second, few groups in the United States who are determined to influence the government—certainly few if any groups of citizens who are organized, active, and persistent—lack the capacity and opportunity to influence some officials somewhere in the political system in order to obtain at least some of their goals.

16

FOUR CASES OF
POLITICAL ACTION

N O GENERAL STATEMENT about policy-making can match the complexity, diversity, and drama of the concrete. This chapter,
therefore, describes a few instances in which individuals or
groups have tried, with or without success, to influence the conduct of
government.

Gideon's Trumpet[1]

One morning in January, 1962, an employee of the United States Supreme Court in Washington opened an envelope from Clarence Earl
Gideon, a prisoner in the Florida State Prison. In the envelope was a
petition from Gideon written in pencil with "carefully formed printing,
like a schoolboy's" asking the Supreme Court to get him out of jail
because at the time of his trial for theft he had been unable to afford the
services of a lawyer. He had therefore been tried—and convicted—without benefit of counsel.

Gideon was no knight in shining armor. One lawyer, from the
American Civil Liberties Union, who vainly tried to help Gideon after

1. This section is based on Anthony Lewis, Gideon's Trumpet, New York,
Vintage Books, 1966, and is quoted herein with the permission of the pub-
lisher.

[387]

the Supreme Court case was decided in his favor, was no doubt still licking his wounds when he wrote:

In the future the name 'Gideon' will stand for the great principle that the poor are entitled to the same type of justice as are those who are able to afford counsel. It is probably a good thing that it is immaterial and unimportant that Gideon is something of a "nut", that his maniacal distrust and suspicion lead him to the very borders of insanity. Upon the shoulders of such persons are our great rights carried.

Clarence Earl Gideon has been described in more measured terms as follows:

Gideon was a fifty-one-year-old white man who had been in and out of prisons much of his life. He had served time for four previous felonies, and he bore the physical marks of a destitute life: a wrinkled, prematurely aged face, a voice and hands that trembled, a frail body, white hair. He had never been a professional criminal or a man of violence; he just could not seem to settle down to work, and so he had made his way by gambling and occasional thefts. Those who had known him, even the men who had arrested him and those who were now his jailers, considered Gideon a perfectly harmless human being, rather likeable, but one tossed aside by life. Anyone meeting him for the first time would be likely to regard him as the most wretched of men.

On August 4, 1961, Gideon was tried in a Florida state court on the charge that on June 3, 1961, he "did unlawfully and feloniously break and enter . . . the Bay Harbor Poolroom . . . with intent to commit . . . petit larceny." Specifically he was alleged to have stolen a pint of wine, a few bottles of beer, and some small coins from a cigarette machine and a juke box. At the opening of the trial, this exchange took place:

THE COURT: What says the Defendant? Are you ready to go to trial?
THE DEFENDANT: I am not ready, your Honor.
THE COURT: Did you plead not guilty to this charge by reason of insanity?
THE DEFENDANT: No sir.

THE COURT: Why aren't you ready?

THE DEFENDANT: I have no counsel.

THE COURT: Why do you not have counsel? Did you not know that your case was set for trial today?

THE DEFENDENT: Yes sir, I knew that it was set for trial today.

THE COURT: Why, then, did you not secure counsel and be prepared to go to trial?

The Defendant answered the Court's question, but spoke in such low tones that it was not audible.

THE COURT: Come closer up, Mr. Gideon, I can't understand you, I don't know what you said, and the Reporter didn't understand you either.

At this point the Defendant arose from his chair where he was seated at the Counsel Table and walked up and stood directly in front of the Bench, facing His Honor, Judge McCrary.

THE COURT: Now tell us what you said again, so we can understand you, please.

THE DEFENDANT: Your Honor, I said: I request this Court to appoint counsel to represent me in this trial.

THE COURT: Mr. Gideon, I am sorry, but I cannot appoint counsel to represent you in this case. Under the laws of the State of Florida, the only time the Court can appoint counsel to represent a Defendant is when that person is charged with a capital offense. I am sorry, but I will have to deny your request to appoint counsel to defend you in this case.

THE DEFENDANT: The United States Supreme Court says I am entitled to be represented by counsel.

THE COURT: Let the record show that the defendant has asked the court to appoint counsel to represent him in this trial and the court denied the request and informed the defendant that the only time the court could appoint counsel to represent a defendant was in cases where the defendant was charged with a capital offense. The defendant stated to the court that the United States Supreme Court said he was entitled to it.

Unfortunately, Gideon was wrong. Twenty years earlier, in the case of *Betts v. Brady*,[2] the Supreme Court of the United States had held precisely the opposite. Their decision may seem somewhat surprising. It

2. 316 U.S. 455 (1942).

is true, of course, that the Sixth Amendment guarantees that "in all criminal prosecutions, the accused shall enjoy the right . . . to have the assistance of counsel for his defence." But the eight amendments were intended to restrain only the federal government—not the state governments. Hence the Sixth Amendment applies to federal courts but not to state courts. To be sure, the Fourteenth Amendment provides the famous words that have borne such an extraordinary amount of judicial weight: "No state shall . . . deprive any person of life, liberty, or property, without due process of law." However, in an opinion upheld by six Justices and opposed by three dissenters, in the Betts case the Court specifically rejected the contention that due process in criminal cases necessarily required states to guarantee that the accused be represented by counsel. Whether or not due process of law was denied, said Mr. Justice Roberts for the majority, "is to be tested by an appraisal of the totality of facts in a given case. That which may, in one setting, constitute a denial of fundamental fairness, shocking to the universal sense of justice, may, in other circumstances, and in the light of other considerations, fall short of such denial." In later cases, the Court held that "special circumstances"—illiteracy, ignorance, youth, mental illness—would serve to justify a constitutional claim to counsel in criminal trials in state courts. But in the absence of special circumstances, such a claim would not be upheld. By itself, poverty was not one of these special circumstances. Unfortunately for Gideon, he had asserted no special circumstances: he simply believed, and never ceased believing, that under the Constitution of the United States even a poor man was entitled to have a lawyer to defend him in a criminal case.

The stand of the Court, it is important to note, was subject to severe criticism in the law schools, the law journals, and other professional forums. The Justices are, after all, human; they are highly sensitive in the long run to the professional opinions of distinguished legal brethren; and a large number of eminent students of the law insisted that the Court's doctrine of "special circumstances" was an absurdity. The discomfort of the Justices was probably compounded as the Court itself became increasingly entangled in the subtle metaphysics of its own doctrine. What special circumstances distinguished the cases in which the Court upheld the claim from those in which it rejected the claim was sometimes totally undiscernable to everyone, including, some observers suggested, the learned Justices—who were, as in the Betts case, quite unable to agree among themselves.

For all these reasons, when Gideon's petition arrived early in 1962 the time was ripe for a fresh look at the Betts doctrine. The Court agreed to review Gideon's case and asked Mr. Abe Fortas, a distinguished Washington lawyer, later appointed to the Supreme Court by President Johnson, to take the case. Now in the world of the American lawyer, such an appointment is a signal distinction, quite possibly enhanced by the fact that to accept the honor may entail considerable personal sacrifice; for neither the Court nor any other part of the government pays a cent to the lawyer for his services; the Court pays his transportation to Washington and home again and it prints the briefs, but provides no other expenses—not even his Washington hotel bill. It goes without saying that Fortas accepted; having accepted he threw himself wholeheartedly into the case and lavished the considerable resources of his eminent law firm on the attempt to establish the principle that under the American Constitution Clarence Earl Gideon, a penniless man with a record of petty crimes, was entitled to be represented by counsel.

The Court heard the oral argument on January 15, 1963—an hour to each side and (an unusual step) an additional half hour for a "Friend of the Court" on each side. For Gideon, there were two highly distinguished lawyers, Abe Fortas and, as a friend of the Court, J. Lee Rankin, a former U.S. Solicitor General now intervening on behalf of the American Civil Liberties Union. For the State of Florida there was Bruce R. Jacobs, a twenty-six-year-old assistant attorney general of Florida who was only two years out of Stetson Law School in St. Petersburg and had never before set foot in the Supreme Court Building; as a friend of the Court appearing in behalf of Florida there was also the Assistant Attorney General of Alabama.

Fortas had steeped himself in his case. He was superbly prepared. Both he and Rankin were impressive and persuasive in the surprisingly informal but often sharp discussions with the members of the Court that take place during oral argument. Jacobs "looking extremely young and earnest . . . was deluged by questions. There was scarcely a five minute period when he could talk without interruption." Both he and his colleague from Alabama were sometimes caught badly off-base by the shrewd and practised Justices; after one exchange in which Justice Black questioned the adequacy of his reply, Jacobs confessed, "I'm sorry, your honor, that was a stupid answer."

Three months later, Justice Black, speaking for a unanimous court in the case of Gideon v. Wainwright[3] over-ruled Betts v. Brady, rejected the doctrine that special circumstances were needed to justify a claim to counsel in a criminal trial, and held that the right to due process of law prescribed by the Fourteenth Amendment necessarily included the right

3. 372 U.S. 335 (1963).

to counsel in criminal prosecutions. After citing earlier cases in order to show that *Betts v. Brady* was really "an abrupt break" with precedents, Justice Black went on to say:

> Not only these precedents but also reason and reflection require us to recognize that in our adversary system of criminal justice, any person hailed into court, who is too poor to hire a lawyer, cannot be assured a fair trial unless counsel is provided for him. This seems to us to be an obvious truth . . . That government hires lawyers to prosecute and defendants who have money hire lawyers to defend are the strongest indications of the widespread belief that lawyers in criminal courts are necessities, not luxuries. The right of one charged with crime to counsel may not be deemed fundamental and essential to fair trials in some countries, but it is in ours.

Clarence Earl Gideon was now entitled to a new trial—this time with counsel. The American Civil Liberties Union offered him the services of their lawyers; however, Gideon, "irascible but spunky," as one of these lawyers described him, quarreled with the counsel provided by the ACLU, refused his services, and accepted instead—perhaps wisely— the services of a local lawyer. On August 5, 1963, he was tried again. After considering the matter for an hour, the jury announced that Gideon was Not Guilty.

> After nearly two years in the state penitentiary Gideon was a free man. There were tears in his eyes, and he trembled even more than usual as he stood in a circle of well-wishers and discussed his plans. His half-brother, the Air Force sergeant, was coming home from Japan and would adopt Gideon's children. Gideon would see the children the next day, then go off to stay with a friend in Tallahassee. That night he would pay a last, triumphant visit to the Bar Harbor Poolroom. Could someone let him have a few dollars? Someone did.
> "Do you feel like you accomplished something?" a newspaper reporter asked.
> "Well I did."

How can we account for Gideon's victory? Two aspects of the case go a long way in explaining his success.

First, although the decision in Gideon's case required the Supreme

Court to do something it is always reluctant to do—to reverse itself—by 1962 the Justices did not have to change their views very much to arrive at their decision about Gideon. There is very good reason for thinking that what Gideon (and Fortas) contributed most was a strong and highly persuasive case that confirmed the views of the majority of Justices and crystallized the views of uncertain members. The evidence is this:

❡ The composition of the Court itself had almost completely changed in the two decades since the Betts case. The only remaining members from the Court that had decided *Betts* were Justices Black and Douglas; Black had written the dissenting opinion in the Betts case and Douglas had joined in that dissent. By chance, Mr. Justice Frankfurter, who was the most likely source of continuing support for the Betts doctrine, had retired from the Court because of illness a few months before the case was heard.

❡ The justices were already dissatisfied with the Betts doctrine and the logic-chopping about special circumstances that it gave rise to. It was increasingly obvious to everyone that some new and clearer doctrine was needed. Each case that arose under the old doctrine gave rise to dissent. A case in April, 1962, led to three dissents—Chief Justice Warren and Justices Black and Douglas. In a 1961 case, a fourth member, Justice Brennan, had joined with Douglas in asking that *Betts* v. *Brady* be overruled; and in a public lecture Brennan had later said that to refuse counsel to an indigent accused seemed to violate the guarantee in the Fourteenth Amendment to the equal protection of the laws. In his four years on the Court, a fifth member, Justice Stewart, "had never voted to affirm a criminal conviction where the de- defendant claimed that he should have had counsel at his trial." Thus at least four members were already convinced and a fifth justice was probably in a mood to crystallize his his views if the right case came along—and, one should add, if that case were presented in the right way by a lawyer as skillful and respected as Abe Fortas.[4]

❡ In a series of important decisions the Supreme Court itself

4. *Cf.* "A Scalogram of Right-to-Counsel Decisions of the Warren Court (1953–1958 terms), Glendon A. Schubert, *Constitutional Politics*, New York, Holt Rinehart and Winston, 1960, Table 27, p. 625.

had staked out new claims to constitutional rights in many areas. The ideology, commitment, and mood of the Court all thrust it strongly toward decisions that enhanced claims to libertarian and egalitarian values.

¶ Informed professional legal opinion had been moving rapidly away from the Betts doctrine toward the position taken in the Gideon case. The members of the Court, who are not immune to these tidal movements in professional attitudes, were aware of the strong criticism their doctrine was evoking.

¶ Moreover, practise in the states had moved overwhelmingly in the direction the Court took in Gideon's case. By the time Gideon's case was heard in the Supreme Court, "thirty-seven states provided counsel for the poor in all felony trials, eight others frequently did so as a matter of practise, five made no regular provision for counsel except in capital cases."⁵ For once, constitutional doctrine was lagging well behind the practises of most states.

The second factor contributing to Gideon's victory was that even if he had had almost no resources himself, his letter happened to unleash a prompt and massive mobilization of energy and talent in his support:

¶ By appointing Abe Fortas to represent Gideon, the Supreme Court insured help for Gideon from one of the nation's distinguished lawyers and the resources, when needed, of his firm.⁶

¶ The American Civil Liberties Union, which is rich with volunteered legal talent of very high quality, also intervened in the case. As we have seen, a former Solicitor General of the United States appeared as a friend of the Court in behalf of Gideon.

¶ A quite unexpected flood of assistance for Gideon was touched off by Jacobs, the young Florida prosecutor, when he innocently wrote to the attorneys general in all fifty states inviting them to join with Florida. As a result, two states did support Florida in the case—but twenty-three states filed a brief that made many of the same arguments Fortas

5. Lewis, op. cit., 172–3.
6. These contributions are described in detail by Anthony Lewis in Chapter 9, pp. 118–138; for Fortas' conduct during the oral argument, see p. 169 ff.

made and asked that *Betts v. Brady* be overruled! In addition, the State of Oregon submitted a brief arguing that its experience "tends to indicate that it would provide greater protection of constitutional rights, and would be less expensive, to insist upon counsel in each original criminal proceeding than to attempt by a post-conviction proceeding to recover justice lost by defects at the trial." Thus the Justices learned that the states were overwhelmingly on Gideon's side.

¶ Against Gideon and supporting Florida, it is worth noting, were two lawyers considerably less experienced than those appearing in Gideon's behalf.

What consequences did the Gideon case have? Not least, it freed Gideon. More generally, alongside the existing constitutional right to counsel in criminal cases that was already guaranteed to defendants in federal courts, the Gideon case affirmed a new constitutional right to counsel in state courts as well. (Incidentally, the State of Florida applied the principle retroactively, and within a year nine hundred seventy-six prisoners were released from Florida penitentiaries; another five hundred were given new trials—this time with counsel.)

It would be an exaggeration to say, however, that the Gideon case automatically produced equality under law for the needy or indigent defendant.

Gideon's petition to the Court was one of about fifteen hundred paupers' cases that arrive each term from prisoners and other persons too poor to hire counsel. Most of these are thought by members of the Court not to be worth their time; a great many are said to be frivolous or absurd; the Court agrees to review only about 3 per cent of the cases raised in these petitions. Even if the Court were to hear all fifteen hundred cases, these are but the merest trickle from the gigantic flood of incidents in which the poor, the indigent, the ignorant, the mentally deficient, the culturally handicapped run afoul of the law. It is estimated that about 33 per cent of the criminal defendants in federal courts and around 60 per cent in the state courts are indigents.[7] Even if all courts, federal and state, must as a result of Gideon insure that every defendant in a criminal case who is too poor to engage a lawyer must be provided with one if he so wishes, the poor are not likely to receive the kind of legal aid the better-off can afford. The chief judge of the Second U.S. Circuit Court of Appeals has portrayed a process typical of many courts:

7. Lewis, *op. cit.*, p. 197.

When advised that an indigent needs counsel, the judge usually picks out some lawyer who happens to be in the court-room . . . The lawyer then spends a few minutes with his new client at the side of the courtroom, or perhaps in an anteroom under the scrutiny of the bailiff or the marshall. In most of such assignments, after a few minutes of conference, the defendant is advised to plead guilty and he feels he has no choice but to do so . . . This mock assignment of counsel and the cursory hurry-up job of a busy uncompensated lawyer makes a farce of due process of law and our Bill of Rights. Every one who participates in the farce knows this—the judge, the district attorney, the assigned lawyer, the bailiff, and of course the defendant himself.

Happily, one of the most consequential results of the Gideon case in the long run was to give new strength to already existing efforts to insure that the indigent defendant is represented not simply by counsel but—and this is quite another matter—by adequate counsel. After their decision, many of the Supreme Court Justices themselves urged upon their legal brethren the gospel according to Gideon. Legal aid societies were formed in many communities to provide free legal assistance to the poor. A number of states decided to follow the path of pioneering sister states by establishing the post of public defender; as the opposite number of the prosecuting attorney, the public defender's job is to serve all those who do not have counsel. The Ford Foundation made grants totalling over two and a half million dollars for projects involving legal aid. Two months after the Gideon case, the Florida legislature passed a law creating a public defender in each of its sixteen judicial circuits. After the federal poverty program was established, officials in that program turned their attention to the problems of legal aid for the indigent. Federal appropriations for poverty made possible a rapid swelling of funds for legal aid. Whereas in 1965 the nation's two hundred and eighty-six legal aid organizations operated with a budget of 5.8 million dollars, federal funds from the poverty program allocated in 1966 for legal aid programs amounted to more than twenty-five million dollars.[8] By mid-1966, federally financed legal aid programs were operating in about one hundred twenty-five communities, including all but four of the largest thirty cities in the country.

Thanks to the persistence of the "irascible but spunky" Clarence Earl Gideon, then, the Supreme Court not only announced a new con-

8.   The New York Times, May 16, 1966, p. 13.

stitutional right but indirectly it also affirmed a new obligation for Americans: the obligation to provide adequate counsel for criminal defendants who cannot afford it.

> It will be an enormous social task (Anthony Lewis writes) to bring to life the dream of Gideon v. Wainwright—the dream of a vast, diverse country in which every man charged with crime will be capably defended, no matter what his economic circumstances and in which the lawyer representing him will do so proudly, without resentment at an unfair burden, sure of the support needed to make an adequate defense. England already approaches that ideal. No poor man there is tried for at least a serious crime without the offer of counsel; assignment in such cases is an expected part of a barrister's life, and he receives a fee from the state comparable to what a private client would pay in that kind of a case. But England is, by comparison, a small and homogeneous society, with a simpler legal system and a much less serious crime problem. There is a long road to travel before every criminal court in the United States reaches the goal that appears on the façade of the Supreme Court building: Equal Justice Under Law.

Dixon-Yates[9]

During 1954 and 1955, American politicians and newspapers gave prominent attention to the Dixon-Yates case—or, as one set of partisans sometimes called it, the Dixon-Yates scandal. Gideon was an obscure man who fought his case almost unaided; as the Dixon-Yates matter progressed, it drew in the President, his chief of staff in the White House, the chairman of the Atomic Energy Commission, the chairman and board members of the Tennessee Valley Authority, Senators, Representatives, important financiers, heads of large utilities, and numerous other nationally prominent persons. Few people have, even now, heard of Clarence Earl Gideon; by the end of 1954, 37 per cent of the people in a Gallup poll said they had heard of the Dixon-Yates proposal—though only a third of these could furnish a reasonably accurate explanation of what it

9. The material for this section is drawn from Aaron Wildavsky, *Dixon-Yates, A Study in Power Politics*, New Haven, Conn., Yale University Press, 1962.

was all about. If, despite its notoriety, the Dixon-Yates case never gained wide comprehension, it is easy to see why: Even in retrospect, the issues seem inordinately complex.

By 1953, twenty years after its creation in the springtime of the New Deal, the Tennessee Valley Authority was a gigantic producer and distributor of electric power; and the giant was still growing.[10] For years a fierce battle had raged between advocates of publicly owned electric power—of which TVA is the prime example—and spokesmen for privately owned utilities; so bitter was the controversy that one scholar who interviewed participants in the Dixon-Yates case reported that in private conversations, "the most common term used to describe the other side was 'those bastards.' "[11] General Eisenhower, as the first Republican President in twenty years, was committed ideologically both to private enterprise and to a balanced budget.

When, therefore, the TVA renewed a request (previously rejected by the Truman Administration) for funds to begin construction of an additional steam plant for generating electric power at Fulton, Tennessee, thirty miles north of Memphis on the Mississippi River, Eisenhower's Director of the Budget, a past president of the American Banking Association, opposed it; a few days later President Eisenhower announced sharp cuts in TVA's budget, including the elimination of the proposed Fulton plant. Had it wished, Congress could of course have overridden the President; but a Republican Congress went along with a Republican President and defeated attempts by TVA supporters, mainly Democrats, to restore the funds for the Fulton plant.

The matter might have died, or perhaps it might have been postponed for some years, had there not been a growing threat of a power shortage in the area serviced by the TVA. Two consumers of TVA's power created a particularly embarrassing problem: the city of Memphis, whose officials were politically close to TVA's officials, and the Atomic Energy Commission (AEC), which had an installation in Paducah, Kentucky, that depended on TVA power. If the Fulton plant were built,

10. "At the end of fiscal 1964, the TVA's total fixed assets of all types (power and nonpower) after depreciation were $2,469,355,000—about equal to the total assets of the Bethlehem Steel Co., the nation's 12th largest manufacturing firm . . . The TVA power program was the nation's largest. The 13.3 million KW generating capacity at the end of fiscal 1964 was the largest of any single power producer in the country, public or private, and was only slightly less than the combined generating capacity of all electric plants operated by all other federal power agencies. TVA's power production in fiscal 1964 was more than double that of the next largest single power producer, public or private." *Congress and the Nation*, p. 917.
11. Wildavsky, *op. cit.*, 6.

TVA could continue to supply power to the atomic energy installation at Paducah and still meet the expanding requirements of Memphis. Without the Fulton plant, however, Memphis would be in difficulty.

Confronted with this dilemma, the Director and Assistant Director of the Budget looked for a way out consistent with their ideological commitments to private enterprise and balanced budgets. In the process of exploring alternatives, they appointed as an unpaid consultant to the Budget Bureau Adolphe Wenzell, vice president and director of the First Boston Corporation, one of the largest underwriters of private utility securities in the nation.

The appointment was, as it turned out, a serious blunder for the Eisenhower Administration; later on, discovery of Wenzell's appointment was to give the Administration's critics a handy brush with which to tar the solution the Administration had proposed.

This solution, a complex and ultimately rather bizarre product of much pulling and hauling in the White House, the Budget Bureau, the AEC, and TVA, was for AEC to contract with a specially formed corporation to supply its power, thus enabling TVA to divert some of its power from AEC to fill the rising demand from the city of Memphis. This new firm, the Mississippi Valley Generating Company, was formed by Edgar H. Dixon, President of Middle South Utilities, a utility holding

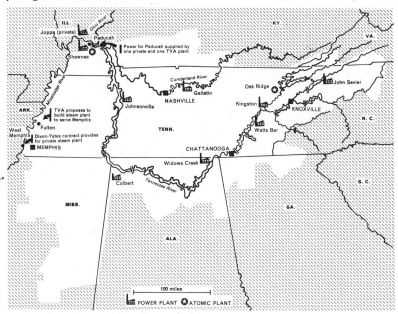

FIGURE 16.1—TVA POWER AREA

Wildavsky, op. cit., p. 44.

company with subsidiaries along the western border of the TVA system, and Eugene A. Yates, chairman of the board of the Southern Company, a utility holding company with subsidiaries bordering on TVA's southwestern edge.

The original proposal, which came from the TVA chairman, naturally envisioned that AEC would buy power from private utilities in order to replace TVA power for its installation at Paducah. But it turned out that private utilities were unwilling to build near Paducah, where they foresaw an inadequate market if AEC should stop taking their power; they would, instead, build near Memphis, where they would be assured of future demand if the arrangement with the AEC fell through. Unfortunately, however, AEC needed power at Paducah, not at Memphis; the Administration, on the other hand, needed power to supply the city of Memphis in order to justify turning down TVA's proposal for a new steam plant at nearby Fulton. Confronted by this new dilemma, the Administration now proposed a truly rococco design: Dixon-Yates would contract with AEC to provide power—not at Paducah but at Memphis; AEC would not use the power itself but would deliver it to TVA, which would deliver it to Memphis! Thus TVA could furnish the new power to Memphis and at the same time continue to provide AEC with power for its installation in Paducah. If the reader is by now hopelessly confused, he will doubtless feel some sympathy with the Senators, Congressmen, and newspaper readers of the time.

The President and perhaps most of the members of his Administration generally seem to have underestimated the potential fury of the opposition their proposal would stir up. To opponents it looked like a jerry-built device for starting to dismember TVA. When word reached Congress about the proposed contract, the Joint Committee on Atomic Energy (a joint committee of both House and Senate) undertook hearings that furnished opponents of the Dixon-Yates contract with an opportunity to investigate it and to express their opposition. The public power forces in Congress and throughout the nation rallied and attacked. Wildavsky writes:

> . . . Barrow Lyons, a public-power advocate who observed these events at close hand, has written a running account of the mobilization of the public power group.
>
> On the afternoon of Thursday, July 15, 1954, a group of liberals employed by consumer, farm, and labor organizations accidentally ran into each other in the hall of the Senate Office Building. They were Alex Radin, General

Manager of the American Public Power Association; Dr. Clay Cochran, research economist for the National Rural Electric Cooperative Association; George Taylor, a director of the National Hells Canyon Association; Angus McDonald, legislative counsel for the National Farmers Union; and Donald Montgomery, economist for the United Automobile Workers. Each on his own had been talking to Senators about the Atomic Energy Bill. Most of those to whom they had talked had not had time to read it. Very little hope was entertained . . . to prevent its passage in the form presented to the Joint Committee. Liberal members of the Senate were gloomy. The five men took counsel together. Then, in a body, they went searching for a Senator who would make a fight on the measure.

The first encountered who showed signs of fight was Senator Warren G. Magnuson of Washington. He was "willing to go along if you can round up a few more." He sent them to Senator Lister Hill of Alabama. "You boys go and line up your forces to get some support for a real fight, and I'll do my best to get together a group in the Senate that will put up a real battle," Hill told them.

A hard core of some twenty senators was organized and met under Senator Hill's direction several times during the debate. Pressure was applied by getting as many votes as possible on the public record so that local public-power groups might hold their senators accountable.

The five original public-power groups, coordinating their activities through the Electric Consumers Information Committee, brought in additional farm and labor organizations and the Cooperative League of the United States of America. The Public Affairs Institute was hired to do special research on a rush basis. Teams of researchers worked around the clock to supply speeches for the Senate debate. Public-power organizations throughout the country sent telegrams to their senators protesting against Dixon-Yates as well as provisions of the Atomic Energy Act.

By the middle of July the debate over revisions of the Atomic Energy Act had been converted into a free-for-all over the merits of the proposed Dixon-Yates contract.[12]

12. *Ibid.*, 101–103.

Nonetheless, when the contract came to a vote in the Senate, the Administration, backed by almost all Republican Senators and a handful of Democrats, won. The Senate rejected a Democratic amendment barring the Dixon-Yates contract by a vote of 55-35 (44 Republicans and 11 Democrats vs 33 Democrats and 3 Republicans). At the same time, however, an amendment favored by public-power advocates and opposed by the Administration authorizing the AEC to produce electric power passed 45-41.

Dixon-Yates was featured by the Democrats during the campaigns for congressional elections that fall. It would be difficult to show that it had any effect on the elections; but as a result of that election the Democratic party did take control over both houses by modest majorities.

The public power forces kept up their attack. Until his term expired in May, 1954, the Chairman of the TVA, Gordon Clapp, fought the proposal. Though his successor, appointed by President Eisenhower, was favorable to it, other TVA board members and staff continued to place roadblocks in its way. The AEC itself was divided; the chairman, Lewis Strauss, backed the Administration; but one of the leading Commissioners, a Democrat, opposed it as uneconomic and absurd. Congress got into the act again with new hearings. Then, to confound matters even more, Walter Von Treskow, a New York financial and economic consultant who had long been interested in the electric utility field, came forward with a wholly new proposal: He would enable the city of Memphis to build its own plant, which his financial and engineering firm would finance, construct, and operate for the city. City officials, though friendly toward TVA, looked upon this as a way out of their difficulties. Von Treskow made sure that his proposal gained publicity and he amplified the volume of attacks on Dixon-Yates as an economic absurdity.

Meanwhile, Dixon-Yates had turned to questions of financing. By something more than a coincidence, the First Boston Corporation agreed to market a large share of the Dixon-Yates securities. But Adolphe Wenzell, their vice president and director, had grown increasingly uneasy about the possibility that his role as unpaid advisor to the Bureau of the Budget would lead to charges of conflict of interest. The First Boston Corporation, perhaps sharing this sense of unease, decided to accept no fee for its services. This precaution was not enough to head off the denouement. For the long and carefully guarded secret of Wenzell's association with the Bureau of the Budget during the period when the Dixon-Yates solution was developed was finally discovered and, on February 18, 1955, unveiled on the floor of the Senate by Senator Lister Hill, one of the most vigorous opponents of Dixon-Yates. Tarred, however faintly, by the brush of scandal, Dixon-Yates was tottering. The coup de grace was delivered by the city of Memphis: in June, the City Commission accepted Von Treskow's proposal to build a municipal power plant.

Dixon-Yates was dead. The Administration now cancelled the contract. All construction at the site stopped. The Government Accounting Office insisted that since Wenzell's role may have violated conflict-of-interest statutes, the government should not pay Dixon-Yates for the costs incurred under the contract. Dixon-Yates thereupon sued the government for $3.5 million expenses incurred under the contract. In January, 1961, the Supreme Court held that the Dixon-Yates contract was unenforceable because of a conflict of interest involving Wenzell. Thus the episode passed into history—at a cost of almost two million dollars in out-of-pocket expenses incurred by the Dixon-Yates companies for their little venture.

What are some of the lessons of this incident?

¶ Despite some well-known theories to the contrary,[13] a coalition of a pro-business administration, utilities magnates, and leaders of 'finance capital' was unable to win.

¶ Debate on the issue turned not only on practical questions, such as the relative costs of power under different schemes, but also on moral questions (e.g., Wenzell's role) and ideological perspectives (public vs. private ownership).

¶ The President was never able to mobilize the administrative agencies as a single, disciplined, hierarchical force: His policy was openly opposed, for example, by some TVA members and AEC commissioners.

¶ Although Wenzell's role was kept secret for a long time, ultimately the press and the politicians pried it loose, despite very strenuous effort by the Administration.

¶ As a minority party, the Democrats had no great difficulty in keeping the issue before the public.

¶ Elections made a difference. When the Democrats won majorities in both houses, they were in a better position to hammer at the administration. Even then, however, the opponents of Dixon-Yates might not have won were it not for unexpected help.

¶ Unforeseen factors that developed during the dispute finally played a decisive part: Von Treskow's proposal and the revelations about Wenzell. One is reminded of some remarks of Machiavelli about *fortuna* (luck):

13. Most notably, C. Wright Mills, *The Power Elite*, New York, Oxford University Press, 1956.

[403]

... if a man governs himself with caution and patience, and the times and circumstances are in accord so that his course of procedure is good, he will go along prospering; but, if times and circumstances change, he is ruined, because he does not change his course of action. Nor does one find a man wise enough to know how to adapt himself to this; not only because he cannot deviate from that to which he is naturally inclined, but also because, having always prospered while following along one path, he cannot be persuaded to leave it.[14]

Foreign Trade[15]

Gideon's case directly involved Gideon himself, a handful of lawyers, and the Justices of the Supreme Court. The direct participants in Dixon-Yates were business leaders, the White House, and administrative agencies, with some crucial action in Congress. For our third case of political action, we now turn to the Congress and the environment of political forces in which it makes decisions about foreign trade.

From the First Congress until the passage of the Reciprocal Trade Act in 1932, Congress was the center—and for the most part exclusively the center—of decisions about the tariff. Except for two brief periods (1832-61 and 1913-22), throughout this whole period the trend was toward higher tariffs, first in response to a need for revenue and later from a demand for protection from foreign competitors. After the Civil War, the Republican party emerged as the champion of protectionism, the Democrats as advocates of lower tariffs. Republican protectionism reached its apogee with the passage of the Smoot-Hawley Tariff Act of 1930, which on the very eve of the Great Depression erected the highest customs barriers in American history.

In making the key decisions that fixed tariff rates in voluminous detail, the Congress of the United States became little more than an instrument for negotiating, reconciling, and accomodating the demands of American businessmen for high tariffs. Tariff-making by Congress was pressure politics in its most undiluted form. Passage of the Smoot-Hawley Tariff displayed Congress in a triumphant and climactic performance

14. Machiavelli's *The Prince, A Bilingual Edition*, Mark Musa, trans. and ed., St. Martin's Press, New York, 1964.
15. The information in this section is mainly from Raymond A. Bauer, Ithiel de Sola Pool, and Lewis Anthony Dexter, *American Business and Public Policy, The Politics of Foreign Trade*, New York, Atherton Press, 1963.

as the unabashed exponent of protectionist interests.[16] This was the last time, however, that Congress was to occupy the center of the stage in the perennial drama of fixing specific tariff rates. As long as the commitment to protectionism was dominant, Congress was a suitable, if often clumsy, instrument for expressing that ideology in policy-making on tariff matters. But it was obvious that to reduce tariffs significantly would require other techniques than the familiar congressional practises of log-rolling, mutual concessions, and unlimited compromise.

Consequently, when Franklin D. Roosevelt sought to translate the low-tariff platform of the Democratic Party into policy, he and his advisers chose an entirely new method. The Trade Agreements Act (often called the Reciprocal Trade Act) of 1934 represented a revolutionary departure from previous practises not only because of its aims—to reduce rather than keep or maintain high tariffs—but also because of its methods. For the first time, tariff-making ceased to be a monopoly of the Congress. Instead, the President was authorized to negotiate agreements over a three-year period with other countries for mutual reductions in tariffs, down to 50 per cent of the Smoot-Hawley rates. In essence, this new process of policy-making, which transferred the initiative in tariff matters from Congress and industry to the President, has since become the accepted practise in the United States, for Congress has regularly renewed the President's authority to reduce tariffs within general limits set by statute.

As might be expected, the first two renewals—1937 and 1940—were strictly party battles in which Democrats supported the President and Republicans overwhelmingly opposed his request for authority. But public opinion was moving with the Democrats, and in 1943 a majority of Republicans in both House and Senate voted for renewal. Throughout that decade Republicans in Congress remained divided with Republican leaders unable to marshall their full following against renewal. In the elections of 1952, a spokesman for the more internationalist and liberal wing of the Republican party was elected President; with less than six months to go between his inauguration as the first Republican President since 1932 and the expiration of the Reciprocal Trade Agreements Act in June, President Eisenhower chose not to challenge his party's historic position by seeking an open reversal on the tariff, and asked instead for a one-year renewal of his authority. His compromise was received by a willing Congress. For even if many Republicans continued to oppose low tariffs, by 1953 few men in Congress, whether Republicans or

---

16. That performance is superbly described in a small classic of American political science: E. E. Schattschneider, *Politics, Pressures, and the Tariff,* Englewood Cliffs, N. J., Prentice Hall, 1935.

Democrats, had any hankering to return to the old, irresponsible, irrational, and troublesome system of tariff-making that had been employed until 1934. By 1953, a new consensus on policy-making had come into existence: not on the aims but on the *methods* of tariff-making. For almost everyone agreed that specific tariff rates should be negotiated and fixed not by Congress but the President, acting under a broad grant of congressional authority. Just as 1934 was an historic turning point, so too in a less obvious way the renewal of 1953 marked the end, for all practical purposes, of the historic view that Congress was the appropriate body for setting tariff rates.

If they agreed, by and large, on methods, many congressional Republicans nonetheless remained opposed to low tariffs as a goal. As he was on most other issues, President Eisenhower was inclined to be conciliatory about tariff problems. In the absence of aggressive leadership from the White House, in 1954 Congress settled again for a one-year extension. In the congressional elections that year, however, the Republican majority was replaced by a Democratic majority in both houses of Congress; the opportunity was thereby created for a three-year renewal and presidential authority to cut tariffs lower than the one-year renewal legislation had allowed. But the Democratic victory was offset to some extent by the fact that Congressmen from Southern textile areas who had hitherto upheld the traditional Democratic position on low tariffs now began to feel pressures from the growing Southern textile industry, which was fearful of foreign competition. Meanwhile, the President persisted in his familiar conciliatory approach; hence the burden of passing new legislation fell heavily on Democratic leaders in Congress. Indeed, at one critical point when the protectionist forces were on the verge of a major victory on a crucial amendment by means of which they hoped to emasculate the bill, Sam Rayburn, the extraordinarily influential Speaker of the House

> did something a speaker does only once or twice a session. He left his rostrum, went down as a member, and took the floor ... "As an old friend of all of you," [Rayburn pleaded] "as a lover of the House of Representatives and its procedures, I ask you to vote down this amendment." The House went from silent listening to feverish activity. The whips worked on the votes ... Among the Democrats the influence of Rayburn paid off. The end was a photo finish. As the roll call proceeded, the protectionists seemed to win by seven votes. Then the "corrections" began. One man after another rose to ask how he was recorded and then corrected his vote from "for" to "against" the amendment. The amendment lost 193 to 191.

Under the closed rule, one, but only one, amendment was permitted: a motion to recommit the bill to committee, that is, to kill it. The one amendment permitted under the rule was offered by Reed [a leading Republican opponent of low tariffs]. Carefully, he made it a very modest one which some middle-of-the-roaders might be able to accept . . . The debate went on all day Friday. Among the many speeches, one deserves to be noted. Henderson Lanham of Georgia, one of the most respected members of the House, who had previously been a lifelong low-tariff supporter, spoke in favor of the Reed motion. He was a weathervane and also an influence on a substantial group of votes . . .

Once again there was a roll-call vote. Once again the protectionists really won until the "corrections" came in. Martin [the Republican minority leader, supporting the President on this issue], Rayburn, and the whips called on their credits. The Reed motion to recommit was rejected, 206 to 199 . . .

The Reed proposal was beaten and the Eisenhower administration saved for one major reason—Sam Rayburn. As Rayburn himself said in conversation, the bill was a "Rayburn bill," not an "Eisenhower Bill." Had there been a new speaker, a weaker leader, or one less devoted to reciprocal trade, the Reed motion would have won.[17]

Before the "Rayburn Act" expired in 1958, reciprocal trade was renewed with little dispute and few changes—this time, however, for four years. In 1962, some of President Kennedy's advisers proposed a stop-gap renewal in order to prepare for a much bolder proposal in 1963. Instead, Kennedy chose to advance the bolder proposal immediately. The new legislation would give authority to the President for five years (i.e. until 1967) to reduce duties by 50 per cent of the 1962 levels, to eliminate tariffs entirely where the current rate was 5 per cent or less, and to negotiate the reduction of tariffs to zero on entire categories of goods where the United States and members of the European Economic Community jointly supply 80 per cent or more of the world trade (not counting trade within the Soviet bloc). The bill passed the House by 298-125 with overwhelming Democratic support (218 Democrats for, 35 against, mainly Southerners) and a majority of Republicans opposed (80 for, 90 against). In the Senate, after a number of restrictive amendments were beaten down, a few by only several votes, the bill passed by a lop-sided majority of 78-8.

Kennedy's bolder strategy had proved successful. He had won a

17. Bauer et al., op. cit., p. 63–5.

resounding victory in his bid for powerful new authority to reduce tariffs.

What were the political forces acting on Congress as it made decisions about tariff policies and procedures in the 1950s? Thirty years earlier an appropriate answer might have been cast in terms of classic pressure politics: Congressional decisions about tariff rates, one might reasonably have said, were simply the resultants of the pressures for higher rates put upon it by American businessmen seeking tariff protection. For the 1950s and 1960s, however, a far more complex answer is required.

To begin with, American public opinion has shifted decisively toward lower tariffs. In 1945, a survey showed that 36 per cent of a national sample favored high tariffs, 33 per cent low tariffs, and 30 per cent had no opinion. In 1945, among 'informed voters' (i.e. that 46 per cent of the population that had heard about the tariff controversy), 27 per cent favored higher tariffs, 49 per cent supported lower tariffs, 27 per cent would keep tariffs the same, and 8 per cent had no opinion. This distribution of opinions was evidently fairly stable throughout the 1950s. Moreover from 1937-62 those who supported continuation of the Reciprocal Trade Act outnumbered by two, three, or more times those who opposed it.[18] It might seem, therefore, that a Congressman who voted against reciprocal trade legislation was likely to alienate more voters than he would win. But estimating the effects of one's vote on 'public opinion' was not so simple. For one thing, a Congressman might represent a particular district in which the threat of foreign competition was, for some reason, salient. For another, throughout the fifties public interest in foreign trade was modest. Survey evidence indicates that a majority of the public had little or no interest in the subject; from a quarter to a half of the adults interviewed could not even provide an accurate definition of a tariff.

As a political force, public opinion was complicated in still other ways—as it generally is. College educated adults favored low tariffs over high tariffs by much larger proportions than those with high school and grade school education. People at the lowest economic levels were more protectionist than the rest of the population. Paradoxically, then, because the Democratic Party drew its support more heavily from the lower economic and educational levels, and the Republicans more from the higher economic and educational groups, among ultrafree traders Republicans greatly outnumbered Democrats, while among ultra protectionists there were somewhat more Democrats than Republicans! Thus it might be thought that Republican protectionist sentiment in Congress should have been blunted by the attitudes of the Republican rank-and file.

18.   *Ibid.*, pp. 81–2, 84.

Moreover, because political activity, as we have seen, is highly related to education and economic position, protectionist opinion among rank and file Democrats would have been muted in action, and the active expression of public opinion should have been even more heavily weighted in favor of free trade than general opinion. This was, in fact, the case. A 1953 survey showed that among those who were most active politically, 63 per cent were opposed to additional restrictions on foreign trade as against 24 per cent among the least active. And among the political actives, the ultraliberal traders outnumbered the ultra protectionists by 17 to 1![19]

Why, then, did not Reciprocal Trade go through Congress easily and by overwhelming votes in 1953 and 1954? Why did a solid phalanx of Republicans in Congress continue their opposition? Why did Sam Rayburn, a Democrat, have to rescue President Eisenhower, a Republican, from defeat?

A substantial part of the explanation is to be found in factors other than public opinion. But one interesting aspect.of public opinion itself may help to account for the resistance Eisenhower had to overcome. The debates over reciprocal trade in 1954-1955 combined with the efforts of groups like the Committee for a National Trade Policy to mobilize public support for *low* tariffs may very well have had the effect of generating more *opposition*. For these events and efforts probably activated more interest in the issue among hitherto uninvolved strata; and as we have already seen it was among the less interested citizens that high tariffs found their greatest support.

> The public may be thought of as an iceberg. Visible at the top are the active, the alert, the influential few who are always in the open air of political activity. Invisible below water are the generally apathetic many who appear only on rare occasions, such as in election campaigns, when strong tides of politics expose them. On some issues, and trade is one, distributions of attitudes at the top and bottom of the iceberg differ. The appearance of public opinion changes when something raises the iceberg higher out of the water.[20]

Congressional controversy, newspaper coverage, and pressure group activity (including that of groups for lower tariffs) all combined to "raise the iceberg higher out of the water."

General public opinion, we know, is not necessarily as influential as

19. All data on public opinion are from Bauer, et al., *op. cit.*, pp. 80–104.
20. *Ibid.*, p. 95.

Table 16.1. Attitudes Toward Foreign Trade Policy

| | SIZE OF FIRM | | |
	LARGE PER CENT	MEDIUM PER CENT	SMALL PER CENT
Protectionists	14	15	12
Liberal traders	49	50	44
Leave as is	19	24	22
Don't know	17	9	21
No answer	1	2	1
	100%	100%	100%
Total number	(166)	(404)	(333)

SOURCE: Bauer et al., op. cit., p. 121.

the opinion of specific segments of the public. In particular, where did businessmen stand on the tariff issue in the 1950s? Was there a business viewpoint? A careful survey of the views of over nine hundred businessmen in large, medium, and small firms shows that by 1954 the gospel of lower tariffs had penetrated to the business community. Only a tiny minority of businessmen were in favor of raising tariffs. The largest number favored further reductions. (Table 16.1)

American businessmen not only lack a unified point of view about foreign trade; but the most popular view now favors low tariffs. The contrast with what was surely the case in the 1920s and 1930s is sharp and definite. Why do so many businessmen support lower tariffs where their predecessors supported higher tariffs? Do their recent views simply reflect changing conceptions of economic self-interest?

In part, no doubt. But one difficulty with this explanation is that a businessman's economic interest in tariffs is very far from clear. Economic explanations of politics assume that an individual or group has a clear-cut interest which serves as a goal and a criterion of benefit. But

> only a small proportion of American industries have a clear, uncomplicated interest in a high-tariff policy and . . . a majority are affected by foreign trade policy only as they have a stake in the economy as a whole . . . The interests of larger and more complicated firms are seldom wholly in the direction of one or another over-all tariff policy.[21]

Because economic interest is often too vague or contradictory to serve as a criterion, businessmen's attitudes on the tariff seem to be influenced by a variety of factors:

21. Ibid., p. 131.

¶ Protectionists were more likely than liberal traders to say business "was worse last year."[22]

¶ The interests of smaller firms were likely to be clearer than the interests of larger firms . . . "The heads of larger firms are more likely to find themselves in a situation of cross-pressure—the condition of a firm simultaneously having tariffs important (a protectionist force) and having export markets important (an antiprotectionist force)."[23]

¶ Although businessmen were overwhelmingly "internationalist" in their foreign policy attitudes, among those who favored raising tariffs there was a smaller proportion of "internationalists" than among low-tariff advocates.[24]

¶ Foreign travel tended "to counteract the force of self-interest. It made a man see the trade issue in national terms, rather than in the parochial terms of his own industry."[25]

But even 'business opinion' as revealed in a sample survey is not necessarily what Congressmen perceive to be the dominant opinion among businessmen nor what they see as the most influential opinions among businessmen. As we saw in Chapter 5, what Congressmen see, hear, and respond to depends, among other things, on what views get through to them, which in turn depends upon who makes an effort to get through to them.

During the period 1952-1954, businessmen in favor of liberal trade outnumbered protectionists by something like three-to-one. But protectionist businessmen were more likely to write to Congressmen than liberal traders, and they were likely to write more often. Consequently, from the point of view of a Congressman's office keeping a rough tab on the mail, it could easily have appeared that business favored higher tariffs!

What about the pressures on Congress generated by businessmen and business organizations operating at the grass roots? The authors of the study from which I have been quoting conducted studies in eight communities in which activity might reasonably have been expected, including Detroit, where the Board of Commerce and Henry Ford II had come out solidly for low tariffs, Wall Street, which was "conspicuously silent," Delaware and Dupont, which is traditionally protectionist,

22. *Ibid.*, p. 135.
23. *Ibid.*, p. 139.
24. *Ibid.*, p. 145.
25. *Ibid.*, p. 168.

a New England city given the pseudonym New Anglia, and three other communities. Among their conclusions are these:

> Most communications bypassed the local community, either by being sent directly to Congress or by originating within industries and being channeled into the national scene by trade organizations.[26]
>
> . . . . If there is an agency which is regarded as the legitimate voice of the community on economic matters, it is probably the local Chamber of Commerce. But in very few areas with which we were acquainted did the Chamber become such a voice . . .
>
> Detroit looms as an obvious exception to what has been said. The Detroit Board of Commerce actually did take a good deal of initiative. And, as we have pointed out, protectionist voices on the Detroit scene were rather effectively quieted . . .
>
> . . . Yet, the volume of protectionist communications to Congress was at least as great as the volume of liberal-trade communications, and we have no way of knowing to what extent the congressmen and senators from Michigan were impressed by the fact that the Detroit community had to some extent gone on record as favoring a liberal-trade policy. When we looked at Detroit from the vantage point of Congress, it did not appear very different from any other city.
>
> . . . It is interesting to note, however, how often a community is perceived as organized and united when our studies showed that this was not so. New Anglia is perhaps the most striking example. Within a few years it was seen by its congressional representatives as militantly organized against the protectionist Simpson bill and then as strongly protectionist. Yet, our investigation showed that only a few men were actively involved in the opposition to the Simpson bill and that some of them had entirely forgotten about the issue within a year. Similarly, of the variety of business interests in New Anglia, probably only the textile ones were in any significant way actively protectionist.
>
> . . . A relatively few voices, well exercised, sometimes created the impression of unified community sentiment and . . . this happened on both sides of the issue.[27]
>
> . . . The practice of "corporate restraint" by large firms came as something of a surprise. . . . Even before we began our com-

26. Ibid., p. 313.
27. Ibid., pp. 314–315.

munity studies, we ran into evidence that very large firms were reluctant to appear to be throwing their weight around too much . . .

. . . The men from the larger firms were considerably more active in communicating with Congress. . . . Although the doctrine of corporate restraint does not prevent the head of a large firm from stating his case, it does inhibit him from using his full power against a congressman who does not agree with him. In addition, the small businessman is likely to evoke more sympathy from the congressman. His plight usually appears more acute. . . .

The curse of bigness is most significant where the company fears adverse public reaction, which may result in further governmental regulation or in prosecution. But this was not the primary factor which immobilized Wall Street banks. The banks were caught in cross-pressures from their clients. Similarly, Atlas and Hercules in Wilmington did not come out for a liberal-trade policy apparently partially because of pressures within the chemical industry.[28]

. . . Finally, the community studies, show that foreign-trade policy was only one among many issues with which American businessmen were concerned and that for most it was an item of relatively low priority. Our selection of communities was strongly biased toward those in which we expected to find active interest in the debate over the Reciprocal Trade Act. Our selection of men to interview was similarily motivated. Nevertheless, in every community that we studied, foreign-trade policy was less important than one or more other issues. For some individuals, it might have been vital, but it was never so for the community as a whole.[29]

If grass roots pressures were weak, what about the lobbies and pressure groups that had been so conspicuous during the passage of the Smoot-Hawley tariff three decades earlier? They did exist in the 1950s. In fact the American Tariff League, founded in 1885 to promote high tariffs, was still active; and the chairman of the League's executive committee was a vice president of Dupont. In 1953 a new protectionist organization was formed; it called itself by the sonorous title of the Nation-wide Committee of Industry, Agriculture, and Labor on Import-Export Policy, and it was supported by some labor unions, particularly

28. *Ibid.*, pp. 317–318.
29. *Ibid.*, p. 319.

the United Mine Workers, and certain tariff-conscious industries: wool, bicycles, glassware, chemicals. A liberal-trade lobby was also formed in 1953, calling itself The Committee for a National Trade Policy; its officers included business executives in several large national corporations and its president was Charles Taft, brother of the late Senator Robert Taft of Ohio. Another low-tariff lobby, the Committee on Foreign Trade Education, was organized by a young public-relations man and included a number of young business and professional people, most of them one-time Young Republicans.

A variety of established organizations also had something to say: the AFL and CIO, the Chamber of Commerce, the National Association of Manufacturers, the League of Woman Voters, etc. In addition, literally hundreds of trade associations, ranging from the American Dental Trades Association and American Farm Bureau Federation to the United Textile Workers and the Wyoming Wool Growers Association displayed at least some interest in the issue.

Yet the importance of these pressure groups is easily exaggerated. In the 1950s their role was at best only a remote approximation to the classic portrayal of Congress as the passive instrument of aggressive lobbyists.

. . . Our initial expectation [the authors of the study report] was that, the facade once penetrated, we would find the decisive events in tariff legislation to be a series of deals worked out between subtle and richly financed interest groups and congressmen pressured by them. It thus came as a surprise to discover that the lobbies were on the whole poorly financed, ill-managed, out of contact with Congress, and at best only marginally effective in supporting tendencies and measures which already had behind them considerable Congressional impetus from other sources. We do not deny that there were large numbers of pressure groups. We are certain that, whatever the outcome, it would have been quite different if all the organized interest groups on one side had been silenced while all those on the other had remained vocal. However, it is in the nature of the democratic struggle that that does not happen. When we look at a typical lobby, we find that its opportunities for maneuver are sharply limited, its staff mediocre, and its major problem not the influencing of Congressional votes but the finding of clients and contributors to enable it to survive at all.[30]

Thus those giant spokesmen for corporate enterprise, the National

30. *Ibid.*, p. 324.

Association of Manufacturers, the Chamber of Commerce, and the industry associations, were inhibited by the very diversity of views and interests among their members. These organizations ordinarily take positions only when their members are more or less united. But their members were far from agreed on tariff matters. Hence these associations avoided taking firm stands, and their influence was correspondingly watered down. The single-interest organizations listed above that were specifically organized to fight for or against high tariffs could and did act more decisively. Yet despite impressive expenditures of funds, they too were far more ineffectual than the historic portrait of lobbyists and lobbying would lead one to expect. The plethora of gold proved to be something of an illusion because the funds were divided among a number of uncoordinated organizations each one of which lacked enough money for an effective job. "The reciprocal trade controversy cost the participants many millions of dollars a year. Yet, wherever one looked at the persons actually spending that money, one saw only harassed men with tight budgets and limited campaign funds, once their essential organizational overheads had been met."[31] The lobbyists themselves were by no means a highly talented lot. Generally they lacked adequate information. And they rarely had enough time to do an adequate job. "Most pressure-group activity is emergency fire-fighting. There is seldom time to do much more. Long-range planning goes by default."[32]

One other major source of influence must be taken into account: the White House. But as we have seen, the importance of the White House varied with the particular occupant, his personality, his strategy, his concern with foreign trade. Eisenhower played a conciliatory and almost passive part, Kennedy a more active and agressive role. Eisenhower's lack of leadership gave Congressmen greater opportunity to respond to other pressures or to vote their own views. Kennedy, on the other hand, by bringing the influence of the White House to bear, contributed decisively to the victory of his foreign trade program in 1962.

On the whole, what is perhaps most surprising is the large amount of elbow room in which Congressmen were free to act. "A congressman is free," the authors conclude,

> . . . because each district is ordinarily a complex and he can choose the elements out of which he wishes to build his coalition . . . He is freed from a slavish dependence on the elements in his coalition, not only because he can change it, but, even more, because, once he has built a coalition, he tends to lead it . . . He is free also because the voters seldom know just

31. *Ibid.*, p. 345.
32. *Ibid.*, p. 349.

what they want . . . Indeed, even where the constituent frames his appeal to his congressman as a highly specific demand, the congressman is quite free to disregard it. Few constituents deny their vote to a congressman who generally listens to them just because he differs on any one issue . . . Finally, a congressman is free also because . . . the procedure of Congress is so complex that it is easy for him to obfuscate where he stands on any issue and what he has done about it.[33]

The Civil Rights Act of 1964[34]

In 1964, almost a full century after the end of the Civil War, the Congress passed the first sweeping civil rights legislation since Recontruction days. This legislation had been preceeded by much milder civil rights acts in 1957 and in 1960, by a number of presidential orders, and by epoch-making Supreme Court decisions. It was followed by another important civil rights act in 1965. But there can be little doubt that in the perspective of Negro rights in American history, the passage of the Civil Rights Act of 1964 marks a milestone of profound significance, for it meant nothing less than the closing of an era of congressional impotence on civil rights legislation and the start of a new era of greater firmness.

In the course of this book and particularly in Chapter 12 we have witnessed some of the origins of the problem which the Civil Rights Act of 1964 was designed to meet. Although the Civil War put an end to slavery as a legal institution, neither Civil War nor Reconstruction enabled Negroes to gain their rights as American citizens. The Compromise of 1877 effectively ended serious efforts on the part of the federal government to free American Negroes from their political, economic, and social subjection. Thereafter the federal government stood aside as Jim Crow laws and practise became the pattern in the South, and de facto segregation became standard in the North.

33. *Ibid.*, pp. 423–4.
34. This section is based mainly on materials dealing with the passage of the Civil Rights Act of 1964, supplied by Raymond E. Wolfinger and David B. Filvaroff. I am deeply grateful to the authors for their generosity in permitting me to draw on their knowledge of these events, which in many instances have not been reported in full. The background of events prior to 1961 is taken from Congressional Quarterly Service, *Revolution in Civil Rights*, Washington, Congressional Quarterly Service, 1965.

There the matter stood for fifty years. By its economic programs, the New Deal won the support of Negroes to the Democratic Party. But Franklin Roosevelt was unwilling to challenge the enormous power of Southern Democrats by seeking to upset white supremacy in the South. In 1941, on the eve of war, only under strong pressure from Negro leaders, Roosevelt issued an executive order creating a Committee on Fair Employment Practices, with very limited powers to deal with discrimination by firms or unions engaged in war work. The war over, FEPC was promptly killed in 1946 by a congressional rider on an appropriations measure.

Following the Second World War, a slow ferment over civil rights began among white liberals and Negroes. But Congress was a formidable obstacle to the passage of civil rights legislation. In the decade after the War, a bill or two dealing with civil rights was introduced almost every year, but even with presidential support these bills failed to win passage. Thus in 1948, President Truman presented a comprehensive legislative program to establish a Fair Employment Practices Commission; to outlaw poll taxes, segregation in public transportation, and lynching; and to protect the right to vote. None of these measures was passed. On the contrary, infuriated by Truman's actions, a group of seventy-four Southern Democrats was organized in the House to join Southern governors in opposing Truman's program; and at the Democratic nominating convention in July, after a strong civil rights plank was inserted in the Democratic platform, a number of Southerners bolted and formed the Dixiecrat party (which cost Mr. Truman the votes of four Southern states in the 1948 presidential elections). Even Truman's re-election and the defeat of the Dixiecrat bid did not change matters very much. Southern white supremacists could still count on Congress to prevent the passage of effective civil rights legislation.

In the late 1940s and 1950s, the opposition in the congress to civil rights legislation still held all the trumps. Sometimes civil rights bills were killed by the powerful House Rules Committee which was dominated by a conservative and anti-civil rights majority led by Representative Smith of Virginia. Because of the opportunity to filibuster, the Senate was a graveyard for civil rights bills. If these barriers showed signs of toppling, the venerable coalition of Southern Democrats and Northern Republicans could usually be counted on to prevent passage of an effective civil rights bill.

In the absence of legislation, any federal action on behalf of the rights of Negro citizens had to occur through institutions other than the Congress, i.e., the Presidency and the judiciary. Thus by executive orders,

President Truman abolished segregation in the military services and, later, created a committee to promote compliance with the anti-discrimination clauses in government contracts; under President Eisenhower, the Secretary of Defense ordered an end to segregation in schools on military posts. But more far-reaching were the actions of the Supreme Court, which from 1938 onward had made small judicial inroads on the "separate but equal" doctrine set forth by their predecessors in *Plessy v. Ferguson* in 1896. Then in 1954, in *Brown v. Board of Education* the Court dramatically reversed the whole doctrine and ordered the states to make an end to school segregation "with all deliberate speed." Thereafter, in a series of cases the Court struck down discriminatory practises in public transportation, in public parks and facilities of all kinds, and in voting.

Yet it was clear to the growing and increasingly impatient civil rights coalition that executive and judicial actions were inherently inadequate: There had to be a statutory basis for bold executive intervention to protect Negroes in the exercise of their rights; and only Congress could constitutionally provide that basis. In 1957, President Eisenhower gained from Congress the first Civil Rights Act passed since Reconstruction days. In its final form the Act was mild enough so that Southern Senators chose not to use the filibuster to defeat it, lest their strategy backfire and create both a stronger bill and more Senate votes to tighten the rules against filibusters.[35] Moreover, Northern Republicans failed to mount their old coalition with the Southerners, in part because the 1956 elections revealed the potential importance to Republican candidates of votes cast by Negroes in Northern cities. Then again in 1960, under President Eisenhower and with leadership from Senate Majority Leader Johnson of Texas, the Republican Minority Leader Dirksen of Illinois, the House Speaker Rayburn of Texas, and the House Republican Minority Leader Halleck of Indiana, a coalition of Northern Democrats and Republicans passed another Civil Rights Act. However, like the act passed three years earlier, the Civil Rights Act of 1960 was a rather weak measure.

At their presidential nominating conventions in 1960 both parties adopted strong planks on civil rights. The Democratic plank was surely the most ambitious in the party's history; among other things it called for legislation to eliminate literacy tests, to establish a permanent FEPC, and to authorize the U. S. Attorney General to bring suits to prevent the denial of equal rights.

During the campaign of 1960, John F. Kennedy asked that legisla-

35. Senator Strom Thurmond of South Carolina fought alone in a marathon speech of twenty-four hours and eighteen minutes—a record for a single Senator.

tion embodying the platform be drafted by congressional Democratic leaders and committed himself to backing it when it was introduced in Congress. After his narrow election victory, however, Kennedy decided that civil rights legislation could not be passed; that any serious attempt to pass such legislation would jeopardize other bills with higher priorities, and that in any case it was politically unnecessary. Thus he decided to focus his civil rights activities on intensified use of executive powers: a significant expansion of law suits, administrative action, and executive orders. President Kennedy adhered to this policy throughout 1961 and 1962, even though feeble attempts were made in Congress to pass civil rights bills.

Following the 1962 elections, moderate and liberal Republican Congressmen introduced mild legislation soon after the Congress met, partly to beat the administration to the punch and be in a position to point to their record. Since their action was mainly symbolic, they made no great effort to push their bills. Some weeks later, the Kennedy Administration submitted its first legislative proposals: amendments to the voting provisions of the Civil Right Acts of 1957 and 1960, a four-year extension of the Civil Rights Commission (appointed under these Acts), and aid to desegregating school districts. The White House did not press for action, however, and there was still a general expectation that nothing important would happen on the civil rights front.

But events outside Washington were speeding up the timetable for civil rights. Sit-ins, Freedom Riders, bus boycotts, James Meredith's admission at Ole Miss, and other militant activities heightened racial tensions in the South in the early 1960s and, in reflex, triggered off white violence. The brutal suppression of Negro demonstrations in Birmingham in April, 1963, amply photographed for all America to see, had two consequences: The Administration became convinced of the need for dramatic federal action, both to remedy racial injustices and to forestall future violence. And Northern sympathy for the plight of the Southern Negro multiplied. Thus the Birmingham demonstrations mark a new stage in civil rights politics: they moved the Administration to propose significant legislation and, by focusing national attention on the growing racial crisis, helped generate the public pressure and support necessary to the passage of the legislation.

The President and his brother Robert, the Attorney General, had sent Burke Marshall, Assistant Attorney General and head of the Justice Department's Civil Rights Division, to Birmingham as a mediator. As soon as Birmingham started to quiet down and Marshall returned to Washington, a task force of Justice Department lawyers began to draft a new and stronger civil rights bill. Since a major focus of both the sit-in movement and the Birmingham demonstrations had been the denial of commercial public facilities—chiefly eating places and hotels and motels —to Negroes, the key to the new bill was to be its provisions prohibiting racial discrimination in "public accommodations." Other sections incorporated and expanded the Administration's earlier proposals on voting, schools, and the Civil Rights Commission.

Meanwhile, the heightened public concern about civil rights was accompanied by a sharp increase in the expectations of the established civil rights organizations,[36] the intensified involvement of the labor movement in the civil rights struggle, and, of major importance, the entry into this field of the principal churches. In April, 1963 the papal encyclical, *Pacem in Terris,* had condemned racial discrimination. Two months later the National Council of Churches established its Commission on Religion and Race to coordinate Protestant activities in this field. All these groups saw that the changed climate of opinion offered a major opportunity to pass significant civil rights legislation. In July representatives of all the major interest groups met in New York, agreed to invest time, money, and effort to press for a strong civil rights bill, and decided to make the Leadership Conference on Civil Rights[37] a major lobbying organization with a considerable Washington staff.

Throughout May and early June, the Kennedy Administration deliberated on the civil rights problem: How big a commitment should it make to civil rights legislation and just what provisions should its draft bill include? The labor unions and civil rights groups put extremely heavy pressure on the Administration to include provision for FEPC. Because he feared that FEPC would be defeated and that asking for it would jeopardize chances of passing the rest of the legislation, President Kennedy finally decided to make a favorable reference to pending FEPC legislation in his message accompanying his bill but not to include an FEPC provision in the bill itself. Nor did the Administration's bill include another key part of the 1960 Democratic plank on civil rights:

36. The National Association for the Advancement of Colored People (NAACP) founded in 1909; the NAACP Legal Defense and Education Fund, founded in 1938; the National Urban League, founded in 1910; Congress of Racial Equality (CORE), founded in 1941; Southern Christian Leadership Conference (SCLC) founded in 1957 by the Rev. Martin Luther King, Jr.; Southern Regional Council, founded in 1942; Student Non-Violent Coordinating Committee (Snick) founded in 1960; and the Negro Labor Council, founded in 1960 by A. Philip Randolph.

37. Formed in 1949 as a coordinating agency for twenty civil rights groups, by 1963 it had seventy-nine participatory groups.

broad and general authority for the Attorney General to institute suits to enjoin denials of constitutional rights, a provision generally viewed as intended to protect civil rights demonstrators from violence and harassment by the police. The Administration had doubts as to the political and practical feasibility of such a broad provision and believed it wiser to deal directly with the conditions which provoked demonstrations than simply to protect the demonstrators. Thus it proposed more specific legislation authorizing the government to bring suit to desegregate schools and public accommodations.

The bill was submitted to Congress in mid-June. By this time Republicans in both House and Senate had introduced their own legislation, as had various Democratic Congressmen and Senators.

Several strategic considerations were clear: (1) The Administration's proposals would be the basis of the ensuing negotiations. (2) Since almost all Southern Congressmen and Senators could be counted on to oppose the legislation, success would hinge on many Republican votes, particularly in the Senate, where the votes of two thirds of the Senators who voted would be required to end the inevitable Southern filibuster. (3) Because the vote to close off debate would be so important, and because it would be much more difficult to get a cloture vote if Senators were not confident of the ultimate nature of the bill, it was advisable to obtain passage of the bill in the House first. Moreover, the difference in the relevant committees of the two houses also promised speedier action in the House. The Senate Judiciary Committee, to which the bill must go for hearings, was headed by James Eastland of Mississippi, an implacable opponent of civil rights; the three ranking Democrats were also Southerners. By contrast, the Chairman of the House Judiciary Committee was Emanuel Celler of New York, a friend of civil rights legislation.

The appraisal of the committees, and the need to start action first in the House, proved sound. The Senate Committee met eleven times in hearings on the Administration's bill, but for Senator Ervin of North Carolina, the leading constitutional expert among the Southerners, to question the Attorney General.

In the House, the key man was William McCulloch, a Representative from a rural Ohio district, and the ranking Republican on the Judiciary Committee. McCulloch, a cautious and generally conservative man, was also a supporter of civil rights. He was viewed as the key to gaining necessary Republican support and the Administration actively tried to enlist his help. Marshall and Nicholas deB. Katzenbach, the Deputy Attorney General, began to work closely with him in the belief that it was essential to build bipartisan support for the bill before it left the

Judiciary Committee. While McCulloch negotiated with Katzenbach and Marshall, he kept in close touch with Charles Halleck, the House Republican leader. McCulloch, out of concern that Republican Congressmen not be pushed out on a limb by voting for civil rights provisions which would be deleted in the Senate, insisted that the Administration agree not to weaken the bill passed by the House in order to make a deal with Southern Democratic Senators to get the bill through the Senate. The Administration agreed to McCulloch's demand. This meant, in effect, that it was agreeing not to press for provisions that had poor prospects of surviving a Senate filibuster.

The Leadership Conference, however, continued to insist on broadening coverage of the voting provisions (Title 1) and the public accommodations section (Title 2), strengthening the provision for the cut-off of federal funds (Title 6), and adding both FEPC and broad authority for the Attorney General to initiate suits. Together with many liberal Congressmen, particularly those active in the Democratic Study Group, they were opposed to the Administration's decision not only on substantive grounds but also for tactical reasons. The best strategy, they felt, was to press at every opportunity for the strongest possible bill in the belief that subsequent bargaining inevitably would cut back some provisions of the bill anyway.

All during the summer, then, the Administration was negotiating with the Republicans, a sympathetic subcommittee of the House Judiciary Committee was holding hearings and off-the-record executive sessions, and the civil rights lobbies were pressing vigorously for a stronger bill. Meanwhile, the church groups had added highly critical re-enforcements on a most strategic front, the largely rural, nonethnic, all-white Midwest and Rocky Mountain areas. The hard lobbying of the civil rights and labor organizations, the desire of several members of the subcommittee to avoid looking conservative on the issue, Democratic mistrust of the Republicans, and general impatience with the Administration's bipartisan strategy—all culminated in a 'revolt' of the Democratic members of the subcommittee. The subcommittee broadened the sections on voting and public accommodations and added two new parts, a strong FEPC provision and an increase in the authority of the Attorney General to initiate suits in order to prevent denial of constitutional rights. The bill was promptly reported to the full committee. Administration leaders were profoundly disturbed. The subcommittee's bill could not be passed, they believed, and it jeopardized crucial bipartisan support. Except for a few liberals, the Republicans were infuriated. McCulloch felt that he had been betrayed by Democrats seeking to embarrass the Republicans by making them look conservative on civil rights. Southerners were over-joyed; they, too, believed that the bill could not be passed; if it were reported out of the House Committee, it would be cut to pieces on the floor of the House, or recommitted, or both. But some liberal Democrats and their allies were also overjoyed.

The Administration held it essential to re-establish close relations with the Republicans. Both Halleck and McCulloch insisted that while they would continue to cooperate with the Administration, they would not allow themselves to be put in the position of appearing to be less favorable to civil rights than Democrats. Attorney General Robert Kennedy testified against the subcommittee's bill. McCulloch and Katzenbach worked out a compromise, substantially like their earlier bill, with one important exception. Katzenbach told the Republican leaders, Halleck and McCulloch, that the bill must include FEPC, for otherwise the Northern Democrats on the Committee would not support the bill. They then agreed on a somewhat milder version than the subcommittee had proposed.

After a month of negotiations, moves, counter-moves, claims of being double-crossed, conciliations, and close votes, the latest compromise was introduced to the full House Committee in late October, 1963, read in its entirety, discussed briefly by McCulloch and Celler, and reported out with strong bipartisan support.

The major outlines of the Committee bill were these: Title 1 on voting rights had been stripped of a key section providing for the early appointment of federal registrars of voters, and was fairly innocuous. Title 2 outlawing discrimination in public accommodations did not apply to all retail facilities, as the Leadership Conference had wished and as the Administration had originally proposed; nevertheless, it prohibited discrimination in most kinds of facilities where it had been a serious problem, and provided that desegregation could be enforced either by individual complaints or by initiatives taken by the Justice Department. In Title 3, the Attorney General was authorized to institute suits to protect some constitutional rights; but the broadest grant of the earlier bill, authorizing him to sue in order to prevent denial of any federal right was omitted. Title 4 dealt with desegregation of public schools. Title 5 preserved the Civil Rights Commission. Title 6 provided for cutting off federal funds from state and local programs which practised discrimination. Title 7 established an FEPC with powers to secure court enforcement for its orders. It was generally felt that Titles 6 or 7, or both, would have to be deleted in order to pass the bill in the Senate.

In November the bill was referred to that historic executioner, the

Rules Committee. For once, however, there seemed to be no real doubt that there were enough votes on the Committee to force the bill out of committee. Yet there was a serious question of timing. Partly in order to speed up Rules Committee proceedings and partly in order to embarrass the Republicans, the Democrats began circulating a petition requiring the Rules Committee to discharge the bill. The civil rights organizations, notably the church groups and unions, then stimulated a flood of letter-writing and other communications to Congressmen, who thus came under considerable pressure to sign the petition. Ultimately the pressure became so great that many Republicans who had not signed the petition began to be distressed, and prospects brightened that the petition would be successful. Anxious to avoid the ignominy of being forced to act by a successful discharge petition, Howard W. Smith, the chairman of the Rules Committee, gave in; the bill went to the floor of the House of Representatives in February, 1964.

Meanwhile, President Kennedy's assassination had put a Texan in the White House. Tragic as John F. Kennedy's death was and ominous as the succession of a Southerner to his office might have seemed for the fate of civil rights, President Johnson may have provided more vigorous and decisive leadership in behalf of a strong civil rights act than President Kennedy had done. The first President out of the South since Wilson and the second since the Civil War, President Johnson was aware that he labored under the handicap of being a Southerner and that he must demonstrate to the country and particularly to Negroes that he stood solidly for civil rights. With Kennedy, conciliation and compromise would be laid to political necessities; with Johnson, to lack of conviction. Johnson, therefore, had to be a more vigorous advocate than Kennedy had been. In addition, Johnson had acquired extraordinary skill and a reputation for unequalled success in dealing with Congress from his long years in the House and Senate.

In the House, the chief requirements were: first, to maintain the precious bipartisan support, and, second, to keep a sufficient number of friendly Congressmen present in the Committee of the Whole to maintain a constant majority on teller votes, which can be held at any time and which are over too quickly to permit Congressmen to arrive on the floor from their offices. Extraordinary efforts and a high level of coordination by the Democratic Study Group, the White House, the Justice Department, and the Leadership Conference maintained adequate majorities on the floor during the nine days of debate. The bill cleared the House without major difficulties or significant change; on the final vote, the bill passed 290–130. Northern Democrats supported the bill 141–4; Republicans 138–34. The greatest opposition was, of course, from Southern Democrats who opposed it 11–92.

It had been assumed all along that because of the filibuster, the Senate would be the more dangerous passage. The key man was the Republican Minority Leader, Senator Dirksen, who had announced the previous summer that he was opposed to Title 2, and therefore was thought to be opposed to Title 7 as well. It was assumed that if Senator Dirksen supported the bill, enough Republican Senators would join him to obtain cloture. The Senators in question were conservative Republicans from the Midwest and Rocky Mountains, who had neither Negroes nor many union members among their constituents. These regions were more important in the Senate than in the House, and it was here that the church groups in favor of civil rights became crucial. Although some western Democrats had customarily favored unlimited debate in the Senate and had never voted for cloture, it was nonetheless expected that the President's pressure could win them over.

Almost all of the interest groups actively concerned with the bill were in favor of it. The only lobby organization actively and openly opposed to the bill was the Coordinating Committee for Fundamental American Freedoms, which was run by a Mississippi lawyer, John Satterfield, and an experienced right-wing public relations man, John J. Synon, and had on its board of directors two or three well known conservative figures. Although most of its funds came from the Mississippi State Sovereignty Commission, not all of this money consisted of public funds of the State of Mississippi, since the Sovereignty Commission was a means for people outside the state to contribute without having their names recorded in Congress. The Coordinating Committee spent most of its time and money in extensive newspaper advertising and public relations campaigns in midwestern and western states, and made some unsuccessful attempts to enlist major business organizations in the fight against the bill. Most major business organizations, however, apparently believed that their basic economic interests were not directly involved, and active opposition to the entire bill could easily be harmful to them.

After a debate of some three weeks, the Southerners allowed the Senate to vote on the question of whether it would make the bill pending business without sending it to the Judiciary Committee, as normal procedure called for. A motion to refer the bill to the Judiciary Committee was then defeated and shortly thereafter the filibuster began. Southern strategy was to delay as long as possible and hope for a change in public opinion which would discourage Senator Dirksen from negotiating with the Administration. For his part, Dirksen refused initially to have any serious talks with the Administration, and some Southern Senators thought that he was sympathetic to them and would not give in without forcing the Administration to cripple the bill.

The manager of the bill in the Senate was Senator Humphrey, assisted by several other liberal Democratic and Republican Senators. If in previous years civil rights forces had been disorganized in their efforts to break the filibuster and haunted by a conviction of failure, in 1964 they were moderately confident and meticulously organized, with incessant coordination between administration strategists in the Senate and in the Justice Department. Since the filibusterers' favorite weapon was to suggest the absence of a quorum, which would stop proceedings until fifty-one Senators could be mustered, elaborate machinery was established to maintain quorums at all times while the Senate was in session. Humphrey's strategy was to make an extensive and continuing favorable case for the merits of the bill, to maintain enough organization of his forces to avoid embarrassing failures to meet quorums, to intensify public interest in and pressure for the bill, and to avoid doing anything to stigmatize Senator Dirksen as an enemy of civil rights. During the entire Senate consideration of the bill, President Johnson kept in the background; so far as can be discerned, after promptly making clear his firm commitment to the bill in his address to both houses of Congress, he did not play a major active role.

Senator Dirksen announced that he would introduce a number of amendments to the bill. In a confusing performance, over a period of several days Dirksen offered almost one hundred amendments. Altogether, these would have crippled or seriously limited most major sections of the bill. Negotiations took place between Dirksen, other Republicans, and spokesmen for the Administration. The eventual outcome was to make many minor or inconsequential changes, and several important ones; it was generally thought among fellow Senators that Dirksen was really interested in only two or three out of his innumerable amendments and that his whole performance had been motivated by a desire to 'leave his fingerprints on the bill'.

After an agreement was finally reached, the forces in favor of passing the bill moved to hold a vote on cloture early in June. There are some indications that supporters of Senator Goldwater's presidential candidacy won a postponement of the cloture vote until after the forthcoming presidential primary in California; Goldwater expected to vote against cloture, and his supporters felt, probably correctly, that his vote would damage his chances of winning that primary. (Incidentally, if the vote on cloture had preceded the primary, and if, as a result, Goldwater had lost in California, quite possibly he would have lost the nomination and the campaign of 1964 might have taken a markedly different turn.) Further difficulties arose with several conservative Republican Senators, some of whom were resentful of the role that Dirksen had played in the civil rights bill. They insisted on the opportunity to vote on three amendments before voting on cloture; their own votes in favor of cloture, they made manifest, were contingent on having this last opportunity to alter the bill. Neither the pro- nor anti-civil rights forces wanted to offend these Republicans, whose votes on cloture could be critical. As a consequence, another opportunity was provided for amending the bill. But the three amendments submitted by dissident Republicans did not represent major changes in the bill, and only one of them passed.

On June 10, 1964, for the twelfth time since 1938, the Senate was confronted with the opportunity to end debate on a civil rights measure in order to move on to a vote. But, for the first time, cloture won. With every member of the Senate present and voting, the motion to close debate won four more votes than the sixty-seven needed for a two thirds majority. The favorable votes came from forty-four Northern Democrats and twenty-seven Republicans; twenty-three Democrats (twenty from the South) and six Republicans constituted the defeated minority. Thus was the Southern filibuster finally halted.

After the critical vote on cloture, the Senate required 106 roll-call votes to complete action on the bill. The Senate accepted ten amendments and decisively rejected ninety-nine amendments offered by opponents of the bill. On June 19, exactly one year after the bill had been submitted to Congress by President Kennedy and ninety-nine years after Appomattox, the Senate passed the bill by a vote of 73–27. The opponents were twenty-one Southern and border-state Democrats and six Republicans, including the imminent Republican candidate for President, Senator Goldwater.

The Senate's bill was promptly passed by the House without change (thereby avoiding a conference committee) and signed by President Johnson on July 2 in the East Room of the White House while millions of television viewers looked on. The reasons for the discrimination that had made the Civil Rights Act of 1964 a necessity, the President said upon signing, "are deeply imbedded in history and tradition and the nature of man. We can understand—without rancor or hatred—how this happened. But it cannot continue."

Thus, it is no exaggeration to say, an era came to an end, and another began. The power of the South to block civil rights laws in Congress was broken. But if the Civil Rights Act marked an end of one era, it was, in spite of all the effort that had been required to pass it, only a beginning of the new.

The four cases examined in this chapter are a tiny sample. No four cases can be said to typify the unspeakably vast range and variety of policy-making and political action in the American system. These four cases will serve, however, to illustrate many of the points presented in more abstract fashion in the last chapter; the interaction of some of the major political institutions and forces described separately in Part Two of this book; the play of easily overlooked factors like personal disposition, skill, and accident; and something of the extraordinary complexity and variety of forces at work in making American national policies.

Several additional points may need emphasizing. Success or failure in securing adoption of a policy seems to depend on historical circumstances which an individual can manipulate and modify only in part. Ten years earlier Gideon would doubtless have lost his case. In the 1920s, when protectionism was the dominant ideology, the doctrine of free trade was expounded by a fiery and seemingly insignificant and powerless minority of academic economists. If the Republicans had won the congressional elections of 1954, Dixon-Yates might have stood. For decades, Congress resisted civil rights legislation; passage in 1964 came only after a tidal change in public attitudes, brought on by a collection of events and circumstances beyond the power of any one person to shape, control, or even channel.

Success, if it ever arrives, often takes years; many defeats may occur during the intervening generations. An idea born out of its time may struggle desperately to survive.

Considered in this perspective, the citizen interested in political action may feel himself to be a helpless victim of forces over which he can exert no control. As a result he may be tempted to believe that there are no alternatives to naked opportunism or alienation and despair.

This, I think, is too one-sidedly pessimistic a view of man's fate. It is true, as these cases illustrate, that no one individual, even the President of the United States, can master all the forces necessary to guarantee success in policy-making. In a democratic republic numbering several hundred million people, it could not—and surely should not—be otherwise. But what these cases also suggest is that in important ways changes in policy depend on the actions of individuals: on their skill, knowledge, resolution, persistence. The day of victory may be long in coming; for some ideas that day may never dawn. But unless individuals were to act, like Gideon, in the confident expectation that their actions had significance, if not now at least some day, then the changes we all witness in our own times would, surely, never occur.

17

ALTERNATIVE STRATEGIES
FOR POLITICAL ACTIVISTS

THE AMERICAN POLITICAL SYSTEM does not encourage or even facilitate revolutionary changes; obviously no stable political systems
do. Comprehensive changes in government policies do sometimes
occur in the United States, as in the period of Republican innovation
during and after the Civil War or in the New Deal period of the 1930s.
But even compehensive changes are, as we have seen, uncommon. The
typical pattern of American politics is one of stability, moderate conflict,
and incremental change.

Suppose then, that a body of American citizens wishes to bring
about changes in government policies by peaceful and democratic methods. How can such a body proceed?

There are, roughly speaking, four strategies available to a political
movement in the United States:

1. The movement can organize a separate political party of its
own.
2. The movement can form a new coalition party by combining
with another group or movement that has similar, overlapping,
but not identical objectives.
3. Although it remains neutral between the two major parties, the
movement can act as a pressure group to secure favorable legislation and the nomination and election of sympathetic candidates.
4. By entering into one of the existing parties, the movement can

[429]

become an element in a major party coalition; it can then use
its bargaining power to gain influence for the movement within
the party.

Each of these alternatives has its own inner logic, its special advantages and disadvantages. Perhaps this is why all four strategies have been tried so often. The first strategy has been tried by Free Soilers, Socialists, Greenbackers, Communists, Prohibitionists, Single Taxers, America Firsters, Vegetarians, and the Church of God Party, among others. The first strategy enables a movement to maintain its ideological purity and avoid compromising its goals. Yet the usual price is political isolation, defeat, and ineffectuality. The second strategy helps a movement break out of its isolation; but in doing so the movement may lose at least some of its purity and still fail to become a major party. The second strategy was that of the Populists, until they went all the way in 1896 and backed the Democratic candidate, Bryan. It was also the strategy of Progressive movements in 1924 and 1948. The third strategy may yield high pay-off if the goals of the movement are narrow and group-oriented. But as a price, the movement must do nothing to alienate the major parties. This is the strategy of most pressure groups; in some states and localities it has also been the strategy of third parties, like the Liberal Party in New York. The fourth strategy may yield a movement more influential over a greater range of goals than the third strategy, a better chance of winning elections than the second strategy. The price, however, is a willingness to negotiate, to bargain, to compromise in order to form a winning coalition, and to run the risk of turning members of the other party into opponents. This is the strategy that some unions have adopted at the state level, like the United Automobile Workers in Michigan. It was also the strategy the Populists were moving toward when they supported Bryan in 1896.

Weighing the advantages and disadvantages of the four alternatives is a recurrent task in American politics. Few choices are so important to the destiny of a political movement. It is instructive, therefore, to examine the experience of a movement that has had to face these four alternatives. An obvious candidate is the American labor movement, for from its earliest years down to the present day the labor movement has debated the pros and cons of the various strategies. As in so many other cases, Americans once again chose a path different from that taken in most European countries. Yet the debate over alternatives is not yet ended; perhaps it never will be.

Democracy and the Proletariat

Not only in the Western world but throughout much of the globe, industrialization has gone hand in hand with the growth of cities and the rapid expansion of the urban working classes. A nation of traders and farmers, as Britain still remained in the eighteenth century, was already well on the road to becoming a nation of urban employers and urban workers before the end of the nineteenth century. If the United States began as a nation of farmers and if, as a result, Americans have not yet wholly given up a romantic assessment of the virtues of rural life, the country was nonetheless destined to become a nation of urban workers, white collar employees, technicians, and businessmen.

The Civil War not only stimulated the growth of Northern industry but liberated economic development from the dead hand of Southern slavocracy. In the last half of the nineteenth century, the proportion of Americans employed in commerce and industry rose steadily as the proportion in farming declined. By 1880 farmers and farm workers outnumbered nonfarm workers. By 1930 the urban population exceeded the rural population. Between 1910–20 the absolute number of farmers reached its peak and thereafter the total number of farmers steadily declined. By 1960, farmers and farm workers were only about 8 per cent of the gainfully employed.

The workers who were employed in urban industries represented a new class. It was all too obvious that they were not farmers, even if they might once have been farmers, farm laborers, or peasants who had come to the cities from an American or European countryside. They were not middle class. They were not, at least to any great extent, property owners. They were definitely not employers. Nor were they small businessmen. Huddled in the cities, often living in execrable slums, working long hours, with little or no protection from the hazards of unemployment, illness, injury, and old age, they constituted a new and separate interest in society, a social and economic class. On this point, Marx said no more than what was widely assumed in his time.

In the nineteenth century, not only Marx but many other observers took it for granted that the relative expansion of the industrial working classes would continue more or less indefinitely. A few observers like the German socialist critic of Marx, Eduard Bernstein, foresaw that industry and commerce might also expand the size of the white-collar classes. Bernstein, it turned out, was closer to the truth than Marx. The propor-

[431]

Table 17.1.   Rise of the White-Collar Strata, Decline of
Farmers and Blue-Collar Strata—1900–1963

White-collar strata:	1900	1963
Professional, technical and kindred workers	4.2%	12.0%
Managers, Officials, and Proprietors	5.9	10.6
Clerical, sales, and kindred workers	7.5	21.2
Total	17.6%	43.8%
Blue-collar strata:		
Craftsmen, foremen and kindred workers	10.6%	13.0%
Operatives and laborers	25.2	23.4
Total	35.8%	36.4%
Service and household workers	9.0	13.2
Farmers and farm laborers	37.6	6.7
TOTAL	100.0%	100.0%

Sources: 1963, *Congress and the Nation*, 586
1900, *Historical Statistics*, Series D 72-122, p. 74.

tion of blue-collar workers, the authentic proletariat, would rise less
rapidly than the proportion with white-collar occupations. Between 1910–
1920 this trend showed up markedly in the most advanced industrial

FIGURE 17.1—GROWTH OF THE WHITE COLLAR WORKER, 1950-1964

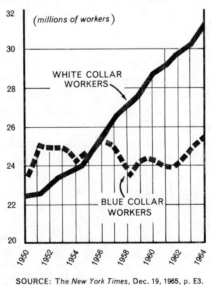

SOURCE: The *New York Times*, Dec. 19, 1965, p. E3.

[432]

nation, the United States, though the full political significance of the development is far clearer in retrospect than it was to most observers at the time. In the mid-1950s, the white-collar strata began to outnumber the historic 'working class' (Table 17.1 and Figure 17.1).

Nonetheless, during the half century or so following the American Civil War, it was not unreasonable to hold that urban working classes constituted a distinct political, social, and economic stratum with interests antagonistic to much of the rest of industrial society. To many people in both Europe and America it was an open question whether these two strata, the working classes and the newer business classes—employers, industrialists, bankers, traders, investors, and executives and professionals of many sorts—could live at peace in the same political system. Anyone concerned with the future of democracy might well have wondered whether the allegiance of both strata could be won to democracy and to an agreed set of constitutional principles. For how could either of the two strata peacefully accept the principles of majority rule and constitutional decision-making if this meant that spokesmen for the other stratum, apparently their natural enemies, might determine policy?

Patterns of Successful Democracy:
Europe vs. America

In some countries, democratic ideas and institutions failed to win enough allegiance from both strata; from a democratic point of view, the results were disastrous. One of the most advanced industrial countries in the world, Germany, and two of the least industrialized in Europe, Italy and Spain, plummeted into violence, dictatorship, and war. In France, the urban proletariat developed into a country within a country, hostile, resentful, alienated, and after the Second World War predominantly Communist.

Yet in most countries with sturdy traditions of constitutionalism and representative government, the conflict eventuated in a victory for democracy. These countries include a number of north European nations like Britain, Norway, Sweden, Denmark, Holland, and Belgium, and the English-speaking democracies of Australia, Canada, New Zealand—and the United States.

There were conflicts, often severe, over economic issues. Yet these conflicts were settled peacefully, and in the end the allegiance of the population to democracy was held or won.

In the United States, as in the north European countries, conflicts over economic issues were often harsh and brutal. "Violence in labor disputes," a leading student of the subject has said, "is more common in the United States than in any other industrial nation."[1] Not only was violence more common; in the United States labor conflicts took on a ferocity seldom equalled in Europe. An authority on both the French and American labor movements has remarked that "American workers had to fight bloodier battles than the French for the right of unions to exist and to function."[2] Nonetheless, despite occasional setbacks and fierce opposition from employers, union membership grew from 447 thousand in 1897 to over two million in 1904.[3]

Government and employers frequently formed a coalition against workers. State governments, and on occasion even the federal government, were brought into industrial disputes. In the strike of the American Railway Union against the Pullman Company in 1894, the U.S. Attorney General Richard Olney who had formerly been a railroad lawyer sought an injunction in Federal Court against Eugene V. Debs and other strike leaders on the ground that the strike interfered with the mails and interstate commerce and violated the Sherman Anti-Trust Law. The Federal Court issued a sweeping order against the strike leaders. When the U.S. Marshall claimed that he was unable to enforce the court order, Olney persuaded President Cleveland to send federal troops to Chicago, although neither the Mayor of Chicago nor the liberal governor of Illinois, Atgeld, had requested federal help and both protested against the presence of the troops. Extensive rioting erupted. The strike failed. "It was not the soldiers that ended the strike," Debs concluded; ". . . . it was simply the United States courts." Debs was sentenced to six months in jail for contempt of court, and three other strike leaders to three months.[4] Later, Debs was to run five times as candidate for Presi-

1. Philip Taft, "Violence in American Labor Disputes," *The Annals of the American Academy of Political and Social Science*, 364 (March, 1966) 127–140, esp. 128.

2. Val R. Lorwin, "Reflections on the History of the French and American Labor Movement," *Journal of Economic History* (March, 1957), p. 37.

3. Philip Taft, *Organized Labor in American History*, New York, Harper and Row, 1964, p. 162.

4. See Taft, *ibid.*, pp. 148–158, for a description of the strike, and the statement by Debs.

dent on the Socialist ticket. It is altogether likely—and fitting—that Debs became a Socialist while he was serving his prison sentence.[5]

In the United States and the north European countries, reforms in capitalism tended to come in bunches, usually as a result of elections that put reform administrations in office. In the United States the main waves of reform came about twenty years apart: Wilson's New Freedom from 1913–1916, Franklin Roosevelt's New Deal from 1933–1937, and the Kennedy-Johnson program from 1961 onward and particularly after the overwhelming Democratic sweep in the 1964 election.

By the beginning of the final third of the twentieth century, the results of reforms were in many ways similar in both the United States and Europe: a good many levers of economic control in the hands of governments; a mixed economy regulated by a vast variety of different instruments—trust-busting, competition, regulatory commissions, public corporations, government contracts, government ownership, fiscal measures, monetary controls; extensive expenditures for a broad range of welfare purposes; large national organizations of employers, farmers, workers, and countless numbers of more specialized interests; and strong interest-group organization and participation in policy-making. There were differences, too, and some of these were important. Thus by 1960 the distribution of incomes was much closer to equality in Australia, New Zealand, Britain, and Norway than in the United States—whereas the distribution of wealth was somewhat more equal in the United States than in Britain.[6]

In none of these countries, however, did unregulated, politically uncontrolled, laissez-faire capitalism exist. Nor, on the other hand, were these economies 'socialist'. The economies were politicized, oriented toward welfare and high consumption, but a major share of production and distribution was not carried on by government-owned enterprise. Indeed, by 1960 the democratic socialist parties of Western Europe had abandoned nationalization of industry as a goal and advocated concrete

5. On Debs' conversion to socialism, see Ira Kipnis, *The American Socialist Movement 1897–1912*, New York, Columbia University Press, 1952, p. 47.
6. On income distribution, see Bruce M. Russett *et al.*, *World Handbook of Political and Social Indicators*, New Haven, Yale University Press, 1964, Tables 71, 72, pp. 245–246. On property distribution in Britain and the United States see H. F. Lydall and D. G. Tipping, "The Distribution of Personal Wealth in Britain." *Bulletin of the Oxford University Institute of Statistics*, 13 (1961), 97. Robert J. Lampman, *The Share of Top Wealth-Holders in National Wealth 1922–1956*, Princeton, N. J., Princeton University Press, 1962, pp. 210–215.

programs distinguishable only in details from platforms adopted at their national conventions by the Democratic Party in the United States. If by the 1960s working class movements in the United States and in many parts of Europe had reached a rather similar destination, they had arrived by distinctly different routes. In Europe the typical path led to the first and second strategies: formation of a separate and independent labor or socialist party that ultimately became one of the major governing parties and helped to bring about extensive reforms. The American labor movement deliberately and with full awareness that it was deviating from the path of European labor chose a different route. It explicitly and self-consciously rejected the first and second strategies. For many decades it favored the third strategy, political neutrality. Then from the time of the New Deal onward, the fourth alternative has more and more become the policy of key labor unions and the unofficial policy of the AFL-CIO.

U.S.: HOME OF UNSUCCESSFUL WORKING-CLASS PARTIES. Surprising as it may seem, the first authentic party of the urban working classes was born not in Europe but in the United States. Called the Working Men's Party, it was organized in Philadelphia in 1828 and lasted about three years.[7] After the Civil War, a number of American socialists affiliated themselves with the First International. Socialist parties proliferated in what now seems a bewildering profusion of names, programs, and ideologies: in 1875 the Social-Democratic Party of North America dominated by followers of Lassalle, the German socialist and rival of Marx; in 1875 the Working Men's Party of the United States, a coalition of Lassalleans and Marxists, which the following year became the Socialist Labor Party of North America; in 1883, the International Working People's Association, a union of militant revolutionary socialists and anarchists; in 1897 the Social Democracy of America; in 1901, the Socialist Party. In every presidential election since 1892 voters in most states have had an opportunity to vote for socialist candidates for the presidency. But the socialist vote never went beyond 6 per cent of the total votes cast (1912), and finally all but died out.

The Pattern of Conflict

Why did the first strategy, which succeeded in many European democracies, fail in the United States? It was not for lack of conflict

7. Philip Taft, *Organized Labor in American History*, New York, Harper and Row, 1964, pp. 15–20.

over capitalism, the role of government, and the power of labor and business in society and the economy. As we have already seen, the relations between workers and employers frequently displayed the most visible symbol of severe conflict—violence. Moreover, two more of the principal conditions of severe conflict were also present: *conflicting views* on matters involving *high stakes*.

In describing the conflict between labor and business we are handicapped, as we were with slavery, by the lack of good data on attitudes and views among the general public or among urban laborers and businessmen. What we have instead are expressions by leaders in politics, speeches and party platforms, statements in the press, demands presented by interest groups such as the AFL, the Farm Bureau Federation, the National Association of Manufacturers.

In the conflicts between these spokesmen, the stakes have never been insignificant and often they have been high. Who is entitled to control decisions on wages, working conditions, and personnel? According to what standards? How and by what standards are prices and employment to be regulated? How shall incomes be distributed? Who is to be protected and who harmed by government intervention? Whose freedom is to be expanded or reduced? These are the weightier if not always visible stakes involved in disputes over the role of labor unions, regulation of business, antitrust, the forms and incidence of taxes, welfare measures, monetary, fiscal, tariff, and agricultural policies.

At times, important blocs of national leaders have diverged widely on these issues: in the 1890s, certainly, and again in the 1930s. From all the evidence at hand, both decades were periods of severe conflict. During both periods there was a sharp divergence of views; and during both periods the stakes were high. (To repeat a point made earlier, the leaders involved obviously *thought* the stakes were high, and for our purposes that is all that matters.)

Yet the conflict was never successfully pressed by a distinct labor party nor a party bearing a classic socialist ideology and program. The political conflicts occurred between and within parties that were conglomerate coalitions, coalitions that lacked ideologies as distinct as European socialism was from European liberalism or conservatism.

No doubt the absence of a labor party with a socialist ideology and program as a major competitor of the other parties helped to keep down the size of the stakes involved in American politics. The absence of a powerful socialist party also meant that political views did not diverge so sharply as in the north European democracies. Yet it is worth noting again that even if the northern European countries took a different route

FIGURE 17.2—SECULAR GROWTH OF REAL NATIONAL INCOME
PER HEAD IN U. S. A. AND GREAT BRITAIN (1929 PRICES)

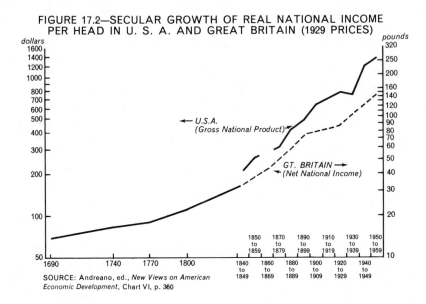

SOURCE: Andreano, ed., *New Views on American Economic Development*, Chart VI, p. 360

they arrived at roughly the same place as the United States. Their socialist parties gradually abandoned much of the distinctively socialist ideology they had begun with; they turned pragmatic and reformist *a l'Americain;* they gave up the classic socialist instrument, nationalization of industry; and they became, or tried hard to become, conglomerate catchall parties uniting urban labor with rural labor, white-collar workers, farmers, fishermen, government employees.

The United States did not then, avoid sharp and sometimes severe conflicts over economic issues; yet it did skip a transitional stage that was universal among the northern European democracies and quite possibly essential to their success in winning over business and labor to democratic institutions and a common set of constitutional procedure. Why did the United States and Europe diverge? Why did labor-socialist parties fail to thrive in the United States?

One part of the answer is perhaps to be found in the fact that while the stakes were high in the United States, the contest was not 'zero-sum'. An expanding economy created an ever available surplus to be distributed.[8] Gross National Product and personal consumption grew faster than population; from 1839–1959 they increased at the rate of

8.   David Potter, *People of Plenty*, Chicago, University of Chicago Press, 1957.

Table 17.2. Trend of Gross National Product and Personal
Consumption, 1839–1959: Percentage Increase per Year.*

	ENTIRE PERIOD	FORTY-YEAR PERIODS		
	1839–1959	1839–	1879–	1919–
	%	%	%	%
Gross National Product				
Aggregate, constant prices	3.66	4.31	3.72	2.97
per head, " "	1.64	1.55	1.76	1.64
Personal Consumption				
Aggregate, constant prices			3.68	3.17
Per full consumer, constant prices			1.64	1.85

*Calculated from values in first and last year of period.
SOURCE: Raymond W. Goldsmith, "Long Period Growth in Income and Product,
1839-1960" in Andreano, ed., *New Views on American Economic Development*, 1965.

about 1.6 per cent a year per capita (Table 17.2). These seemingly
modest rates amounted to a doubling about every forty years, a five-fold
increase in a century (Figures 17.2, 17.3, 17.4). Working-class hostilities
were vastly weakened by rising living standards; it took major depres-
sions, as in 1893-1894 and the Great Depression after 1929 to deepen
hostilities to a point where the working strata could be mobilized to
support extensive reforms.

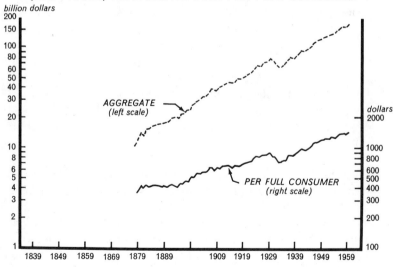

FIGURE 17.3—PERSONAL CONSUMPTION EXPENDITURES
(1929 PRICES) AGGREGATE AND PER FULL CONSUMER

FIGURE 17.4—THE TREND IN REAL GROSS NATIONAL PRODUCT PER HEAD, 1839-1959

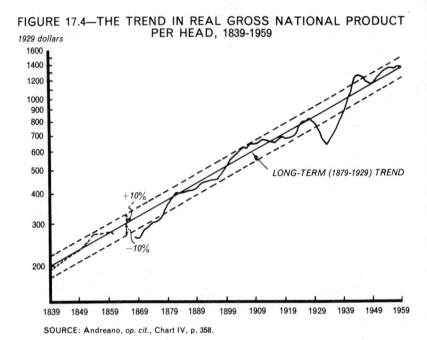

SOURCE: Andreano, *op. cit.,* Chart IV, p. 358.

Yet the European economies were also expanding (Figure 17.2). And it is often argued with persuasive evidence that revolutionary movements prosper most when improving conditions stimulate hope and confidence. Hence to call on the expanding American economy to explain the inability of a labor-socialist party to grow in the United States is not a wholly satisfactory explanation. Was it then because the fruits of economic growth came earlier in the United States than in Europe? Possibly, but there were other differences.

To what extent is the explanation, or a part of it, to be found in the other two sets of factors described in Chapter 10, as influencing the course of political conflict: the pattern of cleavage and the political institutions?

CLEAVAGES. As to cleavages, it seems clear that a pattern of overlapping cleavages was never fully displaced by a pattern of superimposed cleavages cumulating along a single fault-line. One cannot be dead sure that the overlapping cleavages were greater in the United States than in the European democracies, but there is an impressive amount of evidence suggesting that they were, and that in any event neither workers nor businessmen were sharply cut off from one another or from the rest of American society.

Three factors helped to maintain a pattern of overlapping cleavage lines even during times of considerable stress. One of these was the extraordinary consensus among Americans on a number of basic ideological issues. In Europe, the socialist parties often battled for democracy against their 'bourgeois' opponents; it was the socialists, often, who fought for parliamentary government, cabinet responsibility, and an equal and universal suffrage. In Norway and Sweden, for example, in the early stages, socialist and middle-class parties fought more over democracy than over socialism. In the United States this ideological, institutional, and constitutional conflict had been pretty well settled before the urban laboring population began to expand. The American labor movement of the 1880s and 1890s did not have to fight for political democracy; the institutions of political democracy were already here and a democratic ideology widely accepted. To be sure, the constitutional structure was at stake in the Civil War, but it was never again seriously contested. The labor movement joined in the broad consensus on democracy that has been such a pronounced aspect of American life. What is more, the labor movement never mounted a strong opposition even to the traditions of private property and competitive self-advancement.

Another factor that helped to maintain overlapping cleavages was the fact that class lines were weaker than in Europe, while other cleavages were relatively strong. The "solidarity of the working classes" predicted by Marx was weakened in the United States by ethnic differences, language, religion, and region. In many cities where the socialist parties drew most of their proletarian strength from the foreign born, the very parties that most strongly stressed the importance of working-class solidarity had to establish separate branches to accommodate their different and sometimes unfriendly ethnic groups.

Finally, the course of American economic development doomed both labor and business, like all other economic interests, to remain minorities. Until 1880, urban workers were outnumbered by farmers. Yet when the number of farmers began to decline, the number of white-collar workers rose. Hence a party that drew its support exclusively or even mainly from urban labor could not hope to win majorities in national elections. Businessmen were equally condemned to minority status. Owners and executives of business firms were bound to be outnumbered by their employees. Hence they too could not hope to win majorities in national elections with a party that appealed only to businessmen.

Operation of the Political Institutions

The political institutions also offered a powerful and quite possibly a decisive resistance to the creation of a successful labor-socialist party or even a labor-farmer coalition.

First of all, the institutions of federalism made it risky for the labor movement to identify itself exclusively with a single party. The failure of the Working Men's Party of Philadelphia in the early 1830s taught labor leaders the disadvantages of a workingmen's party.[9] For in a federal system many of the specific aims of labor could be achieved more quickly through state action than by federal laws. A separate party which ran candidates against those of the major parties would antagonize state legislators otherwise responsive to demands made on them by workingmen's organizations. A leading student of American labor history has written:

> Only a state legislature could compel defaulting employers to pay wages earned, impose safety rules on hazardous occupations, and define minimum sanitary standards in work places. The state legislatures prescribed standards for schooling, voting, and minimum ages for working, the employment of women, and limitations of hours of labor in certain occupations. . . . Union representatives appealing for legislative concessions understood that frequently only a beginning in the reform of a given problem could be made, and they were usually confident that additional improvements could be subsequently introduced. They also knew that the great majority of legislators were not ideologically committed to or opposed to many pieces of legislation sought by organized labor, and the members of legislative assemblies would respond to the pleas and pressures at slow or rapid rates depending upon the problem and the forces arrayed against labor on a particular issue. Promotion of an independent labor party would have necessitated the sever-

9. Taft, op. cit., p. 19: "According to Professor Frank T. Carelton, the Working Men's party of New York made an important indirect contribution to future labor tactics. 'When in 1833–1837, the strong trade union movement arose, the fate of the Working Men's Party was accepted as a conclusive argument against direct political effort. Hence the trade unions kept aloof from party politics and merely questioned candidates as to their position on measures which were regarded as affecting the interests of labor.' Frank T. Carelton, 'The Working Men's Party of New York City,' *Political Science Quarterly* (September 1902), p. 415."

ance of relations with many members of the legislatures, who, assured of organized labor's political hostility, would have been more reluctant to support the bills labor annually or biennially presented to the legislatures.[10]

Thus the strategies of the American labor movement were shaped, during its formative years, by the political realities of the federal system.

In the second place, there was the sobering matter of the election system, the effects of which we have already explored. In no country in Europe did the labor-socialist parties ever manage to gain a majority of popular votes. But they did obtain the introduction of systems of proportional representation, which reduced or eliminated the multiplier effect of the winner-take-all system. In the United States, not only in national but also in state elections, the single-member district and the winner-take-all system had depressing consequences for a third party trying to make its way against the two existing giants. The evidence of American experience was clear enough to anyone who cared to examine it: For a third party to cross the magic threshold to major party status was a formidable, discouraging, and probably hopeless task.

It is true that in Britain, which was also a two-party country, the Labor Party in the 1920s became the main opposition party; and though it never acquired an absolute majority of popular votes in subsequent elections, thanks to the winner-take-all system it has gained a majority of seats in the House of Commons on four occasions—1945, 1950, 1964, and 1966. The majority it won in 1945 enabled the Labor Party to carry out most of the program it had developed since 1918. However, by the time the successful experience of British Labor became available as an example to encourage the advocates of a separate labor party in the United States, that strategy had long since been firmly rejected by the American labor movement.

In any event, another aspect of American political life greatly reduced the relevance of British experience with the Labor Party. This was the fact that the urban workers had already been won over to the two existing parties before the American labor movement itself developed.

As the number of urban workers multiplied rapidly after the Civil War, there were already on the scene two major parties accustomed to assimilating workers into their organizations. In Europe, in Britain, in the Scandinavian countries and elsewhere in Europe working men faced

---

10. Philip Taft, "Labor History and the Labor Issues of Today," *Proceedings of the American Philosophical Society*, 106 (August, 1962), 306. See also the same author's "On the Origins of Business Unionism," *Industrial and Labor Relations Review*, 17 (October, 1963), 20–38.

existing parties—Liberals, Conservatives, and the like—which were run by members of the middle classes and the aristocracy. These middle-class parties had little or no grass-roots organizations extending down to the wards and precincts. They lacked the kind of organization that was created for American parties during Jefferson's Presidency, perfected during Jackson's, and adopted as a matter of course by the newly organized Republican Party in the late 1850s. In Europe the middle class and aristocratic parties could ignore the urban workers, for workers were deprived of the suffrage.[11] But in the United States, where the working classes had enjoyed the franchise from the early decades of the nineteenth century, to ignore these potential voters would have been political stupidity of a sort alien to party politicians. The urban machines of the Democratic Party were particularly adept at using primitive social welfare devices to gain the votes and often the permanent loyalties of immigrants. Thus, unlike Europe, in the United States there was no vacuum into which a labor party could rush.

The Democratic and Republican parties not only had the advantages of organization; they also profited from the crushing inertia of established party loyalties. A successful labor party would need more than a program or an ideological appeal to workers; to be successful a labor party would first have to break down well established attachments to one of the existing parties. There was nothing peculiar to the mentality of a worker (despite the romantic notions of some socialists) that inhibited him more than other citizens from incurring emotional ties to the Democratic or the Republican Party.

A realistic appraisal of the American political scene, then, would lead inexorably to the conclusion that the two major parties could not be thrust aside by a labor party organized by the labor movement.

11. In Britain, a substantial proportion of urban working class householders were enfranchised in 1867–68; further reforms enlarged the franchise in 1884; virtually universal male suffrage came in 1918. It has been estimated that "perhaps one in twelve adult males could vote before 1832, one in seven thereafter, one in three after 1868, and three in five after 1884: Allen Potter, "Great Britain: Opposition with a Capital 'O'," in Robert A. Dahl, ed., *Political Oppositions in Western Democracies*, New Haven, Yale University Press, 1965, p. 3. The dates for universal equal manhood suffrage in some other European countries were: Norway, 1898; Sweden, 1909; Denmark, 1901; The Netherlands, 1917; Belgium, 1919; France, 1848; Prussia, 1919; Germany, 1867; Italy, 1912.

Difficulties in the Second Strategy

There was, however, another possibility: a coalition party drawing its strength from both farmers and urban workers. This strategy was doubly tempting, for the farmers of South and West were much more responsive than labor itself, oddly enough, to new parties that advocated labor-socialist programs. Even the Socialist Party, although organized and led mainly by urban socialists, gained more electoral support in the agricultural states than in the industrial states. In 1912 at the high-water mark of the Socialist vote, Eugene V. Debs, the Socialist candidate for President, received 5.9 per cent of the national vote. The highest percentage he won in any state was 16.6 per cent which he won in—of all states —Oklahoma. The five other states in which Debs won more than 10 per cent of the vote were Nevada, Montana, Washington, California, and Idaho—none at this time a highly industrial state.

The greatest success for the strategy of a farmer-labor coalition—and the most consequential failure—was achieved by the Populists in the 1890s. As we have seen, the period from 1892–1896 marked a series of critical elections in which party loyalties were re-aligned for over three decades. The defeat of Bryan in 1896 amounted to a profound defeat not only for Populism but for the prospects of a new third party that would unite farmers with labor in a powerful national coalition.

Even though industrial labor and farmers constituted a shrinking proportion of the electorate, proponents of the farmer-labor strategy did not wholly die out. Both farmers and urban wage earners were injured in the economic turbulence of the usual cycle of inflation and depression that followed the First World War. In 1920 a combination of socialists, trade unionists, and liberals organized a Farmer-Labor Party that nominated a presidential slate; however it gained only 265 thousand votes— less than a third of the perennial Socialist Party total and barely more than the Prohibition Party.

Although "the Farmer-Labor Party did not attract many top labor or agricultural leaders,"[12] during the next few years a far more serious effort was launched, mainly on the initiative of trade union leaders, and these chiefly in the railway unions. Their instrument, the Committee for Progressive Political Action, nominated Senator Robert M. LaFollette, a nationally known Progressive Republican, as their presidential candidate;

12. Taft, *Organized Labor in American History*, p. 384.

as his vice presidential running mate the Committee selected a well known progressive Democrat from Montana, Burton K. Wheeler. Despite the fact that the American Federation of Labor had not sponsored the Committee for Progressive Political Action nor proposed the nomination of a third-party slate, in a departure from standing policy the executive board of the AFL publicly endorsed the election of LaFollette and Wheeler.[13]

Although LaFollette and Wheeler carried only LaFollette's home state of Wisconsin, they won 4.8 million votes, or 16 per cent of the total, and they ran second in eleven states. As in the past, the Progressive candidates won their biggest share of the votes in rural, not industrial states. In 1925 the Committee for Progressive Political Action was dissolved.[14]

In 1948, a group of liberals and communists organized the Progressive Party and nominated as its presidential candidate the well known New Dealer, the one-time Secretary of Agriculture and ex-Vice President, Henry Wallace. The Progressive Party was a sad caricature of the authentic farmer-labor parties that had preceded it. The national labor movements opposed it. The AFL maintained its traditional policy of neutrality, though in fact its leaders were hostile. The head of the CIO's political organization announced that it had been "the Policy of the CIO Political Action Committee not to support a third party." The CIO Executive Board decided by 33–11 that "it was politically unwise to inject a third party into the political scene of 1948." In late August, the CIO Executive Board endorsed the Democratic presidential slate of Truman and Barkley. Deprived of trade union support and leadership, the Progressive Party and Wallace's candidacy became little more than an instrument of the Communist Party. In the election of 1948, Wallace was crushed; not only did he fail to carry a single state but he actually won fewer votes than a dissenting group on the Right, the States' Rights Party, managed to pick up in the South.

With the passage of time, the prospects for a separate farmer-labor party have been dimmed beyond hope by the facts of economic growth. In 1964 less than one person out of four in the total United States working force was a member of a trade union; only four persons out of ten in the working force were farmers, farm laborers, or blue-collar workers. No party that attended exclusively or even primarily to the interests of labor and farmers, and ignored the claims of service and white-collar workers, could hope to become a majority party.

13. *Ibid.*, p. 387.
14. *Ibid.*, p. 388.

The Third and Fourth Strategies

It was not from want of a fair trial, then, that the first two strategies were rejected. Nor was it from any failure to consider the pros and cons of each alternative. For decades, in fact, socialists and others who advocated comprehensive social and economic reforms and an independent labor or farmer-labor party put their case during the annual meetings of the AFL. The discussions were highly sophisticated; it is doubtful whether working class leaders in any other country more thoroughly canvassed the consequences of the various alternatives. The first leader of the AFL, Samuel Gompers, a social radical in his native England in his youth, knew the arguments for third-party action; he heard them again and again; but he rejected them as inapplicable to the American scene.

At the first conventions of the AFL in the late 1880s and the 1890s, the question was argued out. The AFL then adopted the position from which it has never deviated:[15] It rejected an independent party of workers and instead chose to be neutral as between the major parties, to endorse candidates favorable to the labor movement, and to secure favorable legislative and administrative action by pressure-group activities.[16] As the controversy over Populism approached its peak in 1895, the annual convention of the AFL declared that "party politics, whether they be democratic, republican, socialist, populistic, prohibition or any other, should have no place in the convention."[17]

The AFL adopted one more position of some importance: It permitted complete autonomy on political matters to the constituent unions and to state and local federations. These departed more frequently than the parent body from the practice of political neutrality, but even they were politically neutral more often than not.

Although leaders of the labor movement pretty consistently found the Democratic Party more sympathetic to their demands than the Republicans,[18] so long as the Republicans were the dominant party in the North, where trade unionism, industrialization, and urbanism were strongest, while the strength of the Democrats lay in the least industrialized region, the South, the Democratic party did

15. Even in 1924 the AFL endorsed Lafollette and Wheeler by name and made clear that it did not endorse any party as such.
16. Taft, *Organized Labor in American History*, pp. 230 ff. and passim. See also Taft, *The AFL in the Age of Gomper*, New York, Harper & Brothers, 1957, pp. 289–301.
17. Taft, *Organized Labor in American History*, p. 232.
18. For the period from 1900 to 1920, see Taft, *ibid.*, pp. 241–245, 372–382.

not appear to be a particularly good risk for the labor movement.

As we have seen, however, the critical presidential elections from 1928–1936 saw a realignment of party loyalties. This time the balance in national support tilted decisively toward the Democrats. Urban workers, North, South, and West flocked to Democratic candidates and identified themselves as Democrats. If it was by no means a labor party or even a farmer-labor party, the Democratic Party was nonetheless highly dependent on and highly responsive to urban labor in general and to organized labor in particular.

Organized labor made great gains under the New Deal. The National Labor Relations Act guaranteed the right of workers to join unions. For the first time, the powers of the national government were now definitely on the side of unionism, not against it. From 1935 to 1941 trade union membership expanded from 3.6 million to over ten million. Unemployment insurance, old age annuities, and other New Deal measures gave benefits to blue-collar workers. Then in 1947, a Republican Congress passed the Taft-Hartley Act over President Truman's veto; this act banned the closed shop, which was prized by many AFL union leaders, allowed employers to sue unions for broken contracts, and imposed other restraints on unions. Perhaps the most offensive provision to the labor movement was Section 14b, which dealt with the closed shop and the union shop, both highly prized among various unions. The closed shop—where union membership is a condition for obtaining a job—was banned outright by 14b. The union shop—where union membership is a condition for holding a job—was not banned directly; but 14b permitted states to outlaw the union shop if they chose. The Democrats pledged themselves to repeal the Taft-Hartley Act.

Confronted with Democratic leaders more friendly to labor than the Republicans, the AFL-CIO became more and more deeply involved in partisan politics despite its formal neutrality. It established a Committee on Political Education to press for policies favorable to labor, promote the registration of voters, and support specific candidates. During the 1960 campaign, COPE spent almost 800 thousand dollars and in 1964 almost one million dollars in behalf of various candidates, mostly Democrats. In 1964 it also spent around 250 thousand dollars on voter registration.[19] In that campaign, two experts on campaign finance report, "organized labor, as always, ranked among the Democratic party's most open-handed

19. Herbert E. Alexander, *Financing the 1960 Election*, Princeton, Citizens' Research Foundation, 1962, p. 42; Herbert E. Alexander, *Financing the 1964 Election*, Princeton, Citizens' Research Foundation, 1966, p. 64; *The New York Times*, Dec. 3, 1965, p. 39M.

allies . . . Thirty-one different labor committees were active at the national level, disbursing a reported total of $3.7 million. Four fifths of it was paid out as contributions or transfers to other committees or candidates—mostly Democratic."[20] Organized labor's expenditure at the national level was, in fact, larger than that reported by the Democratic National Committee (three million dollars) and almost two fifths the size of the expenditures reported by all Democratic national campaign committees (eleven million dollars).[21]

The AFL-CIO also lobbied in Congress, not only for bills directly bearing on unionism, such as the attempt to repeal the Taft-Hartley Act, but also to promote Medicare, federal aid to education, civil rights, and other measures. Since the Second World War the AFL and CIO have reported expenditures of 125–150 thousand dollars a year for lobbying in Congress—in some years, a good deal more. In terms of reported expenditures, the AFL-CIO is generally among the half dozen largest lobbyists in Congress.[22] Legislation supported by the AFL-CIO has frequently been backed by a majority of Democrats and opposed by a majority of Republicans.

More and more, then, in spite of its official policy of neutrality, the labor movement has become one of the major coalition partners in the Democratic Party. In fact, the CIO (which was separate from the AFL until 1955) began life under the aegis of the New Deal and rejected the notion that the labor movement must necessarily remain outside the Democratic Party. In 1944 the CIO Political Action Committee openly worked for the renomination by Democrats of FDR and Henry Wallace and for the election of Franklin Roosevelt and his vice presidential candidate Harry Truman. In 1948, the CIO Executive board officially endorsed Harry Truman for President. In a number of industrial states and cities, the main leaders of organized labor became deeply involved in Democratic Party politics—nominations, campaign finances, elections, policies. Opinion poll after opinion poll revealed that trade union members were among the staunchest Democratic voters in the North. Then in 1964 when the labor movement was offered a choice between a Democratic presidential candidate who supported most of its goals, including

20. Herbert E. Alexander and Harold B. Meyers, "The Switch in Campaign Giving," *Fortune* (November, 1965).
21. Alexander, *Financing the 1964 Election*, p. 43, Table 4.
22. In addition, subdivisions of the AFL–CIO—international unions, the AFL–CIO Industrial Union Department, etc.—generally spend sizeable amounts. Cf. *Congress and the Nation*, op. cit., "Top Lobby Spenders, 1946–1963," pp. 1585–1592, reproduced in part as Table 15.2 of this volume.

the repeal of Section 14b of the Taft-Hartley Act, or an avowedly conservative Republican who opposed practically all of the existing laws and new legislation which the labor movement most ardently supported, the general board of the AFL-CIO rejected neutrality and publicly endorsed the election of President Johnson and Vice President Humphrey.

Despite its endorsement of Democratic candidates in 1964 and its *de facto* involvement with the Democratic Party, however, the AFL-CIO did not officially reject its classic position: The labor movement may have embraced the Democratic Party—but it did not officially endorse the party. Nonetheless, that possibility was weighed more and more favorably by leaders of the AFL-CIO. In 1965, in fulfillment of his campaign promises President Johnson sought to persuade Congress to repeal Section 14b of the Taft-Hartley Act. The Republican majority leader in the Senate, Senator Dirksen, mounted a filibuster that contributed mightily to the defeat of the repeal measure. President Johnson thereupon pledged that he would again fight for repeal in 1966. The president of the AFL-CIO, George Meany, announced to his fellow unionists that "If they (the Republican leaders) are going to conduct their business on the basis of absolute bias against the organized trade union movement . . . then I think labor, itself, is going to take a new look at this entire question of our relationship with the political parties."[23] However, after President Johnson failed again in 1966 to persuade the Democratic majority in Congress to unite behind the repeal of 14b, Meany's ardor for the Democrats cooled. The AFL-CIO did not "take a new look at . . . our relationship with the political parties"; instead it remained, as before, technically neutral but *de facto* an element of the Democratic coalition.

Conclusion

Every group, every organization, every movement that seeks changes in government policies faces the same alternatives as the labor movement. Weighing the pros and cons of alternative strategies is no easy task. Ideologues are drawn toward the first or second strategy; pragmatists toward the third or fourth. A strong desire to maintain the purity of its aim beckons a movement toward independent political action; a strong desire to be effective beckons a movement toward negotiation and coali-

23. Political Memo from COPE, November 29, 1965.

tion. Idealism cries: Reject compromises! Realism asks: Of what value is ideological purity when it leads merely to political futility?

If success is measured by the ability to win elections, then historically the first strategy has been the least successful. The history of the first strategy is, in plain fact, a record of very nearly total failure. Why this is so should by now be all but self-evident. The first strategy is likely to appeal most to a movement committed to goals which are unacceptable to either of the two major parties. Yet, if the goals of the movement are unacceptable to either of the existing parties, is there not good reason to think that these goals will also be unacceptable to the followings of the major parties and hence to most voters? If one goal of a political movement is to win elections, the first strategy will work only if at least one of the two major parties has fallen down badly on the prime job of the politician: to find out what appeals to voters and to act accordingly. The one clear historical instance of atrophy among the existing parties and the emergence of a new major party is furnished by the birth of the Republican Party; the newborn Republican organization rapidly acquired the support of dissident Whigs and Democrats throughout the North and West. Yet this example remains the only case in which a third party has attracted enough support from discontented followers of the major parties to develop into a major party in its own right.

If this is so, why does the first strategy have any appeal at all? Partly, no doubt, because its advocates ignore the historical regularities in American politics; partly because a movement with goals unacceptable to the major parties may simply have no other alternative open to it; and partly, one suspects, because of faith in the 'doctrine of the hidden majority.' The doctrine of the hidden majority, which is sometimes propounded by movements on both the extreme right and the extreme left, is the belief that a majority of like-minded citizens already exists waiting only to be mobilized, since the two major parties are for some reason ignoring and frustrating that latent majority. Belief in the doctrine of the hidden majority is not always confined to people on the most extreme fringes; in 1964 Senator Goldwater seems to have assumed the validity of the doctrine and to have fashioned his campaign accordingly with disastrous results.[24]

Choice of the first strategy by a movement that is already divorced

24. Cf. Philip E. Converse, Aage A. Clausen, and Warren E. Miller, "Electoral Myth and Reality: the 1964 Election," *American Political Science Review* (June, 1965), pp. 321–336. See also, however, the comment "On Electoral Myth and Reality," by William C. Baum, *ibid.* (September, 1965), p. 693.

FIGURE 17.5—THE VICIOUS CYCLE OF POLITICAL ALIENATION

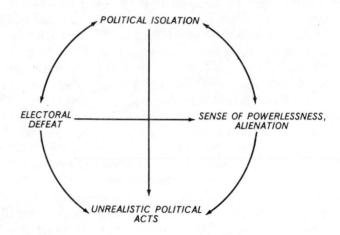

from the main currents of American opinion may establish a vicious cycle of political alienation: defeat, political isolation, and powerlessness reinforce a sense of political alienation and lack of realism in the movement, while alienation and lack of realism in turn increase the likelihood that the movement will be badly defeated in elections and will remain politically isolated and powerless.

The second strategy has been, at least in national politics, no more successful than the first. The second strategy has some of the appeal of the first, for it enables a group to adhere to most of its goals even though it enters into a coalition with one or two other groups with slightly divergent (but in the main overlapping) goals. The strategy reached its zenith of success in the Populist Party; but the needed majority was not forthcoming. Neither 'labor' nor 'farmers' constituted a homogeneous body of like-minded citizens, and the combination of the two groups created an even more heterogeneous coalition. Bryan and the Populists gained a good deal of support in some farming areas, especially in the South and West. But they lost badly in others and failed to win urban labor. If the American citizen body was already highly heterogeneous in the 1890s, it is probably even more heterogeneous today.

Just as the appeal of the first strategy may lie in the doctrine of the hidden majority, so the appeal of the second may be drawn from the 'doctine of the pure and simple coalition': a belief in the possibility of forming a majority coalition that is *pure*, in the sense that the coalition partners do not need to modify their goals in order to create or maintain a coalition, and that is *simple*, in the sense that it can be formed from only two or three groups, movements, classes, strata, each of which is internally homogeneous. Hence the appeal of a pure and simple coalition of workers and farmers; of the civil rights movement and the peace movement; of conservatives and property owners. . .

Yet if the interpretation set out in Chapter 14 is roughly correct, the doctrine of the pure and simple coalition must also be largely mythical. For where are these two or three internally like-minded groups that can combine to form a majority? Blue-collar workers are a minority of the working force, and a declining minority at that. Trade union members are an even smaller minority—a fifth to a quarter of the employed population. The white-collar strata constitute a complex of occupational minorities, from clerical workers to professional men and employers. Professional men and women are a small minority of the working force; doctors are a minority of professionals; psychiatrists, a minority of doctors. The poor are a minority, but so are the rich; the middle-income strata are only a statistical category, not a homogeneous group. Negroes are a minority; so are white Southerners; so are Southerners, white and black. Jews and Catholics are minorities; the Protestant 'majority' is largely a fiction, for it is a congeries of minorities as different as Southern Baptists, Lutherans, Episcopalians, and Quakers. What is more, none of the categories just mentioned are, in fact, collections of like-minded people—blue-collar workers, trade union members, white-collar workers, professionals, doctors, psychiatrists, the poor, the rich, the middle-income strata, Negroes, white Southerners, Northerners, Jews, Catholics, Protestants, Democrats, Republicans, liberals, conservatives. . . . No major category of the population defined by a single criterion, whether occupation, income, religion, ethnic group, region, or any other, consists altogether of like-minded voters.

The third strategy offers a fair chance of success for any group smaller than a majority, when the members of the group agree on relatively narrow or specific goals that do not run sharply counter to widely prevailing beliefs. The third strategy is the strategy of the pressure group. For limited purposes it can be highly successful. Farm organizations, representing at most a small and diminishing minority, have used it with enormous success. So, in varying degrees, have literally thousands of other organizations, representing or claiming to represent trade unionists, veterans, businessmen, industrialists, taxpayers, bankers, oil companies,

Table 17.3. Four Factors Relevant to the choice of
Political Strategies by a Group

A. GOALS	Goals of the group are:	
1. Breadth	1a. Oriented to NARROW objectives.	1b. Oriented to COMPREHENSIVE objectives.
2. Acceptability	2a. ACCEPTABLE to both major parties.	2b. UNACCEPTABLE to either major party.
	Members of the group are:	
B. MEMBERS		
3. Number	3a. FEW in number	3b. NUMEROUS
4. Homogeneity	4a. HOMOGENEOUS in political outlook.	4b. DIVERSE in political outlook.

copper importers, doctors, women's clubs, nature-lovers, stream pollutionists, conservationists, foreign policy groups, old people. . .

But a movement that seeks something more than its own group interests may conclude that as a pure pressure group it will exert too limited an influence over the policies of the American republic. If a movement also has a numerous following of prospective voters, like the labor movement, it may find the fourth strategy more reasonable than the third.

Is the fourth strategy perhaps the 'best' all round strategy? Not necessarily. A very small and well organized group without many votes behind it may retain more influence as an independent pressure group. A large group whose members are divided among people loyal to both parties would run the risk of splitting its following if it adopted the fourth strategy. A group with narrow goals more or less acceptable to both parties may succeed better as a pressure group. A group whose goals diverge widely from those supported by both parties could not find a home in either party.

Thus each strategy has its advantages and disadvantages. Since enthusiasts are prone to believe that they can have the advantages of a strategy without its disadvantages, a choice among the four strategies is often a somewhat irrational process colored more by hope and faith than by hard-headed analysis.

It is probably impossible, and in any case not very useful, to lay down a set of of hard and fast rules according to which one strategy or the other would always be the most 'rational' in the American political system. Instead, let me try to draw the discussion together by pin-

Table 17.4. Appropriate Strategies for Four Kinds of Groups

Thus if a group's

Goals are	Members are	An appropriate strategy would be to:
I. Comprehensive Acceptable to neither party	Few Homogeneous	Form an independent party.
II. Comprehensive Acceptable to neither party	Numerous Diverse	Form a new coalition party.
III. Narrow Acceptable to both parties	Few Diverse	Form a pressure group.
IV. Comprehensive Acceptable to one party	Numerous Diverse	Join coalition with existing party.

pointing four factors that seem relevant in choosing among strategies (Table 17.3).

Theoretically, these factors can be combined, in a number of different ways. For many combinations it might be difficult or impossible to say that one strategy was more 'rational' than another. For others, however, one strategy does seem more appropriate than the others. Table 17.4 shows one type of group for which a particular strategy seems appropriate.

Why is it that every strategy seems to have certain disadvantages? The main source of trouble is an apparently inescapable fact: In the United States, any group of people who have virtually the same views on political questions, the same political loyalties and identifications, is certain to be a *minority*. Whether the group is microscopic or relatively numerous, it will be a minority of the total body of citizens, even a minority of voters, and a rather small minority at that. To make the same point in another way, every aggregate of American citizens large enough to constitute a majority of voters is necessarily a rather heterogeneous collection of individuals and groups who may agree on some matters but are sure to disagree on others. No group of like-minded citizens can ever win a national election merely by mobilizing themselves and others who think exactly the way they do. To win national elections, even to win influence over national policies, every group must participate somehow in the politics of coalition building. To be sure, it can pursue its own goals; and it must engage in conflict; but it must also conciliate, compromise, negotiate, bargain—and in the process often forego its lesser goals for its greater objectives. In this sense, no single group can win national elections—only heterogeneous combination of groups can.

Some people, particularly if they happen to be highly confident of their own political virtue, the rightness of their own goals, and the evils of compromise, find this a most repugnant interpretation of American political life. Either this interpretation is false, they say, and the strict, undiminished pursuit of the goals held by the group, the movement, the cause will one day eventuate in political success uncontaminated by compromise. Or if the view is true, then politics is a dirty and evil business.

This, I think, is too crabbed, too inhuman a view of political life. For it seems obvious that, in a democratic republic, freedom and diversity lead inexorably to conflict. Yet they need not lead to inexorable conflict. For among a people guided, even in their conflicts, by a talent for conciliation and a commitment to the principles and institutions of a democratic republic, both freedom and diversity might flourish.

———•—•—•———

INDEX

Printed in U.S.A.